Using
The Human Record
Sources of Global History

Fourth Edition
Volumes I and II

Suggestions from the Editors

Alfred J. Andrea
The University of Vermont

James H. Overfield
The University of Vermont

Houghton Mifflin Company   Boston   New York

Sponsoring Editor: Nancy Blaine
Associate Editor: Julie Dunn
Editorial Associate: Gillie Jones
Editorial Assistant: Marie Bernard-Jackson
Senior Manufacturing Coordinator: Priscilla J. Bailey
Senior Marketing Manager: Sandra McGuire

We dedicate this little book
to our friends and colleagues of the World History Association.

May it serve in some small way to help promote the WHA's
program of education and service.

Printed in the U.S.A.

ISBN: 0-618-04248-2

123456789-VGI-04 03 02 01 00

Contents

Preface

To the best of our knowledge, no sociologist has yet focused on professors of global history as fit subjects of inquiry. This is a shame, and we hope this ill-deserved oversight will be rectified one day soon, but not by someone who specializes in the study of deviant behavior. If and when this long-overdue and important study is done, we would be surprised, even shocked, if it did not uncover a number of common characteristics among us—its subjects. It would reveal, in all likelihood, that as individuals we tend simultaneously to be supremely self-confident that we can do the apparently impossible—teach global history in a reasonably coherent fashion—and exceedingly humbled by an awareness of the limitations of our historical knowledge. It would probably also show that most of us who teach the subject are true believers, convinced of the importance and relevance of offering world history to today's undergraduates.

This seminal sociological study would also discover that our fervor is due in part to the fact that most of us were converted to global history somewhere in mid-career. It would find that during our graduate school days, and for some years thereafter, few of us included in our life plan teaching survey courses in world history. The study would demonstrate, by means of carefully analyzed statistical data derived from numerous interviews with randomly selected subjects, that teaching world history was either something we grew into because of our expanding historical interests or, more commonly, was a task we assumed due to the importunate entreaties of a persistent chairperson and a cohort of colleagues who agreed that we, and we alone, were just the perfect people to assume this burden that no one else felt worthy of bearing.

Our own experiences at The University of Vermont are probably typical. When our department began to offer a survey course on world history over two decades ago, we were a small part of the *departmental team*, captained by a course coordinator, who directed us to appear on certain days to deliver our one or two lectures each academic year in our areas of special expertise. For various reasons, the team plan never quite worked as well as we had hoped it would. Time went by, the years passed, and as personnel changed and the curriculum evolved, it became apparent one year that the once team-taught course on world history was, for better or worse, exclusively…ours. And it is that experience—more than a combined third of a century of teaching global history on our own—that has gone into the preparation of this instructor's manual.

This manual offers *suggestions* on how the fourth edition of *The Human Record* can be used in different classroom situations and as the basis for a variety of writing assignments. It explains the reasons behind our choice of sources and suggests ways of using them in and out of the classroom. It outlines suggested answers to some of the Questions for Analysis that precede each source selection (even though we realize that single, definitive answers do not exist for most of those questions) and proposes ideas that might prove successful in generating student discussion. Virtually all of the suggestions that appear in these pages are tactics that we have employed in our own classrooms with at least some success. We have spared you most of our failures.

Although we have labored both in the book and in this accompanying manual to be as clear and as helpful as possible, we could not anticipate every question or problem you and your students might encounter as you use *The Human Record*. If you have any questions about a source or reference, please do not hesitate to contact us. Our address is:

> Department of History
> Wheeler House
> The University of Vermont
> Burlington, Vermont 05405

Because of our division of labor and expertise, address all questions relating to Volume I to Al Andrea and all queries relating to Volume II to Jim Overfield. We will let you in on a little secret: Al did the Prologue and Volume I, and Jim did all of Volume II; we divide our interests chronologically rather than culturally. You can reach Al by phone at (802) 656-4488 and Jim at (802) 656-4513. Our shared FAX number is (802) 656-8794. In this age of electronic mail, you might find it faster and easier to use e-mail (we prefer it). In that case, contact us at: <aandrea@zoo.uvm.edu> or <joverfie@zoo.uvm.edu>.

> Collegially yours,
> *A.J.A.*
> *J.H.O.*

Introduction

We present this instructor's manual with the full realization that global history courses are taught under many different conditions and according to a wide range of formats. At The University of Vermont we have taught classes in world history with enrollments as small as three and as large as 250. We have taught sections in which we did nothing but lecture and others in which we spent every class discussing readings and responding to student questions. Most frequently and recently, however, we have sought a balance between lectures (two per week to the entire class, which averages between 70 and 120 students) and discussions (once a week, with each discussion section no larger than twenty students). In all these different teaching conditions, we believe we have been able to use the documents and other sources now contained in *The Human Record* as effective instructional aids.

Professors with large enrollments, little time, and no graduate teaching assistants are often discouraged from using collections of primary source material, believing that without opportunities to discuss the sources, students will find such readings more confusing than helpful. We have adopted several approaches that we trust have enabled us to involve our students in analyzing sources largely on their own, and we offer them for your consideration.

Journals

Student journals can provide students with an opportunity to record observations, speculate, raise questions, develop ideas, and draw conclusions about what they have read and about what they have heard in class, and they can do so without making major demands on a professor's time and energy. When properly used, the journal has the dual benefit of forcing students to think seriously about the course matter and to articulate their ideas in written form while at the same time largely freeing the professor from the laborious (and, let's be honest, often deadly dull) task of seemingly endless hours of reading and commenting on essays.

A journal falls somewhere between a private diary that records a person's inner feelings and private thoughts and a class notebook that records what a student has read or heard from an outside source. Journal writing also differs from formal writing assignments in which students are expected to pay close attention to organization, grammar, and style. Because its purpose is to stimulate thinking and encourage the generation of new ideas, journal writing inevitably includes digressions, false starts, and a certain amount of disorganization. Furthermore, because journal entries are essentially unedited, single drafts they are likely to contain a larger than usual number of misspellings and stylistic flaws. If you are able to accept such work comfortably, then maybe you should consider making the journal an integral part of your global history course.

Journal writing can take several different forms. At one end of the spectrum the instructor can give students a free hand to record their personal comments on and reactions to a week's reading assignments and lectures with no formal direction other than stipulating a minimum of three or four (or however many) entries each week. The advantage of this approach is that it affords students the greatest latitude to react to the material and make their own connections between the past and their own experiences. The disadvantages are several: unimaginative (or lazy) students inevitably will claim they "can't think of anything to write about"; inexperienced students will fill their journals with entries that focus on the peripheral rather than the significant; clever but disinterested students will compile one lengthy entry after another but without serious attention to the reading; historically unsophisticated students will compose entries that focus totally on personal feelings and present-day concerns without ever trying to understand on its own terms evidence that reflects alien cultures and long-past phenomena. At the other end of the spectrum, the instructor can provide specific questions as the basis for journal entries. This more controlled approach ensures that the students will write on what the instructor believes is important and that they will not shy away from difficult problems and issues. At the same time, it might discourage spontaneity.

When we use journals, we prefer an approach that each week includes several *assigned* journal topics and at least one *personal* entry. Thus, in a week in which the topic is World War II, an instructor might assign such journal topics relating to sources in *The Human Record* as:

1. Compare the political views of Hitler in *Mein Kampf* and those of the authors of *The Way of Subjects*. Which strike you as more significant, the similarities or the differences?

2. To what extent does the nationalist philosophy expressed in *The Way of Subjects* resemble Japanese nationalism before and during the Meiji Restoration?

In the personal entry for the same week, students might explore their feelings about the Holocaust, based on the memoirs of Rudolf Höss, or the dropping of the atomic bomb on Hiroshima, based on the accounts of the Japanese students who lived through August 6, 1945.

We have found it best to collect journals several times during the semester to make sure that students are keeping up with their work and that the work meets expected standards. Although instructors should feel free to write comments in the journal, we suggest they refrain from placing a grade in the journal during these periodic collections. We have discovered that a grade is best given only at the end of the semester, when we have the opportunity to consider the entire semester's entries as a whole. That grade then reflects the number of completed entries and the extent to which they reflect a serious, ongoing, semester-long involvement with the course material.

The Portfolio

One variation on the journal is the portfolio of student masterpieces, based on the model of the student art portfolio. Each student purchases a small portfolio in which to place all out-of-class work. This work consists of essays and exercises.

Exercises follow a variety of forms. Some might be map assignments; others are *thought pieces* along the lines of free-thought journal entries; still others are what we call *factual/inferential exercises*. Here students are asked to discover a certain number of important facts in a particular source and then to note the major inference(s) they have drawn from each fact. This exercise helps students to learn how to distinguish between factual data and historical interpretation. For example, suppose the class is studying *The Judgments of Hammurabi* (Vol. I, Chapter 1, source 2). A typical exercise of this sort would be:

> Draw three parallel columns. In the first, copy verbatim three significant judgments from this collection. In the second, list the most important, indisputable *fact* you are able to garner from each judgment you chose. In the third, write the most important *inference* you have drawn from each fact.

A good entry would look something like this:

Law	*Fact*	*Inference*
142. "If a woman hates her husband, and says 'You shall not possess me,' the reason for her dislike shall be inquired into. If she is careful, and has no fault, but her husband takes himself away and neglects her, then that woman is not to blame. She shall take her dowry and go back to her father's house."	A woman who is clearly not to blame for the ruining of her marriage, may, upon investigation, legally divorce her husband and return to her father's house with her dowry.	Although women do have certain rights and protections, insofar as they can divorce their husbands who have abandoned them, their freedom is strictly defined and narrowly limited by a patriarchal society. They have to prove that they are not at fault for the breach in their marriage in order to divorce their husbands and they then return to their father's house. Women are not considered capable of controlling their own lives.

Another type of exercise we favor is what we call *the spurious primary source.* Here we ask students to fabricate a historical document as a way of developing and demonstrating understanding of a particular historical culture, phenomenon, or person. For example, we might ask them to compose a dialogue between a Muslim and a Hindu in sixteenth-century India in which they discuss their respective views of Divine Reality. Another exercise might be to write Tokugawa Ieyasu's farewell address. Letters home by Chinese Buddhist monks traveling in India, Europeans at the court of Akbar, and so on are especially popular items with our students because such assignments enable them to get a firm grasp on two different cultures by forcing them to look at one culture through the eyes of another. One assignment that invariably draws rave reviews from students on end-of-semester evaluations is the following:

Imagine you are a follower of *one* of the major schools of Chinese philosophy: Daoism, Yin-Yang theory, Confucianism, or Legalism. You have traveled westward, arriving in Athens in 431 B.C.E. There you hear the Funeral Oration given by Pericles and witness the plague that devastates the city the following summer (Volume I, Chapter 4, source 28). Write a letter home to your teacher describing and *interpreting,* in the light of your chosen philosophy, what you have heard and witnessed.

This is not an easy assignment, but most students seem to view it as nonthreatening because, we believe, they are given choices and are allowed to exercise their imaginations. In fact, students seem to enjoy such exercises, and often the results indicate that they have worked hard to try to enter the mind and world of the fictional author. At best, this type of exercise results in very sensitive and insightful pieces. Moreover, when the subject matter is not overly serious, our more creative students also are capable of producing some deliberately funny and quite entertaining pieces. We often ask students to read their spurious documents in discussion section, especially when there is good reason to believe that one or more will have produced a humorous piece.

The heart and soul of the portfolio, however, is the serious, formal essay. This is where we assign our students the task of writing thoughtful and coherent essays on questions we have given them relating to a variety of primary sources. Many of the Questions for Analysis that appear in *The Human Record* come from our stock of essay topics. The number of such essays we require in a semester varies, but generally we try to space three or four formal essays over the span of fifteen weeks.

No matter how many or few, the essay assignments follow a standard pattern. Unlike journal entries, we expect these essays to be as free as possible of misspellings, grammatical errors, punctuation flaws, and literary gaffes. More important, the essays must present coherent and complete analyses of the documents or other sources in answer to the question presented. Given the almost universal availability of word processors on our campus, we require students to pass in typed (is the proper term now *printed?)* papers. By essentially requiring them to use word processors (does anyone still have a typewriter?), we hope to help them learn that revision is fairly quick, almost painless, and invariably necessary, no matter how facile one might be as a writer. We mandate no particular length but advise our students that most essays cannot adequately cover an issue in less than two to three pages.

Each assignment presents students with a choice of five or six different essay topics relating to a common theme or issue. Providing a variety of choices seems best suited to the needs of both the students and the instructor. Students feel better about the task when given a choice of topics. Similarly, by allowing students to write on a variety of topics that relate to the common theme of a particular week, the instructor is spared the burden of reading too many essays on the same issue—a mind-deadening experience—and is also provided with an effective means of covering quite a bit of matter in the space of one discussion section meeting.

Students bring their essays to the discussion section. We ask the students to hold their essays until the end of class but to pass in before class a slip of paper with their name, the topic on which they wrote, and a one-sentence summary of their argument. This enables us to see immediately the range of topics and to plot at a glance the way we will guide discussion in order to incorporate as many different perspectives and topics as possible. We begin by asking a student to read or summarize his or her essay, and from there we try to direct discussion in a way that enables all class members to share, no matter how briefly, the conclusions of their essays.

After receiving the essays, we read them over carefully, making comments where appropriate, *but we assign no grades.* Comments revolve around the following points: literary style and organization; thoroughness of source analysis; and the apparent validity of interpretation. In dealing with the last two areas, we prefer to offer comments in question form rather than stating boldly that we disagree with some interpretation or think (as is often the case) that the student has not adequately exhausted the evidence. Students may then revise their essays if they wish. We usually urge that course on about forty percent of the class, but most students whose essays have fallen short of the mark have already learned from the points raised in class discussion that they have not fully explored the topic. If a student chooses to write a revision, we require that the revised essay be appended to the original essay and that it be kept in the portfolio, along with all other work.

As with the journal, each student passes in a portfolio at the end of the semester. Then and only then do we assign a grade after reviewing the whole portfolio and gaining a picture of the student's semester-long effort, improvement, and grasp of the material.

The portfolio approach does take up more of an instructor's limited time than the journal because helping students to craft essay masterpieces demands a good deal of hard work. When not carried to extremes, however, this approach can be very satisfying for both students and instructors. One valuable lesson that students learn from this exercise is that the craft of writing is the craft of rewriting. At the same time, instructors must be careful not to overdo essay assignments or criticisms. We have been guilty of assigning too many formal essays in the past and needlessly working our students and ourselves to exhaustion. Learn from our mistakes. We suggest that instructors who choose to use portfolios should give weekly writing assignments but only two to four of those assignments should be formal essays, and these should be well spaced over the semester. None should come so close to the end of the semester as to prevent revision. Let the bulk of the writing assignments be exercises, such as outlined above, and even informal journal-type entries. The important thing is that students be required to conduct some sort of written dialogue every week with the sources. Most of them will soon catch on that this is meaningful and can even be fun.

Group Projects

The image of the historian as the solitary researcher is somewhat misleading inasmuch as we belong to a community of scholars in which we constantly learn from and are stimulated by one another. The discussion section, where students bring their individual insights and work to share with one another and offer up their ideas for consideration by their peers, is the undergraduate equivalent of that process of communal scholarship. Historians, however, rarely work in teams, unlike their colleagues in the physical and social sciences, and perhaps something is lost by adhering so strictly to the cult of the individual interpreter of the past.

Although we believe that students should engage in most of their out-of-class exercises and assignments solely by themselves, we understand the value of group work, where several or more persons are engaged in a common effort to create a superior product. When used judiciously, the group project can significantly enrich student understanding of the material while simultaneously lifting a great burden of work from instructors, especially those with heavily enrolled classes and no teaching assistants. Another benefit is that, especially when used early in the semester, the group project is an effective tool for bringing students together and helping them become comfortable with one another.

We favor several types of group projects. First and most elementary, four or five students are assigned a source or group of related sources. They must exhaustively study the assigned material, using the Questions for Analysis as their starting point, and then report, in any manner they wish, to the class or discussion section regarding their work. In their report they must directly deal with the issue of how study of this evidence has deepened their understanding of the general topic to which it relates. A second type of group project revolves around the spurious primary sources outlined above. A manageable group, four to six people, is assigned the project of creating a ten-to-fifteen-minute docudrama on some particularly important topic or group of related topics. The easiest and often most rewarding type of docudrama to present is a debate in which the representatives of two or more different cultures or groups discuss or debate their respective visions of reality. For example, question 6 for source 25 of Volume I, which asks the student to imagine a conversation among a Daoist, Legalist, and a Confucian, is exactly the type of thought-provoking matter we like to interject into our classes. When the material is presented in debate form, the instructor can empanel a second group of students to act as judges. They should not be charged with determining which side is right or who won the debate. Rather, their sole judgment, which they should openly discuss in front of the class before taking a vote on their decision, should be which side more faithfully and fully presented the position of the group it represented. In order to make this decision, the judges must have already read and studied the relevant sources. Following the judges' rendering of their decision, the instructor might wish to invite the class's comments on the debate and decision.

In addition to being fun and serving as ways to enliven discussion, these docudramas also provide a means for some of our more creative and artistically oriented students to engage themselves fully in the material. We encourage our students to suggest to us ways in which they as members of a group or as individuals can contribute to the class's understanding of this material. We hope that one of these days some of our students will write and perform an hour-long docudrama with a full cast.

Peer Evaluation

One of our most important responsibilities as instructors is to evaluate the work of our students and to offer helpful criticism of their ideas and modes of expression, and we must never shirk that duty. At the same time, however, we must also be aware of the fact that students have a lot to offer one another and probably learn more from their peers than they ever learn from us—painful as that might be to admit. Moreover, as we all learned when we began teaching, the best way to learn something is to teach it. For these reasons we have begun incorporating limited peer evaluation into our courses in global history.

Peer evaluation, as we use it, is simple and straightforward. Members of the discussion section exchange journal entries or other pieces of work. On one occasion we will ask them to pass the work to the person on the left; on another occasion to the person two seats down on the right. (We are always formed in a circle, often around a table.) Our purpose is to keep the process random. Each person has one week to read and comment on the work received. The reader is to make no marks on the paper itself nor assign any grade. All comments are to be typed on a separate sheet and that sheet must be legibly signed and appended to the work that has been evaluated. Additionally, all evaluators must pass in to us photocopies of the papers they have evaluated and their comments. A quick scan of these photocopies enables us to monitor everyone's work and to identify those who take this assignment seriously. Before passing the evaluations back, we make brief comments on them to let each evaluator know how we judge his or her comments.

When students approach the task conscientiously, and most do, peer evaluations prove valuable to both parties. This process of evaluation also lessens somewhat our own burden of closely reading and commenting in depth on student work.

Prologue

We like to focus on the Prologue and its accompanying sources in our initial discussion section meeting. We ask our students to read these pages with special care and to write down any and all questions they have regarding the material. Everyone is to bring to class at least one written question relating to any point made in the Prologue or a brief statement of any insight our words might have sparked. Questions can deal with the nature of historical understanding and the uses and limitations of history as an area of human inquiry or the nuts and bolts of source analysis. In the spirit of Cole Porter, anything goes, and we are always especially happy when one or more students chooses to take exception to something we wrote.

We also require our students to bring two lists to class as bases for class discussion, and we encourage them to join into small, informal groups in preparing these lists. In this manner they quickly come to know at least a few members of the class; they become comfortable with the often intimidating process of sharing their ideas openly with one another; they learn that global history is something that should command their attention outside of the classroom, as well as within; and they benefit from this give and take to the point that they generally produce thoughtful and thought-provoking lists.

The first list is of sources the future historian of their class might want to consult that have not been mentioned in the essay. Suggested additional sources that our students have thought of include tapes of the university's radio programs, local town newspaper accounts of college activities and town-gown relations, and the records of the campus and city police departments! (We will not comment here on that last item.) This exercise usually provides plenty of material for a lively discussion on the nature of historical evidence and knowledge.

The second list relates to question 7. We ask students to enumerate all of the qualities and characteristics of Taino society that Columbus recorded. We tell them simply to list as many *facts* as they can about this Caribbean people. Most will come to class with fairly long lists. They will note, for example, how the Tainos appeared to be timid and unwarlike and had essentially no weapons, except for sharpened canes. The more historically sophisticated members of the class will note where Columbus's observations are contradicted or modified by a footnote, such as on the issue of the Tainos' presumed lack of idolatry.

These lists of Taino characteristics, some of which seem to have been the product of Columbus's imagination or his wishful thinking, provide an opportunity to help students understand more clearly several of the major points raised in the Prologue: the need to understand the perspectives and limitations of one's sources and the distinction between fact and inference.

Take, for example, the Tainos' apparently pacific nature—an item that appears on almost every student list and which we try subtly to focus on early in the discussion, while simultaneously attempting to make it appear that we are not trying to bend discussion in any particular direction—not always an easy feat. Later accounts of the Tainos by other Spanish visitors support Columbus's observation that these people were not generally aggressive. Indeed, the word *Taino* means "good" or "noble," and these people became known to the Spaniards by this term because several of their members used it to describe themselves to Columbus as a way of saying that they were not warlike Caribs. Notwithstanding the Tainos' normally pacific behavior, note 22 provides some interesting information that should cause us at least to modify the admiral's statement. Prior to leaving behind his garrison at Navidad del Señor, Columbus thought it prudent to try to impress upon these supposedly unwarlike people the fact that it would be foolish to test the military might of the Spaniards. Despite this display, the Tainos wiped out the garrison in 1493. Moreover, Columbus's letter contains a statement that seems crafted to protect him from possible repercussions should the Tainos ever attack the garrison. He writes that those holding the fortress will be able easily to keep the whole island in check without endangering themselves, "if they know how to govern themselves." Apparently the admiral, knowing his men, had reason to fear that they would act imprudently and incite native hostility. And he was right. Those left behind did not learn to control themselves and did not survive the year.

In our commentary on Columbus's letter in the Prologue we deliberately do not mention this important but almost throw-away phrase in the hope that students will pick it up themselves. After all, we have to leave something for them to discover, and if they think they see something that we overlooked, it is all the sweeter. If luck is with us, someone in the discussion class will take note of that phrase and use it as a launching pad to discredit Columbus's account and to argue against our overall evaluation of his letter's worth. If no one notices it, we will try to bring it to their attention as subtly as possible, hoping for a reaction.

When we ask students to explain the dichotomy between Columbus's official assurances and the Tainos' subsequent attack on the garrison, they usually raise several interesting points. Someone often suggests that the appearance of Columbus and his great ships had so overawed these people that they acted more timid than usual. Once the Tainos realized that the Spaniards were humans like themselves, they lost that initial fear. Someone else might suggest that it was not that simple. These people had rudimentary weapons at best and seemed to live in fear of the advancing Caribs, who had more advanced weapons and preyed on them. It is logical to conclude that Columbus was basically correct when he characterized the Tainos as unwarlike, even though his judgment seems to have been influenced at least in part by his interest in seeking out people who could easily be converted to Catholicism and subjected to Spanish royal control. However, even peaceful people will often react violently to abuse, as the Admiral himself seems to fear will be the case. This then leads to a discussion of what sorts of abuses, such as rape, might have caused that reaction. Now this is where we want the discussion to go, but we want the students to bring it there. After all, source analysis is an exercise in discovery.

Following this, we return to the core issue of what we can learn about Taino culture from this letter. Students will come up with all sorts of other facts from which they can draw interesting inferences and which likewise provide a context for raising questions relating to both the validity of this particular source and historical epistemology in general. We have discovered that this initial discussion hour passes too quickly, and we rarely have enough time to work through all the student questions and lists. Some years we barely get through fifty percent of them. No matter how many questions and lists remain undiscussed, we collect all lists and written questions. In addition to making quick comments on the papers, by way of encouragement for the students' effort, we also select any intriguing insights or questions that we did not get to in class and devote five minutes to reading them aloud at the next discussion meeting, without identifying the authors. We have found this to be an effective means by which to remind students that there is always another way to look at the evidence before us and that none of us, the instructors included, has the final word on any subject. It is also a gentle way of demonstrating to the class the high level of thought and work we expect of each student.

If class discussion seems to have exhausted the dual issues of the nature of historical inquiry and what Columbus's letter allows us to infer about Taino society, and if time miraculously remains (something that rarely happens), we suggest spending the few remaining minutes discussing the problems that confront the historian using artifactual evidence. We have discovered that even our quietest students have something to say about the artifactual evidence that we ask them to analyze. Whenever class discussion lags, an artifact will revive it. Indeed, over the years we have discovered that discussion classes in which an artifact is being examined tend to be the liveliest. Notwithstanding the natural attraction of this sort of evidence, which our students largely find unintimidating, in our initial venture into the topic of the overall worth of artifacts as historical evidence we fall back on a sure-fire, time-tested tactic to initiate class discussion. We ask someone to take some coins out of a pocket, back pack, or purse and to describe the symbols and words on them. We then ask the class to imagine that they know absolutely nothing else about the society that produced these coins and to try to draw as many reasonable inferences as possible from the evidence at hand about that culture. The results are usually amusing and instructive. Many of the points we make in our essay on the value and limitation of artifactual evidence are underscored in this exercise.

VOLUME I
To 1700

CHAPTER

1

The First Civilizations

Chapter Theme

Most students are initially confused about the meaning of the term
civilization. Many see it as a value judgment. Civilizations are good, and
cultures that have not developed civilized institutions are barbaric. This, of
course, is nonsense. We recommend that you review our introductory
comments with the class. By definition, a civilization is simply any human
society that has produced a *state*—a political and social body that supersedes
the loyalties and functions of the food-gathering clan, of the herding tribe,
and of the food-producing village. This distinction is important because we
have noticed a tendency on the part of some students to mistake neolithic
agrarian communities for civilizations. For this reason, an instructor cannot
emphasize too often that a state binds people together at a level that
transcends the ties of blood or local community. Some of the attributes
common to most civilizations are: clearly delineated political and social
hierarchies; large areas of concentrated population that serve as sites of
manufacture and commerce, areas of communal worship, and centers of
political and social control; building on a monumental scale; an organized
priestly class with an enunciated theology; wide economic specialization and
far-ranging trade networks; military organization; and often (and, from an
historian's point of view, most important of all) *written records*.

In both the Prologue and Chapter 1, we have tried to make it clear that
most historians concentrate their research on civilized societies because that
is where they find the bulk of their evidence. Indeed, without documentary
evidence historians are unable to reconstruct a detailed, coherent historical
picture of any past society.

Why These Sources?

The documents and artifacts chosen for this chapter illustrate the historian's
dependence on the written word and also some of the significant social and

intellectual achievements of humanity's first *known* civilizations. Moreover, these sources not only reveal some of the concerns and generic institutions that all civilizations have shared, they also point out that humans have evolved a variety of often radically different responses to their problems. Here the student encounters the distinctive and quite different cultural trademarks of early Mesopotamian, Egyptian, and Chinese civilizations and, we trust, begins to understand and appreciate the rich variety of the human historical experience. Additionally, the student also has glimpses of Tassili, Nubian, Harappan, Minoan, and Olmec cultures through some of their artifacts.

Several documents, specifically *The Epic of Gilgamesh* and the Egyptian funerary texts, deal with issues we all must someday face: death and the meaning of life (and they are themes that recur throughout the two volumes, as the topical indexes show). We have discovered that the vast majority of our students want to grapple with these questions, and for this reason asking students to compare the Mesopotamian and Egyptian visions of life and death seems to be a fruitful starting point in the class discussion devoted to Chapter 1. The three Egyptian funerary texts serve a second important function in that they nicely illustrate the evolution of Egyptian thought on the issue of life after death, thereby putting to rest the misconception that Egyptian civilization was static and also underscoring the fact that historians study change over time. Although we begin with these two sources, we should not neglect the interesting insights provided by the other sources from the ancient world's first civilizations.

The Judgments of Hammurabi's prologue and epilogue, *The Classic of History*, the first poetic selection from *The Classic of Odes*, and the two temple reliefs from the Nile present self-images of people at the pinnacle of authority, whereas other sources, notably the actual judgments of Hammurabi, the Egyptian scribal exercise on crafts and trades, the second and third poems from *The Classic of Odes*, and the Tassili rock painting provide glimpses of the activities and concerns of common folk. Although most of the documentary evidence left behind by the world's earliest civilizations reflects the concerns and perceptions of their rulers, students must never lose sight of the place of common people in history.

Students must also not blind themselves to the ways in which these early cultures perceived the cosmos. *The Epic of Gilgamesh* and the three funerary texts provide perspectives on the perceived roles of some of Mesopotamia's and Egypt's chief deities. On its part, *The Classic of History* shows us the *Mandate of Heaven*, China's traditional explanation of the human and cosmic forces that govern the fortunes of "all under Heaven," namely the

Chinese. Finally, our last three artifacts provide vivid evidence of the interplay of the human and the divine as perceived by the cultures of the Nile, Harappan India, Mesopotamia, Crete, and the Olmec people of Mexico.

The seals of source 8 serve an additional function by introducing students to two core themes that run throughout both volumes: cultural encounter and exchange. The seals of Mesopotamia, Harrapan India, and Minoan Crete represented here strongly suggest that certain notions and motifs were carried along routes that ran from the eastern Mediterranean to the northwest regions of the Indian subcontinent, and in the process the migrating ideas were adapted by their new hosts through a process we term *syncretism*—the blending of foreign influences with native traditions as a way of making imported concepts intelligible and acceptable. Because syncretic fusion is one of the primary driving forces of global history, it is necessary to introduce students to this phenomenon as early as possible. And in case they somehow miss the point in source 8, we return to the theme of cultural syncretism in source 9, where students are asked to compare two temple reliefs from the upper Nile: one an Egyptian piece, the other a Nubian creation. Juxtaposed as they are, these artifacts suggest a southward flow of Egyptian influences into the land called Kush, but they also indicate how the Nubians reshaped these imports.

Analyzing the Sources

All eight questions that accompany *The Epic of Gilgamesh* are variations on a single theme: What do these excerpts tell us about the Mesopotamian view of life and death? The answer is obvious to most students who take time to read the selection carefully. In life humans appear to be little more than pawns in the hands of willful deities, and in death they enter the bleak house of dust. No human achievement or pleasure is permanent; the grave is the end of all. At the same time, it is simplistic and wrong to characterize this philosophy as joyless and pessimistic. Mesopotamians recognized that, within the limited destiny accorded humanity, people could and should enjoy life's pleasures. Moreover, by making the most of their lives, mortals can achieve heroic dignity. Question 6 is the key to a student's realization of this Mesopotamian view of life. Gilgamesh, who prior to his confrontation with the realities of life and death had self-centeredly abused his royal office, returns a transformed man and becomes a model king—"without an equal among men." Although he dies, he achieves an immortality of sorts in his deeds and in the memory and affection of his people.

The Judgments of Hammurabi offers a treasure-trove of evidence into the heroic efforts of the Mesopotamians to create a just and ordered society. Question 6 is the key question, and it often becomes the topic for the class's initial formal essay. Students can only adequately answer the question after they have considered and attempted to answer the first five questions. Those initial (and admittedly leading) questions help students realize that although inequality based on differences of class, age, and sex was built into the fabric of Hammurabi's Babylon, these judgments were an honest attempt to provide measures of protection for all members of society. Certainly the punishments are severe by most modern standards of criminal and civil law, and some of the sanctions, such as we see in judgments 117 and 230, will strike students as cruel and unfair. If, however, students are first helped to understand the social structure that these laws were intended to uphold, they then should perceive that Hammurabi's goal, like that of Gilbert and Sullivan's Mikado, was "to let the punishment fit the crime." No more, no less.

The first of our two Egyptian sources gives another view of reality, as seen from the more secure world of the Nile. The three funerary texts that constitute source 3 are especially telling for two reasons. Singly and collectively they allow the student to draw some interesting comparisons with Mesopotamian views of life, law, death, and the afterlife; they also illustrate the evolution of the Egyptian concept of life after death. Both Gilgamesh and Hammurabi reveal a society that believes nothing is permanent in this life, and there is no meaningful life after death. Therefore, the only security available to humans is the order that good kings impose upon their people. Egyptian civilization created a radically different notion. The funerary texts reveal the growing idea in Egypt that eternal life was available to all who followed the proper procedures in life. To be sure, many of those procedures were purely ritualistic and magical. As understood by most, the *Pyramid Texts*, the *Coffin Texts*, and even the so-called *Book of the Dead* were no more than sets of spells and incantations that assured the corpse protection from evil spirits as it journeyed to the Land of the West. Yet, as more Egyptians laid claim to an afterlife, those procedures also took on a moral tone, as the "Negative Confession" suggests. Here we see someone claiming the right to live eternally in the Land of the West because he has conformed to the universal and immutable laws of Ma'at, which is best understood here as meaning Justice, Truth, and Harmony. More than a moral abstraction, Ma'at is divine and eternal. Indeed, the goddesses Isis (Right) and Nephthys (Truth) are the Double Ma'at. By living a life that conforms to Ma'at, one becomes Ma'at in death. In essence, the dead person becomes a living god.

One important manifestation of this Egyptian focus on Ma'at, which unhappily is not explicit in any of the texts in this chapter, was that ancient Egyptians perceived the god who lived in their midst—the pharaoh—to be the embodiment of Ma'at. His every word and action was Truth and Justice. Consequently, Egyptians (or at least Egyptian rulers) perceived no need to set down elaborate, detailed collections of law and legal precedent such as we find in Mesopotamia. In essence, ancient Egyptians lived in a world that was permanently ruled by Ma'at. What is more, and this is clear in our third funerary text, they could assure themselves eternal enjoyment of this cosmic harmony by conforming to its moral strictures.

Lest our students mistakenly think that ancient Egypt was a utopia, source 4 vividly describes the hardships and meager rewards of those who daily toiled for their living. To be sure, the document is filled with hyperbole and heavy-handed expressions of class prejudice, but its picture of labor-intensive work and precious little return is not far off the mark. Moreover, the dichotomy that it draws between the privileged few who were literate, and therefore had the power that such knowledge confers, and the illiterate masses is right on target. A few facts might help your students better understand the status that Egypt's scribes enjoyed: (1) the patron of scribes was Thoth, the god of wisdom who gave humanity the art of writing, *recorded* the names of all who passed to the afterlife, and served as judge in the Hall of Two Truths; (2) the Egyptian word for what we term *hieroglyphs* (a Greek word that means "priestly writing") literally translates as "words of god." Anyone who had the ability to share Thoth's work and write divine words obviously was a person of great power.

Just as this scribal exercise gives us a glimpse of antiquity's lower classes (as seen from the top), so the second and third poems from *The Classic of Odes* (source 6) also reveal the views of some of history's often silent elements. Poem 2 compares the foppish court dandies of Zhou with the exploited Chinese of the East whom Zhou had subjugated; poem 3 is the lament of a conscripted rank-and-file soldier serving in the armed forces of Zhou. Some things seem to be universal realties.

Just as universal is the need for ruling classes to justify the authority that they exercise, and we see such justification in the first poetic selection from *The Classic of Odes*, "The Ideal Minister," as well as in the excerpt from *The Classic of History*, which precedes it (source 5). Both documents illustrate the *Mandate of Heaven* (*tianming*), an idea that has served as one of Chinese civilization's core doctrines for well over two thousand years. Anyone who does not understand the central elements of this principle cannot begin to understand Chinese culture. For this reason alone we spend a fair amount of time in lecture and discussion on the Mandate of Heaven. Happily, the concept is not difficult to comprehend, and we have discovered that students easily grasp it. According to this doctrine, the entire cosmos is ruled by an impersonal, all-pervading, and all-powerful Heaven *(tian)* that confers on a monarch the responsibility and right to rule "all under Heaven" *(tianxia)*, whereby the monarch becomes the Son of Heaven *(tianzi)*. Furthermore, the monarch will exercise effective power as long as he rules conscientiously, behaves morally, and selects equally conscientious and moral ministers to put his wise policies into practice. Should, however, the ruler lose his moral compass and act in improper ways, he will lose Heaven's mandate to rule and cease to be the Son of Heaven. The reason is simple. Once a monarch begins acting immorally in private matters, he naturally abandons the benevolence and wisdom required of him as a ruler. Not only does his judgment suffer and result in decisions and ministerial appointments that injure "all under Heaven," but Heaven shows its displeasure by unleashing natural disasters. Famine, flood, drought, plague, and invasions occasion rebellion through which Heaven transfers its mandate to a new ruler. In the words of one ancient Chinese proverb: "The voice of the people is the voice of Heaven." Although the doctrine as articulated by the Zhou implicitly contained the notion of the right of rebellion against tyranny, it was the Confucian theorist Mencius, or Mengtze (ca. 372–ca. 289 B.C.E.), who first fully carried the principle to its logical conclusion by stating that it is the duty of right-minded individuals to depose unworthy rulers.

One of our favorite assignments in regard to Chinese political theory is to ask students to compose a journal entry on question 6 of source 5. Even though all seven questions for analysis have served well in discussion and as topics for written assignments, question 6 is especially effective because it forces students to see the differences between modern American political attitudes and assumptions and those of traditional China. To be sure, a number of ideas articulated by Yi Yin in this excerpt are Confucian, an ideology that only began to become an important part of the intellectual framework of China's ruling classes in the age of Han (202 B.C.E.–220 C.E.), as source 35 of Chapter 5 suggests. There is, however, no good reason to doubt that these Confucian ideals antedated the historical Confucius (ca. 551–ca. 479 B.C.E.) and were an important element of Chinese thought from at least the age of Western Zhou. These include the implicit belief that the ways of the past are a model for present behavior, the notion that old age confers wisdom, and the idea that the wise ruler leads by example and moral force and does not unwisely follow the fashions of the moment.

Unlike the documents, the artifacts in the section "Mute Testimony" are best dealt with in a freewheeling class discussion and informal journal entries. Few students can find much to write when asked to analyze any single artifact in a formal essay, but they seem to be able to talk (and write) almost endlessly on these pieces when allowed to do so in an unstructured medium.

In order to build the students' confidence in analyzing such sources, we have deliberately posited questions for analysis that largely lead the students to certain conclusions. Consider, for example, the Tassili rock painting. The obvious answer to question 1 is that the harvesters are women, and so probably is the person who is entering the field in the lower right. In answer to question 2, most of our students conclude that the person in the upper left is male and seems to be hunting. These answers in turn lead most of our students to infer, in answer to question 3, that women and probably children (our students have pointed out that the two smaller figures at the top of the second row of harvesters appear to be younger people) gathered the wild grains, whereas men hunted. This was, so it seems, a society that had gender- and age-specific tasks.

Equally leading is the first question that accompanies the two Nile temple reliefs. The answer to question 1 is that, as in Egypt, the Nubians perceived royal power as divine, insofar as a god conferred power on a monarch who, while he lived on Earth, was the incarnation of that god. One clue that strongly hints that the Nubians borrowed more than just a few artistic forms from Egypt is that, like Seti I, the anonymous Nubian monarch is on an equal plane with the god who is handing him the scepter of power. Both monarchs look their respective gods directly in the eyes, as equals. Question 2 is not as difficult to answer as it might first appear. Here we expect students to comment only on the obvious. When we take a few minutes to compare the two reliefs, we see a good deal of evidence of Egyptian influence on Nubian culture. Consider the similar ways in which the figures are dressed (the tight, skirt-like garments, the necklaces, bracelets, and arm bands worn by kings and deities alike, the royal crowns, and the gods' headdresses), the strikingly similar way each artist represented bodies in profile, and most significant of all, the similarity of motif. At the same time, the differences are equally important. The Nubian form of writing is radically different from that of Egypt. The Nubian king's crown, albeit influenced by the double crown of Egypt, is decidedly un-Egyptian. The lion god Apedemak might wear ornaments modeled on those of Horus and might strike a similar pose, but this is truly a deity of deeper Africa.

Of all the artifactual sources, the Indus, Mesopotamian, and Cretan seals are probably the most challenging. Although undoubtedly instructors and their students will discover insights in these artifacts that we have not perceived, we owe you a few words on what we are looking for in the Questions for Analysis that accompany source 8.

Question 1 asks the students to discover the obvious. Without necessarily being Freudian, we can say with assurance that the horned creature represents male sexual potency and muscular dominance and is often, but not invariably, a figure of reverence and authority in a warrior society. (One of the titles of the Aryan warrior-god Indra was "mighty bull"; the bull was also sacred to Lord Poseidon, the Earthshaker, the Greek god of the sea and earthquakes.) The same is true of the hairy male (question 2), such as Enkidu (source 1) and the biblical Samson (Judges, Chapters 13–16), who apparently was modeled on Gilgamesh and Enkidu.

Question 3 regarding the figure in seal 6 is intriguing. Many scholars believe this is a Harappan prototype of the god Shiva, the Hindu god of fertility and wild beasts, as well as the Destroyer. The fact that this putative fertility deity is surrounded by powerful wild beasts and a rather puny human stick figure suggests his centrality in the Harappan cosmos (and the relative insignificance of humans?). Moreover, if he is three-faced, as some viewers of the seal maintain, he might also anticipate later three-faced Hindu effigies of the divine trinity of Brahma, Vishnu, and Shiva. All of this speculation leads to the further theory that important elements of ancient Harrapan religion—specifically what and how much we will probably never know—survived the Aryan influx. There is another possible explanation of whom this figure represents. The oversized buffalo-horn headdress, his yogic posture, and the apparent look of trance on his face suggests that he *could* be a shaman (see source 10, as well) in a priest-dominated society. If he is, does he claim the ability to become each of these wild creatures? And what does that mean? Yes, the mysteries contained in these Harappan seals make them all the more fun to analyze.

Question 4 gets to the heart of the matter of cultural exchange and syncretism. Even a casual glance at these nine seals reveals striking similarities. (For example, compare the bull leapers in seals 4 and 9, the hairy heroes in seals 1, 7, and 8, and the horned animals flanking an apparent sacred tree in seals 3 and 8.) We ask our students to make as exhaustive a list as possible of all such similarities. We ask them further to note the ways in which similar motifs have been altered to fit different environmental realities (e.g., compare the animals being vanquished in seals 1 and 7). After they have done this, we then ask the question: Who do you think influenced whom? Given the early dates of the Mesopotamian seals and the geographic centrality of Mesopotamia, sitting as it does between the region of the Persian Gulf and the eastern Mediterranean, it seems logical to conclude that Mesopotamia was the matrix from which most of these motifs and ideas flowed east and west. This does not preclude, however, the generation of some of these themes in either Harappan India or the eastern Mediterranean. For example, there are no bull leapers in any Mesopotamian seal. Possibly the bull leaper was a Harrapan motif that traveled westward to Crete by way of Mesopotamia. Of course, all of this is speculation, but there can be no doubt that there was significant cultural exchange of some sort taking place.

The four Olmec figurines in source 10 are quite a bit easier to interpret, given the source's rather full introduction and leading questions. It is clear that what we have here is a sequence of magical moments in which a shaman metamorphoses into a were-jaguar, a divine creature of mystery and power, as well as of courage, cunning, and stamina. Question 3 is the key question here, and we hope that, in considering and discussing it, students will see that, so far as Olmec society was concerned, humans could embody these qualities of the jaguar only in an environment in which there was no sharp dichotomy between humans and the rest of the natural world. But is that also not the message of the nine seals in source 8? Perhaps students should be asked to compare the two sets of artifacts with an eye toward discovering and analyzing the world views that they shared.

Other Ways to Use the Sources

You will never exhaust all of the sources and the seemingly endless Questions for Analysis that we have provided. We never have. At the same time, however, we enjoy coming up every year with totally new journal and spurious primary source problems to test students' understanding of the material, to challenge their historical imagination, to enliven class discussion, and to keep us fresh. Here are a few that we tried recently.

1. An aged Gilgamesh is reflecting on his life as he awaits death. Compose his memoirs in two pages.
2. Hammurabi is asked to defend his judgments. Give him the best possible arguments in their defense.
3. Compose Gilgamesh's commentary on the three Egyptian funerary texts.

4. Choose any two workers or other nonscribes mentioned in the *Scribal Exercise Book* and compose their responses to the scribes who created this student exercise piece.

5. Imagine that you are an advisor to the president of the United States and are instructing him or her in the nature and workings of the *Mandate of Heaven*. What would you say? Be sure to point out to the president the attitudes and practices that he or she must abandon. Emphasize the consequences that will follow if the president does not prove worthy of the *Mandate of Heaven*.

6. Choose any single artifact, or coherent group of artifacts, from the "Mute Testimony" section, and describe it through the eyes of its artist. What does it represent, and why did the artist craft it?

7. For those who are artistically gifted: Draw or otherwise craft an artifact that expresses the message of any *document* of your choice in Chapter 1.

CHAPTER

2

New Comers: From Nomads to Settlers

Chapter Theme

Nomadic pastoral peoples inhabiting the fringes of settled societies have played important historical roles since the dawn of agriculture and down at least to the seventeenth century C.E. These *fringe peoples*, as anthropologists term them, often interacted with their settled, or *centered*, neighbors as merchants and mercenaries and also served as pools from which sedentary cultures drew new inhabitants and slaves or other types of servants. Conversely, nomads also raided settlements and even conquered civilizations. In time, many of these conquering invaders from the deserts, mountains, and steppes succumbed to the heady delights of civilization and, in turn, became the prey of other fringe peoples.

The sources in this chapter shed light on the early histories of three newcomers: the Aryans, the Greeks (or, more correctly at this time, the Achaeans), and the Hebrews. The three groups exhibited many similarities, especially strong warrior traditions. More significantly, the documents reveal their striking differences and the roots of what became three of Eurasia's major cultural matrices—Hinduism, Hellenism, and Judaism.

Why These Sources?

The excerpts from *The Rig Veda* show us three of the many faces of Indo-Aryan religious thought and hint at the ways in which it evolved. Created between roughly 1200 and 900 B.C.E. in the heart of a period we term the *Vedic Age* and imprecisely dated as ca. 1800 to about 600 B.C.E. (the dates vary with each historian), *The Rig Veda* was one of the major bases for what later became one of the world's greatest social-religious complexes—Hinduism.

The hymn celebrating Indra's victory over Vritra, the earliest of the three poems from *The Rig Veda* that we have put together to make up source 11, is a prayer of thanksgiving for the monsoon rains, a central feature of India's climate. Without the violent rains that come in June there would be no life in most of the Indian subcontinent. Thunder and lightning are harbingers of doom in many cultures; in India they are signs of divine beneficence. Indra, the Thunder-Wielder, has again vanquished the dragon of drought, which has held the land captive since October. As befit a warrior people, the Aryans' chief deity, Indra, was a god of battle, who slew large numbers of *dasas*, the indigenous people of India. But as we see here, his destructive powers brought new life, for he was also a creator deity and a protector god. This apparent contradiction is at the core of the Indian religious vision and is a concept we shall encounter again and again, especially in Chapter 6, source 43.

"The Hymn to Purusha," the third sacred song in our collection of vedic poetry (we will deal with the second hymn in a moment), comes to us from a later and less bellicose period of Indo-Aryan history that we term the *Late Vedic Era*. Like the hymn celebrating Indra's victory, it also underscores the Indian belief that life is born in death, but it does so in a way that is more spiritually complex than what we saw in that first song. This mythic tale depicts the origins of the universe as the result of an act of self-sacrifice by Purusha, the Primeval Being, from whom all forms of life, including the gods and humans, are descended. Here we can glimpse a moment of historical transition in which the ancient religion of the Aryans, which revolved around ritual sacrifices to the gods, was becoming more speculative and transcendental. Most important of all, we can find in this hymn clear evidence of the roots of what will be Hinduism's central religious insight: the unity and, therefore, intrinsic divinity of all being.

Before arriving there, Indo-Aryan society had to depose Indra from his position of divine primacy. The second hymn, which chronologically falls between the hymn celebrating Indra's victory over Vritra and the hymn commemorating Purusha's creative sacrifice, suggests that as the Aryans settled down and were absorbed into Indian society, their ancient god of war became less central to their lives and worship. Indra never disappears from the Hindu pantheon. Indeed, nothing ever seems to be discarded in Hinduism. He became, however, a far less important deity in the Late Vedic Era and eventually assumed a minor function as the god of weather. This poem's attempt to assert Indra's supremacy in the face of doubts about his very existence is a sure sign of changing religious values and perceptions.

The Odyssey shows us another world, one whose values and religious ideas were much closer to those of the earliest Aryan invaders of Harappan India than they were to India's Late Vedic Era. By 1600 B.C.E. the Achaean cousins of the Aryans had forged a decentralized, warrior civilization in the

Greek Peninsula—a civilization that we usually call *Mycenaean*, in acknowledgment of the primacy of Mycenae, a principality in the Peloponnesus. By at least 1400 B.C.E. the Achaeans were writing an early form of Greek in a script known as *Linear B*. We chose not to include any Linear B texts because, as valuable as they are for shedding light on Mycenaean society, these records are solely palace inventories and, therefore, too difficult for an average undergraduate to analyze with any reasonable degree of success. We consequently turned to Homer, whoever he, she, or, more likely, they were. Although *The Odyssey*'s Homer flourished four to five hundred years after the era celebrated in this epic (assuming that the poem was crafted largely by an eighth-century genius), the poet (or poets) surely drew the basic story, as well as many of the vivid scenes and stock phrases that enliven the poem, from a bardic tradition that served as Greek society's living memory of its Mycenaean past.

Homer's contemporary audience saw Mycenaean civilization through the prism of a newly reemerging Greek civilization, for Homer was on the cusp of what we term the *Ionian Renaissance*, which was centered in the coastal Greek cities of Anatolia (modern Asiatic Turkey)—an area known as *Ionia* because of the settlement there of Greek colonists who spoke the Ionic dialect. The problem of separating thirteenth-century Mycenaean cultural elements from eighth-century Hellenic attitudes and institutions is one that vexes even the most expert Homeric scholar and should not be tackled in an introductory course in global history. We believe the value of the selection we have chosen lies in what it allows the student to discover about certain basic Greek beliefs and attitudes: to wit, the respective roles of fate and the gods in human affairs; the state of the dead; and the Greek focus on human beings and their concerns. These notions were certainly integral to Homer's society and remained constituent elements of the Hellenic worldview for ages to come. How Mycenaean they were is anyone's guess. References in *The Rig Veda* to a House of Clay, where the dead dwelt indefinitely do strongly suggest that the early Aryans had a notion of an afterlife that paralleled the realm of the dead that we see in both *The Epic of Gilgamesh* and *The Odyssey*, and this in turn allows us to guess (and that is the operable word) that the Mycenaean Greeks had a similar view of the Beyond.

Because the Hebraic religious tradition has largely centered on humanity's relationship with the Divine in this world, rather than in any afterworld, our first excerpts from the Bible revolve around the theme of an evolving covenant between the Hebrews and their special God and the earthly consequences of that agreement. The selections also allow the student to perceive that Hebrew society and religion did not develop within a vacuum. A comparative analysis of the story of Noah with its Mesopotamian prototype in *The Epic of Gilgamesh* should enable students to see how the Hebrews drew from the traditions of the older civilizations around them and how they turned what they borrowed to their own purposes.

Many instructors will, undoubtedly, be disappointed that we decided not to use the sonorous and familiar King James translation of the Bible. Our decision, painful as it was, was based on several criteria. We desired to present students with a translation they would find comfortable and readable, and we also wanted a translation based on up-to-date scholarship. For those reasons, we chose the Revised Standard Edition.

Analyzing the Sources

The first question relating to *The Rig Veda* is straightforward and should not overly tax students. Indra, a warrior sky deity, releases rainstorm clouds by slaying Vritra, thereby breaking a drought. The imagery and theme of this poem suggest that it was the product of a people who were abandoning their pastoral ways but still retained many of their traditional values and modes of life. The poem's theme strongly hints at the fact that the Aryans were becoming settled agriculturalists because drought is a far greater menace to a settled, agrarian people than to pastoral nomads who could move their flocks to wetter areas. At the same time, the poet's use of cattle imagery (e.g., "like lowing cows," "impetuous as a bull") suggests that cattle remained an important element in the cultural fabric of the Aryans. Likewise, it is significant that this god who brings rain is a warrior god. This suggests that Aryan society still retained many of its ancient warrior traditions and was probably still warrior-dominated.

The remaining five questions are not so easily answered and demand more probing analysis. With a bit of help from the instructor, however, students should be able handle the questions successfully. Questions 2, 3, 4, and 6 should be examined as a unit. In attempting to answer them, the student should arrive at several important insights. First, the Indra whom we see in the second hymn is much more and a bit less than the Indra of the first hymn. The priestly poet of the hymn "Who Is Indra?" declares that Indra is the chief god of the cosmos and the bringer and preserver of life, as well as the destroyer of enemies. Yet this god's very existence was being questioned by some, and the hymn seems to protest just a bit too much. Indra's days as premier deity were numbered. Second, "The Hymn to Purusha" shows us where late-vedic religious thought was headed. Here we see a culture in which warriors and their special gods were no longer unquestionably dominant. To lead students to this second insight, we find it helpful to ask them how this third hymn explains and justifies an emerging caste system. Even though the caste system was not fully articulated until many centuries later (We deal with it in detail in Chapters 3 and 5, sources 17, 38, and 39.), "The Hymn to Purusha" clearly indicates that this uniquely Hindu form of social-religious organization had begun to take shape before the end of the Vedic Era. We suggest that you first ask your students to identify the four *varnas*, or great castes, and to describe the place of each in the scheme of life. Then refer them back to the first hymn. As we saw, that poem seems to support the generally accepted notion that the *Rajanyas* (later known as the *Kshatriyas*), or warriors, were the earliest dominant Aryan class. A large body of evidence further leads us to conclude that the warriors gradually lost their position of preeminence to the *Brahmins* because of the priests' monopoly on sacrifice, the making and drinking of *Soma*, recitation of the sacred vedas, and teaching. The hymn extolling Purusha's self-sacrifice hints at this shift when it mentions the Brahmins first, noting that they were generated from and simultaneously became this cosmic spirit's mouth. (In Hindu culture the mouth is an especially sacred and clean orifice that serves as the organ of humanity's highest functions.) The hymn then puts the Rajanyas in second place, noting that they were generated from (and also became) Purusha's arms—noble limbs but definitely inferior to the mouth.

You might want to inform your students that this shift in caste dominance was not complete until after the Mauryan period (ca. 315–183 B.C.E.). You might also want to ask them to speculate on why the Brahmins eventually emerged as the dominant caste. Of course, we should always keep in mind that throughout Indian history strong *rajas* (princes) were often able to check brahminical pretensions and power.

After warming up with questions 1 through 4 and 6, students will be ready to wrestle with question 5, whose answer is far more difficult for a Westerner to arrive at and understand. Why? This question forces the student to confront the very essence of Indian religious truth. The principle of logical contradiction—an entity either is or is not but cannot simultaneously be both—holds no validity so far as Hindu cosmology is concerned. Life and death are not mutually exclusive states, and there is ultimately no substantial separation between humanity and the divine. We shall return to these ideas in more fully articulated form in later sources, but it is necessary to introduce students as early as possible to the Hindu idea of the unity of all being.

Unlike "The Hymn to Purusha," *The Odyssey* revolves around a society in which warriors were the unrivaled masters, but even these heroes could not outrun the gods, fate, and death. Homer's characters are fully responsible moral agents and exercise a wide latitude of freedom in their choices and actions, but ultimately they, and even the gods, must bow to the superior power of the *Moirai* (the three goddesses of fate). Here we see Odysseus of the Nimble Wits fleeing the enmity of Lord Poseidon the Earthshaker. Poseidon has buffeted Odysseus's passage home and is bent on his destruction. Ultimately, Odysseus's crew will perish, but their deaths will largely be a consequence of their own ill-considered action. Odysseus will arrive home—battered and late. Although Poseidon's power is great, even he cannot frustrate Odysseus's destiny or defeat a hero so filled with courage, determination, and quick wit. When death does come to Odysseus, as come it must, it will be gentle and befitting a great mariner-hero.

The place of dead shades to which he will go is very much like the house of dust that Enkidu had seen in his vision in *The Epic of Gilgamesh*. There former kings functioned as servants. As Achilles tells Odysseus (and us), dead princes and heroes in the Greek underworld would gladly exchange the empty honors of death for life as the poorest of unfree persons on Earth. Yet that is not the whole story. Even in death these shades continue to focus on the world they left behind. Achilles grieves over the state of his aged father and swells with pride over his son's heroic deeds. The Hellenes might believe that life on Earth, with all of its sorrows and its inevitable end, is the sum total of the human portion, but they glory in that life.

The instructor should not miss the opportunity to compare this passage with *The Epic of Gilgamesh*. Perceptive students will inevitably note the close parallels between both selections and will conclude correctly that what we have here is, at least in part, a Greek recasting of the Gilgamesh tradition.

The story of Noah is likewise a recasting of a Mesopotamian myth but a retelling with an important difference. It is hardly possible to exaggerate the impact of Mesopotamian and Egyptian ideas and institutions on the various cultures of Syria-Palestine, and that includes the Hebrews. However, as is almost always the case with such borrowings, the Hebrews added their own cultural twist. All six Questions for Analysis clearly hint at this fact, and the first four questions are so framed as to stimulate a student's perceiving that YHWH is a moral god who demands certain proper actions on the part of humans. According to *The Epic of Gilgamesh*, Enlil called for the destruction of humanity because of the noise it made, and the council of gods concurred. In the Genesis story, to the contrary, YHWH decided to destroy humanity because of its evil ways, especially its violence. Ea, for no apparent reason other than his oath to protect civilization, frustrated Enlil by warning Utnapishtim and later denied that he was the one who whispered the warning. According to the Hebrew version of the flood story, YHWH saved Noah and his family because Noah alone was righteous. YHWH's rainbow, a visible token of the covenant between this single god and all of humankind, reminds us of Ishtar's necklace of rare lapis lazuli (source 1, note 14). Yet there is a significant difference. Ishtar's rainbow was a reminder of Utnapishtim's ritual sacrifice to all the gods (except Enlil) and the fact that by so doing he acknowledged his servantship. YHWH's rainbow reminded humans that never again would all life on earth be threatened with extinction by a flood, but in return for this promise all living creatures were now subject to a moral code that sanctified human life.

The striking similarities and even more important differences between these two flood accounts often lead students to ask why YHWH differs so markedly from the gods of Mesopotamia, especially in light of the fact that Hebrew culture borrowed so heavily from Mesopotamia, and the Hebrews even traced their ancestry back to Ur (Genesis 11:27-31). Evidence does not allow us to posit a definitive answer to this important question, but it seems that the key to understanding the phenomenon of the rise of an all-powerful god of morality among the Hebrews is the proximity of Egypt and the consequent deep influence that Egypt had on the land of Syria-Palestine, especially in the age of Egypt's New Kingdom, or Empire (ca. 1550–1069 B.C.E.). As *The Book of the Dead* shows, during the later stages of the Middle Kingdom (ca. 1700–1550 B.C.E.) and throughout the era of the New Kingdom, Egypt evolved the notion that an afterlife of eternal bliss (an idea not yet current among the Hebrews) depended upon one's moral behavior in this world. Moreover, there was a growing tendency among the Egyptians to merge their various deities into one all-powerful god of the universe. This was true so far as the chief deity of the New Kingdom, Amon-Re, was concerned, and it was certainly true in the case of the short-lived primacy of Aten, the sun disc, the sole god worshipped by Amenhotep IV, or Akhenaten (ca. 1369–1353 B.C.E.), the "heretic king." Both of these Egyptian religious ideas probably had a profound influence on the evolution of Hebraic (and later Judaic) religion in antiquity. Sources 13–15 of this present chapter, and source 22 of Chapter 3, trace some of the high points of that evolution in religious vision.

Questions 5 and 6 deserve attention simply because answers to them nicely illustrate how a careful reading of a document often enables us to place it within a temporal and social context.

The answers to the two parts of question 5, of course, are that this is a rigidly patriarchal society, and Ham has dishonored his father. In such a patriarchal culture, the guilt for a father's heinous crimes, such as this act, could be inherited by the children, especially male children, and even down to distant generations. Compare this, for example, with judgment 230 in *The Judgments of Hammurabi,* where if a father's shoddy construction work has resulted in the loss of a client's child, his own child can be killed in retribution and as a social deterrent.

Answers to the two segments of question 6 are, likewise, not difficult to reach. The story was obviously an attempt to explain why YHWH had given the Children of Israel permission to conquer the land of Canaan. As a justification of the Hebrew invasion of this land, the story, as we have received it, cannot be dated any earlier than ca. 1200 B.C.E., and it probably dates from no earlier than the tenth millennium (900s) B.C.E.

The excerpts from Deuteronomy and Judges deserve explication in class largely because they illustrate the continued development of the idea of a *covenant*—the central religious concept of what becomes Judaism. Because they develop a single theme, they are probably best analyzed as a unit.

The selection from Deuteronomy is significant for a number of reasons. Note that the idea of the Children of Israel as a Chosen People predominates here. In return for keeping YHWH's commandments, and this especially means honoring no other gods, they are promised a homeland and prosperity. They are not to marry any people who worship other gods, and they are to mercilessly wipe out all memory of these alien neighbors and their cults. Such strong prohibitions suggest that a fair amount of intermarriage and cultural interchange was taking place in Josiah's kingdom of Judah. Should the Children of Abraham and Israel not honor their special covenant with YHWH, then, as the Book of Judges tells us, they will suffer disaster. When they repent and cry out for mercy, however, YHWH will hear them and send a deliverer.

What is also worthy of note here is that apparently at this time Israel's Covenant with YHWH was not predicated upon a notion of strict monotheism. YHWH seems to acknowledge the existence of other deities and simply commands exclusive worship. Such a phenomenon is termed *monolatry*—exclusive devotion to a single deity while not denying the existence of other divine beings. Note also that YHWH promises only temporal, or earthly, prosperity in return for keeping the Covenant. There is no mention here of any Heaven or blissful life after death—an idea that the Hebrews did not embrace at this time.

Other Ways to Use the Sources

1. Compose Odysseus's personal account of his journey to the Underworld. In this memoir, lay bare the man's soul, and show what he learned from this extraordinary adventure.
2. You are an eyewitness to both the flood of Utnapishtim and Noah's flood. Compose a newspaper account of these two disasters in which you compare and contrast them. In this account you must quote Mesopotamian and Hebrew witnesses (Yes, we know, they all drowned, but indulge us here.) in such a way as to illustrate how the two cultures perceived these floods and their aftermaths.
3. You are one of those Children of Israel to whom Moses gave his farewell address. What is your understanding of what he said?
4. People often look upon religions as static entities. Some prophet has delivered the word of God, and the faithful followers of that word maintain it through the ages that follow. In Chapters 1 and 2 we have studied sources that illustrate evolutions of religious perception in three different cultures. Choose any one of those cultures (the Egyptians, the Indo-Aryans, or the Hebrews), and show how their religious insights and ideas took shape over time.

CHAPTER
3

Transcendental Reality: Developing the Spiritual Traditions of India and Southwest Asia: 800–200 B.C.E.

Chapter Theme

In this chapter we concentrate on the early stages of two major spiritual traditions. The first, which we see manifested in Brahminical Hinduism, Jainism, and Buddhism, is a world- and self-denying transcendentalism that emerged in India between roughly 800 and 200 B.C.E. The second, which we see manifested in Zoroastrianism and Judaism, is a world- and self-affirming ethical monotheism that became an important tradition in Southwest Asia between roughly 600 and 200 B.C.E. (although Zoroaster might have lived and taught as early as the fourteenth century B.C.E.).

Judaism and Hinduism present the instructor of global history with special problems because neither traces its origins to a single prophet, saint, or founder. Judaism slowly grew out of the varied experiences and religious visions of an entire people, and Hinduism slowly grew out of the varied experiences and religious visions of many different peoples. Consequently, anyone who attempts to fix precisely the historical point at which each emerged as a fully articulated faith is doomed to frustration.

This is particularly true for Hinduism, which is a family of religions, rather than a single religion. It has no single creed that it enjoins on all believers, no single set of rituals common to all Hindus, and no single organized church. It does not even have a single, universally accepted pantheon, although most Hindus tolerantly accept all the deities of India, especially the great trinity of Brahma, Vishnu, and Shiva, even as they simultaneously believe in an all-pervading Divine Reality, or *Brahman*. Just as significantly, Hindus almost universally belong to one of India's four great castes, or *varnas*—Brahmins (priests), Kshatriyas (warrior-rulers), Vaisyas (farmers, artisans, and merchants), and Sudras (servants)—that define and regulate essentially every aspect of a person's life. Of these religious-social groups, the Brahmin caste is considered the highest and purest. In addition to organizing the most public and private aspects of their lives according to the dictates of caste law (*dharma*) and tradition and also accepting, at least in a religious sense, the primacy of the Brahmins, most Hindus also share certain basic cosmological beliefs. The most important of these core assumptions are: (1) the tangible, observable world is unreal, in contrast to the real world of the spirit; (2) the world of the spirit, or *Brahman,* is all-encompassing; (3) each individual possesses an *atman,* or soul, which is identical to Brahman, the universal absolute; (4) the atman is the Real Self, as opposed to the unreal sensory self, which is a mass of corporeal desires that serve as the focus of the self-absorbed person; (5) as long as the atman remains in a state of unrealized unity with Brahman, it is a *jivatman* and migrates from body to body in a process of reincarnation known as *samsara*—the painful transmigration of unperfected souls; (6) samsara will continue until the soul has been cleansed of all taint of blind attachment to this world and the concomitant selfishness (concern with the desires of the unreal corporeal self) that results; (7) *karma,* or the fruits of one's deeds in a previous incarnation, determines the life form a soul enters into at each rebirth; (8) the law of karma is that good deeds, that is deeds that one *selflessly* performs in obedience to one's caste obligations (*dharma*) and the general laws of the universe (also known as dharma), cleanse the soul of selfish desire; (9) finally, the soul so cleansed, usually after numerous incarnations, achieves liberation (*moksha*), or unity with Brahman, and an end to the chain of karma and samsara.

Despite the foolhardiness of any attempt to place the emergence of Hinduism and Judaism into precise historical settings, we have chosen, respectively, the age of the *Upanishads* and the period of Second, or *Deutero,* Isaiah as the eras when these two religious forces clearly emerged into the light of history. In so doing, we deny neither the preceding centuries of development nor the uncontroverted fact that Hinduism and Judaism, as we know them today, were not fully formed until, respectively, the Gupta Age (320–ca. 550 C.E.) and the centuries following the destruction of Jerusalem in 70 C.E. We justify our interpretation on the following bases.

The Upanishads, which were composed between roughly 800 and 500 B.C.E., were the culmination of the vedic-brahminical traditions and a breakout into new spiritual frontiers. Without rejecting sacrificial ritualism or emerging caste distinctions, the Upanishads stressed the individual's interior search for the Divine One. Rejection of the unreal self (the body and its ego) in order to discover and release the Real Self (the atman, which is actually Brahman) took center stage. Moksha, or release from the endless cycle of reincarnation and the bonds of matter, was now the highest goal of the spiritual seeker. Hinduism had developed its characteristic spiritualism and otherworldly orientation.

The special characteristic of Judaism is the belief that Jews are a divinely Chosen People who have entered into a unique covenant with the sole God of the universe, a God who is Goodness. As a consequence, these People of the Covenant serve as God's moral agents in the world, helping to realize the divine plan for all humanity. It is only with Second Isaiah in the sixth century B.C.E. that we see a clear articulation and integration of all of these elements. The earlier prophets, dating back to the middle ninth century B.C.E., had preached the primacy of the Covenant and the need for conduct that was pleasing to YHWH, and they were, thereby, essentially practical monotheists. Yet, they did not explicitly state that only YHWH exists as God. This changed with Second Isaiah, for whom the Lord (*Adonai,* which is a title, as opposed to the earlier personal name YHWH) is the sole creator and ruler of the universe. The Lord is the God of all peoples, whether they know him or not. Because Israel knows and is bound to the Lord by a special covenant, it alone is God's *suffering servant,* and through its tribulations and patient witness it will bring all nations to the Lord.

This chapter presents the instructor with the additional challenge of wrestling with the issue of how to present Jainism and Buddhism in relation to Hinduism's Upanishadic tradition. We believe that, when studying them in the context of their sixth-century B.C.E. origins, one must not view these two spiritual schools as rival religions to mainstream, or Brahminical, Hinduism. What is more, using the model of Europe's Protestant Reformation to explain Jainism and Buddhism's relationship with Brahminical Hinduism is equally inappropriate (although many commentators have chosen to use this analogy). Much more appropriate is the analogy of China's roughly contemporaneous Age of a Hundred Schools. Just as China's sages of the Late Spring and Autumn Era (722–481 B.C.E.) produced a broad spectrum of secular philosophies in answer to the troubles that plagued late Zhou society, so India's gurus created a rich variety of answers to spiritual questions that vexed Indian society, and in that variety demonstrated the fluidity of Indian spiritual thought. At the same time, whatever their differences (such as the Buddha's and the Mahavira's rejection of caste and brahminical ritual), all three spiritual schools that we are considering here addressed directly India's central spiritual question and offered answers that in essence were strikingly similar. The central question was: How does one escape the sorrows of earthly life, especially the sting of death? Their answers, although variously presented, were the same: Escape is only possible through rejection of that ephemeral and unreal *ego* which is rooted in the world of matter.

Why These Sources?

There are as many as 108 Upanishads (depending on who is doing the counting), but of them several early texts enjoy special authority, especially the *Chandogya* and *Brihadaranyaka*. The excerpt from the *Chandogya* illustrates the central message of the Upanishadic school: *Eternal divinity lies within each mortal being because Brahman (the Universal Soul) and atman (the individual soul) are one and the same.* The selection from the *Brihadaranyaka* makes it clear that this human soul is not some transitory or world-immersed personality. It is a divine spark that, following the law of karma, travels from body to body (human and nonhuman) until it is released to return to the One. That release comes when a person fully comprehends that divinity lies within and puts aside all earthly desires. Then even caste and its law (dharma) become unimportant because one has reached the plane of Brahman.

Until one reaches that state of pure soul (a state that transcends mere intellectual affirmation of one's Brahmanhood), there are caste, dharma, and karma. The excerpt from the much later *Bhagavad Gita* defines karma and dharma more fully and emphasizes that in order for caste actions to be fully meritorious they must be performed with absolute selflessness. One cannot earn meritorious karma if one *desires* it. Consequently, release through Upanishadic self-knowledge and release through faithful performance of caste duty both involve rejection of all desires and egoism.

The Mahavira and the Buddha rejected caste, the Vedas, and brahminical ritual but not the concepts of karma and dharma and certainly not India's central spiritual value—selflessness. They also equally accepted the notion, which runs through all Indian religious teaching, that the soul can be perfected through discipline, even though the Buddha refused to speculate on the existence of the soul and appears to have assumed that neither atman nor Brahman existed. Well, we never promised you this was easy.

The selections from *The Book of Good Conduct* reveal that, for the Jains, dharma is the universal law of absolute asceticism and nonviolence toward all life (*ahimsa*). From this central principle it follows that karma, by definition the fruit of action, is always negative and never positive. Why? Because all activity involves some level of violence toward living beings, no matter how unintended. This violence produces karma, which is nothing more than a weighty dust that adheres to the soul, weighs it down, and prevents its upward movement to a purely spiritual plane. Any and all karma means continued existence and reincarnation, and that in turn means pain. Escape and release to *Nirvana* can only be achieved through an extreme rejection of activity and sensual experiences and an asceticism that outweighs and burns up the karma gained through even minimal actions.

Like the Mahavira, the Buddha preached that life is sorrow. Unlike the Mahavira, however, the Buddha embraced the *Middle Path* of passionless, disciplined, nonactive action that avoided the fierce asceticism of the Jains because, to his mind, any extreme action is the product of desire (or passion), and desire is the root of all suffering. Such a moral, well-ordered life, he believed, would lead to the total cessation of all desires and, thereby, release from this world of pain. Like the Mahavira, he envisioned dharma (or Dharma—a convention we employ when referring to the Buddhist law as opposed to Hindu caste law) as a universal law, but for him it was encapsulated in the Four Noble Truths.

There are a number of different versions of the Buddha's sermon on "Setting in Motion the Wheel of the Law," and all of them date from long after his death. All, however, present essentially the same message contained in our selection. This leads us to conclude that what we have here is a valid memory of the Buddha's original moral philosophy. A few scholars, to the contrary, doubt that this sermon in an way reflects the Buddha's teachings. If they are correct, then we shall never know what the historical Siddhartha Gautama thought and taught. Whatever the case, this sermon preserves the essential doctrines of Buddhism as it came to be known and spread throughout northern India and beyond.

The second sermon of the Buddha, which makes up the other half of source 19, is almost equally famous. "Questions That Tend Not to Edification" illustrates the essential agnosticism of the Buddha's original teachings so far as many basic religious issues are concerned. Nowhere in the record of his teachings is there mention of a Divine Other, an immortal soul, or an afterlife. In fact, as we noted above, the Buddha seems to have gone so far as to deny the existence of an atman, or substantial soul. Although he accepted the principle of karma, he rejected the idea of samsara, or transmigration of souls, because he appears to have believed there are no souls to migrate. It seems that, as far as he was concerned, karma is the migration at the time of death of the moral state of one individual to another. One life, therefore, builds upon another, just as a flame passes from one candle to another (one of his favorite analogies). As to the questions of whether or not there is a Divine Reality and whether or not liberated persons exist in some manner after death, the Buddha chose to have no stated position, considering such issues irrelevant to the person on the path to ending selfish desire.

Our next Buddhist text tells the story of the successful attempt by the Buddha's aunt, Maha-Prajapati, to gain permission for women to enter into the monastic life. The Buddha was a spiritual teacher, not a social reformer, and consequently he was initially reluctant to stray too far from social norms by allowing women to participate in such supposedly unwomanly activities. But he was forced by the very nature of his spiritual message to accord women the opportunity to reach Enlightenment through monastic discipline. The value of this document is twofold. First it sheds light on the meaning of the Buddhist message for women in the age of the Buddha and for ever after. Second, it gives us a glimpse, however imperfectly, of the status of Indian women. But the question is: Indian women when and where? As the introduction to this source suggests, the document's strongly misogynistic sentiments might well reflect the attitudes of a society far removed in time and space from that of the Buddha.

The teachings of Zarathustra and Second Isaiah provide another view of the meaning of human existence and humanity's relationship with the Other. Perceptive students will ask what influence Persians and Israelites had on one another's religious development, especially in light of the fact that Syria-Palestine became a Persian satrapy. The fact is, no one knows for certain if there were any lines of influence. The *Gathas* make no reference whatsoever to the cultures of Mesopotamia, Hellas, or Syria-Palestine, and it is equally impossible to demonstrate any direct Zoroastrian influences on the teachings of Second Isaiah. Despite this lack of evidence, it seems almost inconceivable that there was no religious interplay between Persian Zoroastrianism and Judaism.

As noted in the introduction to source 21, Zarathustra was not a strict monotheist. Indeed, we usually term his faith *dualistic* because, in addition to Ahura Mazda, the God whom he worshiped and served, this Persian prophet acknowledged the existence of a coeternal, almost coequal enemy god of evil, the Liar. What is more, he also accepted the existence of a host of lesser spirits (the angelic *yazatas* and the demonic *daevas*). Notwithstanding all of this, Zarathustra centered his faith on a single ethical God of history. That is, he envisioned Ahura Mazda to be the universe's sole creator God—a God who is purely spiritual, totally good, and uniquely worthy of devotion. What is more, this God of Goodness calls upon humans to act on Earth as his agents in a cosmic struggle with evil—a struggle that will result in victory. By using humans in this manner, Ahura Mazda has elevated human history to a new plane of significance. Put another way, Zarathustra perceived human history as a divine morality play.

The same can and should be said about Second Isaiah. As suggested, the selections from the Book of Isaiah that appear here are the expression of a new stage in the spiritual journey of the Israelites, in which they now perceived themselves as a people with a world mission. Chapters 1 through 39 of the Book of Isaiah were clearly composed in an eighth-century B.C.E. setting in which Assyria was a major power and a threat to the independence of Judah, and the concerns of this prophet were largely local and focused on Jerusalem, the holy city. Chapters 40 through 66 present different settings and visions. Scholars generally divide these latter chapters into the prophecy of Second Isaiah (Chapters 40–55), which they date to around 540 B.C.E., or just prior to the fall of Babylon in 538, and the writings of Third Isaiah (Chapters 56–66), which they place in the period immediately following the return of the Jews to Judah after Cyrus's victory over Babylon. Both of these later, otherwise unknown "Isaiahs" were universalists.

The words of Second Isaiah proclaim a new Exodus and, by implication, a new Covenant. Earlier, as we saw in Chapter 2, source 14, the Israelites were enjoined by YHWH not to mingle with any alien people. Indeed, YHWH even commanded the Israelites to show no mercy and to put them all to death. Failure to do so resulted in the Israelites being sorely tested and even seduced away from worship of their God (source 15). Now, however, certain gentiles, namely King Cyrus and the Persians, appear as servants of the Lord (albeit unknowing servants) and protectors of Zion. The Lord is now sole God of all people. When Cyrus frees the captive Israelites and rebuilds Jerusalem, those who have suffered bitter exile in Babylon will return in triumph and will serve as "a light to the nations, that my salvation may reach to the end of the earth."

Analyzing the Sources

In our remarks on why we chose these particular sources, we have implied answers to many of the questions for analysis. A few questions require some additional comments. Moreover, here is probably the best place to emphasize again our belief that it is necessary for the instructor to help students realize, as they read these particular sources that seem initially so alien and incomprehensible to most of them, that all of the documents, with the possible exception of Second Isaiah, directly address the core issues dealt with in *The Epic of Gilgamesh* and the Egyptian funerary texts--the meaning of life and death. Now on to the yet unaddressed Questions for Analysis.

Question 6 for source 16, "Why do good and evil cease to have any meaning to the soul that has found Brahman?" often perplexes students, especially those who approach the issue of good and evil from a Judaeo-Christian-Islamic perspective, where God is Absolute Good. From a Hindu perspective, good and evil are simply categories of change (and, consequently, imperfection) in a material world and have no meaning outside of a constantly changing material creation. Here we should keep in mind the words of Lord Krishna in *The Bhagavad Gita*: "One should not abandon a natural duty though tainted with evil; for all actions are enveloped by evil, as smoke by fire." It follows from this that *once a soul has united with Brahman all change ceases, and good and evil have no meaning*. Moreover, because acts and values that we in the West generally perceive as either good or bad are in Hindu eyes equally good and bad, we encounter many Hindu deities, such as Shiva, who present what to Westerners seem to be dual, contradictory identities—malevolence and benevolence. We will deal with this issue in greater detail when we comment on source 43, the *Shiva Nataraja* statue of Chapter 6.

Question 8 of source 16, "How is the upanishadic view of Brahman a logical development from the message of the `Hymn to Purusha'?" is important to address, if only for the fact that it underscores the historical perspective. The historian never views the past as a static phenomenon. We are always aware that institutions and ideas change over the course of time, even in so-called traditional, or conservative, societies. Although historical developments rarely, if ever, follow straight or rational paths, it is necessary that we help our students see how the upanishadic vision of Reality had antecedents in some of the last vedic songs. Review what we have written in Chapter 2 of this manual concerning "The Hymn to Purusha."

Question 4 relating to *The Bhagavad Gita* also deserves careful attention. Students often assume that modern egalitarian values are timeless and universal. Hindu society, as we saw in "The Hymn to Purusha," attempts to provide a metaphysical explanation for the obvious fact that people are not born into equal situations, and many are exploited throughout their lives. Moreover, Hinduism also attempts to give hope to those in such a condition that their status will improve, but certainly not in this incarnation. If one's low caste is a consequence of evil deeds performed in a previous life (the law of karma), then one deserves that caste and must complete the full life-time penalty, no matter how long that might be. Conscientious and *selfless* devotion to caste obligations, no matter how demeaning, will earn one sufficient merit for a higher caste in the next incarnation and possibly even liberation (moksha) from the cycle of rebirth (samsara), if performed in perfect selflessness.

Today Jains number not much more than three million individuals in India and Sri Lanka combined, so demanding is the selfless life required of the followers of the Mahavira's call to heroic asceticism. Buddhists, to the contrary, number in the hundreds of millions throughout South and East Asia, in large part because of the comforting message of the Buddha's self-denying Middle Path. Although the Buddha was destined to have the greater impact on world history, we suspect that their sixth-century B.C.E. contemporaries in northeast India viewed the Mahavira and the Buddha as equally significant teachers.

The Mahavira and the Buddha, both Kshatriyas, spiritualized the martial values of their warrior caste, and both claimed to have conquered the cycle of suffering. (*Jina*, or Conqueror, is one of the Mahavira's titles, and a Jain is "one who conquers.") One had done it through heroic asceticism, the other through a moderate but demanding discipline, and both had done so selflessly, as befits any warrior hero. Moreover, the fact that both were Kshatriyas who rejected the constraints of caste is probably evidence that many warrior-rulers of this era, and particularly of the Ganges region, were resisting the Brahmins' claims to caste superiority.

As students grapple with the first three questions of source 19, which force the reader to distill the essence of the Buddha's message, we have found it desirable to ask them, as a class, to recast the Four Noble Truths (the Law, or Dharma, of Buddhism) into their own words. In this way they are forced to think about what those words really mean. At the same time, because Buddhism is not a subject that most students easily understand when they first confront it, we offer an important hint by telling them to notice two things about the Four Noble Truths. First these truths delineate a systematic, rational analysis of the problem confronting all humans—suffering. Following that analysis, the Truths offer a *progressive* eight-step program of spiritual development guaranteed to relieve humans of this pain. (Apparently the Buddha did not need twelve steps—unless one wishes to count the Four Noble Truths as four preliminary steps that bring the seeker to the Holy Eightfold Path.) Consider the following schematic analysis and rewording of the Four Noble Truths:

1. First one comprehends that life is unhappiness.
2. Next one comprehends that this unhappiness is caused by a self-centered craving for gratification.

3. One then realizes that we can put an end to such selfish craving.
4. One understands that the means of destroying self-centeredness is an ordered and measured program of spiritual development known as the Holy Eightfold Path.

Although understanding these four truths is necessary for one's Enlightenment, understanding them is not Enlightenment because Enlightenment cannot be achieved solely by an act of the intellect. It can only be achieved by a total and radical reformulation of one's whole being through a long process of self-discipline. Once the person seeking release from pain has reached this preliminary level of insight, then that person is ready to undertake the eight, progressively steeper steps along the Middle Path that leads to *sambodhi,* or Enlightenment. The Enlightenment sought is such a total, *suprarational* understanding of the emptiness of selfish desires that one is, by that very fact of total understanding, purged of all such cravings. One reaches this state not in a moment of initial enthusiasm but only through a long journey of spiritual endeavor that progresses through three increasingly steep plateaus. We might call these the levels of *preparation, action,* and *contemplation.*

The plateau of preparation (or commitment) involves the first two steps along this holy path. One begins by understanding that the goal of ending all attachment to selfish desires is attainable and worthy of effort *(right belief).* One then resolves in mind to undertake the journey and also prepares one's psyche for the upcoming task *(right aspiration).* The second plateau of spiritual growth involves steps three, four, and five. One now acts morally by speaking the truth *(right speech),* acting honestly *(right conduct),* and earning one's living in a manner that does not coarsen one's psyche *(right means of livelihood).* The moral foundation laid in the first five steps enables the searcher after Enlightenment to move on to the third level, and that level culminates in sambodhi. In the sixth step *(right endeavor)* one not only acts morally, one disregards all distractions, or temptations, of the flesh. Step seven *(right memory)* means that one can finally focus the whole mind on the issues that are important, such as life and death. When this is achieved, one is then capable of total contemplation *(right meditation),* out of which comes Enlightenment and liberation from the chains of matter and suffering. As we can see, this eight-step process is totally rational and the product of a master psychologist, even though its goal of Enlightenment transcends reason.

As source 20 shows us, the Buddha believed that all persons, women and men, are capable of Enlightenment. Given this insight, he could not logically exclude women from full discipleship as monastic beggars. Yet, as *The*

Discipline Basket shows, tradition records that he was initially reluctant to admit them to the mendicant life, and when he finally did, he laid upon them eight special rules through which they were subordinated to male monks. In order to understand this apparent contradiction, we must distinguish between the Buddha's spiritual egalitarianism and the social norms and assumptions of his day (or of a later day that reshaped the early history of female Buddhist monasticism). The Buddha probably accepted the notion that women are inferior to men by nature, being weaker both in body and temperament, and probably equally accepted the customs of his society that were predicated on such a view of nature. This does not necessarily mean, however, that he was a misogynist. It appears that the eight special rules for female mendicants (if, indeed, he ever articulated them) represented the Buddha's attempt to assist these naturally weak followers to achieve Enlightenment. In fact, sex and gender issues were largely irrelevant to the Buddha, *as far as we can judge from his spiritual message*. For this reason, most scholars believe that the misogynistic statement at the end of this passage (by allowing women into the monastic profession, the good Law as taught by the Buddha will only survive for five hundred years) is a later interpolation and does not reflect the Buddha's words or sentiments. We think it likely that a male monk from the conservative wing of Buddhism, the Theravada School, penned this interpolation as a jab at what he considered to be a new heresy—Mahayana Buddhism. Established roughly half a millennium after the Buddha's lifetime, the Mahayana School attracted large numbers of women by virtue of its message of universal salvation. We shall look at Mahayana Buddhism in Chapter 6.

Despite these special rules, which effectively subordinated Buddhist nuns to male rule, and despite, undoubtedly, a fair degree of male hostility toward female mendicants, many women found the monastic profession attractive. Question 6 asks students to speculate why any woman would freely choose such a life. Apart from the obvious spiritual motives that surely impelled many pious women into monasteries, there is the possibility that in a male-dominated society celibacy can empower a women, especially when she joins forces with other celibate women. Despite the fact that they lived a highly structured life and were subordinated to male monks, these women were free of any direct control over them by fathers and husbands. That, in and of itself, meant they had achieved a degree of freedom and power normally not available to women. What is more, Buddhist (and later Christian) monasteries became major centers of economic, social, and political power. Consequently, abbesses (women who direct monasteries) and their subordinate female officials could and did become people of wide-ranging influence. Moreover, in a society that reveres holy people, holy women (as well as holy men) enjoy the authority that comes with respect.

In addition to asking students to formulate answers to the various specific questions regarding Hinduism, Jainism, and Buddhism, we have found it useful to ask them to compose a one- to two-page essay in which they compare and contrast the religious visions of India and Southwest Asia in this period of intellectual and spiritual revolution. Question 7 of source 22, which centers on a spurious quotation (all of the unascribed quotations that appear in the Questions for Analysis are the products of our imaginations), is a good focal point for the paper.

Occasionally we have turned this paper into the initial draft of an extended, semester-long masterpiece project. Subsequent chapters contain sources that illustrate the historical developments of these two great religious traditions. As students trace the history of religion in India and Southwest Asia, they will be able to create, in stages, a fairly detailed comparative analysis of the major religious forces that arose in the southern regions of Asia and their combined impact on the entire world. We have discovered that if we assign such a project, we must collect and comment on the work in at least three stages of its preparation. These collections normally follow the class's discussion of Chapters 3, 6, and 8 in Volume I.

Other Ways to Use the Sources

1. Assume for the moment you are a follower of the teachings of either the Mahavira or the Buddha. Compose a spiritual analysis of *The Bhagavad Gita*. What are your major agreements and disagreements with this sacred text?

2. What would Zarathustra think of Krishna's view of evil as expressed in *The Bhagavad Gita*?

3. Do you see any inconsistencies in source 20 concerning the Buddha's supposed attitude toward admitting women as full disciples? What are those inconsistencies? How might you explain them?

4. Compose Maha-Prajapati's response to the Buddha's permission to allow her to live the life of a mendicant disciple. Try to express what you infer would have been her sentiments and try to leave your values out of this response.

5. Imagine a debate between two persons: one a Jew, the other a Brahmin. What would be their major point of disagreement? Now that you have identified it, write the text of their debate over that issue.

CHAPTER

4

The Secular Made Sacred: Developing the Humanistic Traditions of China and Hellas, 600–200 B.C.E.

Chapter Theme

Perhaps the fact that the Chinese and Greeks lived on the outermost edges of the civilized core of the Afro-Eurasian World enabled them to develop societies that were different in basic perspective from those of southern Asia. China's greater distance from the religious ferment of India and Southwest Asia (until the coming of Buddhism into China in the early centuries C.E.) might also explain in part why its thought and society are the most secular of all. Concern with the affairs of the visible, material universe, and especially human relationships, have characterized Chinese philosophy since the civilization's earliest days. Whereas the equally secular-minded Greeks produced great schools of metaphysical speculation, the Chinese overwhelmingly focused on the tangible, physical world and particularly the place and role of humanity within it. Practical ethics rather than metaphysics was the arena for China's classical sages, until the coming of Buddhism and the subsequent development of Neo-Confucianism during the twelfth and thirteenth centuries (Chapter 9, source 74).

This is not to say that the Chinese do not believe in spiritual forces. Nothing could be farther from the truth. They have traditionally viewed the cosmos as inhabited by numerous spirits. Natural phenomena, such as mountains and rivers, are infused with spiritual powers; anthropomorphic deities abound; and then there are the spirits that are most characteristically Chinese—the ghosts of ancestors. As we saw in Chapter 1, there is also the impersonal, all-pervading moral force of Heaven, whose Mandate endows monarchs with legitimate earthly authority. To understand and placate these spirits, the Chinese developed a wide spectrum of rituals that ran the gamut from geomancy (consider the oracle bones of Shang and the later *Yi Jing*, or *The Classic of Changes*) to elaborate family and court ceremonials (e.g., the three books that comprise the *Li Jing,* or *The Classic of Rituals*). However, these spirits were not a focal point of theological speculation, and the ceremonies performed were largely magical insurance.

The same can be said of Hellenic religion but with less emphasis. At first glance this statement might seem surprising in light of the fact that religion played a major role in Greek life. Political and cultural events were religious celebrations (e.g., Athenian drama sprang out of the six-day festival in honor of the god of wine, Dionysus), and even war and athletics were imbued with religious significance. One theory that has received widespread approval is that the Parthenon, a temple erected to the honor of the goddess Athena and Athens's chief religious shrine, was built as a memorial to the Athenian heroes who had fallen at Marathon. In the arena of athletics one term suffices to remind us of the close interplay between competition and devotion: the Olympic Games. And these quadrennial games were only one of many regularly scheduled series of contests that had a religious core. Hellenic medicine, arguably classical Greece's most significant scientific breakthrough, began within the priesthood of Aesculapius. As the cult of this snake god of healing suggests, Hellas borrowed deeply from the widely variant religious traditions of the Aegean islands, Southwest Asia, Egypt and other areas of North Africa, and the Balkans, as well as building upon its native Indo-European roots. One consequence of all of the borrowing was the prominence of a number of mystic resurrection cults, such as the Eleusinian mysteries and Bacchism, which Euripides celebrated in his last masterpiece, *The Bacchae.* Though a champion of reason, the playwright realized that humanity also has suprarational needs that must be met.

Despite all of this piety, religion in Greek society tended to be human-sized and practical. The Olympian deities were human in their behavior and performed their godly tasks in mundane fashion. Very much as in China, Hellas's most common religious rites were aimed at either keeping the gods at arm's length or enlisting their superhuman powers for specific earthly gain. Consequently, the essence of religion and the nature of the divine Beyond were not the concern of most Greek thinkers. Greek philosophy tended to concentrate on such tangible objects as the human individual, the good life here and now, and the essence of the natural and social worlds.

Why These Sources?

Daoism, Confucianism, Legalism, and the theory of Yin and Yang do not collectively encompass all Chinese thought. The Age of a Hundred Schools that flourished in the latter stages of Eastern Zhou produced a broad spectrum of philosophies ranging from the abstract and theoretical to the concrete and practical. These four schools of thought, however, became China's preeminent intellectual forces and over the ages that followed proved to be the four most important ideological influences in the development of Chinese classical culture. They also demonstrate the sweep of Chinese thought and the humanistic secularism that stands at its core.

Secular and *humanistic* do not necessarily mean non-mystical, as Daoism, the philosophy of the Way, shows us. What can we say about our first selection, except that to leave out the *Dao De Jing* is unimaginable? Daoism, whose roots are so ancient as to be beyond the scope of historical records, became a major school of Chinese thought, despite the opposition of Daoist ideology to all activity and system-building, and it has profoundly influenced Chinese culture, particularly its aesthetics, down to the present. We chose our selections to illustrate the intrinsic paradoxes within Daoism and, thereby, to shake the student reader out of a mindset based on the yes-and-no certainties of computer logic. As was also the case with the selections from Hindu literature, Western students are forced to come to grips with the fact that their own way of relating to truth, which they probably have assumed is valid for all peoples and cultures at all times, is not universal.

We have discovered that most students enjoy studying Daoist thought and feel comfortable discussing its illogical logic once they have had an opportunity to see the richness of this philosophy. They feel even more at home with Confucian principles, perhaps because of the Master's commonsensical practicality. As is true of most great teachers who spoke rather than wrote and whose words were preserved by those who followed, it is difficult (many would say impossible) to separate the teachings of Kong Fuzi from that of his disciples. *The Analects* is as close as we shall ever get to the mind and words of Confucius. In addition to shedding some light on a historical philosopher (and we do not accept those theories that deny his historicity), this work demonstrates how his ideas were remembered, and that is historically more significant.

The first excerpt from the writings of Master Han Fei, one of the chief architects of Legalist thought, demonstrates the central principle of his political philosophy: The well-governed state is one in which monarchs and their ministers administer a set of rational laws dispassionately, evenhandedly, and never arbitrarily. Roman legal dictum 'The will of the prince has the force of law," held no appeal for Legalists such as Han Fei. As far as they were concerned, the *law* was sovereign. A corollary of this primary Legalist principle is enunciated in the second excerpt: The ruler must control all subjects, particularly ministers, by the threat of sure and severe punishment for all transgressions of the law and the promise of equally certain and generous reward for meritorious behavior that conforms to the law.

More interesting and insightful than any theoretical treatise are the records of Qin Shi Huangdi's Legalist regime. The selection we have chosen from Sima Qian's historical survey of the Qin regime presents us with a document that articulates the First Emperor's vision of himself and his rule. By studying this list of trumpeted accomplishments, the student is able to perceive the Qin Dynasty's political program and the ideology that drove it.

Chinese thought focused on more than just social and political philosophy, as *The Yellow Emperor's Classic of Medicine* demonstrates. Here the student meets the cosmological theory of Yin and Yang and also has the opportunity to study an example of the Chinese approach to disease and healing. Indeed, what we have here is a treatise on holistic preventative medicine. It sounds almost New Age!

Half a world away and at about the same time, the Greeks were also studying human diseases as natural phenomena and attempting to deal with them in an equally rational and natural manner. *On the Sacred Disease*, a treatise on epilepsy ascribed to Hippocrates of Cos, demonstrates early Hellenic medical science at its best. A classic example of the Hippocratic School's application of careful clinical observation and reasoned inference in order to understand the nature and course of a disease, the document underscores the strengths and weaknesses of ancient Greek medicine and also illustrates how typically a Greek scientist was able to balance religious belief and rational analysis. For most ancient Hellenic thinkers, there was no intrinsic conflict between religion and rationalism.

Some Greek rationalists, however, totally ignored the gods and their generally presumed influence on human fortune. One example is Thucydides, who possessed one of his age's finest intellects and is universally regarded as one of Greco-Roman antiquity's two or three greatest and most original historians. (Whether or not he was the equal of China's Sima Qian, however, is a hotly debated but unresolvable question.) The excerpt we have chosen from Thucydides demonstrates two aspects of fifth-century B.C.E. Hellenic rationalism and its secular concerns: history writing and political-social analysis. Hellenic *historia*, or understanding achieved through rational inquiry and expressed in prose, was born in mid-fifth-century Athens with the *Histories* of Herodotus, a transplant from the Ionian coast of Anatolia. A generation later Thucydides raised Herodotus's art to a science with his demanding emphasis on careful assessment of evidence, objectivity, and truth. (Consider what he says about the shortcomings of Homeric poetry.) Even though he fell short of his ideal (and what historian does not?), Thucydides composed a sober, carefully researched and crafted history that analyzed the Peloponnesian War in the moral terms of contemporary Athenian tragic drama. Believing that history is a didactic science, he turned his energies toward creating "a possession for all time" and succeeded brilliantly.

Thucydides's chief purpose was to measure the increasingly deleterious and ultimately disastrous effects that the war had on Athenian society, and in order to do that he first had to show his readers Athens in all of its glory and pride in the early stages of the conflict. He adroitly achieved that through Pericles's Funeral Oration of 431/430 B.C.E., a speech in which Athens's "First Citizen" praises the democracy he has helped mold and indirectly defends his stewardship of city affairs. Actually, the words we read are probably those of Thucydides, but the sentiment and major points are surely Periclean. Thucydides had undoubtedly been present at this public funeral, and the speech was so memorable and sufficiently recent as to make any major misrepresentation of it unimaginable. (Even more unimaginable is the suggestion raised by some modern commentators that Pericles never delivered such a speech.) To heighten his praise of Athens, its citizens, and their special form of life, Pericles contrasts his native *polis* with oligarchic Sparta, Athens's enemy at the time. As is always the case with wartime propaganda, Pericles's observations should not be accepted at face value, but they certainly give us a good picture of the Athenian self-image as the city and its allies embarked on a military adventure aimed at humbling Sparta and assuring the continued prosperity of the Athenian empire.

After showing us a self-confident, even arrogant Athens that glories in its rule of self-imposed law and civic responsibility, Thucydides's history turns to a darker reality——a plague-devastated Athens in which most social norms and restraints are violated. Playing a little loose with chronology in order to reach a higher truth, Thucydides artfully juxtaposed the Funeral Oration's moment of civic pride with the plague of 430. Pericles had boasted that Athens was a *polis* whose citizens respected authority and law. The plague gives the lie to that claim, thereby prefiguring greater moral collapses as the war wears on. Like Athens's contemporary tragedians who studied the relationship between *hubris*, or overbearing pride, and *nemesis*, or retributive justice, Thucydides studied Athens's fall from grace due to its own flaws of character and a blindness born in arrogance.

The plague also allowed Thucydides to demonstrate his mastery of the clinical research techniques of the Hippocratic school of medicine. This, in turn, allows us, the editors, to do something we deeply believe in—to juxtapose and combine sources. One point we constantly try to make in the pages of this book and in our own classrooms is that no historian bases a historical judgment on a single, isolated source. We study sources in context, and that means assembling all relevant documents and artifacts. Throughout this book we ask students to relate one source to another. Here students (and instructors) have the opportunity to relate Thucydides's clinical approach to the plague with the principles articulated in the Hippocratic treatise on epilepsy.

Just as Thucydides's text can be fruitfully compared with the source that precedes it, so the source that follows *The History of the Peloponnesian War* sheds further light on Thucydides's art and message. Thucydides was not alone in his attempt to study the way in which stresses can adversely affect human behavior. Euripides, a contemporary of Thucydides, also analyzed psychic disorders and antisocial behavior occasioned by intolerable pressures and unusual circumstances. His medium was the tragic stage. *Medea* is by any standards a theatrical masterpiece, and it clearly illustrates for the student the serious nature of Greek rationalism. Like a significant number of other fifth-century Greek male authors (Aristophanes, Plato, and Sophocles come immediately to mind), Euripides often turned his powers of analysis to a study of the role and status of women in Hellenic society.

Students should study Medea's speech not only as an example of Hellenic psychological and sociological analysis but also as evidence of the status of women and foreigners in late fifth-century Athens. The whole excerpt, and especially the speech, will enable the perceptive student to read Pericles's Funeral Oration more critically. Whereas Thucydides has shown us an idealized Athens as perceived by the man who had dominated the city's affairs for thirty years and was its unrivaled leader for the past decade, Euripides shows us Athens, in the guise of mythical Corinth, as perceived by a female outsider. Significantly, the playwright presented this drama in 431, the first year of the Peloponnesian War. Equally significant is the fact that toward the very end of his life Euripides voluntarily left Athens, a city that had become a far less pleasant place in which to live as a result of the on-going and increasingly brutalizing war with Sparta and its allies.

Plato's *Crito*, with its focus on the rights and responsibilities of citizenship, also sheds light on concerns that Thucydides and Euripides struggled with. Plato, who once considered becoming a writer of tragedies, had a gift for presenting complex philosophical issues in an entertaining and intelligible form. In this excerpt we meet Socrates, the gadfly of Athens, as he faces execution for impiety and corrupting youth. Post-war Athens was fertile ground for hysterical scape-goating, and this aged curmudgeon was a ready target. Here, in one of the most famous texts in all of ancient Greek political thought, Socrates (or Plato) wrestles with the issue of how a loyal citizen should react to injustices laid upon him by legitimate civic authority. His answer is that the social contract, which a citizen freely accepts and lives by, demands that he bow to the ultimate authority of the polis, no matter how badly the state's officials might have misapplied or perverted its law. This terrible burden is the price of citizenship's many blessings. To do less is to forsake one's citizenship, and without citizenship a Hellene was considered less than a freeman. Whether or not Thucydides, who was exiled from Athens, would have agreed is another issue. Indeed, one wonders what Plato truly thought on the subject. Unlike his teacher, Plato spent two extended periods of time away from Athens: one for twelve years, following Socrates's death, and later for six years. This leads us to suspect that the *Crito* is one dialogue that truly expresses the ideas and teachings of Socrates who, even upon the point of death, defended the ideal of citizenship with all of its obligations, including residence in one's polis.

We have added a fourth Hellenic source—three examples of the artistic vision and genius of fifth-century B.C.E. Hellas. In choosing these works we were guided by several criteria. First, we wanted pieces that illustrate Hellenic artists' concentration on the idealized human being. Second, we wanted pieces that students could profitably compare with the Hellenistic works of art that appear as source 32 in Chapter 5. Third, we wanted pieces that combined to demonstrate the wide range of Hellenic artistry, such as pottery, vase painting, and small relief, as well as sculpture. Fourth, we wanted pieces that most students (and possibly professors) would not have otherwise seen, so that they could approach these works of art with fresh minds. For that reason we chose not to include such well-known works of art as Myron's *Discobolus* (*The Discus Thrower*). Fifth and last, we wanted pieces that were not hidden away within the sacred confines of some inaccessible temple (such as Phidias's *Athena Promachos* of the Parthenon) but which represented the types and forms of art that fifth-century Greeks would encounter in the normal course of their lives. Arguably several of our choices violate this last criterion. The *Demareteion* is a commemorative ten-drachma coin that was minted for expensive transactions and Syracuse's treasury reserves The vast majority of Syracusans would never have seen, much less held, the coin. Nevertheless, it is representative of the artistry of Hellenic coinage. One-drachma coins were just as carefully crafted as this ten-drachma masterpiece. The *Amazon Rhyton* was probably created for Athens's flourishing export trade. After all, it was uncovered in Sudan.

Moreover, a rhyton was not an everyday drinking vessel. It was too heavy and cumbersome for that. Rhytons were used for ceremonial occasions, and this particular example might well have been created (and purchased) to serve only as a curiosity in some well-to-do foreigner's home. Nevertheless, although this signed masterpiece is not a piece of common earthenware, it does nicely represent the way in which Hellenic potters raised their craft to a high art and the way in which painters decorated Greek ceramics. Pottery was a major industry in the Hellenic World for both export and domestic use, and decorated vases and other ceramics were known to all Greeks and most of their neighbors. As for the maiden of the *Erechteum*, there can be no doubt that she (along with her five sisters) was a beloved public statue, standing as she did on the south porch of this small, exquisite temple.

Analyzing the Sources

Many of the Questions for Analysis ask the reader to compare Chinese and Hellenic systems of thought with one another and with the spiritual traditions of India and Southwest Asia. We believe this approach is eminently rewarding for both student and professor. It enables the instructor to cover a large amount of material fairly quickly and compactly, and it gives the student the double opportunity of reviewing the materials from the previous chapter and of placing the new schools of thought encountered in Chapter 4 into a broad and comprehensible context.

Like the Indians, the Chinese have historically tended to assume that adherence to a particular philosophy or religion does not preclude the integration into one's life of the tenets, insights, and modes of behavior of another school of thought or system of belief. A person could comfortably, therefore, accept the basic values of Confucianism and still be deeply influenced by Daoist thought. Both are equally part of a complex cultural heritage. This Chinese ability to harmonize what seem to Western eyes to be dissonant philosophies needs emphasis and should be compared to India's approach to spiritual truth.

Nowhere is this intellectual flexibility more evident than in Daoism—the Way of limitless ways (or, perhaps better, the Unlimited Way). Students should be encouraged to compare Brahman with the Dao, for the similarities are as telling as the differences. One is incorporeal Soul without limit; the other is Nature with no boundaries. Both can be only be discovered within one's self and not in the conventional wisdom of society.

Daoism's negative attitude toward social norms and worldly concerns (a reasonable enough reaction to the chaos of the Eastern Zhou Age) deserves comparison with the teachings of the Mahavira and the Buddha insofar as all three rejected such worldly values as fame, wealth, and power. Indeed, the parallels with Buddhism were striking enough that, when Buddhist thought began to infiltrate into China in the early centuries C.E., many Chinese originally accepted it as a variant form of Daoism, translating Nirvana as *wuwei* (active nonaction). Yet, in the final analysis, Daoist wuwei is not a path to liberation from the world nor is it a state of reality outside of space and time; it is a way of living in the world. This insight is crucial because students must perceive the differences as well as similarities among these schools of thought if they are to avoid trivializing them. The inactivity of the ascetic Jain or the meditative, passionless Buddhist is the spiritual struggle and self-imposed discipline of a person actively seeking Nirvana. The nonstriving follower of the Dao, on the other hand, embraces emptiness as both means and end—the end being a good life here and now. Wuwei, therefore, is a positive value unto itself.

For all of its presumed mysticism, Daoism is eminently unmysterious and very much oriented toward this world. The homely aphorisms of the *Dao De Jing* reduce this philosophy to understandable and human-sized proportions. In so doing, Daoism might be said to be one side of the coin of Chinese secular humanism. The other side is Confucianism.

Confucius and Socrates deserve comparison. Neither philosopher concerned himself with seeking answers to theological or spiritual issues. Humanity, human relations, and human virtue were sufficient to engage their total energies. Each man believed that there are absolute standards of right and wrong and also confidently assumed that in knowing what goodness is, one would, as a matter of course, always choose the virtuous act. Each felt compelled to seek wisdom, no matter where it led him. Each suffered rejection for his teachings, but each also became the philosophical watershed of his civilization. Yet, as our remarks in the text suggest, significant differences, particularly of culture, temperament, and perspective, separated these two philosophical giants. We have found it useful to require students to focus on those similarities and differences in some sort of written exercise. Exercise 6 in "Other Ways to Use the Sources" has proved worthwhile. In writing that suggested spurious primary source, most students recognize and come to grips with the fact that a Confucian would be quite ambivalent about Socrates and his teachings, and probably could not even begin to understand how he could think and act as he did.

One important element that separated Confucius and Socrates was the fact that one philosopher functioned within the context of a social and political system where a ruling father commanded the obedience of his subject children. The other lived within a *polis* where, in the words of Thucydides/Pericles, "we...regard a man who takes no interest in public affairs, not as a harmless, but as a useless character." This single difference helps explain their respective approaches to moral action and leadership. Confucius assumed that the male individual perfected himself by conscientious application of the rules of propriety—traditional rules of decorum that China inherited from its revered past. By becoming a proper gentleman, a man became a model ruler and subject, father and son, brother and friend. Socrates assumed that the male individual who sought *within himself* (and not in tradition) truth and personal perfection was, thereby, an effective and valuable citizen. Conversely, a good citizen was a good man. Thucydides says as much when he puts into Pericles's mouth the words: "When a citizen is in any way distinguished, he is preferred to the public service, not as a matter of privilege, but as the reward of merit."

The Funeral Oration is a panegyric for Athens and its peculiar system of government—peculiar because democracy was rare in the ancient Hellenic world. Oligarchies and tyrannies were much more common forms of political organization, and most fifth-century B.C.E. Greeks, including Thucydides, regarded democracy as an unnatural and unworkable system of government that invited class warfare and social instability. Many, in fact, saw it as a uniquely Athenian perversion. Athenian democracy only emerged in full form after 462 B.C.E. (but its origins reached back to 507); outside of Athens, Hellas's few democratic governments were to be found almost exclusively in some, but not all, of the tribute-paying Greek poleis that were answerable to the authority of the Athenian Empire—an empire that emerged after 478 and was dissolved in 405. In the case of most of these subject democracies, Pericles and the Athenians supported democratic factions as a means of maintaining control over their unpopular empire. We make this point in order to emphasize that when dealing with the issue of Athenian democracy we must be careful to avoid certain pitfalls. One of these is the tendency to assume that democracy was a pan-Hellenic phenomenon; it was not.

Another common error made by students is to think of the democratic Athenians as morally superior to the oligarchic Spartans. Many Hellenes, possibly a majority, saw the Spartans as defenders of Greek freedom and the stability of the Hellenic world against Athenian imperialism—a not unreasonable attitude because Athenian imperialism, in the form of the Delian League, subordinated a number of unwilling maritime poleis to

Athenian power and interests. The instructor should make liberal use of Euripides's *Medea*, as well as Plato's *Crito* and Thucydides's description of the social consequences of the plague of 430, to disabuse students of any romantic notions they might have of the ancient Athenians.

Another anachronistic error that many students fall prey to is to apply late-twentieth-century ideals of political and social egalitarianism to their study of Greek history and, therefore, to judge that Pericles and his supporters were hypocrites when they called themselves democrats. Why hypocrites? Well, we all know that Athens's democracy in the Age of Pericles was the private preserve of its free, adult (age thirty and over), native-born (both parents had to have been free-born Athenians), male citizens. Most people living in Attica, therefore, did not qualify for citizenship. In 431 B.C.E. Athens and the surrounding countryside of Attica counted about thirty thousand citizens out of a total population of about three to four hundred thousand. That is less than a 1:10 ratio of citizen to noncitizen.

The charge of sham democracy, however, misses the point. As noted in the introduction to *The History of the Peloponnesian War*, all of classical Greece's poleis, Athens included, were brotherhoods of warriors, and adult males usually shared in the duties and privileges of citizenship in direct proportion to their military worth to the polis. Note, for example, all of Pericles's references to military duty and deeds in his Funeral Oration. Indeed, Athens's democratic system was directly traceable to the fact that the city, as a naval power, needed the military service of its lowest economic and social class, the *thetes*, or laborers, who functioned as rowers and sometimes as light-armed marines in the fleet. Pericles hints at this fact when he says: "Neither is poverty a bar, but a man may benefit his country whatever be the obscurity of his condition."

Finally, based probably on what they learned in grade school, most students enter our world history course believing that modern democratic institutions can be traced in a direct line back to the Greeks. That simply is not so. Athenian democracy lasted less than a century and a half; its traditional dates are 462–320. By the end of the fourth century B.C.E., it was dead. When various forms of popular government reemerged in the West over two millennia later, they rose quite independently on foundations laid in Europe's so-called Middle Ages and not from Hellenic or Roman roots.

There are no direct connections between modern forms of democracy (none of which even vaguely resembles the Athenian form of participatory democracy) and democracy in ancient Hellas, but Greek medicine surely survived into the early modern era and served as one of the roots of the modern science of medicine. That, of course, is not the main reason we should study it. The fact that Greek medicine sheds light on the intellectual revolution that took place within the Hellenic world is sufficient reason. For this reason, the third Question for Analysis, which asks the student to apply the same analytical categories to Hippocratic medical theory that she/he has to Chinese medical theory, is key.

Students often have a naive notion of physical science. For them, valid physical science deals only with incontrovertible facts and unchanging laws, and any scientist who misses these truths is practicing bad science or even pseudoscience. Question 4 for source 26 and question 3 for source 27 suggest a broader and, we believe, more correct definition of physical science. It is true that modern science, which uses the controlled experiment and other exacting techniques of investigation, allows us to discover many otherwise unknowable truths about the physical world. Notwithstanding this high degree of reliability, science, whether ancient or modern, can only provide partial answers and convenient models for understanding the ambient world, and those scientific perceptions of reality are, at least in part, reflections of the culture that produced them. Of course this was more true for premodern science than for modern science, but it also applies to the most up-to-date research and discoveries. In short, no science can be divorced from its cultural setting. By this definition, the authors of *The Yellow Emperor's Classic of History* and *On the Sacred Disease* were both good scientists insofar as they attempted, with some success, to apply the best and *most rational* methods of analysis available to them to the study of the human body and physical maladies. The Yin-Yang and humor theories of illness might today strike us as quaint and decidedly wrongheaded. Any Western physician who held such opinions today would probably be labeled a charlatan. But the Yin-Yang theory provided medical practitioners in classical China with a rational structure, just the humor theory provided Hippocrates and his colleagues with an equally rational base on which they could practice good medicine. Each theory made sense and enabled Chinese and Greek physicians to treat illnesses as natural and *treatable* phenomena.

Reason is also a key to understanding the three Hellenic works of art. Contrary to popular opinion, Hellenic art was not naturalistic. It was, however, rational and logical (as well as idealized and human-centered). Consider the drapery of *The Maiden of the Erechtheum*. The folds and drapes are stylized and even exaggerated in order to frame and reveal the body beneath the cloth, but they make sense and are harmonious. There is nothing about them that violates the laws of the physical world or that strikes the viewer as bizarre or impossible, even though probably no gown has ever had vertical folds such as we see here. All three Questions for

Anaylsis, each of which asks the student to respond to a particular statement regarding the nature of Hellenic art and the values that underlie it, are aimed at helping the student understand the essentially rational and humanistic qualities of this artistic vision.

Other Ways to Use the Sources

1. The class will conduct a debate among Daoists, Confucians, Legalists, and Yin-Yang theorists on the issue "What is the correct *Dao*?" Each of you has been assigned one school; be prepared to defend its ideals ably and in a manner consonant with its basic principles.
2. Compose either Hippocrates's commentary on *The Yellow Emperor's Classic of Medicine* or a Chinese physician's commentary on Hippocrates's *On the Sacred Disease.*
3. Compose Hippocrates's commentary on the plague at Athens.
4. Compose a commentary on *Medea* by a Chinese teacher of Yin-Yang theory.
5. Compose Euripides's commentary on the plague of Athens.
6. Imagine you are a follower of the teachings of Confucius. You have traveled westward from China, arriving in Athens in 399 B.C.E. There you are privileged to meet Socrates as he prepares for death and to hear his discussion with Crito on the laws of Athens. Write a letter home to your teacher describing and *interpreting*, in the light of Confucian ideology, Socrates and his philosophy.
7. Compare the balance and sense of proportion exhibited in the three Hellenic works of art with the Chinese theory of Yin and Yang. Which strike you as more significant, the similarities or the differences? What do you conclude from your answer?

Regional Empires and Afro-Eurasian Interchange: 300 B.C.E.–500 C.E.

Chapter Theme

This chapter considers the first great age of Afro-Eurasian linkage and the four major cultural pools (China, India, Southwest Asia, and the Greco-Roman Mediterranean) that flourished within that first *ecumene*, or world community. By the end of the first century B.C.E., four great empires, each dominating to a significant degree one of those cultural areas, connected the Afro-Eurasian world from the Pacific to the Atlantic, from the South China Sea to the North Sea, from the Indian Ocean to the Mediterranean.

Our sources concentrate on two major issues: the interchanges and cross-cultural exchanges that took place in this era; and the maturation of Greco-Roman, Chinese, and Indian cultures, each of which entered its classical era in the time of the First Afro-Eurasian Ecumene.

Why These Sources?

The sources from the Greco-Roman World come first because we need a starting point, and we also want to demonstrate an example of Hellenistic sculptural drapery early in the chapter in order to make it possible for students to interpret a later collection of artifacts, namely the robed statues of source 41.

The four Hellenistic statues of source 32 have been chosen because they reflect nicely some of the important *isms* of the Hellenistic World. Touches of cosmopolitanism, individualism, realism, and romanticism (Yes, these contradictory elements were equally part of the Hellenistic cultural fabric.) are certainly to be found here, as well as the Hellenistic World's simultaneous fascination with the common and the eccentric, with the familiar and the foreign, and with the secular and the sacred. Some modern critics have dismissed Hellenistic art as the over-ripe fruit of Hellenic experimentation in technique and composition. It is a judgment that proceeds from a failure to appreciate the rich complexity of this ecumenical age and the dynamic tensions within its art. The secure, rather parochial Hellenic World that produced the harmonious and serene human forms that we saw in Chapter 4, source 31 was far removed from the much larger, more confusing Hellenistic World inhabited by the five people portrayed in these statues.

Sources 33 and 34 continue that theme by illustrating the Greco-Roman World's cultural complexity. The well-known scene of Aeneas's visit to the Underworld from Virgil's *Aeneid* (source 33) obviously begs comparison with the visions of the Hereafter that we saw in *The Epic of Gilgamesh* (Chapter 1, source 1) and *The Odyssey* (Chapter 2, source 12), and a careful comparative analysis is revealing. But we have included the source for more reasons than this. It provides one of the best available expressions of the pride, optimism, and self-confidence of those who accepted and supported Augustus's *Pax Romana*. Beyond that, it suggests rather strongly how religious ideas that originated in India were adopted, in somewhat altered form, by at least some inhabitants of the Mediterranean World.

Source 34, three funerary monuments of the second century C.E., illustrates the Roman Empire's diverse population and the many different cultural streams that flowed through the empire. Petronia Hedone and her son are classic Romans in dress and bearing (as is also Empress Vibia Sabina in source 41), but the same cannot be said for Sosibia and Aththaia. Sosibia is clearly a Greek devotee (possibly even a priestess) of Isis. Devotion to Isis began in Ancient Egypt, but during the Hellenistic Era it incorporated a wide variety of other eastern Mediterranean religious traditions and became probably the single most popular religion throughout the Greco-Roman World before the triumph of Christianity. Aththaia's religious beliefs are not revealed in her tomb effigy, but her northern Syrian ethnic heritage is abundantly clear from her costume, jewelry, and even facial features. The craftsmanship of her abundant jewelry marks her as a woman of wealth and reminds us that Palmyra, the city in which she was interred, was one of the great commercial centers of the Eastern Mediterranean. As an oasis town that stood near the end of the Silk Road, Palmyra served as one of the Roman Empire's many entry points for foreign goods and cultural influences. Her mode of dress and decoration also reminds us that Palmyra looked culturally eastward across the Euphrates to Parthia rather than to the Mediterranean, as will become obvious when we compare Aththaia's portrait with that of the Parthian noblewoman in source 41.

Han China, the focus of our second section, was similar in size and population density to the Roman Empire, but whereas Rome's empire was heterogenous and centered around a great sea, China's Han Empire was largely homogenous (although it did include Turco-Mongol tribal groups in its western and northern regions) and centered on a solid mass of land. To be sure, the two civilizations shared some other striking similarities, not least of which were their family-centered religions and the secular-humanistic orientations of their educated elites. Nevertheless, the basic cultures of these two empires were quite different, and it is to Han China, the other end of the Afro-Eurasian World, that we must now turn.

Source 35 is another excerpt from Sima Qian's *Shiji*, or *Records of the Grand Historian*. Whereas our first reading from the *Shiji* showed us the workings of Qin Shi Huangdi's Legalist state, this second reading shows us Confucianism's acceptance as an officially sanctioned school of thought in the reign of Han Wudi. The decree of 124 B.C.E. that established an imperial Confucian academy did not usher in any sudden and total triumph of Confucian philosophy, but it did signal the beginning of a process whereby Confucianism became the dominant ideology of China's ruling elites.

The very nature of the Confucian message meant that, once it was adopted by China's rulers, it would touch the lives of countless Chinese who had never read the Confucian classics. Confucian emphasis on family relationships (as Confucian thought evolved in the era of Han) and the centrality of the father within the family had a profound effect on the roles and status of men, women, and children in traditional Chinese society. Family and, by extension, society at large were hierarchies where each person's place, or relationship to others, was defined by age, sex, and function. This meant that each position, or rank, had its own responsibilities and virtues. We have already seen in the excerpts from *The Analects* the moral qualities expected of a superior man, or *lieshi*. The feminine counterpart of a male exemplar of Confucian rectitude was the *lienu*, or virtuous woman. During the Former Han Era male Confucian writers began producing collections of biographies of notable women to serve as models of proper female behavior. The greatest of all of China's ethicians in the field of womanly morality, however, was a woman—Ban Zhao. Madam Ban departed from the convention of using biographies and, instead, composed a code of practical feminine behavior along Confucian lines, for although "female Confucian" might sound like an oxymoron, that is exactly what Ban Zhao was. Her *Lessons for Women* provides detailed insights into both the expected norms of feminine conduct and the workings of Chinese society on the level of the family.

When we turn from China to India we see a quite different approach to such basic human concerns as the family and society at large. The Greek historian Eusebius preserved the legend of certain Indians who traveled to Athens and engaged Socrates in conversation. When they asked him to explain the object of his philosophy, he replied, "an inquiry into human affairs." This answer resulted in one of the gurus bursting into laughter and asking, "How can a person grasp human things without first mastering the Divine?" How typically Indian. Our documents from India provide evidence of transcendental religious principles translated to the practical levels of society and family—in other words, the spiritual defining the material.

Excerpts from the rock and pillar edicts of Asoka, which serve as the first source in our section on India in the age of empires, show how one ruler attempted to lessen the level of suffering in the world by applying the teachings of the Buddha, as he understood them. This paradoxical attempt to alleviate misery by creating a political-social system based on *Dharma*, or the Law of Righteousness—a law which maintains that the world of matter and desire is a place of suffering and must be rejected—demonstrates the way in which at least one highly influential person in northern India was reinterpreting the Buddha's message in the third century B.C.E.

The period from the age of Asoka to the end of the Gupta Empire in the sixth century C.E. witnessed production of the great lawbooks of Hindu dharma, or caste law, which helped bring together so many different ethnic groups and religious traditions into a single, inclusive religious-social complex. Of them all, *The Laws of Manu* is the most widely accepted and all-embracing. A reading of the canons of this complex collection reveals the rich layers of Indian history and society. Many of the laws appear to uninitiated Western readers to contradict one another. (Consider the apparent contradictions in the rules regarding female dependence and divorce.) What else could one expect of laws that reflect an evolving tradition that was already over two thousand years old? To Hindus, however, there are no contradictions. Rather, the various laws reveal the boundless nature of dharma.

The travel account of the Chinese Buddhist monk Faxian to this land ruled by dharma is important for several reasons. It provides external evidence for the wide degree of harmony in Gupta society. One of the most extraordinary achievements of Indian civilization has been its ability to balance so many different elements, and this is particularly apparent in the Gupta period, arguably the golden age of classical Hindu civilization. In Faxian's day, India was probably the most peaceful and prosperous region of the entire Afro-Eurasian World. His travelogue shows us not only Hindus and Buddhists peacefully living side by side but also worshiping together. Once again, if we followed the Western tendency to separate these two traditions into competing religions we would misunderstand the realities of Indian thought and history. At the same time, Faxian's account provides a good deal of information on different Buddhist and Hindu practices. Here we see caste in action and not just the idealized abstractions of the laws of Manu. We also get a glimpse of Mahayana Buddhism as a folk religion, a phenomenon we will explore in greater depth in Chapter 6, sources 44 and 45. Finally, Faxian represents the long-range interchange of peoples and ideas in this age of Afro-Eurasian linkage.

The fourth section of Chapter 5, "Long-Distance Travel and Exchange," has been recast for this edition and expands upon the theme of Afro-Eurasian linkage by focusing on the routes that connected the cultural areas that we have just studied and the ideas and people that traveled along them. Our first source, which details Faxian's homeward voyage from Ceylon to China, serves as a corrective to the pronouncements of those bookish persons who, never having hazarded the perils of open water in small craft, blithely speak and write of the "easy and regular" water-borne commerce that supposedly existed between China and Southeast Asia.

When we study the age of the First Afro-Eurasian Ecumene we might want to think in terms of regional, multi-cultural units that formed a long chain stretching across Inner Asia from China to the Roman Empire, but tied into this main east-west chain were many subsidiary chains going off in various directions (e.g., through the islands of Southeast Asia or down the Red Sea to the Indian Ocean). Within each link of the main chain that connected the Pacific to the Atlantic (Have we lost you yet with our metaphor?) there was plenty of cultural interchange, and direct contact and exchange obviously existed between contiguous links (e.g., China and the steppe lands to its west), but the links at either end (namely China and Rome) had little or no direct contact; their indirect contacts, however, were significant, as the five robed statues that comprise source 41 illustrate.

The five statues serve as examples of the spread and reinterpretation of the artistic motif of sacred (and redemptive) authority across the expanse of Eurasia in the period from the second century C.E. to the late fifth century. There is nothing subtle about this source and its Questions for Analysis. Its very simplicity makes it one of our favorites, because it brings home so vividly and painlessly one of the two main themes of the chapter: encounters and cross-cultural exchanges.

Analyzing the Sources

As is usually the case, we prefer to adopt a comparative approach when attempting to create some intellectual order out of what seem to students to be a dizzying array of disjointed sources and an overwhelming avalanche of new information. Happily, the sources are such that we can construct some interesting comparative problems for our students. The status of Hindu women as revealed by *The Laws of Manu* begs for comparison with the status of women in Confucian China (see source 38, question 7). Because of our students' normal willingness to engage in a spirited discussion of artifactual evidence, we also favor a comparative study of the five statues contained in source 41.

The relative status of women in various societies is a topic we began considering in Chapter 1, and it is a subject to which we often return in both volumes. Needless to say, it is a marvelous essay issue. To initiate student thought and discussion on the respective positions and roles of traditional Chinese and Hindu women and possibly to lay a foundation for an extended essay on the topic, we ask students to list in two parallel columns all of the similarities and dissimilarities they can discover regarding the status and societal perceptions of Chinese and Indian women as revealed respectively in Ban Zhao's *Lessons for Women* and *The Laws of Manu*. We provide the following categories, or headings, but encourage students to add their own. We also tell them to be prepared to discuss in class the inferences they have drawn. A good student paper might look something like this example:

The Status of Women in Traditional Chinese and Hindu Societies

Innate Female Qualities

China

Women are "by nature stupid." They are lowly creatures who possess the weakness of Yin.

India

By nature they seduce men. They are impure and cannot hear the Vedas and by themselves are not worthy to perform religious ceremonies.

Highest Acquired Virtues

China

Gentleness, humility, industry, chastity, a good reputation earned by proper behavior.

India

Avoidance of the six causes of ruin. (See the next category.)

Improper Feminine Behavior

China

Contempt of one's husband; rebuking and scolding a husband; acting like a "tiger"; lack of respect for others; failure to "yield"; immodesty, even with one's husband; lack of industry; gossiping/silly chatter.

India

Drinking spirits; associating with wicked people; separation from one's husband; rambling about; sleeping at unreasonable hours; dwelling in another man's house; infidelity; hating one's husband unjustly.

What Do Women Bring to a Marriage?

China

Her Yin complements and completes her husband's Yang—especially her gentleness; homecare.

India

Children, religious rites, faithful service, prosperity, the highest conjugal happiness, and heavenly bliss.

Women and Family Religious Rites

China

Her primary duty is the continuation of the ancestral rites.

India

She assists the husband.

The Consequences of Improper Feminine Behavior

China

A woman who is not well trained for marriage will humiliate her birth family and its ancestors. By implication, disharmony will result from improper behavior.

India

If she disgraces her husband, her next incarnation will be a vile one.

The Status of Women in Traditional Chinese and Hindu Societies (continued)

The Reciprocal Responsibilities of Marriage

China	India
A man controls; a woman serves. Women are not to be beaten. Husbands and wives must respect one another. They must be mutually modest.	Mutual fidelity.

The Blessings of a "Good Woman"

China	India
Harmony in the family.	Where women are honored, the gods are pleased; where women are happy, there is prosperity.

Protections for Women

China	India
Other than that women are not to be beaten, no specific, built-in protections are mentioned. However, by implication, husbands (and all other males) are to control at all times their innate power (Yang) and to exercise decorum. Ban Zhao assumes that a husband will respect and love a "proper" wife.	Women must not be sold into marriage. Wives who do not produce living male heirs may be superseded after a stipulated period of time but cannot be divorced if they behaved properly. A virtuous wife who is ill must never be disgraced.

Independence?

China	India
A woman belongs to her husband and in-laws once she is married. Property rights are not mentioned. No mention of divorce.	A female is always dependent on a male, before, during, and after marriage (father, husband, and son). After three years of marriageability, a woman may select her own husband, but he must be of equal caste. Her husband may divorce her for just cause but cannot divorce her if she legitimately has an aversion to him. What she earns in marriage belongs to her husband, yet she retains possession of her six-fold property. She can also inherit property from her mother and pass property on to her heirs.

This exercise should produce some good insights and spirited discussion. Most students tend to conclude that each society recognized the importance of women, although it considered them innately inferior to males, and each, in a manner consonant with its basic cultural principles, sought to protect them, even as it subordinated them to men. Many will probably also argue that the evidence in these two sources suggests that *The Laws of Manu* gave Hindu women marginally more safeguards and freedoms. Others will disagree with that assessment and conclude that the differences are too insignificant to be worth discussing. One thing is almost certain: Everyone will have something to say on the subject.

A comparative analysis of the five statues of source 41 is best dealt with in a free-wheeling class discussion in which students who have some background in or special sensitivity toward artistic expression can help their fellow students. Even an untrained eye can see that certain Greco-Roman sculptural techniques and forms of composition were passed along from the eastern Mediterranean to East Asia and, in the process, were changed and adapted to local needs, tastes, and preexisting styles. While that is obvious, many students have trouble identifying exactly what was adopted and adapted. To focus their inquiry, we ask them to concentrate on three typically Greco-Roman sculptural techniques to which they were introduced in source 32: facial expression, drapery, and *contrapposto.*

It is instructive to turn back to source 32 for a moment and study the Hellenistic sculptures there. All four use facial expression to great effect, but let us only consider two: the bust of King Euthydemos and *The Boxer.* The hard, battered, unsentimentalized face of King Euthydemos reflects the roughness of his Bactrian kingdom and his career as a soldier in the Central Asian fringes of the Hellenistic World who clawed his way to power. Age has added flesh to his face, but it is clear that he is a hard man—hard in body and lacking any compassion for his enemies and those who frustrate him in any way. He is not someone whom one would wish to anger. The boxer's face is similarly revealing. It is brutish. (Lest we be accused of insensitivity to the athletically battered, we should point out that the person writing this analysis has broken his nose five times—and it looks it.) The boxer's nose has been broken and flattened to the point that he breathes with difficulty, as the open mouth suggests. Likewise his ears are cauliflowered. We have to wonder what damage has been done to his internal organs, especially his brain. One commentator has interpreted the boxer's scowl as a peevish manifestation of displeasure at being disturbed while at rest and at having to jolt his brain back to activity in order to understand some question or instruction. That interpretation seems eminently reasonable. But leaving aside the details of the stories that are lined in their faces, it is safe to say that here are portraits that clearly show two hard, brutal men.

Only two of the statues, *The Gaul and Wife* and *The Old Woman*, employ drapery, so this allows us a nice symmetry as we consider these other two Hellenistic statues, each of which shows a dramatic use of drapery meant to evoke certain emotions from the viewer. The clothing that hangs from the limp corpse of the Gallic wife emphasizes her lifelessness and the pathos of death; the clothes that hang from the old woman present an equally pathetic view—an aged, time-ravaged body whose imperfections cannot be hidden by clothing but, rather, are made more obvious by it.

Both statues, as well as the bronze boxer, show the use of contrapposto, the technique of turning the hips, legs, and feet in a different direction from the shoulders and head to give a sense of balanced dynamism and motion to a sculpted figure. Normally this technique was employed for standing statues, but Apollonius's genius was such that he could impart motion to a seated figure. Note how the angles created by his out-turned feet and the twist of his neck give this exhausted athlete at rest a certain vitality. Note also how the anonymous sculptor of *The Gaul and Wife* twists the head and limbs of the man to impart a sense of violent motion as he plunges the sword into his chest. Note also how the feet of *The Old Woman* point in opposite directions to impart a sense of her moving through the marketplace at a shuffling pace that was her fastest.

After we have pointed out and commented on these techniques in the Hellenistic statues in source 32, we turn to the statue of Vibia Sabina. Students who have a sensitivity to art note that her face conveys a sense of sobriety. The Romans had a word rich in connotations for the quality that the sculptor hoped to capture: *gravitas*. Given the Roman self-image, it was a highly esteemed quality and one that every Roman of high status wished to convey. The drapery that covers Vibia Sabina underscores her dignity and womanly virtue by imparting a sense of rectitude and grace. The same can be said of her stylish but severe hairstyle and the veil that covers her head. The sculptor's use of contrapposto is subtle and effective. Note the slight turn of her left foot and the bend in her left knee. When combined with the dramatic use of drapery, a statue that otherwise would be static comes alive. Turning to the Parthian statue, we see attempts to use facial expression, drapery, and contrapposto that fall short of what Hellenistic artists achieved. Of the three, the attempt to convey the woman's piety and sobriety by crafting a square, stolid face is the artist's greatest success (a face that reminds us of Aththaia in source 34). Elsewhere, he is less successful. Bluntly put, the drapery (which is purely Parthian dress; compare it with Aththaia's dress and jewelry) is flat and crude by Greco-Roman standards. It does succeed, however, in conveying through its opulence the woman's wealth and high status (again, compare Aththaia with her). Because this is not the clearest photo we have ever seen (due to political problems with Iraq that preclude our securing a better photo) and also because the woman's long gown reaches the ground it is difficult to see her feet. They are there, however. There is a slight turning of the right foot and a modest attempt at balancing that rather inactive action by having the woman lift the top layer of the left side of her gown. Note also the attempt to create some sort of sense of motion by having the woman's right fingers point upward and her left fingers point down. This is contrapposto of a sort, but it is awkward and static. The sculptor never quite caught the spirit, much less mastered the techniques, of Hellenistic sculpture, but his art was surely influenced by the Greco-Roman West.

East of Parthia was Gandhara, which produced great works of Buddhist art. As was true of all works produced by this school, the Hellenistic influences on it were profound, but equally significant were the ways in which it departed from Greco-Roman models. Consider the Gandharan Buddha's face. Here again we find gravitas, sobriety, or whatever else we wish to term it. It is the same seriousness that we saw in the faces of Vibia Sabina and the Parthian noblewoman. Obviously, this was a common artistic way of expressing the inner qualities of those who properly commanded respect. Note also the statue's drapery. The clothing covers a clearly recognizable and rather masculine body, and it certainly is more expressive than the gown that we just saw on the Parthian statue. Nowhere near as fashionable as Vibi Sabina's clothing, this robe conveys the simplicity of the monastic *sanghati* while simultaneously imparting to the Buddha's body a sense of sacred authority. There is an ever-so-subtle turning of the right ankle and foot, apparently inspired by Hellenistic models but not as technically developed, and it certainly fails to communicate any sort of motion. One wonders if the artist even understood why Hellenistic sculptors turned feet in this manner. A lack of motion, however, is entirely appropriate for a statue representing the Buddha, whose eighth Noble Truth was Right Meditation. Indeed, there is no way this work could be mistaken for a Hellenistic sculpture, especially in light of all of the Buddhist symbols that are to be found here. Nevertheless, the lines of influence are quite clear.

We have to admit a particular fondness for all Gandharan sculpture, but regardless of the unquestioned, deep devotion that underlay this art and the Buddhist symbols that permeated it, the school's works do often strike us as being at variance with the world-rejecting message of the Buddha. The muscular, quite masculine Buddha who appears here seems more like a

Greek hero or Roman general (even with the inward gaze of his eyes) than a spiritual teacher. But that's very much a subjective observation, is it not?

The body of the Gandharan Buddha seems too real for the Buddha, even though his ankles and feet are slightly out of proportion to his torso and head, as apparently also were his forearms and hands. We find the same dichotomy in the Chinese Buddha, whose body is partially ill-proportioned (look at those feet) but quite of this world. Given what we read in source 19, we reasonably expect to find a Buddha image that expresses the nonreality of all earthly bodies. Well, we are not going to find it here. The drapery outlines a decidedly sensuous human body that appears to be almost androgynous. Gone is the masculinity of the Gandharan Buddha and in its place we have an expertly crafted nonsexual sensuousness. To be sure, this is Hellenistic drapery several steps removed from its source, but it is also evidence of the transmission of Hindu temple-sculpture influences, without the overt sexuality. It also brings to mind the soft, nonsexual sensuality of contemporary Gupta India's Buddhist sculptures. Influenced by several currents from lands to the west, the sculptor also uses contrapposto, but here his art departs radically from distant Greco-Roman prototypes. Motion has nothing whatsoever to do with the central message of this Mahayana masterpiece. Just as Enlightenment (and Nirvana, which is essentially the same thing) is a state of nonmotion and nonchange, so the draped robe and the slightly angled right foot convey no sense of motion. The drapery certainly is much more than decoration, as we have already suggested, but the angled foot serves only to impart a sense of balance and nothing else. Even the wonderfully expressive hands seem static and changeless. This Buddha seems to be locked in eternity, forever welcoming all who come to him.

As marvelous as the drapery is, it is the Buddha's face that carries the brunt of the artist's message. Forming the apex of a triangle created by two balanced hands, one pointed up and the other down in gestures of comfort, the face presents us with a decidedly Chinese piece of true Mahayana art. The Buddha's face and hair style are distinctly Chinese, but such matters aside, it is that glorious, endlessly comforting smile of welcome that captivates the viewer. Indeed, the Buddha's smile conveys a sense of absolute inner tranquility and, in good Mahayana fashion, infinite compassion. As we shall see in Chapter 6, the artist has captured the essence of Mahayana Buddhism's message of universal salvation.

The same eternal smile of warm welcome is also evident in the Funan Buddha. Here we see a Gandharan-inspired Buddha that lacks the sternness (or sobriety) of the Gandharan statue that we just studied and which also lacks all clearly identifiable Hellenistic elements. To be sure, the drapery vaguely outlines the body and brings to mind the folds in the robe of the Gandharan Buddha, and there is a certain substantiality to the body, which is also reminiscent of Gandharan art. But this body is totally static, for there is no attempt at contrapposto. What we have here is Gandharan forms transformed into a distinctly Southeast Asian style. Although nowhere as delicate or as sophisticated as the Northern Wei Buddha, this work of art from Funan reminds us as much (maybe even more) of the Chinese Buddha as it does the Gandharan Buddha.

Well, the final question is: What does this all mean? Darned if we can give a definitive answer. The whole exercise has been to see how artistic motifs and techniques traveled and changed across Eurasia. The result of our investigation should be the realization that the process of transmission and adaptation was neither linear nor simple.

Before leaving this chapter, we want to direct your attention to source 40, which chronicles the hazardous and even death-defying journey of Faxian from Ceylon to China. We favor asking students to compose a journal account in which they write a newspaper account of Faxian's return voyage—an "as told to" story. There is nothing especially difficult about this assignment. A person would have to be exceedingly obtuse to miss the danger, uncertainty, and large amount of time involved in this monk's homeward journey. Faxian's ship, for example, missed its intended port by hundreds of miles and narrowly averted total disaster. The point of this exercise is simple. We speak and write facilely of the increasing volume of commerce through the waters of South Asia during this age of interchange. The fact is, at its best the sea routes connecting the lands of the Indian Ocean with China were dangerous and not easily navigated at this time in history. We should never forget the hazards of long-distance travel at this time, the courage (and naive foolhardiness) of the relative few who undertook it, and the unknown numbers who perished in the process.

Other Ways to Use the Sources

1. Compose Virgil's commentary on the statue of Vibia Sabina.
2. The Chinese character for "woman" (*fu*) is a combination of two elements; one signifies "female", the other "broom." What is the implication, and would Ban Zhao agree with it? What is your evidence for your answer?
3. Write Ban Zhao's commentary on *The Laws of Manu.*

4. "Citizens of the United States are taught to value their individual rights. The subjects of imperial China were taught to think in terms of the responsibilities they owed by virtue of their relationships to other people." Please comment on this anonymous statement in light of evidence provided by Ban Zhao's *Lessons for Women*.
5. What do you think Asoka would say about the India that Faxian described? What would he find praiseworthy? What would he fault? On balance, would he approve or disapprove of Gupta society?
6. Assume the identities of two people, each an artist of one of the twelve sculptures that appear in this chapter (sources 32, 34, and 41). Choose two sculptures from two different cultures; only one of your choices may be Greco-Roman. Compose a paragraph on each sculpture in which you explain the ideas or feelings you have attempted to convey through your art.

CHAPTER
6

New Developments in Three Ancient Religions

Chapter Theme

Around the beginning of the Common Era, Hinduism, Buddhism, and Judaism spread far beyond their birthplaces, and in the process underwent significant changes. Brahminical Hinduism, whose origins lay in the Indus Valley of the northwest but which took more definitive shape in northeastern India's Gangetic Plain, moved into southern India and from there traveled across the waters of the Bay of Bengal into the coastal regions of Southeast Asia—an area often termed *Greater India*. Of all the forms of Hindu culture introduced into Southeast Asia, two of the most important and lasting were the new cults of Shiva and Vishnu, which largely sprang from Tamil, or southern Indian, sources. Buddhism also traveled far beyond the place of its birth. As Buddhism moved westward out of its northeastern Indian homeland in Bihar and into the north-central region known as the Punjab, it evolved the doctrine of the Great Vehicle (*Mahayana*), and it was largely this form of Buddhism that became a dominant force in East Asia. Judaism found itself without a religious capital following the destruction of Jerusalem in 70 C.E., and after the unsuccessful rebellion of Simon Bar Kokhba, which was crushed in 135 C.E., relatively few Jews continued to reside in their ancestral homeland. Scattered all over the Greco-Roman-Persian Ecumene and beyond, Jews faced the greatest challenge in their long history of religious and political crises. The story of *Diaspora Judaism* is the struggle to retain cultural identity and to remain faithful to the Covenant with their Lord.

In India, as the religion of the Indo-Aryan north spread into the Dravidian south, it encountered forms of ecstatic piety that, in turn, influenced the rise of a form of devotional Hinduism known as *bhakti*. One consequence was the creation of a body of popular religious literature available to all, even men and women (!) of low caste. Although the *Vedas*, *Brahmanas*, and *Upanishads* remained Hinduism's preeminent holy books and were studied only by those initiated into their mysteries, new forms of religious literature appeared—epics (source 17 of Chapter 3), *Puranas*, books of Sacred Law (source 38 of Chapter 5), and numerous devotional poems and hymns—all of which addressed the emotional and spiritual needs of Indians of every caste and race. Hinduism in all of its rich variety now permeated Indian life from the mountains of the north to the subcontinent's southern coastal tip. From the first through sixth centuries C.E., Hinduism, especially in its bhakti form, also made significant inroads in Funan, Champa (southern Vietnam), Srivijaya (southern Sumatra), and elsewhere in Southeast Asia, where it merged with native cultures.

Already during the age of Asoka, Buddhism was moving into Ceylon and Burma, where it took root in a conservative, monastically oriented form known as *Theravada* (the Way of the Elders). It also moved into northwestern India, where it came into contact with certain Southwest Asian religious concepts, especially the Zoroastrian notion of a savior who successfully leads the forces of Light against those of Darkness. It seems likely that this Persian vision influenced the development of the ideal of the *Bodhisattva* and the phenomenon of Mahayana Buddhism, just as it might also have played a significant role in the evolution of the Christian view of Jesus as the savior deity. When Buddhism crossed northwestern India's Hindu Kush mountain range and entered the trade routes of Central Asia, it did so largely (but not exclusively) in the form of the Great Vehicle. Although Theravada Buddhism eventually came to predominate in most of Southeast Asia (except for Annam, or northern Vietnam), it was Mahayana Buddhism that became a key element in the histories of Tibet, China, Korea, and Japan. In return, each civilization placed its own mark on this great East Asian faith.

In the more western regions of the Afro-Eurasia World, we see another form of the story of the interplay between host civilizations and an ancient religion that has taken up residence in their midst. The cultural tenacity of Judaism, and its successful struggle to avoid total absorption by a variety of other ways of life and belief, is one of history's great stories of survival. For about nineteen hundred years, Jewish history was the story of scattered communities throughout the world clinging to the essence of their Southwest Asian faith and identity but also adapting to the varied circumstances in which they found themselves.

Why These Sources?

The form of bhakti exemplified in the *Bhagavad Gita*, when Krishna reveals himself in his full divinity and Arjuna falls to the earth in terror,[1] is rather restrained and impersonal. The emotions engendered in this passage are awe and respect rather than unequivocal love. The later Puranas, which date from the Gupta Age and following, express a fuller development of the bhakti tradition. In *The Vishnu Purana* Vishnu appears as a personal and loving manifestation of Brahman. His compassion and powers are unlimited, for he is Divine Reality, and even karma has no hold over him and those who trust in him. Total devotion to Vishnu assures release from karma, samsara, and the bonds of material existence.

In like manner, Shiva offers his devotees immediate release from the consequences of their sins. *Shiva Nataraja* is one of the most venerated sacred images in the world. A product of the Tamil people of southern India, this statue artfully symbolizes Shiva's double nature, as well as his diverse historical origins. He was a composite of the fierce vedic god *Rudra* (the Howler), a deity of disease and death (but, like the Greek Apollo, simultaneously the god of healing), and ancient non-Aryan hermaphroditic gods of fertility from both Harappa and the southern forest regions. In fact Shiva/Rudra's origins are even more complex than that sentence suggests because Rudra himself seems to have had not only Indo-European but also Harappan origins. We see this in Rudra's manifestation as "Lord of the Animals." Reminding us very much of Harappan seal 6 that we studied in Chapter 1, source 8, the later Indo-Aryan lord of the animals was clad in animal skins and enjoyed the power of life and death over animals and humans alike—functions that Lord Shiva continued to perform long after Rudra ceased to be a major Hindu deity. For all these reasons, Shiva represents, perhaps more than any other deity, the merging of so many different Indian cultures—Harappan and Aryan, as well as southern and northern—into that rich complex we term Brahminical Hinduism. It was this Hindu complex that reached its first great period of efflorescence in the Gupta Age (320–ca. 550 C.E.). Moreover, perhaps also better than any other Hindu deity, Shiva represents the core Hindu religious concept that Divine Reality generates and *is* all things—both the apparently good and beautiful and the apparently evil and ugly. (See what we say about the Bodhisattvas Guanyin and Hevajra a bit farther down.)

---

[1] We chose not to include this scene in Chapter 3, source 17.

Our two sources relating to Mahayana Buddhism during these post-classical centuries can only hint at the richness of this compassionate faith of salvation that become the dominant religion through much of East Asia. The selection from *The Lotus Sutra* is, as far as we are concerned, one of the clearest and most beautiful expressions of the Bodhisattva's infinite compassion for all of humanity in all of its needs. Theravada Buddhism teaches that a person is able to help another to Nirvana only by example and advice, but ultimately each individual must achieve Buddhahood alone. In the Greater Vehicle, to the contrary, we come face to face with the notion of Bodhisattva saviors who redeem *all* humanity and, just as significant, prior to leading humans to Nirvana the Bodhisattvas protect and bless them in this world. What a marvelous win-win situation: eternal salvation and temporal prosperity. No wonder such diverse people as the Chinese pilgrim Faxian (source 40) and the Japanese warrior Kusunoki Masahige (source 68), as well as unknown hundreds of millions of other devotees, looked to the Bodhisattva Perceiver of the World's Sounds for comfort and protection.

Perceiver of the World's Sounds, originally known as *Avalokitesvara* in India, is only one of Mahayana Buddhism's many Bodhisattvas (*The Lotus Sutra* suggests that there are at least as many as the grains of sand in sixty-two million Ganges Rivers), but arguably he/she was (and remains) the most beloved and prayed-to savior in all of East Asia. Source 45 introduces us to the sculpted images of three Bodhisattvas, of whom the first is Guanyin, the Chinese version of Avalokitesvara. Guanyin entered China as a male Bodhisattva but metamorphosed into a goddess of mercy. Perhaps by studying this exquisitely crafted statuette from the era of the Sui Dynasty (a short-lived dynasty that apparently did not profit from Guanyin's help), we can begin to perceive the reasons for the high level of devotion to this graceful enlightened being. (One popular Chinese aphorism is: In every household there is a goddess of mercy.) Whereas Guanyin is beautiful by any standard, Hevajra is ugliness personified, at least by some standards. Reminiscent of Shiva Nataraja, of whom he is the Tantric Buddhist counterpart, this Bodhisattva appears to us as an eight-faced, four-legged, sixteen-armed deity. To complete the picture, he holds a skull in each hand and dances on a corpse. The point, of course, already made in our study of Shiva Nataraja, is that Tantric (or Exotic) Buddhism, a branch of the Mahayana Doctrine, is based on the principle of *non-dualism*. Here we clearly see the close connections between popular Buddhism and Hindu belief and devotion—a point also clearly brought out in Faxian's account of his travels in India and Ceylon (source 39). Guanyin offers the gentle, unquestioning love of a mother; Hevajra offers victory over death;

Arapacana offers the comfort and peace of meditation. This, our third Bodhisattva, whose statue was carved in fourteenth-century Java, wields the sword of interior knowledge, the knowledge that is Enlightenment and comes from Right Meditation, and holds the book of knowledge, a true knowledge that comes from contemplation. Arapacana, whose cult was far less popular than those of Guanyin and Hevajra, appealed (and still appeals) to persons with a more contemplative bent—Mahayana Buddhists with Theravada temperaments. In short, these three Bodhisattvas suggest in their differences and similarities that Mahayana Buddhism offered something for everyone, and each of their gifts was simply one of the infinite faces of inner peace.

With our two Jewish sources students return momentarily to a religion where truths appear to be more fixed and absolute and, thereby, more understandable to the Western mind. Rabbinical Judaism, which began to take shape around the beginning of the first millennium C.E., normally rejected the notion of saviors, save for the Messiah who was to come, and on that issue there was great disagreement about who and what he would be. Instead of looking for help from heavenly spirits and rather than seeking protection in magical rituals, Jews concentrated their religious focus on the Law and the moral and spiritual guidance of the rabbis who interpreted the Law.

Source 48, an excerpt from Flavius Josephus's *Against Apion*, shows us the attempt of a Hellenized Jew of the first century C.E. to define Judaism's legitimate place within the cultural complex of the Hellenistic Ecumene. More than that, Josephus argued for the superiority of Jewish law and its universality. It was, so he argued, the perfect law for all peoples. The Mosaic Law, per se, never became a law for all nations, although much of it would later be universalized by Christianity and Islam. It was, however, a law that proved to be an effective cultural connective for a widely scattered people.

Academies devoted to the Law flourished wherever Jews resided in sufficient numbers, and learned Jews could comfortably travel from one settlement to another, as Benjamin of Tudela did in the twelfth century (Chapter 8, source 64), knowing full well that wherever they went the Law was being studied, interpreted, and lived. As such, the Law was Diaspora Judaism's central cohesive force, and among its many rabbinical expositors whose answers to vexing questions were solicited from near and far, none was more in demand, important, or original than Moses ben Maimon.

Maimonides's *Letter to Yemen* nicely illustrates the ties that bound Diaspora Judaism, wherein the Judaic community of Yemen requested the authoritative opinion of a Sephardic Jew from Iberia who was head of the

Jewish community of Cairo. The issues that Rabbi Moses addresses in this letter—the persecution of Jews and the hope of a Messiah to come—were ones that concerned almost all Diaspora Jews nearly everywhere and well nigh at all times.

We wanted to include a third reading in this section—a letter dating from ca. 960 by Joseph, king of the Khazars, to Rabbi Hasdai of Spain. Unfortunately, space limitations forced us to excise it. The letter sheds important light on the conversion of the Turkic Khazars to Judaism. Toward the middle of the eighth century, rulers of these fierce horsewarriors, who inhabited the region between the Black and Caspian Seas, accepted the Jewish faith, probably as a consequence of the influence of Persian Jews. The kingdom of these Khazar Jews, which continued down to the early thirteenth century, was Judaism's only independent state between the Roman occupation of Judea and Galilee and the establishment of the modern state of Israel. Perhaps, we will include this letter in a future edition, if we can ever figure how to fit it in without excising some equally important source.

Analyzing the Sources

Of all the phenomena studied in our first-semester global history course, which spans the period ca. 8000 B.C.E. to 1500 C.E., we have discovered that students have the most difficulty grappling with Hindu and Buddhist concepts. For this reason, we favor constant redundancy—returning to these two religious traditions time and again—and also grappling with the two religions in class discussion, where students can air their uncertainties and questions, and we can provide help and instruction. When it is time to deal with the salvation movements within Hinduism and Buddhism, we ask our students to compare the message of *The Vishnu Purana* with those of *The Upanishads, The Bhagavad Gita,* and *The Laws of Manu.* We hope by doing this to help them perceive and understand three of Hinduism's major paths, or *yogas,* to *moksha* (release): (1) the yoga of karmic action—selfless action according to the law (dharma) of one's caste (*The Bhagavad Gita* and *The Laws of Manu*); (2) the yoga of knowledge—knowledge of the Real Self through meditation and indifference to the transitory pleasures and pains of the unreal, sensual self (the Upanishadic tradition); and (3) the yoga of bhakti—unconditional devotion to a savior deity who, likewise, loves humanity without reservation or limit. At the same time, we attempt to help them discover for themselves that these three paths to liberation are complementary and not mutually exclusive.

By the way, an interesting point that you might wish to make in class is that the Sanskrit word *yoga* is cognate with the English word *yoke*, both having a common root in the Indo-European *yeug* (Latin *jugum*—"a bond" or "collar"). *Yoga*, therefore, means both a discipline (or path of discipline) and a union. Hence, the ultimate Yoga is union with Brahman, and in order to achieve that one employs a yoga (or yogas). A person who employs a yoga or enjoys a state of yoga is a *yogi*, and even the gods are yogis, as we shall see in our analysis of Shiva Nataraja's statue.

After all these points have been made, we turn to an in-class analysis of *Shiva Nataraja* in an effort to help students further sharpen their skills at interpreting visual evidence, as well as comprehending the Indian vision of reality. This exercise will then prepare them for a journal entry in which they interpret on their own the three Bodhisattvas in source 45. But first let us look at source 43, *Shiva Nataraja*.

Before beginning our analysis, allow us to offer one suggestion. At the beginning of the class in which we are going to discuss the *Lord of the Dance*, we pass around the room a bronze statuette of Shiva performing his cosmic dance of ecstacy. Allowing students to hold the statue and examine it up close seems to be an effective aid to discussion. Let's be frank: The photos in this book often are less than perfectly clear, and it helps to bring an item such as this into class. We do the same for Guanyin, when we discuss her iconography.

The Questions for Analysis that accompany the picture are sufficiently leading to enable the thoughtful student to crack the statue's code of symbols. However, just to make sure, why not supply them with a few additional clues that we deliberately left out of the introductory remarks that accompany the artifact? It always helps when the instructor is able to add something to the information provided in the text.

Ask the students to look at the drum that Shiva holds in his upper right hand and ask them to describe its shape. The correct answer is that it is shaped like an hourglass—a rather obvious symbol of the beating out of the rhythm of time. More than that, within Hindu culture the hourglass drum represents life (because incarnate life is so temporal). Have them also study the crown. Note that it contains a circle and projects rays. The students will probably infer that this represents the sun—a good guess but wrong. It is actually the moon, which in Hindu iconography symbolizes unending time (the moon waxes and wanes endlessly).

Now that you have helped the students discover additional symbolic clues not hinted at in the source introduction or Questions for Analysis, it is time to move on to the symbols that the students, with the help of the text, can reasonably be expected to unravel. Obviously, the circle of fire represents the eternal cycle (circles have no beginning or end) of destruction, purification, and regeneration—the very qualities of fire, especially for a South Indian forest people who practiced slash and burn farming. Shiva's cosmic dance of fire ends each great eon of time in violent destruction, but then begins life anew. Note how the life-giving waters of Mother Ganges, the source of all life and holiness, flow out of Shiva's head as strands of hair and merge into the circle of flames. Water and fire—life and death—are two opposite yet complementary elements that interact and transform one another (water quenches fire; fire turns water to steam). But the symbols do not end here. We have only begun our analysis.

Once the students have seen and understood these basic symbols, we go even farther in breaking down the statue and its component images. What we do next is to project a transparency of this statue onto a screen and using a crayon, we draw an isosceles triangle whose base is a line that connects the hands of each upper arm and whose apex is the top of Shiva's crown (remember the triangle created by the Northern Wei Buddha's hands and head?). By doing this we can now focus on the image's core sculpted message, namely that it is Shiva who presides over the eternal cycle of life and death. The upper left hand (on our right as we face the statue) holds a flame—the symbol of destruction and death. *On an equal plane,* the upper right hand holds the hour glass drum—a symbol of eternal life. Life and death, therefore, balance one another and are equal realities. The moon-crown at the top of the triangle shows us, if ever there was any doubt, that they are balanced for all eternity and are forever reconciled in Shiva.

Shiva's facial expression suggests a state of simultaneous divine ecstasy and meditative peace (compare seal 6, Chapter 1, source 8). The eyes are closed and the mouth forms a smile of contentment. Shiva is, therefore, *Mahayogi,* literally "the Great Meditator," but a better translation is "Total Tranquility." (Remember we noted above that a yogi is a person who practices yoga or enjoys a state of Yoga.) When we combine this with the fact that his upper right arm is entwined by a deadly cobra (but the Tamil snake god Aiyanar, a son of Shiva, was and still is widely revered as a beneficent protector and a fertility deity), while he makes the gesture of "fear not" with his lower right hand, the message is unambiguous: Death is not an end and must not be feared. Hence, Shiva triumphs over the demon of the ignorance of those who fear their own mortality. In Shiva, death brings life, and through Shiva one will attain moksha. (Remember the raised foot toward which his lower left hand points.)

Once students have had a chance to explore in class the iconography of *Shiva Nataraja*, they are ready to write a good journal entry on the three Bodhisattvas in source 45. We have already commented extensively on these Bodhisattvas in the section Why These Sources?, and anything else we might write about them would be superfluous. When we assign this entry, we ask students to write at least one full page that addresses directly source 45's question 6, but only after they have read and answered, at least in their minds, questions 1–5. One thing that we constantly stress is that no matter which Question for Analysis they might be asked to address in an essay or journal entry, they should first read and attempt to answer *all* of the questions that accompany the source under consideration. This is prudent because these questions are intended to lead them, step by step, through a full analysis of that source. To overlook such help would be foolish. Apparently most students take our advice because, by the time we get to this assignment, journal entries are generally quite good. What is especially exciting for us is that students, who a few weeks earlier had never heard of nondualism and similar Hindu and Buddhist concepts and who initially had difficulty (and even resisted) comprehending these alien notions, are now writing some insightful and articulate essays on these Mahayana Buddhist statues.

Statues were not a form of religious expression for Diaspora Jews. Rather, the spoken and written words of their rabbis held their communities together and preserved their sense of unity and mission as they dwelt in alien lands.

The two Jewish sources bring the student face to face with the dual identity of Diaspora Judaism, its exclusivity and its universality. We favor asking students to focus on this issue by first trying to answer all the questions for analysis and then composing a journal entry in response to the question:

> In what ways, if any, do these two selections show Judaism to be a culture with a sense of exclusivity? In what ways, if any, do they underscore Judaism's sense of being part of the family of humanity and its having a special role to play in human history?

If students have read the sources carefully, especially in the light of the very leading Questions for Analysis, they should have little difficulty perceiving that Diaspora Judaism's identity as a Chosen People was, according to most of its teachers, a terrible but wonderful burden laid upon it by its Lord.

Other Ways to Use the Sources

1. Prepare a journal entry in which you compare Vishnu and Shiva with the ideal Bodhisattva. Which strike you as more significant, the differences or the similarities? What does your answer suggest?
2. The deity shown on seal 6 of source 8 in Chapter 1 is often called a proto-Shiva. Can you perceive any connections or parallels between this nameless Harappan god (if it is a god) and Shiva Nataraja?
3. A question for reflection: Shiva is, among his many attributes, the god of music. What is there about music that would make it an art that is especially appropriate to Shiva? (A note to the instructor: A partial answer is that music is the creation of harmony from dissonance or, put another way, the harmonious balance of two extremes into unison.)
4. Compose the Buddha's commentary on either *The Lotus Sutra* or the three statues of source 45.
5. Consider sources 43 and 45. One expert has noted that religious statues are perceived by their creators and those who venerate the statues as having a certain alchemical function, whereby they absorb intense human emotions and release them back to the worshiper as a healing force. Choose any of the four statues and comment in detail on whether or not this insight has any validity in regard to your chosen statue. In other words, how, if at all, did it function as a healing force?
6. Compose a discussion by the sculptors of the three Bodhisattvas that appear in source 45, illustrating their respective visions of the perfect Bodhisattva.
7. Compose a commentary by Second Isaiah (Chapter 3, source 22) on either Josephus's *Against Apion* or Maimonides's *Letter to Yemen.*

CHAPTER

7

Christianity: Conquering
the World for Christ

Chapter Theme

The sources in this chapter reflect a number of pivotal moments in the development of Christianity as a globally significant religion. First there was the appeal of Jesus of Nazareth's ministry and his message of the imminence of the Kingdom of Heaven. Then came the spread of Christianity beyond the ethnic boundaries of Judaism and its formulation of a coherent theology of salvation in the age of Paul of Tarsus, a man who probably deserves the oft-bestowed title *Christianity's Second Father*. The early fourth century witnessed another significant turning point with the almost simultaneous marriages of the Christian faith and its ecclesiastical structures to the Roman Empire and the kingdom of Ethiopia (see Chapter 11, source 95). Of the two, the bond between the Roman state and the Christian Church was the more dramatic and had more far-reaching consequences. So far as the subsequent civilizations of Byzantium and Western Europe were concerned (Chapter 10), Emperor Constantine the Great was *Christianity's Third Father*. Christianity was firmly entrenched as the imperial religion by the death of Constantine in 337, and certainly imperial law over the next century reflected that reality. However, about the same time that Christianity was becoming the state religion of both Rome and Ethiopia, another tradition arose in the wastelands of Egypt and Syria-Palestine—the flight to the desert by large numbers of Christian enthusiasts, many of whom were a living repudiation of the Church's growth into a major institution and its identity with the Roman state. Christian monasticism, which would serve for centuries to come as a periodic force for spiritual renewal within all branches of Christendom, was well underway by 400 C.E.

The process of defining Christianity's core beliefs and structures necessarily involved defining what it did not believe in and what was not part of its accepted heritage. During its first few centuries of existence, Christianity had to come to terms with Gnosticism, a pervasive, dualistic tradition that held as its core belief the idea that each human has within him- and herself an imprisoned spark of divinity that can only be liberated through knowledge (*gnosis*) of one's divine origins and the absolute rejection of this unreal world. Gnostic Christians were a significant force in Egypt and elsewhere in the eastern Mediterranean, especially during the second century. Like Judaism, which also had its Gnostic elements, orthodox Christianity ultimately rejected outright Gnostic beliefs as heresy. The question still remains, and it is hotly debated among scholars: How deeply, if at all, did Gnostic influences manage to penetrate into the body of what became orthodox Christian faith and practice? For example, was Christianity's uneasiness with human sexuality, such as we see in source 53, a manifestation of Gnostic elements that lived on long after Gnosticism was rejected as a pernicious error?

Just as Christianity was born into a Southwest Asian religious milieu in which Gnostic ideas (which apparently had their origin in India) freely circulated, so also early Christianity influenced other religious traditions. As the introduction to the section "Religious Exchange and Interchange" notes, "cultural syncretism was a two-way street during Christianity's formative years." If we try to study the historical evolution of early Christianity without being mindful of the richly variegated cultural context of the ecumene in which it developed, a world that stretched from the western reaches of the Roman Empire to Persia, then we fail to place this new religion into its proper global context. For this reason, it is necessary to look at Manichaeism, as difficult as its metaphysics might be for the average undergraduate. An offshoot of Gnostic Christianity, Manichaeism emerged in third-century Mesopotamia to become a religion that claimed a world-wide mission, and it acted upon that vision. Until its suppression by orthodox Christian authorities, Manichaeism gave Christianity a run for its life in the Late Roman Empire. Although it ceased to be a viable alternative to Christianity in western Eurasia after the fifth century, Manichaeism managed to travel to China where it took root and persisted into early modern times.

Why These Sources?

No survey of Christian literature is complete without an excerpt from the Sermon on the Mount. Here the student confronts the basic spirituality of the message of Jesus and his God-centered code of ethics—a code that idealistically demanded selfless perfection. Paul's Epistle to the Romans is similarly required reading because it reflects the full maturation of Paul's theology of salvation. In this letter we see Paul leading the primitive Church away from its earliest emphasis on Jewish messianism and toward a new focus on personal salvation, or what Paul calls *justification* through faith in Jesus the God-man.

Eusebius of Caesarea's *Ecclesiastical History* reflects the next major moment of development in the historical evolution of Christianity—the persecution and then triumph of the Christian faith within the Roman Empire. Well, at least Eusebius saw it as a triumph. Our purpose in presenting these excerpts from Eusebius is to illustrate how quickly Christianity moved from being the object of imperial scorn and persecution in the early fourth century to an ideology embraced by Emperor Constantine to justify his aggression against his pagan coemperor. And most church leaders, as was the case with Eusebius, applauded and agreed. *The Theodosian Code* continues this theme by illustrating how the Christian Church had become an arm of the Roman state and the consequences that followed for Christians and non-Christians alike. Whereas the message of Jesus' Sermon on the Mount was "Blessed are those who are persecuted for righteousness' sake, for theirs is the Kingdom of Heaven," the message of this source is "Christianity," as defined by the imperial Church, has triumphed. The *Pax Romana* is now the *Pax Christi*, and woe betide anyone foolish enough to oppose the emperor's religion." Source 52, the *Barberini Ivory*, graphically shows us the blessings that an orthodox Christian emperor at Constantinople, the New Rome, expected as his due—the submission of all foreign pagan peoples, including Central Asian nomads and Indians.

Jesus, however, had taught about the Kingdom of Heaven, not the Roman Empire, and was also remembered as having claimed, "My kingdom does not belong to this world" (John 18:36). In response to that initial message and partially in repudiation of the new Christian-imperial order, substantial numbers of laity and clerics, but largely laity, sought to live lives more perfectly modeled on the message of the Sermon on the Mount by retreating to desert hermitages. Over time, this *eremitical* movement was defused of much of its inherent rebelliousness and transformed into varieties of *cenobitic* monasticism that were safely incorporated into the institutional framework of Christianity in both East and West. Monasteries, however, remained refuges from the world where some individuals could live lives that conformed to their interpretation of the otherworldly message of the Gospel. *The Life of Saint Mary the Harlot* expresses more eloquently than any modern commentary the spirit and vision that initially drove men and women into the wastelands of the Eastern Mediterranean and from which sprang over the centuries many different modes of monastic life. Rather than presenting excerpts from *The Rule of St. Benedict* or from one of the many other, often radically different and culturally specific rules of Christian monastic organization (and space precludes our presenting more than one source on this topic), we thought it best to show the student a vivid example of the original monastic model, as described by one of its practitioners, Saint Ephraem of Edessa. The story of Ephraem's two monastic friends, Abraham and Mary, illustrates, more than any collection of rules and aphorisms could, the spirit of love and devotion that drove the most devout of the Desert Elders. The periodic renewals and reinterpretations of Christian monasticism that occurred over the last seventeen hundred years have generally been attempts to return to the ideals of the desert.

The flight to the desert was obviously a manifestation of a contempt-for-the-world philosophy that often expressed itself in extreme acts of asceticism. The Desert Elders saw themselves as soldiers of Christ and athletes of religion, with all of the accompanying self-sacrifice and pain that such notions imply. Even Christians who did not seek out the solitude of the desert (and most did not) were enjoined to live lives of sacrifice and penance and to reject the vanities (literally, the emptiness) of the false allurements of this world. They were instructed to see themselves, as St. Augustine phrased it, as persons who were *in* this world but not *of* it. They were pilgrims passing through this empty world on their way to Heaven. In acknowledgement of that ultimate goal, laity and clerics representing all orders of society accepted asceticism as a manifestation of heroic Christianity in its highest form and venerated these living and dead ascetics as saintly intercessors before the throne of God.

One wonders where Christianity picked up this strong emphasis on rejection of the vain pleasures of the world. The answer is not simple because the roots of Christian asceticism were many. One root, however, seems to be Gnosticism, a pre-Christian religious complex of ideas that apparently had its roots in India. Christian Gnostics were a force to be reckoned with during the first several Christian centuries, especially in Egypt, the home of Christian monasticism. Of all the extant Gnostic Christian texts, *The Gospel of Thomas* is the most important. A collection of 113 *agrapha* (unwritten things), or uncanonical sayings attributed to Jesus, *The Gospel of Thomas* raises many questions. Are any of these supposedly new sayings valid, otherwise unrecorded words of Jesus? Given the oral basis on which the canonical Gospels were constructed, that is theoretically quite possible. What about those instances where we have sayings that echo but depart from the texts of the three synoptic evangelists (Matthew, Mark, and Luke)? Who got it right, the Gnostics or the canonical evangelists? Are all of these sayings simply after-the-fact, creative recastings by a Gnostic author or authors of the essentially non-Gnostic canonical Gospels? Do these sayings attributed to Jesus, whether spurious or not, represent an alternative tradition that, although later repudiated, goes back to Christianity's earliest days? If experts heatedly debate these and other associated issues, we should not expect to be able to arrive at any definitive answers on the basis of the few excerpts here. What we can hope to do, however, is to help students become aware of the rich, complex, and still ill-understood cultural matrix in which Christianity took shape.

Complex matrices are the very stuff of global history. Where would we be without them? For this reason we also include the deeply syncretic Manichaean text *The Parable about the World-Ocean*. Manichaean writings are not easily understood, even by specialists in the field. This particular excerpt is as easy as they get. We chose it in order to illustrate three important and not especially obscure points: Manichaeism's self-conscious syncretism; its essential Gnosticism; and its sense of world mission.

Analyzing the Sources

The author of the Gospel of Matthew expected his readers to appreciate the parallels between Jesus and Moses in the Sermon on the Mount passage, and we would do well to draw our students' attention to Matthew's artistry as a way of helping them interpret the message of this scriptural account. Students have read the Book of Deuteronomy's account of Moses's farewell address to the Israelites, where he reminded them of the Law and Covenant that the Lord had given them on Mount Sinai. Here, on another mountain, Jesus begins his public ministry by calling for adherence to a higher Law of Righteousness (cf. the Buddha's Law of Righteousness in Chapter 3, source 19) and a New Covenant. Without repudiating the Law and Covenant given to Israel through Moses ("Think not that I have come to abolish the law and [the teachings of] the prophets"), Jesus, the New Moses, claims that he is fulfilling the promises the Lord had given through Moses and the prophets ("I have come...to fulfill them"). As Matthew notes, "He taught them as one who had authority." The Kingdom of Heaven, when God's universal sovereignty will be fully realized (See Second Isaiah, Chapter 3, source 22), is at hand and open to all who heed Jesus' call for obedience to a higher Law of Righteousness. Whereas the Old Law is holy ("You have heard that it was said to the men of old, `You shall not kill,'"), the New Law is holier ("But I say to you that every one who is angry with his brother shall be liable to judgment"). By following the New Law, namely by having faith in God the Father (see the so-called Lord's Prayer) and by living a life of love modeled on the Father's love, one will merit Heaven.

To help students perceive the world view and message of the author of this Gospel, we ask them to list as many direct and indirect references as they can find in this passage to the selections from Jewish scripture in Chapters 2 and 3. These lists then become the starting point for a class discussion on the issue: "What is the theological message of the Sermon on the Mount?"

Saint Paul was essentially a mystical, intuitive teacher rather than a systematic theologian, but his theology of salvation helped to transform Christianity into a universal faith. In his Epistle to the Romans, Paul teaches that the Law of Moses is good, but it is incomplete and incapable of saving anyone (that is, of *justifying*, or making one right, with God). In this respect Paul's theology is consonant with Jesus' Sermon on the Mount, but then Paul goes one step farther and in the process recasts Jesus' message. Jesus had centered his messianic message on Judaism's God the Father; Paul centered his theology on Jesus, the Son of God. According to Paul, personal salvation is available to all—Jew and gentile—through absolute faith in Jesus, the God-man (cf. the bhakti movement in India). Only faith and then the love that results from that faith (question 3) can save one. Faith, first and foremost, and then the love that necessarily follows from faith: This is the New Law and New Covenant inaugurated by Jesus, as far as Paul is concerned.

One way to help students see the ways in which Paul interpreted and articulated Jesus' message of salvation, and also reoriented Christianity by making faith in Jesus the means through which one fulfills the New Covenant, is to ask them to answer question 6. In comparing this selection with the Sermon on the Mount, students must consider Paul's statement: "Jesus has set me free from the law of sin and death" in the light of Jesus' words, according to Matthew, "I say to you, till heaven and earth pass away, not an iota, nor a dot, will pass from the law until all is accomplished." These apparently contradictory statements are only that: apparent contradictions. Both Jesus and Paul emphasize the *spirit* behind the Law, a spirit of love and reconciliation through which one gains the Kingdom of Heaven. Jesus teaches love even of enemies, and Paul teaches that the person who has placed total faith in Jesus will "be aglow with the spirit" and will understand that "love is the fulfilling of the law."

This epistle also provides hints about the roles played by a number of prominent women in the early Church as deaconesses and persons in whose houses local Christian congregations gathered. In this respect, Priscilla, who is named *before* her husband Aquila, thereby implying her precedence, is noteworthy. Although the evidence is admittedly ambiguous and fragmentary, it appears that women held important positions in the early Church. We urge you to consider requiring your students to prepare a journal response to question 4.

Eusebius's *Ecclesiastical History, The Theodosian Code*, and the *Barberini Ivory* deserve a few minutes of combined class attention or at least should be assigned as subjects for a journal entry. Why? Well, it is more than just arguable that Constantine I (r. 306–337) ushered in a revolutionary stage in the history of Christianity, and Constantine's imperial successors (with the exception of Julian the Apostate) continued the revolution. As we study these three sources, it becomes clear to even the most casual observer that in the process of becoming Rome's imperial Church, both Christianity and the Roman Empire underwent radical reorientations. In dealing with these three sources as a short unit (and class analysis usually takes no more than ten minutes; this is not overly complex material), we ask students to address the following issue:

> Consider *The Theodosian Code* and the *Barberini Ivory* in the light of Eusebius's *Ecclesiastical History*. Which strike you as more significant, the similarities or the differences in tone and message? What do you conclude from your answer?
>
> Class analysis (or a journal entry, if you wish) faces only one potential problem in regard to this issue. Some students take the opportunity to castigate the imperial Church (and Christianity in general) for having gone wrong or perverted its original message. We try, as gently but as firmly as possible, to remind the entire class that as historians our mandate is not to sit in judgment of the past or to impose our personal standards of right and wrong on it. We try simply to understand the process of historical evolution and gain perspective, understanding and, we hope, a certain wisdom in the process.

The class can gain a more balanced perspective on the early imperial Christian Church if it takes a few minutes to analyze in detail the laws excerpted from *The Theodosian Code*. As these laws clearly show, in the process of becoming Rome's imperial Church, the clergy of the orthodox, state-sanctioned Church had in essence become imperial officials and enjoyed a number of powers and privileges as a consequence of their status. Conversely, Jews, pagans, and heretics now labored under various degrees of state-imposed constraints. It is misleading and even wrong, however, to say simply that pagans, Jews, and dissenting Christians were now persecuted and to leave it at that. The story is more complex than that and deserves to be understood in all of its complexity. Note that, of the three groups, heretics have the most severe penalties laid upon them, Jews are begrudgingly tolerated, and pagans fall somewhere between the two. Because of its emphasis on faith, Christianity in its various forms has throughout the ages been generally most intolerant of heretical, or heterodoxical, belief, far more so than it has been of unbelief and even paganism. The reason for this is simple: The heretic is perceived as an invidious cancer within the Church, whose false teachings can mislead many unsuspecting and otherwise pious believers. Pagans, Jews, and other unbelievers, to the contrary, are not hidden enemies and, therefore, are less dangerous to the body of believers. Moreover, heretics are considered inherently perverse and beyond redemption because they have willingly perverted the true faith (The word "heresy" derives from a Greek verb that means "to choose."). They have, in other words, used a gift from God—free will—to distort God's true revelation. As a law of 391 notes: "For the lapsed and the errant there is help, but for the lost—that is, the profaners of holy baptism—there is no aid." Therefore, the late fourth-century laws enshrined in *The Theodosian Code* prescribe that heretics are to lose a wide range of the normal rights and protections accorded citizens and their places of worship are to be shut down. By barring them from making wills and inheriting property, this family-centered society has essentially turned heretics into non-persons. Pagans, to the contrary, retain their civil rights of family inheritance, but their traditional places of worship are now, in 391, closed to them. Jews enjoy even greater rights than pagans. Not only do Jews retain their traditional civil rights, they also have the right to worship in their synagogues, but that toleration is given only in a most begrudging manner. For example, Jews must desist from certain public ceremonies that appear odious to pious Christians, and "their synagogues or habitations should not be burned *indiscriminately* or should not be damaged *wrongfully* without any reason" (emphasis added). Although Jews must "not become insolent and elated by their own security" and must be vigilant lest they "commit anything rash against reverence for the Christian worship," the imperial Christian Church tolerates Judaism for several reasons. First, because of its triumphant new status the Christian Church does not perceive Jews as a threat. Second, for all of Christianity's antipathy toward a people "who refused to accept their Messiah," Christians perceive Jewish monotheism, Jewish scripture (what Christians call the Old Testament), and even Jewish history as their own. As wrong as Christians might believe Jews to be in their refusal to accept Jesus, Christians still regard Jews as the people who prepared the way for the New Covenant.

If time allows, we like to spend a few minutes with Abraham and his niece Mary as presented by Saint Ephraem of Edessa. Students like this story of love and faith and have no trouble relating the ideals of the desert hermits, as illustrated here, to the Sermon on the Mount's message of uncompromising love. Indeed, in responding to question 2, they see that, at least as exemplified by Abraham, these hermits were not perceived by their contemporaries as self-centered dropouts. Although the strict law of asceticism might require Abraham to remain in his cave and to forswear tavern meals and similar comforts of the flesh, the spirit of the law of love, as preached by Jesus and Saint Paul, compelled him to face these temptations in order to save Mary's soul. Moreover, students have no trouble seeing how, as question 3 suggests, these holy people of the desert excited the popular imagination and became the revered superstars of their day. Their contemporaries believed that saints like Mary and Abraham, who had faced evil and emerged triumphant, had gained extraordinary powers over both nature (consider the passage that informs us Mary earned a reputation for healing) and the supernatural. Indeed, contemporary society perceived these holy people as persons who, through their heroic lives and meritorious prayers, served society by keeping evil at bay and even tempering the stern justice of God.

The Desert Elders played a major role in converting the common people of the eastern Mediterranean to Christianity, but their uncompromising asceticism and simplicity was matched and often exceeded by Gnostic and Manichaean teachers. We would be quite wrong if we saw the Gnostic religions, including Manichaeism, as marginal cults. They attracted significant numbers of devotees, in large part because their leaders were perceived as extraordinarily holy people who offered compelling answers to several basic spiritual questions: What is the nature of evil, and why do evil things happen to the innocent? What is the nature of humanity? Are humans inherently good or evil? What is the destiny of humanity?

In order to help our students perceive the serious challenge that the Gnostic faiths offered to Christianity and the important place they hold in global history, we ask them to compose a journal entry in which they draw two sets of parallels. First they are to note parallels between the message of *The Upanishads* and that of *The Gospel of Thomas* (question 3 of source 54). Then they are to see if they can find parallels between the message of Mahayana Buddhism and that of *The Parable about the World-Ocean*. This exercise helps them see that, contrary to the dismissive statements that one finds all too often in history textbooks, there was nothing bizarre or outlandish about these Gnostic faiths. They comfortably fit into the broad spiritual spectrum of their day. Indeed, they were deeply influenced by religious currents from India and other points in the East.

Other Ways to Use the Sources

1. In your journal, write a commentary on the *Barberini Ivory* by either the artist who crafted it or the emperor whom it represents.
2. In your journal, compose St. Matthew's commentary on Ephraem of Edessa's *The Life of Saint Mary the Harlot.*
3. Consider what Paul says about love. Where does this place him in relation to the Sermon on the Mount? To Saint Abraham (source 53)?
4. In your journal, compose a commentary by either Saint Mary the Harlot or her uncle (source 53) on either Eusebius's *Ecclesiastical History* or *The Theodosian Code.*
5. Saint Mary the Harlot is on her death bed. Compose her memoirs.
6. *Heresy* is a religious belief that deviates from established doctrine. Within a Christian context, it means erroneous teachings that masquerade as the orthodox (correctly thought) faith. Compose a commentary by an orthodox Christian on *The Gospel of Thomas* in which you expose its heresies. If you have questions as to what a mainstream Christian would believe, refer to Saint Paul.
7. Saint Paul also had a vision of a universal mission. Compose his commentary on *The Parable about the World-Ocean.*

C H A P T E R

8

Islam:
Universal Submission to God

Chapter Theme

The sources in this chapter illustrate, above all else, the close parallels between Islam's doctrines, moral principles, and religious practices and those of its sibling Southwest Asian faiths: Zoroastrianism, Judaism, and Christianity. The sources also suggest how the modern Western notion of the need to separate secular concerns from religious beliefs makes no sense to a Muslim who is an obedient member of God's community on Earth. The sources also underscore the rich diversity within Islam, despite the ideal of Islam's being a totally integrated and united community devoted single-mindedly to service to God. Finally we see how various Islamic communities have related to the nonbelievers in their midst.

Why These Sources?

All great civilizations have classics, or sacred texts, that enunciate their most profound values and beliefs. For Islam the most revered of all books is the Qur'an, a sacred text very much like but also quite different from the Judaeo-Christian Bible. Most Jewish and Christian theologians and biblical scholars have historically viewed the Bible as a collection of texts authored by divinely inspired humans who employed a variety of literary devices and idioms to express, often in metaphorical terms, divine truths. Most Muslims, to the contrary, would consider such an interpretation of the Qur'an as blasphemy. Orthodox Muslims of every sect venerate the Qur'an as the coeternal Word of God, finally revealed in all of its beauty, majesty, and clarity to the Prophet Muhammad through the agency of the Angel Gabriel. Human authorship, even the authorship of Muhammad, the most perfect of all God's creatures, plays no role in the formulation of the Qur'an, as far as pious Muslims are concerned. Like God, it is uncreated.

Our first two selections contain qur'anic excerpts that not only convey many of the basic teachings of Islam but also reflect, as well as any translations can, the sonorous beauty of a book that has infused virtually all aspects of Islamic life and expression for the past thirteen centuries.

Source 56, an excerpt from the surah known as *The House of Imran*, should remind the student of earlier readings from Deuteronomy, Second Isaiah, and the Sermon on the Mount, and the reader should be able to see, without any difficulty, the moral and theological affinities among the three monotheistic faiths represented in those selections.

We chose this excerpt because it illustrates many of Islam's basic articles of faith and moral instruction. First and foremost, there is the doctrine of the absolute omnipotence and uniqueness of God: "God there is no god but He, the Living, the Everlasting."*Allah* (The God) is almighty, all-wise, merciful, and loving, and He especially loves those who do good, but He is also a God of justice who punishes disbelievers and evil-doers. None of this is alien to anyone who has studied the other monotheistic faiths of Southwest Asia. We also find here Islam's guiding principle that the revelations given Muhammad were the completion of a history of divine revelation that began with God's speaking through such great *Islamic* prophets as Adam, Noah, the House of Abraham (Abraham, Ishmael, Isaac, and Jacob), the House of Imran (Moses and Aaron), and Jesus, born of the Virgin (as well as through Jesus' apostles). Islam preceded the Torah and the Gospels, and prophets now claimed by Jews and Christians had actually been Muslims, by reason of their faith and submission to the Word of God. Now, however, Jews and Christians had turned away from the truth and were schismatics. Notwithstanding their errors and false pride, Jews and Christians remain *People of the Book* because they received a measure of divine revelation, even though they perverted it. Because they were People of the Book, an all-merciful God continued to call them back to Submission through rightly-guided Muslims. Should these Jews and Christians remain hard hearted and continue to turn away from the truth, after it has been told them, they should be left to God's justice and mercy. If, however, they offer violence to Muslims, they are to be painfully chastized.

This God of goodness, who communicated His eternal truth to Muhammad, requires that all True Believers not only have faith but act piously. Source 57, *Gardens of the Righteous*, contains additional qur'anic quotations that illustrate such principles as peacemaking, humility, charity, treatment of the lowly, male-female relations, and holy struggle (jihad). In addition, the commentaries on these passages show us how *al-Hadith*, or holy Tradition that centers on the remembered sayings and actions of the

Prophet and his Companions, became a source of authority, second only to the Qur'an, for the delineation of proper Islamic behavior.

The single greatest exemplar of perfect Islamic behavior was, of course, Muhammad, and for that reason most of al-Hadith centered on the life and sayings of the Messenger of God. An integral part of Islamic tradition is the biography of the Prophet by Muhammad ibn Ishaq, which records the marvelous story of Muhammad's Night Journey. We have added Ibn Ishaq's telling of this story to this fourth edition for several reasons. As is obvious, the story allows students to compare this Islamic vision of the Afterworld with those presented in *The Epic of Gilgamesh, The Oddyssey*, and *The Aeneid*. The story's various versions as recorded by Ibn Ishaq also underscore some of Islam's core values, practices, and attributes. These include Islam's emphasis on moderation, its proscription of the consumption of alcohol, the belief in a Hell of punishments for the wicked and a seven-layered Heaven for the Just (a vision that later influenced Dante), and the practice of prayer five times daily.

All of Islam's righteous practices can be termed *jihad*, or struggle, in the service of God, as we have already seen in several selections from al-Hadith in source 57. But jihad also has a more commonly understood narrower meaning: armed struggle for God. Source 59, also new to this edition, is an excerpt from the writings of the *qadi*, or Islamic jurist, al-Kayrawani, in which he discourses on the rules governing the jihad of the sword. Here students have an opportunity to see how no topic escaped the study and learned commentary of the jurists who interpreted *Shari'a*, or Sacred Law.

The sources in "Variety and Unity in Islam" illustrate several important aspects of traditional Islam. Chief among these are: (1) some of the essential differences between Shi'ite and Sunni Muslims; (2) the serene mysticism of Sufi devotion; and (3) the purgative qualities of the *hajj*, one of Islam's most serious obligations. More than that, source 62, a description of the fourteenth-century pilgrimage of Mansa Musa of Mali, illustrates the universality of Islam and its ability to encompass so many diverse peoples.

After Islam spread beyond the borders of Arabia, it attracted unknown millions of converts from almost every imaginable ethnic background. Islam, however, was more than just a faith that evolved a sense of universality. It was also a state (and later a number of competing states), which conquered and dominated vast numbers of non-Muslims. Many conquered Christians, Jews, Zoroastrians, Hindus, Buddhists, animists, and others eventually adopted the faith of their Islamic lords. Many others did not. The sources in "Islam and Unbelievers" describe some of the ways in which Muslims dealt with their infidel subjects.

The two documents that comprise source 63, *Ibn Muslama's Pact* and *The Pact of Umar*, provide examples of two stages in the evolution of the *dhimma*, or contract of toleration, that Muslims offered their non-Muslim subjects. Habib ibn Muslama's pact with the Christians of Tiflis, which dates from around 653, exhibits the overall tolerance toward the People of the Book that characterized official Islamic policy in the era of Islam's first four caliphs (632–661) and the Umayyad Dynasty (661–750) that followed. The second document that appears here purports to be a pact entered into with the Christians of Syria around 637, but there is every good reason to conclude that it was created in the ninth century, rather than the seventh, when the Abbasid Dynasty was searching for historical precedents for its more restrictive policies.

Needless to say, we chose to juxtapose these two pacts in order to help students understand that the dhimma was not a static phenomenon. The other two sources in this section also underscore that reality.

The eye-witness account by Benjamin of Tudela of the situation enjoyed by the prosperous Jewish community of mid-twelfth-century Baghdad shows us the dhimma functioning in one of the most open Islamic communities of its day. Regardless of Benjamin's apologetical purposes and apparent exaggerations, the picture he presents is probably not that far from the truth. Other sources make it clear that two of the most notable examples of prosperous, semi-autonomous Jewish communities in the twelfth-century were the Jews of Baghdad in Iraq and of Cairo in Egypt. Under the tolerant rule of their Islamic sovereigns, the Jews of both cities achieved a deserved reputation for piety and scholarship. In the light of present-day Muslim-Jewish relations in the Middle East, it is important that our students examine a source that reveals another side of the history that binds these two religious cultures.

Bitter Muslim-Hindu animosities in the Indian subcontinent have also been a constant feature of late-twentieth- and early-twenty-first-century history. The source we have chosen to shed historical light on this centuries-old problem is *The Deeds of Sultan Firuz Shah*, the memoirs of a late-fourteenth-century Turkish sultan of Delhi. As ageless as India's culture appears, it has undergone moments of severe challenge and change. One of the most significant was occasioned by the Turkish importation of Islam into northern and central India, after 1000 C.E. This document provides vivid evidence of some of the problems engendered by the meeting of a religion that preaches submission to the one and only path to God with a way of life and devotion predicated upon the assumption that there are an infinite number of paths to the Divine.

Analyzing the Sources

One theme binds all of these sources together (including Benjamin of Tudela's *Book of Travels*): *jihad*, or holy struggle. No matter their sect, like Zoroastrians, Jews, and Christians, Muslims see themselves as God's agents in the world, actively working to help realize the triumph of the Divine Plan. The struggle calls for sacrifice and martyrdom (literally, "giving witness") of one sort or another, but the rewards far outweigh the pain and price of victory.

Most citizens of the United States who have bothered to follow current Middle Eastern events have probably concluded that jihad means military action in the name of an intolerant and unforgiving deity. Such a simplistic conclusion does gross injustice to a richly complex and broadly tolerant religion, whose faithful largely agree that the jihad of the sword is less meritorious than the jihads of the soul, heart, mouth, and hand (all of which are defined two paragraphs below). To see all or most Muslims who attempt daily to struggle for God as suicidal fanatics ready to kill everyone whom they cannot forcibly convert is tantamount to assuming that all Christians who claim to take seriously Jesus' injunction that one must daily take up a cross and follow him (Matthew 10:38) are crusaders (those who bear a cross) in a military and not metaphorical sense.

Hadith preserves the tradition that following a successful campaign against the Meccans, the Prophet informed his followers: "We have now returned from the lesser jihad to the greater jihad." That jihad is a moral struggle against evil in all its forms, and the exertions required of the *mujahid*, or warrior of God, in the greater jihad include prayer, study, preaching, teaching, charity, fasting, and pilgrimage. All Muslims, therefore, must daily fight as mujahidin by doing battle with their lower selves, or passions, and working to establish an equilibrium in life according to the norms of Islam.

Consonant with that tradition, Islam's classical-era qadis, or religious jurists, distinguished four forms of jihad, and most Muslims still accept those four categories. In addition to *jihad of the sword*, there is *jihad of the hand* (the good actions, especially charitable deeds, enjoined by Shari'a, or qur'anic law), *jihad of the mouth* (proclaiming one's faith and preaching the Word of God), and *jihad of the heart* (the inner transformation of one's personality as one truly believes and acts accordingly). Sufis add a fifth, the *jihad of the soul*, the struggle of the soul to reach God through a mystical experience.

To assist students in perceiving the moral and devotional aspects of jihad, we favor asking them to study the various sources in this chapter as a block and to respond to the following problem, which is simply an expansion of source 57's question 2:

> Most of the sources in Chapter 8 deal, in some manner or other, with the different forms of jihad, or holy struggle, that Muslims carry on in the name of God. A careful analysis of these documents will show you how complex and variegated jihad is. What types of jihad can you identify? List in your journal each type of jihad that you have discovered and comment briefly on the apparent importance of each. Which forms of jihad do you think would appeal to most Muslims? Why do you conclude this? Be prepared to discuss your findings and conclusions in class.

Of course, the instructor can require students to compose a formal essay on the problem, but we prefer using the journal for this assignment so that students concentrate their full energies on discovering as many different forms of jihad as they can and trying to understand the place that these various struggles play in the lives of Muslims, rather than worrying about the style and form of the essay. This exercise, by the way, makes an excellent group project. We have discovered that small groups of about five students work well.

It is crucial to conduct a class discussion on the issue of Islamic jihad once everyone has completed the assignment. If time and other factors do not allow the professor to divide the class into manageable discussion groups, we believe it is necessary to interrupt lecture for ten or fifteen minutes to carry on some sort of discussion on the varieties of jihad and the conclusions that students have reached. The reason we believe this particular discussion is so important is that, to our way of thinking, it is crucial that we not allow students to leave our courses in global history still harboring the notion, unfortunately all too often fostered by today's popular media, that all or most Muslims are crazed, bloodthirsty fanatics who carry on terrorist jihads against all non-Muslims. In order to get the most out of this discussion, the professor will have to be prepared to point out indirectly through leading questions each of the forms of jihad reflected in these sources.

The Qur'an includes many surahs from the Medinan period, 622–630, when the Muslim community was struggling against Mecca, and many of these chapters reflect the grim reality of armed struggle and the need to raise to a high moral level combat in defense of the Word and Name of God. Indeed, such *defensive* warfare became a sacred duty of all able-bodied Muslim men in Medina, and martyrdom was the reward for all who fell while exerting themselves against Islam's enemies in this fight for survival.

At the same time, Islamic law, especially as canonized in the Qur'an, enjoins restraint. According to the surah *al-Baqarah* (*The Cow*), Muslims must resist those who attack them, but they are also to "aggress not: God loves not the aggressors." Moreover, they are to fight "till there is no persecution and religion is God's; then if they (the unbelievers) give over, there shall be no enmity save for evildoers." Likewise, the surah chosen for this chapter, *The House of Imran*, commands the chastisement only of those who slay God's prophets. Otherwise, the Muslim's duty is done by simply proclaiming before unbelievers his own submission to God.

The tenth-century jurist al-Kayrawani went a bit beyond this but not by much. As we read in his treatise on jihad (source 59), Muslims must resist Jews and Christians, but only to the point that these People of the Book either convert to Islam *or* (and this is an important "or") submit themselves to Islam's overlordship and pay the *jizya*. The implication is that forced conversion to Islam is not a goal of jihad. Moreover, according to al-Kayrawani's mainstream interpretation of Shari'a, when armed jihad is waged against unbelievers, certain rules must be followed.

Three qur'anic passages that appear in Imam Nawawi's *Gardens of the Righteous* (under the heading "On Striving in the Cause of Allah") continue the theme of struggle against the unbelievers. These excerpts from the Qur'an are then followed by a number of hadiths, or tales from oral tradition, that illustrate the Prophet's interpretation and application of the quoted precepts. Even a superficial reading of these selections shows that most relate to military conflict. War was and remains an undeniable component of Islamic jihad. After all, Arabic society in the Prophet's day was what anthropologists term a *courage culture*, which means it granted warriors extremely high status. One manifestation of that was the ancient tradition of *razzias*, or raiding expeditions for fun and profit. If the Prophet had, like Jesus, preached "do not resist one who is evil," few, if any, of his contemporaries would have listened to him. (As it was, he only initially attracted a handful of followers in his Meccan, or purely prophetic, period.) And if Muhammad had not, himself, become a warrior leader, leading razzias from Medina against the caravans of Mecca, Islam would not have survived. Notwithstanding all of this, note that several passages expand jihad beyond armed struggle. Surah 61:11–14 calls upon faithful Muslims to "strive in the cause of Allah with your belongings and your persons," and the last two hadiths in this collection of excerpts equate travel for the cause of Islam and preaching with jihad.

When we study the other excerpted passages from Imam Nawawi's compendium of hadiths we see that quite a few imply that holy striving, or struggle, is so much more than armed conflict. Consider the selections that deal with domestic matters and moral principles. The True Believer is a peacemaker within the family of Islam and acts with kindness and charity toward the lowly. Here we confront the obligation to exhibit amity to friends and relations and kindness to strangers. Here also we see a clear articulation of the obligation to protect the weak and the poor. Indeed, justice in speech and action, leavened by generosity, is expected of all true Muslims. Those who failed in this struggle for justice, such as people who devoured the wealth of orphans, could expect ghastly torments in the Afterlife (source 58).

To underscore the fact that Muslims understand jihad to be a multi-faceted, life-long striving by fallible people who will falter, but who also have God's assurance of help, we ask students to read and comment on the prayer that is found early in our qur'anic selection. As they begin reading the words, "Our Lord, make not our hearts to swerve after that Thou hast guided us; and give us mercy from Thee," many of our students will remark on the striking similarities between this prayer and the Lord's Prayer of the Sermon on the Mount (source 48). In addition to shedding additional light on the depth of jihad, this prayer also clearly demonstrates the close affinities between Islamic and Judaeo-Christian beliefs, values, and modes of expression.

Although Muslims anticipate setbacks and momentary lapses in their struggles for God, success is the goal of all forms of jihad, and success is expected. They expect success for the *umma*, or the universal community of Islam, and success for the individual Muslim. As far as the individual is concerned, this usually means success both in this world and in paradise. Just as Muslims count on evildoers' suffering in this world, as well as in Hell, most Muslims do not envision being unhappy in this world because service to God is, by definition, a happy and liberating experience. Indeed, recitation of the Qur'an brings a state of *sakina*, or divine tranquility. Muslims are also reminded five times daily of the success that God bestows on those who strive when they hear the *muezzin's* call to prayer:

> God is most great! I bear witness that there is no god but God. I bear witness that Muhammad is the Prophet of God. Hasten to prayer! *Hasten to success!* [Italics added.] God is most great! There is no god but God!

More than that, as the story of Muhammad's Night Journey makes clear, the obligations laid upon Muslims as they struggle in the way of God are not unbearable or painful in the extreme. At least this is how most Muslims interpret this story and the traditions of Islam.

One major Islamic branch, however, has historically expected persecution as it strives for God's righteousness, and that is the *Shi'ite* faction. Ever since the death of the Prophet's grandson, Husayn, at Karbala in 680, the followers of Ali's party have colored their interpretation of the obligation of jihad with the notion of redemption through suffering. Many Shi'ites, in unity with their martyred *imams*, expect and even welcome persecution and see their suffering as a sign of the righteousness of their struggle. This view comes across clearly in the *Creed Concerning the Imams*. Shi'ites, however, like all other Muslims, also expect their efforts to be crowned with ultimate success in both this world and beyond. However, in working to usher in this victory over the forces of evil that exist outside of and within Islam, Shi'ite *ulema* (religious scholars) teach that, when necessary, *taqiya*, or pious dissimulation of one's beliefs when surrounded by false Muslims (non-Shi'ites) and unbelievers, becomes an act of jihad. Here the end justifies the means, as long as it serves a higher goal and one continues to strive and oppose evil inwardly.

Another, quite different form of inward striving is that practiced by Islam's mystics—the Sufis. Al-Ghazali's *The Alchemy of Happiness* reveals Sufism's jihad of the heart and soul (as also does Ibn Ishaq's treatment of Muhammad's mystical Night Journey). According to al-Ghazali, the person striving for perfection wages jihad by the act of total surrender to God through an act of love. By renouncing self and becoming totally absorbed in the object of their love, God, Sufis expect to be purified of all earthly concerns and to ascend to a mystical union with God.

Most humans are incapable of such spiritual journeys, and for them the more mundane pilgrimage serves the purpose of cleansing their souls and bringing them closer to the Divine One they seek. The pilgrimage is an important act of worship in Buddhism, Hinduism, Judaism, and Christianity and serves as one of Islam's Five Pillars.

A pilgrimage, any pilgrimage, is a religious journey to a sacred place, often in expiation for one's sins and always to commune with the Sacred Other. The pilgrimage serves as both a symbol of one's personal, special relationship with the Divine and also as an affirmation of one's membership in a special community of believers. Most pilgrimages are expected to be difficult because it is a purgative process. "No pain, no gain" is as applicable to pilgrimages as to marathons. At the same time, they cannot be so arduous as to render them impossible to the average but determined believer.

In Mahmud Kati's description of Mansa Musa's *hajj* we see all of these elements clearly. The king of Mali undertakes a pilgrimage in atonement for his role in his mother's death. The change that comes over him by virtue of his pilgrimage is classic. By striving on this long and difficult journey, he has reached a new level of friendship with God, thereby becoming a *wali*, or special client of God, and he is able, thereby, to raise Islam to a new level in his homeland. He builds mosques, including the great mosque of Timbuktu, and even brings back to Mali presumed Qurayshites for the edification of his people. All of Mali benefits from Mansa Musa's arduous pilgrimage to Mecca. In much the same manner, the pilgrim who returns to his or her community brings back lifelong blessings for that community by virtue of being a witness to the faith and a living religious hero.

The Islamic ruler who maintains a proper relationship with his state's dhimmis, keeping them in a position of subservience, is also striving in the way of God. All three sources in the section "Islam and Unbelievers" present different manifestations of that struggle.

The Pact of Ibn Muslama is typical of early dhimmas in the age of Islam's first conquests, whereas *The Pact of Umar* is typical of the compacts that were entered into with subject non-Muslims in the era of the Abbasids. Although the first pact is less restrictive than the second, both clearly were intended to underline the God-ordained supremacy of Islam. Over time dhimmas such as these served a second purpose, acting as effective incentives for conversion.

Although Benjamin of Tudela's rather sanguine account does not deal directly with restrictions placed upon the Jews of Baghdad, it indirectly serves as testimony of the Jews' subservience to the caliph and their dependence upon the caliph's good will. The struggles of his predecessors to impose their authority over the Jews of Baghdad (as well as al-Abbasi's own struggle to be the upright man that Benjamin assures us he is) have brought great prosperity to the caliph (and, by extension, Islam).

Well, some might think we are stretching it a bit to find evidence of jihad in Tudela's account, but jihad abounds in the fourteenth-century memoirs of Sultan Firuz Shah of Delhi, who certainly saw himself as a person who constantly struggled for Islam. By means of sumptuary laws he outlawed outward signs of sinfulness, irreligion, and ostentation. He upheld Shari'a by ending the practice of his predecessors who imposed illegal punishments upon their Muslim subjects. He attempted to suppress Shi'ism in his lands by threats, censorship, and, when necessary, punishments. He built and endowed mosques, qur'anic academies, and Sufi monasteries and encouraged and aided pilgrimage to Sufi holy sites. Expanding upon the obligation of alms-giving, he built and maintained free hospitals (apparently for Hindus as well as Muslims). He patronized the active preaching of Islam among his Hindu subjects and offered incentives for conversion. Regarding his policies toward the majority of Hindus, namely those who refused to accept Islam, the sultan was a strict constructionist.

Note that whereas *The Pact of Ibn Muslama* fails to mention Christian churches (Apparently the assumption was that the Christians would be allowed to maintain and repair their churches as long as they kept their side of the compact.), *The Pact of Umar* mentions them prominently. This latter treaty shows us that in the time of the Abbasids the tradition of the dhimma had evolved to the point that already-standing non-Muslim places of worship were allowed to remain open but no new ones could be built, and what was even more restrictive, repairs to standing structures were also forbidden. That apparently was the tradition that Sultan Firuz Shah knew and supported. When some Hindus erected new temples, the sultan ordered them destroyed, executed the leaders of the movement, had some of their lieutenants flogged, and raised mosques on the sites, where now "devotions to the true God" were performed. However, he did not punish the entire Hindu community, which enjoyed the security purchased by the jizya. Whereas Firuz Shah's predecessors had laid this poll tax on all their subjects, including Muslims, the pious sultan ended that practice and used tax relief as an incentive for conversion.

All of these forms of religious struggle should give your class more than enough to discuss. We have discovered that we have no difficulty filling an entire fifty-minute discussion period just on this topic of jihad. If any time does remain, there are many other issues raised in the Questions for Analysis that will engender discussion and even debate. We like to try to work in question 6 of source 57: What picture emerges of the place of women in Islamic society?

Other Ways to Use the Sources

1. Some scholars distinguish between Christianity's preoccupation with *orthodoxy* (correct thinking) and Judaism's focus on *orthopraxies* (correct practice). All religions, of course, concern themselves with both doctrine and behavior; the distinction is one of emphasis. Based on all of the available evidence, please compose an informal essay in your journal in which you show where Islam places its emphasis.
2. Compose al-Ghazali's commentary on Muhammad's Night Journey.
3. In your journal, compose al-Ghazali's commentary on Ephraem of Edessa's *The Life of Saint Mary the Harlot* (Chapter 7, source 53).

4. The headline reads: "Mansa Musa, Mandingo Monarch of Mali, Makes Meccan Migration." Write either the lead story or an editorial on the event as it would appear in a 1325 edition of *Mali Today*.
5. Compose Sultan Firuz Shah's commentary on the two dhimmas of source 63.
6. Compose a dialogue between al-Saduq and Sultan Firuz Shah. On what points would they basically disagree? Is there anything on which they would agree?
7. Address the same questions as you compose a dialogue between al-Ghazali and Sultan Firuz Shah.

CHAPTER

9

Asia:
Change in the Context of Tradition

Chapter Theme

We begin our commentary on this chapter with a disclaimer or, at least, a statement that we know better. We realize that it is wrong to think or even to appear to imply that there ever was a single, generic Asian culture. The fact is, Asia is richly multicultural, as one would expect of a massive continent that encompasses steppes, deserts, rainforests, tundra, the world's most formidable mountain ranges, and every other imaginable form of landscape. Although trade routes allowed for a good deal of cross fertilization, the deeply rooted, individual cultures of Asia varied widely, as we have already seen in a number of previous chapters. Had we sufficient space and were this a more perfect world (and a more perfect world history textbook), this chapter would have been expanded into two, more internally coherent chapters: Far East Asia (China, Korea, and Japan) and South Asia (Southwest Asia, India, and Southeast Asia). Maybe we can do so in the fifth edition. We tried to do so for this fourth edition but were defeated by the realities of space. So we are again left with trying to do the next to impossible: cover in fifteen sources a thousand years of change-filled Asian history.

The theme of Chapter 9 is change within the context of tradition. Asia was the focal point of the Afro-Eurasian Ecumene between 500 and 1500 C.E. The civilizations that ringed the steppe lands of Inner Asia enjoyed extraordinarily high levels of equilibrium, sophistication, technical skill, commerce, and artistic and intellectual creativity. Much as the term and the concept behind it disquiets us, we think it fair to state that all of this activity made civilized Asia the most "advanced"region in the world. It certainly was a standard of civilization for its neighbors. Even Byzantium, whose capital city was situated on a peninsula that technically lies in Europe, was Asiatic in orientation and flavor.

Asia's impact and historical importance, however, did not begin and end with its great civilizations. During this thousand-year period wave upon wave of Turco-Mongol nomads—Huns, Avars, Bulgars, Khazars, Uighurs, Magyars, Khitans, Rurchen, Tanguts, Seljuk and Ottoman Turks, the conquering armies of Chinggis Khan and Timur Leng—advanced against and over the borders of their settled neighbors, playing dramatic and often pivotal roles in the unfolding of history from one end of Eurasia to the other. In some cases the newcomers settled down, established states, and became major political and cultural forces. In other cases the invaders largely played the role of devastators.

Asia was many things during this millennium, but static was not one of them. India received into its already complex fabric the culture of Islam; Southwest Asia witnessed the invasions of Islamic Turks and Christian crusaders; China, Iran, and Iraq were conquered by Mongol pastoralists. At the same time, however, despite the absence of stasis, Asia's great civilizations remained largely conservative and tradition-bound. And why shouldn't they be? Even its newest additions, the civilizations of Arabia, Korea, Japan, and Southeast Asia, were based on native and foreign foundations established millennia earlier. Quite simply, Asia's civilizations, especially those of China, India, and the newly Islamicized regions of Southwest Asia, were deeply rooted and in full bloom by 700 C.E. (a rather arbitrary date chosen in order to include the new Islamic Ecumene in this picture). There was no good reason to change the inner fabric of what worked so brilliantly.

China is the best example of this conservative dynamism. Without a doubt, the period from 1000 to 1500 C.E. was, as William H. McNeill has characterized it, "the era of Chinese predominance."[1] China's technology and wealth placed it at the forefront of all the world's civilized societies, and its economic leadership profoundly influenced societies as far away as Western Europe. Paradoxically, this world leader remained wedded to traditional structures and philosophies, especially Confucianism, yet the triumphant Confucianism of the Song Era (960–1278) joined the old with the new to create Neo-Confucianism. Another paradox of the Song Era was the simultaneous final and total victory of the Confucian (or, better, Neo-Confucian) bureaucracy over the hereditary aristocracy alongside China's

---

[1] William H. McNeill, *The Pursuit of Power: Technology, Armed Force, and Society since A.D. 1000* (Chicago, 1982), Chapter 2, " The Era of Chinese Predominance, 1000–1500," pp. 24–62. See also McNeill's comments on China's role in a premodern world system in " The Rise of the West after Twenty-Five Years," *Journal of World History*, 1 (1990), pp. 1–21.

emergence as the world's unrivaled technological giant, despite the Confucian literarchy's prejudice against machines that were created to drive up profits. Classical scholarship and reverence for the Way of the past could not, at least in the short run, stifle innovations in a wide variety of practical fields. For this reason many scholars have labeled the Song Era a period of *change within tradition* or China's *neo-traditional age*. But the same could also be said of India and Southwest Asia.

Why These Sources?

The reason for the inclusion of Yasumaro's *Preface to Records of Ancient Matters* is not too difficult to fathom, inasmuch as it nicely illustrates the many different elements from China that Japanese reformers adapted to their native culture.

Murasaki Shikibu's diary shows us the rarified atmosphere of the Heian court (794–1185) with its highly refined sense of aesthetics and code of courtly behavior. It is not overly difficult to find Japanese adaptations of Chinese cultural influences in Madame Murasaki's account of early eleventh-century Japanese aristocratic society, but so much of what she shows us is also distinctly (one is tempted to write uniquely) Japanese. By the time in which Murasaki Shikibu was flourishing, Japan had long abandoned its self-assumed role of student and emulator of Chinese culture. The last official mission from the Japanese court to China for the purpose of learning Chinese ways had taken place in 838. After the early ninth century Japan self-confidently evolved its own forms of Confucian, Buddhist, Daoist, and Legalist traditions, marrying them to native Japanese ways to create a civilization that owed much to its mainland neighbors, Korea and China, but which was decidedly its own.

Court women of the tenth and eleventh centuries played a prominent role in articulating that Japanese vision, and of all of these female writers, Murasaki Shikibu was preeminent. Madame Murasaki had set for herself the task of creating in her masterpiece, *The Tale of Genji*, a picture of life as it is, with all of its vices and virtues, vanities and accomplishments. Despite the deep romanticism that infused her story, she succeeded brilliantly and established the standard of measurement for all subsequent Japanese novels. The same genius is evident in her memoirs. Here, through the eyes of a deeply introspective, perceptive, and melancholy woman, we confront one of the most important aspects of Japanese civilization, its sensitive appreciation of beauty in all of its forms.

Murasaki Shikibu's sense of melancholy, genuine as it was, was also tinged by the same romanticism that pervades *The Tale of Genji*. In the *Chronicle of the Grand Pacification* we confront another form of romanticism, the idealization of the superior warrior. Confucius and most of his followers had held soldiers in high contempt, believing that war represents an abandonment of reason and decorum. A warrior could, therefore, never be a superior man, at least according to the Confucian definition of that term. Japanese culture, to the contrary, glorified warriors, and one of the most celebrated of all its *samurai* was Kusunoki Masashige, the hero of this excerpt.

While these changes were taking place in Japan, China enjoyed two dynamic periods of prosperity under the Tang and Song Dynasties. Both are justly looked upon by the Chinese as golden ages, and even today the Chinese proudly call themselves the People of Tang. Yet, neither age was without its problems.

Tang China flourished as an empire from the dynasty's seizure of power in 618 to about the mid-eighth century, but then came the rebellion of An Lushan (755–763), which was a watershed so far as Tang fortunes were concerned. The last century and a half of Tang was characterized by militarism, increasing xenophobia, political fragmentation, loss of imperial authority over the northern and far-western provinces, and intense factionalism at the emperor's court. During its last half century, the Tang Empire was a case study of anarchy masquerading as a state. By 907, the official death date of an already lifeless Tang Dynasty, most of North China was ruled by non-Chinese invaders, and local warlords governed elsewhere within the once mighty empire.

In 960 the commander of the palace guard of the last of the Five Dynasties of northern China was acclaimed emperor by his troops. In this manner Emperor Zhao Kuangyin established the Song Dynasty, which managed to put down the warlords by 979. China under the Song enjoyed an era of such material and cultural productivity that some China scholars have gone so far as to characterize it as an age of renaissance (ironically, just as Europeanists are finally weaning themselves from that misleading term). Some even call it China's greatest age. Perhaps the most judicious title for Song is *China's Age of Cultural Maturity*. The paradox is that this efflorescence was achieved in an age of increasing military weakness and diminishing frontiers. Almost from the start, Song China was beset by invaders from Inner Asia who nibbled away at portions of the empire in fits and starts until finally the Mongols swept away the last vestiges of the Song Dynasty in 1279.

We shall see the Mongols in Chapter 12. For the present we concentrate upon five sources that combine to illustrate some of the major trends during the Tang and Song eras.

Our first source, *The Christian Monument* of Bishop Adam, illustrates a little-known but significant phenomenon in the history of the early Tang Dynasty, the establishment of a Nestorian Christian Church in China. That Church enjoyed a marginal existence, at best, and it eventually passed into oblivion, never playing a major role in Chinese history. What is significant, however, is that Nestorian Christianity's arrival and momentary imperial patronage illustrate the manner in which early Tang was open to cultures and peoples from far beyond the Pamir Mountains by reason of its empire, which stretched deeply into the western regions of Inner Asia.

The imperial reach of Tang also brought woes to China. The poetry of Du Fu, our second Chinese source, forces us to confront the stark realities of life, particularly the high level of frontier warfare in the later Tang Era and the weight of the burdens borne by China's peasantry. Albeit realistic, the poems also convey certain ideological messages. These include Confucian contempt for war and the profession of arms and the notion that the peasant is the backbone of society and stands second only to the scholar-bureaucrat in the social hierarchy. Indeed, ever since the Han Era, the traditional Confucian list of China's four occupational classes—scholar (*shi*); farmer (*nong*); artisan (*gong*); and merchant (*shang*)—totally excluded the warrior. As far as Confucians were concerned, military people ranked on a level with prostitutes and other unclassified misfits.

Confucians based their theoretical ennoblement of the peasantry on their recognition that without this class there would be no Chinese civilization. Peasants were the basis of the economy and, in Confucian eyes, the practitioners of all the domestic virtues that Master Kong and his followers held so dear. Early in the Song period Confucian bureaucrats began a concerted effort to revive the state of a Chinese agrarian economy that had been sorely disrupted in the confusion of the late Tang Era and the troubled times that followed the collapse of that dynasty. Part of that program consisted of publicizing the best and often latest methods of agricultural technology. Printed, mass-produced handbooks and pamphlets that trumpeted new farming tools and techniques proliferated and played an important role in Song China's Green Revolution. Chen Pu's treatise illustrates how China accommodated a veritable revolution in agriculture to traditional values and ways of seeing the world.

China's dramatic increase in food production made it possible for its population to increase to around one hundred million in the Song era, and many of those people gravitated toward its great cities, which grew tremendously in size and number from the tenth to late thirteenth centuries. Domestic and foreign commerce boomed to a level unequaled by any other place on the face of the earth. The nerve centers of this activity were the metropolises of Kaifeng, capital city during the period of Northern Song (960–1127), and Hangzhou, the so-called temporary capital of Southern Song (1127–1279).

A Record of Musings on the Eastern Capital enables students to see the prosperity and rich diversity of Hangzhou and, we trust, will enable them to imagine the frenetic activity that characterized this port city. Students who have ever lived in or even briefly visited any large modern city should have no trouble whatsoever comparing their experiences and observations with those of our anonymous author.

In both city and countryside, Buddhism became a major force throughout East Asia, but its success was not without resistance by and accommodation to native elements. "Buddhism in East Asia: Acceptance, Rejection, and Accommodation" deals with this tripartite phenomenon.

Its first source consists of two documents: Han Yu's famous *Memorial on Buddhism* and Emperor Tang Wuzong's *Proclamation Ordering the Destruction of the Buddhist Monasteries.* Buddhism, especially in its Mahayana forms, made major inroads into China during the interdynastic era (220–589) and in the Sui and early Tang Dynasties to the point that it became a permanent part of the fabric of Chinese civilization. There were, however, aspects of Mahayana Buddhism that disturbed traditionalists. The notion of what seemed to many Chinese to be the abdication of personal responsibility (placing one's faith and destiny totally in the hands of a Bodhisattva) ran counter to the spirit of Confucian ethics, and certainly the phenomenon of monasticism seemed to threaten the integrity of both the family and the imperial state. Running off to a monastery could be construed as abandonment of one's family and its ancestors, and the creation of large, richly-endowed monasteries that became independent states within a state disturbed many officials. So it should not surprise anyone that Buddhism encountered strong opposition in China, even as it became one of that society's major cultural forces. Han Yu's *Memorial on Buddhism* addresses some of the aspects of Buddhism that this early-ninth-century Confucian literarch found most disturbing. A generation later, Emperor Tang Wuzong launched an imperial counteroffensive against Buddhist monasteries and sundry other foreign religious establishments. The document that orders the closing down of these centers of foreign religion is revealing for what it allows us to infer about the reasons behind this reversal of the earlier Tang

Dynasty's openness to foreign ideas and its often enthusiastic patronage of Buddhism.

Han Yu's *Memorial* also illustrates how far at least one Buddhist branch had moved from the Buddha's original teachings on the non-reality of the body. The Buddha's dying words are said to have been, "All composite things decay," and with that death he had finally shaken off the shackles of matter. Ironically, pieces of his body or his ashes (the legends vary) were then distributed among his sorrowing disciples. They soon became sacred relics. As with the cult of relics in Christendom, these items left behind by the Buddha and his Companions became objects of devotion, perceived to possess magical properties. Needless to say, the cult of relics disquieted many Confucians who, following the dictates of the Master and the traditions of the past, believed one should keep spirits (and dead bodies) at a healthy distance.

Metaphysical speculation was another aspect of Buddhist culture that ran counter to traditional Chinese ways of perceiving and explaining reality. In the end, however, metaphysics had a profound impact on Confucianism, as Zhu Xi's *Conversations of Master Zhu, Topically Arranged* illustrates. This is a source new to the fourth edition. Neo-Confucian texts are not easy to read, and most would confuse rather than enlighten the average undergraduate. For years we searched for a comprehensible text that we could insert into our book. We believe we found it, and here it is.

Despite the popularity of such tangible objects of divine favor as relics, Buddhism never rejected its essential meditative core. Of all the Buddhist sects that have emphasized this avenue to Enlightenment, none has been more important historically than that school of meditation known as *Chan* in China and *Zen* in Japan. Zen Buddhism found fertile ground in Japan, where its emphasis on discipline appealed to the warrior class. Zen's equal emphasis on humanity's unity with nature also appealed to the Japanese, who saw in Zen a religion that was consonant with their traditional focus on the intrinsic beauty and divinity of the natural world. The selection from the writings of Dogen illustrates Zen Buddhism's central tenet—the Doctrine of Emptiness. This essentially means the cultivation of a mystical viewpoint whereby one is suddenly awakened to a new level of spiritual perception that transcends articulation and reason. From this new plane one intuits one's unity with all being and one's nothingness, thereby realizing simultaneously one's Buddhahood.

The Zen ideology of Japanese monks and samurai warriors is worlds removed from the militant religion of Turkish mujahidin and European crusaders, both of whom appear in our next section, "Southwest Asia:

Crossroads of the Afro-Eurasian World." This section stresses the flux of peoples, goods, and ideas across Southwest Asia during the thousand-year period from 500 to 1500.

First, there were the newcomers, and of them, the ones who had the deepest and most lasting impact were the Turks. Al-Jahiz shows us the Turks several centuries before they became one of Islam's major driving forces and one of its preeminent state-builders. The Turks he describes are still essentially horse nomads, but he is perceptive enough to see the potential advantage these newcomers offer. He notes that just as the Chinese are the world's preeminent artisans and skilled manufacturers, the Turks are the world's toughest and most able soldiers. In fact, he artfully suggests that they are the new Arabs of Islam. Just as the Arabs of the seventh century arose out of a non-literate Bedouin culture to forge one of the world's greatest civilizations, so these Turks would someday soon play their heroic role for Islam and would also, in time, pursue the civilized arts and sciences. How prophetic!

We selected this excerpt for two reasons. It sheds light on the special personal and military qualities of Central Asia's nomads—qualities that enabled them to play such important historical roles throughout this millennium. It also highlights the fact that Islam had not run out of energy after the year 750 and its first century of extraordinary empire-building. It was still able to attract and absorb new peoples and to turn them into warriors of Islam—in all the various senses of that term.

One reaction to the success of the Seljuk Turks was Pope Urban II's call in 1095 for holy warfare against this new Islamic menace in the East. The result was two centuries of crusades and the introduction of a new element in Southwest Asia—the European crusader. The *Franks,* or *Franj,* who carried the cross of the crusades to the Levant were a source of wonder, terror, and often disgust to the indigenous peoples whom they encountered in the land the West called " Holy." Usamah ibn Munqidh's well-known description of some of the customs of the Franks that he found most curious serves several purposes in this chapter. First it helps to break our students out of a Eurocentric way of seeing their civilization's European forebears. We often say: "If only we could see ourselves as others see us." Usamah's often sardonic description of the crusaders whom he encountered is a welcome corrective to the often romanticized vision of the crusades, crusaders, and medieval Europe in general that students have received from the popular media and in their early schooling. At the same time, Usamah's narrative does provide evidence that at least some European residents of the Latin Kingdom of Jerusalem (1100–1187) were able to adopt Levantine ways and to actually enter into friendships with their non-Western neighbors, even Muslims. As we see, the longer a European resided in Syria-Palestine, the more likely it was that he (or she, for some Western women migrated eastward) would undergo a process of at least partial acculturation. Intermarriage, especially between Greek, Armenian, and Arab Christians on the one side, and Latin, or European, Christians on the other, was common enough to create a whole class of mixed-culture inhabitants of the crusader states.

For every warrior who rode or marched across that amorphous region we call Southwest Asia, there probably were many dozens of merchants and other people of commerce. The unfortunate fact is that war and soldiers seem to grab the headlines, even when it comes to narrative sources from the past, while merchants function in relative obscurity. Happily there are exceptions to this rule, and one of the prime exceptions is the Sinbad cycle of adventure stories. The first voyage of Sinbad, Arabic literature's most famous merchant-adventurer, shows us the world as seen from the perspective of Baghdad and Basra, and the view we get is two-sided. The Indian Ocean became, in a sense, an Islamic *Mare Nostrum* as Islam spread into the Indian subcontinent and into the coastal lands of Southeast Asia, particularly from the twelfth century onward. The Sinbad cycle, however, shows us that the waters and lands of this vast region held out not only the allure of untold riches for the enterprising (and fortunate) sea-faring merchant but also the threat of terrible, and often unknown, perils. In the period in which the Sinbad stories were being redacted (tenth through fourteenth centuries?), the Indian Ocean was still a place that held many secrets and yet-to-be-discovered wonders for the Arab merchant-adventurers who plied its waters.

Arab and Persian Muslims traded at the various entrepôts up and down India's western coast, but they were not the only Islamic visitors to the subcontinent. Toward the end of the tenth century, Turkish raiders out of Afghanistan began a series of incursions into northwestern India, thereby setting into motion a series of events that would establish Islam as a permanent presence in the Indian subcontinent. As we already saw in Chapter 8, where we discussed Sultan Firuz Shah's memoirs, the Turkish importation of Islam into northern and central India after 1000 C.E. proved to be one of the most significant long-term events in all of Indian history, ranking on a par with the earlier coming of the Aryans and the later arrival of the British.

Our first source for the section "India: Continuity and Change" comes from the pen of al-Biruni. In it we get a foreshadowing of how Hindu tradition will clash with Islamic innovation. As early as Chapter 3 we saw

how the religious vision of India differed radically from that of Southwest
Asia, of which Islam was an integral part. In Chapter 4 we saw how the
Greek scientific outlook differed radically from the Indian world view. Is it
any wonder that Islam, which drew on the Greek scientific tradition as well
as on the Southwest Asian religious tradition, should be so diametrically
opposed to Hinduism in all its forms? Al-Biruni was a sympathetic student of
Hindu culture who found much to admire in that civilization. Imagine what
less cosmopolitan Muslims thought about the Hindus.

Dandin's *Tales of the Ten Princes* shows us what the Hindus thought
about themselves—at least in regard to the pursuits of virtue, love, and
wealth, or the good life. It is a healthy corrective to all those religious texts
that could easily mislead us into concluding that Hindus are totally fixated
on the reality of the spiritual world—to the point of rejecting the allures and
joys of earthly existence. Nothing could be farther from the truth. Another
strength of Dandin's tale is that it focuses on traditional, rural India. Like
China, India had its great commercial centers and large cities, but even more
so than China, the heart and soul of its culture lay in the countryside. Both
this selection and the excerpt that follows, from *Vikrama's Adventures*, shed
further light on marriage and the role and status of women in traditional
Hindu society, a phenomenon we began studying when we looked at *The
Laws of Manu* in Chapter 5. What is more, and this is quite important and
well worth whatever time one can spend on it in class, *Vikrama's Adventures*
deals with the issue of widow immolation, a subject that continues to have
relevance in contemporary rural India.

Analyzing the Sources

We favor concentrating on the theme of change in the context of tradition
and asking our students to compose either a formal essay or an extended
journal entry in which they comment on how, if at all, these various sources
illustrate the conservative dynamism of Asian civilizations during the period
500–1500 C.E. In preparing students for this task, we have found it necessary
to instruct them that, in order to deal adequately with the topic, they must
minimally analyze the evidence contained in the following records:
Yasumaro's *Preface to Records of Ancient Matters*; all five Chinese sources;
al-Jahiz's treatment of the Turks, Usamah ibn Munqidh's description of the
Western crusaders, and al-Biruni's analysis of Hindu thought.

Obviously, not all of the chapter's sources are relevant to this project. The
two Hindu sources, for example, shed important light on the status of Hindu

women and certain attitudes toward life, happiness, and death in Indian society, but they do not directly address the issue of change. This is unfortunate, especially in light of the fact that the practice of self-immolation by satis appears to have been largely an innovation of the late Gupta period and following (largely the sixth and seventh centuries) and is an excellent example of change in conformity with certain traditional values and religious assumptions. One has to look very closely, however, at *Vikrama's Adventures* to find even the shadow of a hint that sati suicide was a fairly recent tradition. That hint (and it is almost a stretch to call it a even hint) is King Vikrama's initial failure to understand why this new widow would wish to immolate herself.

As far as these two Hindu sources are concerned, we prefer to ask students to compose a separate journal entry in answer to either question 5 or 6 (their choice) of source 81. We ask students not only to compare the two sources but to address the core issue of what the two sources tell us about the perceived role and status of women in Hindu society, suggesting that they refer back to what they wrote on Hindu women in their analysis of *The Laws of Manu* in Chapter 5. If they had earlier composed a journal entry, we ask them to reconsider what they concluded and wrote in the light of this additional evidence. Do these stories support or contradict the picture of female-male relations that emerges from *The Laws of Manu*? If the students are engaged in a semester-long essay project on the relative status of women in the various traditional societies of Eurasia and Africa (and a fairly large number of our students elect this as a research option), then they must deal with not only these two Hindu sources but also Murasaki Shikibu's memoirs.

Murasaki Shikibu's so-called diary is a particular favorite of ours, and we always try to work it into class discussion, no matter how busy we might be trying to deal adequately with our central focus: change in the context of tradition. Question 1 is sure to engender some heated debate and is a marvelous issue to raise about ten minutes before the end of class. It almost guarantees a spirited discussion that will spill over into the halls as class is dismissed.

Another approach that one can take, if the class does not wish to discuss at length the issue of women in traditional Hindu society, is to look at the ways in which Japan both absorbed and refashioned Chinese cultural elements. Some of the suggested journal exercises that appear below ask students to wrestle with this issue on their own, as they try, for example, to figure out what Du Fu would write about the actions of Kusunoki Masashige and how Ban Zhao would view Madame Murasaki, but one of the fastest and best ways to deal with this topic is to attempt to discover in class all of the

Chinese and native Japanese elements in Yasumaro's *Preface to Records of Ancient Matters.*

Other Ways to Use the Sources

1. Compose in your journal a commentary on Yasumaro's *Preface to Records of Ancient Matters* by a Chinese Confucian scholar-official.
2. Compose in your journal Ban Zhao's (see Chapter 5, source 36) commentary on Murasaki Shikibu's diary entries.
3. Write a diary account by another court woman describing Murasaki Shikibu.
4. Compose in your journal Du Fu's commentary on the tone and spirit of the *Chronicle of the Grand Pacification.*
5. Compose in your journal a diary account of your first visit to Hangzhou in 1235.
6. Compose in your journal Han Yu's commentary on Bishop Adam's *The Christian Monument.*
7. Compose in your journal an account and description of Usamah ibn Munqidh by a Frankish resident of Jerusalem.
8. Compose in your journal al-Biruni's commentary on *Shiva Nataraja* (see Chapter 6, source 43).
9. Compose in your journal Sultan Firuz Shah's view of the practice of sati immolation (see Chapter 8, source 65).

CHAPTER
10

Two Christian Civilizations:
Byzantium and Western Europe

Chapter Theme

At the close of the fourth century C.E., the Christian Roman Empire stretched
from the Atlantic to the Black Sea, from the Scottish lowlands to the upper
Nile, from the North Sea to the Sahara. In the centuries that immediately
followed, however, this Mediterranean-centered ecumene underwent a
transformation. Like several contemporaneous civilizations to the east, the
Roman Empire entered a time of troubles. Unlike those Eastern cultures, the
Roman World was essentially and irrevocably changed. Centuries of
upheaval, caused by both internal weaknesses and invasions by various
fringe peoples, eventually resulted in radical mutations of its political, social,
and cultural forms. By the year 600, the empire and its civilization had
passed away. Out of this collapse came two direct heirs—Byzantium and
Western Europe—and one indirect heir—Islam.

   We have already studied Islam, which arose outside of the boundaries of
the old Roman Empire but managed to conquer vast amounts of former
Roman lands and, even more significantly, digested a large body of Greco-
Roman philosophy and science. It is time now to turn to the Roman Empire's
direct heirs, the sibling Christian civilizations of Byzantium and the
European West. In this chapter—the most radically revised chapter of
Volume I—we first study several of the distinguishing characteristics of these
two civilizations, with particular emphasis on how each envisioned itself as
the legitimate manifestation on Earth of divine authority. We then turn to a
study of how these two Christian societies drifted apart to the point that by
the year 1200 they were in a state of schism and mutual hostility.

   While the former western portions of the Roman Empire were in the
midst of a painful process of political breakdown and sweeping cultural
transformation, the empire's eastern half evolved more gently and with
greater continuity into a new cultural synthesis that we call *Byzantine*
civilization, a term created by modern historians to distinguish the Eastern

121

Christian civilization centered at Constantinople, the site of the ancient Greek city of *Byzantion* (*Byzantium* in Latin), from preceding Greco-Roman cultures. This new civilization resulted from the fusion of three key elements: the autocratic structure of the late Roman Empire; Eastern Orthodox Christianity; and the cultural heritage of the Hellenistic past.

In true Hellenistic fashion, the entire Byzantine world revolved around the orthodox emperor, who in theory was answerable to no one on Earth. As a Christian, he could not play the part of a god-king, but he was the next best thing: the living image of God on Earth, insofar as his imperial majesty was a pale reflection of the Glory of God. As such, the emperor was the link between the Christian Chosen People and their God. Emperor Leo III (r. 717–742) most clearly summed up the imperial Byzantine world view when he proclaimed: "I am the vicar of Christ."

Under the leadership of these emperors, who styled themselves *isapostolos* (peer of the Apostles) and *autokrator* (sole ruler of the world), the Eastern Christian Empire experienced close to a millennium of vitality. Some eighteenth-century European historians, such as Edward Gibbon, considered Byzantine civilization merely an unoriginal and degenerate fossilization of late antiquity, but nothing could be farther from the truth. Although the Byzantines saw their state as a living continuation of the Roman Empire and, therefore, called themselves *Romaioi* (Romans), reality was far more complex than that. By the middle of the sixth century Constantinople had become the matrix of a new civilization that persisted and, more often than not, flourished down to 1453, when finally the city of Constantinople fell to the forces of the Ottoman Turks. Over those nine hundred years Byzantium experienced inevitable fluctuations in fortune and creativity, but by and large, Byzantine civilization was noted throughout its long history for economic prosperity and cultural brilliance. Moreover, long after 1453 Byzantine culture remained a living force in Russia and Eastern Europe's other Orthodox Christian societies—such as Bulgaria, Romania, and Serbia—that had adopted Constantinople's religion and many of its other traditions.

Byzantium's Western sibling was a civilization that many historians (we included) prefer to call *The First Europe* (the idea being that Greco-Roman civilization was Mediterranean and not exclusively or even primarily European). Others prefer the terms *The Medieval Christian West* or *Medieval Europe* (the implication being that this was a middle age between Antiquity and Early Modern European civilization, a notion we emphatically reject).

Whatever one calls it, it is clear that around 600 C.E. post-Roman Western society was decidedly far ruder and cruder than Byzantine society. Even during Roman times, the West had been the area of the empire that most severely suffered from Antiquity's endemic economic and political problems. The invasions and settlements in the West of various fringe peoples from the late fourth through the tenth centuries only accelerated the process of political fragmentation and economic breakdown. But this was not the entire story. While Byzantium and Islam jockeyed for power in the Mediterranean, Western European Christendom was forced to look northward, beyond the Alps, to still untamed lands and recently converted peoples. The eighth-century marriage of convenience between two emerging Western powers, the Roman papacy and the Franks, is a clear indication that the West was following a path of historical development that differed radically from that of Byzantium. Indeed, as backward as the West might appear to have been during the era popularly known as the Early Middle Ages (500–1050), these five centuries proved to be the formative period of a tenacious and revolutionary civilization—a new civilization whose ideas and institutions would, in time, transform the world. All of this lay in the distant future, but by the eleventh century Western Christian Europe was ready to take its place as a significant power in western Eurasia. A dramatic turnaround in Western Europe's economy, a rise in its general level of political stability, and a new religious vitality provided the necessary impetus for the Age of the Crusades (1095–1291).

Having developed along two different historical paths for a half millennium and more, it was a foregone certainty that the cultures of the Byzantine and Roman branches of Christendom would be different, even radically different in some respects, by the eleventh century. Consequently, when a self-confident papacy began claiming in the mid-eleventh century that all Christians had to submit to the authority of the Church of Rome and conform to its practices, tension between the Roman papacy and the Church of Constantinople was almost inevitable. One of the earliest manifestations of that tension occurred in 1054 when an emissary of Pope Leo IX, Cardinal Humbert of Silva Candida, traveled to the imperial court at Constantinople on a diplomatic mission. Unfortunately for the pope, who was seeking an alliance with the emperor, Cardinal Humbert was an ideologue with a short fuse. While in Constantinople, the cardinal and his colleagues managed to alienate the patriarch of Constantinople, Michael Cerularius, in a disagreement over divergent ecclesiastical traditions. Cardinal Humbert was a leading theoretician of that faction of the mid-eleventh-century papal reformers who maintained that all churches must bow to the authority of the Church of Rome and follow its practices. The result was a dramatic exchange of excommunications, whereby Cardinal Humbert and Patriarch Michael declared each other to be outside the boundaries of orthodoxy and the one, true Church. Contrary to what one reads in many textbooks, these mutual bans of 1054 aroused little contemporary notice and did not signal an immediate schism between the Churches of Rome and Constantinople. They did, however, symbolize the growing estrangement between the two Christian cultures, and they foreshadowed the problems that future popes and patriarchs would encounter.

One of Pope Leo IX's more embattled successors was Pope Gregory VII (r. 1073–1085), a friend and ideological follower of Humbert. Like the now-deceased Cardinal Humbert, Pope Gregory was an ultrapapalist. His program of reforming Christendom so that it conformed to the world view and directions of the Roman papacy brought him into direct conflict with Henry IV of Germany in a conflict known as the *Investiture Controversy* (1075–1122). Gregory and the popes who immediately succeeded him did not win any clear-cut victory in the Investiture Controversy, but several significant consequences resulted from the half-century-long conflict with the Western emperor and all others who rejected the claims of the radical papalists. Most significant of all, the Roman papacy emerged from the crisis with a new vigor and a heightened consciousness of its unique status in Christendom. This in turn directly contributed to a continued widening of the breach separating the Churches of Rome and Constantinople.

Ironically, it was partially out of a desire to repair deteriorating East-West relations that Pope Urban II (r. 1088–1099) set in motion the First Crusade on November 27, 1095. Urban sincerely believed that by sending Western Christian warriors to the East to fight Turkish Muslims who were threatening the Eastern Roman Empire, he would help engender feelings of mutual Christian charity. The opposite proved to be the case. Undisciplined crusader armies marching through Byzantine lands destroyed most, if not all, of whatever good feelings Latin and Byzantine Christians once had for one another. By the end of the first century of crusading, Greek and Latin Christians largely mistrusted and even hated one another. It was almost an anticlimax when the army of the Fourth Crusade captured and sacked Constantinople on April 13, 1204, thereby effectively making the bitter schism between the Roman Catholic and Eastern Orthodox Churches an accepted reality that has persisted down to our own day.

Why These Sources?

The well-known mosaics of Justinian and Theodora, which serve as source 82, immediately propel us into the sixth-century imperial court of

Constantinople where there was not any clear distinction between what the West would much later term church and state. The emperor was the state, and he and his empress were the God-anointed deputies of God on Earth. Most sixth-century church leaders in East and West, such as Archbishop Maximian who is portrayed in this mosaic, willingly acknowledged that the emperor who resided in Constantinople enjoyed a unique position within and over the Church. Even Pope Gregory Saint Gregory the Great (r. 590–604), whom many historians refer to as "the father of the medieval papacy," called Emperor Maurice "our most pious and God-appointed Lord," and deferred his papal coronation for quite a few months until he had received official imperial confirmation of his election. Yet, Pope Gregory I could and did stand up to that same far-away emperor when he felt compelled to do so by virtue of his Petrine office ("You are Peter, and upon this Rock I will build my Church": Matthew 16:18) and his concomitant duty of serving the beleaguered Western Church. With our twenty-twenty hindsight we can see already in the sixth century the seeds of what will, centuries later, blossom into a major rift between these two branches of Christendom.

Byzantium was dazzlingly powerful, at least down to the late twelfth century, and it achieved and maintained its power not by virtue of its emperors' ideological claims but because of well-trained and well-led armies, an armed naval force second to none, a superior merchant marine, a vibrant internal economy, a tradition of sophisticated diplomacy, and a well-run bureaucracy (and we left out many other factors in this catalogue of qualities). It also depended on the abilities and hard work of its emperors and empresses, many of whom proved quite capable of effective leadership. Source 83, however, from the pen of the sixth-century historian and court gossiper Procopius, suggests not only the centrality of the emperor within Byzantium but also the inherent dangers of autocratic rule. Notwithstanding the fawning exaggeration of Procopius's official *On the Buildings* and the equally exaggerated vitriol of *The Secret History*, Procopius's testimony, especially when one extreme is used to balance the other, allows us to imagine the potential for good and mischief that lay within the powers of Byzantium's monarchs.

The emperors of Constantinople not only captured the imagination of the people of Byzantium and their empire's immediate neighbors, they also served as models of imperial majesty and legitimacy for the Christians of the West from the mid fourth through the mid-fifteenth century. Theodoric the Ostrogoth (ca. 453–526), king of Italy, was not employing empty rhetoric when he informed Emperor Anastasius that "our royalty is an imitation of yours…a copy of the only empire." Of all the early imitators of Byzantine imperial greatness, the most successful was a Frankish monarch named Charles (r. 768–814), also known as Charles the Great, or *Charlemagne.* Charles the Great has been characterized as the "father of Europe." Although it is arguable that the events and personalities of the later ninth and tenth centuries were even more important in the forging of the First Europe and that the period immediately following the breakup of the Carolingian Empire was the true crucible of Europe, no one would deny the pivotal role that Charles played by carving out Western Europe's first empire. What is possibly even more significant is the role that the Charles of legend— Charlemagne—played in fashioning the Western European mind and self image. Charlemagne became in life and legend the archetypal Christian king and emperor—as far as the West was concerned. As protector of the Church and its people, patron of education, letters, and the arts, and a warrior of God who waged Christianity against pagan neighbors, Charlemagne symbolized *the* European ideal of proper royal/imperial behavior. We cannot understand the deeds of such later European monarchs as Otto I, Frederick I, and Louis IX (as well as Charles V, Louis XIV, and Napoleon) if we do not understand the man whom they adopted as a model.

Charlemagne was larger than life to his contemporaries and certainly to later generations that preserved and magnified his memory, but his claims to unrivaled power never went unchallenged. Unlike his Byzantine imperial rivals (and models), Charles had, close to home, a counter claimant to the office of deputy of God on Earth—the pope in Rome. The coronation of Charles as emperor on Christmas Day, 800 is a good example of the tension that existed between Charles (and all of his imperial successors in the West) and the papacy. As Charles's contemporay biographer, Einhard, tells us, Charles was upset by the events of Christmas, 800 to the point that he declared that he would not have set foot in church that day, despite the fact that it was a major holy day, "had he foreseen the pope's design." Other sources strongly suggest that when Charles entered the basilica of St. Peter, he expected to be *acclaimed, anointed,* and *venerated* as emperor, in the style of the emperors of Byzantium, and probably expected to place the crown on his own head. When Pope Leo III, for whatever reason, upstaged Charles by crowning him, one of the basic tensions that runs as a leitmotif throughout Western European history was clearly spotlighted—the struggle between popes and monarchs for supremacy within and over Christendom. Charles never returned to Rome, but many of his imperial successors did, at times to be crowned by various popes and at other times to attempt to dominate the Church of Rome. The struggle was never resolved, and that lack of a definitive resolution played a major role in shaping the West's vision of the proper relationship between religious and political authorities.

But we are slightly ahead of our story. We shall see in the chapter's third section, "A Conflict of Authorities," the different ways in which two influential molders of Western thought dealt with the issue of conflicting claimants to the deputyship of God on Earth. Suffice it to say here that sources 84 and 85 of the second section, "Charles the Great: Europe's First Emperor," show us some late-eighth and early-ninth-century positions on a problem that would vex Western leaders and thinkers for centuries to come. Source 84, *A Lateran Palace Mosaic,* illustrates the tension between Charles and Pope Leo III (not to be confused with Emperor Leo III who was mentioned above). The Roman papacy had been dependent on Frankish military support since the mid-eighth century, and Pope Leo understood his relative political weakness and dependency. But he was still the Vicar of Peter! The Lateran mosaic, which shows Charles receiving a banner of royal-military authority from Saint Peter (while Leo, *sitting on Peter's right,* receives the badge of supreme priestly office), clearly symbolizes the world view of the late-eighth-century Roman papacy. Consonant with one of the many messages of Saint Augustine's *The City of God,* Charles is portrayed here as an armed retainer of St. Peter and the Church. In true Augustinian fashion, the king (Charles was not yet emperor) is seen as a pious, strong-armed warrior who has been employed to keep other, less pious strong-armed warriors in line. He uses the bloody sword and lance of the soldier, weapons prohibited to priests who have a higher spiritual calling, and does so at the command of the Church and in order to keep a modicum of peace so that the members of the City of God might complete in good order their earthly pilgrimage. Of course, Charles, who enjoyed having *The City of God* read to him during meals, interpreted St. Augustine's master work differently. As far as Charles was concerned, he was the man who was instituting the City of God on Earth. His efforts at reforming the Church by raising the level of clerical learning and promoting high standards of clerical behavior, as well as his efforts to spread Christianity by both the word and the sword, captured the imaginations of his contemporaries and became the matter out of which legends were born.

Source 85's two documents illustrate the Carolingian self image rather nicely. The letter of 796 to the newly crowned Pope Leo III clearly delineates the pope's and King Charles's respective duties before God and to the Christian people. As far as Charles was concerned, his duty was to defend the faith from the external attacks of pagans (such as the Saxons and the Avars) and from the internal attacks of heretics (as he had earlier done when he took it upon himself in the *Libri Carolini* to instruct Leo's predecessor, Pope Hadrian I, on how to avoid the dual heresies of iconoclasm and icon worship). The pope's duty seems to have been confined to praying for Charles's success, admonishing the Christian people to obey God's Law, and serving as an edifying example of sanctity. It is clear who, in Carolingian eyes, had the weightier duty. Still four years away from his imperial coronation, Charles looked upon himself as the God-anointed head of Christendom (in other words, the *Christus*, or anointed one). The fact that his closest advisors at his court called him "David," after the ancient king of Israel, speaks volumes on how Charles saw himself and was seen by the intellectuals whom he assembled at Aachen. The second document, *The Capitulary on the Missi*, shows us Emperor Charles's attempts to do his duty, which included supervision of the imperial Church.

Section three, "Constantinople and Rome: Beacons of Christianity," illustrates how both imperial Constantinople and papal Rome drew into their orbits newly converted peoples. Since its foundation as the new Christian Roman capital in 330, Constantinople served as the bulwark of Christian power in the eastern Mediterranean and Black Sea regions, and it was also a major center of evangelization. Late in the tenth century and following, the Rus' of Kiev were brought to the Orthodox Christian faith by missionaries from Byzantium. In the process, the Rus,' like so many Eastern and Southern Slavic groups, adopted Byzantine forms of culture and political organization. Source 86 from *The Russian Primary Chronicle* allows us to see why so many different peoples looked to Constantinople as the holy city without equal and why so many formerly pagan princes adopted Byzantine forms of Christianity for themselves and their people. It seems obvious to us, anyway, that many peoples, such as the Rus', were attracted to Byzantine Christianity because of the magnificence of Constantinople and its culture. Moreover, conversion to the religion of *Tsar'grad* brought leaders such as Vladimir a significant amount of additional respectability and legitimacy, thereby strengthening their power at home.

Of course, conversion to Christianity entailed choosing cultural sides. Whereas the leaders of the Rus' opted for Byzantine Orthodoxy, the leaders of the Magyars chose Roman Catholicism, and those choices have continued to influence the histories of Russia (as well as Ukraine) and Hungary down to the present. Source 88, a letter dated in the year 1000 from Pope Sylvester II (r. 999–1003) to King Stephen of Hungary, illustrates nicely the role that the Roman papacy was assuming in an expanding Europe around the turn of the millennium.

The papacy from the mid-eleventh to the late-thirteenth century produced a long line of capable and powerful popes, and none was more capable or powerful than Innocent III (r. 1198–1216). Source 88 of section three, "A Conflict of Authorities," is the letter *Solitae* that Pope Innocent sent to Emperor Alexius III of Constantinople in 1200. Clearly delineated here is the large gap in ideology that separated Rome from Constantinople at the turn of the twelfth century. In brief, this letter demonstrates the basic *ecclesiological* differences that divided these two great branches of Christendom by 1200. Ecclesiology means one's vision of the nature, or framework, of the Church, and the basic ecclesiological disagreement between Western and Eastern Christianity was the question of *papal primacy*—a primacy that Innocent saw as integral to the very essence of the Church. Of course, many clerics and most princes in the West disagreed with Rome's ecclesiological vision regarding papal claims to ultimate authority over all of Christendom, and in the end the moderate views of John of Paris (source 89) won out over those of Innocent III and the champions of ultrapapalism. But as we also see in John's *Treatise on Royal and Papal Power*, the Western opponents of ultrapapalism were generally willing to acknowledge some sort of papal headship over the ecclesiastical structures of the Church, and they further accepted the Holy Father as chief priest and Christendom's primary moral voice. By the age of Innocent III, the Byzantines refused to go anywhere near as far. For the Byzantines (and most other Eastern Orthodox Christians), the pope was a once-revered patriach whose claims to supremacy separated him from the mystical body of the Orthodox Church.

This Byzantine antipaplism of the so-called High Middle Ages (1050–1350) is quite clear in the first excerpt from Anna Comnena's *Alexiad* (source 90 of the chapter's fourth section, "Byzantium and the West in the Age of the Crusades"). Here a twelfth-century Byzantine princess gives voice to the cultural-political differences that separated East and West in the Age of the Crusades. And speaking of the crusades, consider the second excerpt from Anna's history.

Regardless of contrary voices in East and West, the papacy after Pope Gregory VII (r. 1073–1085) was supremely confident of its position, and it was in that context that popes launched crusades. Although Europe's crusading tradition had many antecedents, it was not until the last decade of the eleventh century that Pope Urban II (r. 1088–1099) pulled all of these elements together to set in motion a movement that brought Western Europe into conflict with two other civilizations, Islam and Byzantium, and created an ideology that remains even today an integral part of the Western mindset.

We do not know for certain what Urban II said at Clermont on November 27, 1095 and how he envisioned the movement he set in motion. A close study of the extant sources does allow us to infer, however, some of the pope's major motivations. It seems obvious, at least to most scholars, that Pope Urban saw this expedition as a way of assisting sibling Christians in the East, thereby engendering a closer feeling of Christian love between the two major branches of Christendom. The pope also wished to lower the level of feudal violence in Europe by exporting that violence eastward in what he believed to be a good cause—the liberation of Jerusalem and the rescue of Eastern Christians. Ironically, the crusades that followed split apart Christendom in large part because of the violence that the crusaders visited upon their Eastern coreligionists.

The culmination of this mutual antagonism was the Fourth Crusade, which witnessed the capture and sack of Constantinople in April 1204. The two accounts of that capture, which appear as sources 91 and 92, present radically different visions of what happened and what it meant. For Nicetas Choniates, a high-ranking Byzantine aristocrat who witnessed and suffered during the city's despoilation, it was a barbarous act that showed the Latin crusaders for what they were: impious hypocrites who treated the Christian inhabitants of Constantinople more mercilessly than the Muslims had treated the Christian inhabitants of Jerusalem in 1187. Gunther of Pairis has a quite contrary view. Here we have a pious German monk justifying the crusaders' capture and rapine of Constantinople as a God-ordained, God-directed venture.

Analyzing the Sources

In his more metaphorical (or pretentious) moments, one of us (the person who is writing these words) has been known to speak of Byzantium and the European West as the antiphonal voices of medieval Christendom. There probably is something positive to be said for this judgment, as long as one overlooks the fact that they were only two of many different Christian cultures that flourished in the period 500–1500. We also pass over in silence that same person's contempt for the term *Middle Ages* and its associated adjectives and nouns (even though he proudly calls himself a medievalist). Go figure. As he also says, consistency is a grossly overrated quality.

Anyway, the image of antiphony works, and it serves as the underlying structural principle of this chapter. Each source has at least one antiphonal counterpart. For example, the most obvious is the juxtaposition of the mosaic of San Vitale with the Lateran mosaic. The antiphony within source 83 is clear, where we encounter two radically different sketches of Justinian by Procopius. Perhaps less clear is the antiphonal effect produced by comparing the second excerpt from Procopius (*The Secret History*) with the mosaic of San Vitale. Equally rewarding is a comparison of Procopius's two accounts with Charlemagne's letter to Pope Leo III and the *Capitulary on the Missi*. These two Carolingian documents also serve as counterpoints to the Lateran mosaic. *The Russian Primary Chronicle's* account of the conversion of the Rus' is balanced by the letter of Pope Sylvester II to Saint Stephen of Hungary. Innocent III's *Solitae* presents us with a nice point-counterpoint exchange of views on the proper relationship of papal power and imperial authority as seen from the imperial court at Constantinople and the papal court at Rome. John of Paris's treatise, however, shows us that neither Alexius III's nor Pope Innocent's vision would ultimately win out in the West. As such, it is a nice contrast to *Solitae*. The two excerpts from Anna Comnena's *The Alexiad*, as well as Nicetas Choniates' account of the sack of Constantinople, clearly stand juxtaposed to Gunther of Pairis's account of his abbot's exploits on the Fourth Crusade.

Sources selected and arranged in this manner lend themselves easily to the following journal assignment. After telling our students that the sources have been chosen in large part because they illustrate divergent visions of reality, we ask them to pair off all of the sources, noting in their journals which Byzantine sources balance or complement which Western sources (and which Byzantine and Western sources contradict or modify other sources from that same culture). We assure them that every source has at least one counterpart and, in some cases, several. A complete list must include all sources and all antiphonal permutations. Assuming that they have read the sources with sufficient care, they should come up with a list pretty much like the one outlined in the preceding paragraph.

Once they have done this, we instruct them to create any grouping of two or more sources they wish, as long as that grouping sheds some light on the issue of "Two Divergent Christian Cultures." They are then to write detailed notes on what a comparative analysis of the sources they chose allows us to infer about the ways in which these two Christian cultures parted ways. They are warned that each person will be expected to serve as a class-discussion expert on the grouping she or he has put together. Prior to the start of the discussion class students are polled as to which sources they have grouped together. We poll them by asking them to bring and to hand in before class a slip of paper on which they have written their selected sources and, in a sentence or two, a short note on what major inferences they have drawn.

With these slips before us, we group the class members accordingly, and we begin. We prefer to begin by discussing the mosaics and then to allow the dynamics of the class to dictate the order to follow, but we have at times set an order of discussion (and have written it on the blackboard) to ensure that all topics get discussed in fifty minutes.

Students generally find this to be an easy assignment. Although they have, in theory, read all of the sources and are (we hope) prepared to discuss them all, they are expected to be experts on only one group of two or more. In this manner students serve alternately as teachers and students in the same discussion meeting. Throughout that class we try to be as silent and unobtrusive as possible, usually limiting our comments only to moments when we think the discussion needs a new orientation or a point needs clarification or correction.

Other Ways to Use the Sources

1. Compose a dialogue between the artists of the mosaics at the church of San Vitale and the Lateran Palace, in which each discusses the message behind his creation.
2. Compose a debate between the artist of the San Vitale mosaic and Procopius on Justinian's qualities as emperor.
3. Compose a Byzantine emperor's commentary on Pope Sylvester's letter to King Stephen.
4. Compose Innocent III's commentary on the Lateran mosaic. Be careful here. His reaction to that mosaic might surprise you. (Note to the instructor: Innocent styled himself *Vicar of Christ* as opposed to the traditional title *Vicar of Peter.*)
5. Compose John of Paris's commentary on the mosaics at San Vitale and the Lateran Palace.
6. Compose Anna Comnena's commentary on Gunther of Pairis's account of the Fourth Crusade.

CHAPTER
11

Africa and the Americas

Chapter Theme

In fifteen weeks, the normal length of a semester, it is impossible to cover, even in the most superficial manner, all of human history from roughly 8000 B.C.E. (or 3500, if one begins with Sumer) to about 1500 C.E. (or 1700, if one really wants to try the impossible). Given this fact, writers of global history textbooks and many instructors of world history concentrate most of their focus on Eurasia and North Africa, spending little or no effort on exploring the histories of Africa south of the Sahara and the Americas prior to arrival in force of Europeans. This is unfortunate and does both our students and global history a major disservice.

We have already glimpsed in a minor way some significant aspects of the history of the Americas and Africa south of its Mediterranean coast. Chapter 11 cannot adequately, through only eight selections, provide anything even approaching a complete picture of the premodern histories of these massive continents, but it can, we trust, give a hint of the rich sophistication, complexity, and diversity of Africa and America's many cultures and civilizations.

Our four selections relating to Africa illustrate two essential aspects of its variegated history. Sub-Saharan Africa was, by reason of its commerce, deeply influenced by cultures from outside, especially by Islam and, in the case of Ethiopia, by Christianity. At the same time the societies of Africa south of the Mediterranean managed to retain much, probably most, of their indigenous (and radically diverse) cultures, despite influences from outside.

In the Americas the story was somewhat different. *Significant* influences from outside seem to have been nonexistent or, at least, minimal, once the Americas had received their initial migrations from northeast Asia. To be sure, we know for certain that Christian Scandinavians around 1000 C.E. established a short-lived colony at a site in northern Newfoundland now known as L'Anse aux Meadows, and they or other Norse adventurers probably also visited and maybe even momentarily settled in other, yet-to-be-discovered sites in northeastern North America. Yet, there is no evidence to suggest that these Norse visitors had any lasting impact on the cultural development of the native North Americans whom they encountered and with whom they occasionally clashed. Similarly, except for brief mention of these adventures in Vinland in a few Icelandic sagas, Norse contact with the *skraelings* ("the wretches"—as the Norse called them) of North America had no demonstrable effect on Scandinavian history or culture. There is not even any evidence of genetic transfer through interbreeding. Most of the other supposed evidence of America's putative contacts with Asia, Africa, or Europe prior to the late fifteenth century C.E. withers under close scrutiny. At one time some archeologists thought that pottery from Valdivia in present-day Ecuador might have been influenced by the ceramic style of Japan's neolithic Jomon culture. Subsequent reexamination of the chronological data (the Valdivian pottery proved to be much earlier than previously thought, dating from as early as 3100 B.C.E.) and discovery of other sites in Ecuador that left no doubt as to the native origins of this pottery showed this theory to be wrong. One also hears on occasion the claim that the famous Olmec colossal heads of Mexico's Gulf region have obvious Negroid facial features, thereby showing the presence of Africans at the birth of Meso-American civilization. More than that, inasmuch as these highly individualized heads probably portray specific chieftains, it has seemed logical to some to conclude that travelers from Africa brought the elements of civilization to the Americas and served as Olmec society's leaders (and gods?). There are many good reasons to reject this theory, but one of the best is that these faces are not Negroid. It is true that some of the sculptures have wide noses and fleshy lips, but people who cite this as evidence that the Olmec chiefs were Negroid fail to take into account the pronounced epicanthic fold of all the eyes, distinctive physiognomic characteristics of only Amerindians and East Asians. Indeed, as one travels through the Gulf region of Mexico today one encounters many inhabitants who still bear resemblances in a general way to these Olmec sculptures, and the broad, fleshy faces that one sees there are definitely Amerindian and not African.

A few other scattered pieces of evidence that suggest but certainly do not prove contacts between the Americas and the outside world prior to the fifteenth century C.E. are less easy to dismiss, but what they mean is unclear. As far as we are concerned, no one has yet adequately explained, if ever it can be explained, what seem to the casual observer to be striking similarities between some of the artistic expressions of the cultures of coastal northwest North America (Alaska, British Columbia, and Washington) and those of various regions of East Asia and even Oceania. Also, although almost all of the staple crops of Polynesia are of Southeast Asian origin (as are the

Polynesians themselves), the sweet potato can only have come from South America by means we can only surmise.

Notwithstanding these few, tantalizing clues of known and possible contact with outside cultures, the weight of the evidence strongly points to the conclusion that Amerindian societies before 1492 were largely unaffected by the Afro-Eurasian World. For example, the Americas produced about one hundred domesticated crops that were unknown to the rest of the world, and almost all of the staple agricultural products of the Afro-Eurasian World were unknown in the Americas. Maize and rice, potatoes and wheat might blend together nicely in today's fusion cooking, but they were worlds apart prior to the arrival of Europeans in the late fifteenth century. So also were the disease pools of the Afro-Eurasian and American worlds, as the natives of the Americas tragically learned after 1492.

Despite this isolation, a number of Amerindian cultures, initially in Meso- and South America and later in North America, evolved exceedingly complex and prosperous civilizations. Our sources highlight three of America's more spectacular civilized societies—the Moche, the Maya, and the Quechua; a fourth source focuses on one of its precivilized, or neolithic, societies—the Tainos.

Why These Sources?

Al-Masudi's description of tenth-century East Africa is filled with fact and fancy. Separating the two is not always easy, but it is always rewarding. The legends, half-truths, and errors that al-Masudi reports tell us much about the way in which the land of the Swahili, which to tenth-century Arabs was a fairly new trading frontier, was viewed from the heart of the Islamic world. The land of *Zanj,* particularly the interior, was still a fabulous region shrouded in mystery. The facts al-Masudi reports are equally important. Here we see a land that was dangerous to sail to (and sailing was the only way to reach this area from the so-called Middle East), but the profits to be gained from its raw materials—leopard skins, tortoise shells, gold, and elephant ivory—made the voyage sufficiently attractive. Islam was already making inroads into the region in the mid-tenth century, as we see was the case with the important trading island of Kanbalu (Pemba), but native societies, both along the coast and far inland, had established strong kingdoms long before they had any meaningful contact with Muslim merchants. Finally, we see an East African coastal world that looks out into the Indian Ocean and is tied into the greater trading network of India,

Southeast Asia, and even China by the sailor-merchants who visit and trade in its ports (most of which, by the way, were located on off-shore islands).

Al-Bakri's description of mid-eleventh-century Ghana gives a strikingly similar picture of the cultures of West Africa. His account shows us the power and wealth of Ghana, the first great sub-Saharan trading empire in West Africa, and the way in which Islam was penetrating Ghanian society and becoming an increasingly important force in its culture. Yet, it also shows us the manner in which native cultural elements, including traditional religious ways, still predominated.

The Glorious Victories of `Amda Seyon reminds us that Islam was not the only outside religious force to penetrate beyond Africa's Mediterranean coast. The ancient Christian state of Ethiopia, unlike Nubia to its north, successfully resisted the incursions of Islam, as this source illustrates.

Source 96, a seated statue of a Yoruba woman, in all likelihood an *iyalode*, suggests the power wielded by *some* women in this West African culture. We would be very much mistaken if, in conformity with the theories of the late Senegalese historian Cheikh Anta Diop, we believed that all indigenous African societies have historically been matriarchal. The fact is, evidence from history and anthropology points to a wide variety of cultural systems in Africa, many of which are, and have been, strongly patriarchal. Note, for example, eleventh-century Ghana. Although, as al-Bakri tells us, royal power was passed matrilineally, to assure that the king was truly of royal blood, power was wielded by strong male monarchs. To be sure, this system of matrilineal succession suggests that Ghanian women enjoyed far greater freedom than many other women across the globe. Why else would there be reason to doubt the legitimacy of one's own son? And Ibn Battuta, as we shall see in Chapter 12, source 109, lends supporting evidence to the thesis that women in many West African cultures had a degree of personal freedom unknown by their sisters elsewhere, especially when it came to forming friendships with men to whom they were not related by blood or marriage. Still, it is a long distance from this form of freedom to matriarchy. Nevertheless, this statuette does show us that among the Yoruba-speaking people of Oyo women did rise to positions of power and prestige and did wield authority.

Each of the first three sources relating to the Americas provides a glimpse, in one way or another, into the religious cosmology of a particular Amerindian culture. The Moche ceramic effigy allows students to study a single, rather complex piece of religious art in depth and to draw from its many symbols insight into the Mochica spiritual world. Fray Ramón Pane's description of Taino beliefs regarding *cemis* provides a nice corrective to

Christopher Columbus's rather vague and misleading description of Taino religious beliefs and practices in his letter of 1493, which appears in the Prologue. Pane was a good ethnographer long before ethnography was a systematic discipline, and his account is an invaluable source for the culture of a people who were largely wiped out by European diseases before the mid-sixteenth century. This document also gives us the opportunity to remind students again that we should be careful of the conclusions we draw from isolated pieces of evidence. Certainly our view of Taino culture is quite different after reading Pane from the image we formed of it while reading Columbus's account. The selection from the *Popul Vuh*, or *The Book of the Community*, illustrates that, very much like the ancient Hellenes, the Maya were a people who were politically and socially divided into constantly changing states and groupings but shared a common culture, despite regional variations. It also shows that, contrary to what was once believed by scholars in the field, the Maya were a warlike people who built their various kingdoms by conquest. Certainly the Quiché kingdom described here is the product of a good deal of warfare. The source also allows us to see that the various Mayan deities, in this case the syncretic god Tohil, demanded constant sacrifice and pain from their people and especially from the ruling classes, in return for prosperity and a good life. We also know, especially from recent excavations, that the Maya provided their deities with the blood of human sacrifice, as did so many other Amerindian societies of Mexico and Meso-America, such as the later Aztec people, whom we shall see in Chapter 13, source 112.

Another people who used war to carve out a state were the Quechuas, who constructed the great Inca Empire of South America during the fifteenth century. Pedro de Cieza de León's *Chronicles* shows us this vast empire whose highly organized system of control allowed its rulers to provide fairly stable and even caring government to a widely heterogenous subject population.

None of our sources illustrates an Amerindian culture north of the Rio Grande, and this is unfortunate, but we are captive to the available evidence. We have traveled extensively to Hohokam, Anasazi, and Mound Culture sites, visited numerous regional and national museums, and talked with experts in the field of the pre-Columbian cultures of North America. As personally rewarding as this has been, we have not yet found any single piece of artifactual evidence or group of artifacts that we believe we could ask our student-readers to analyze with any degree of success. The search continues.

Analyzing the Sources

It is possible to deal with these sources within a fifty-minute discussion period in a variety of ways. One can, for example, concentrate on the twin themes of diversity and complexity, asking students to identify those pieces of evidence that point to the diverse and complex natures of African and Amerindian cultures. We favor, however, using the various Questions for Analysis as guides for a wide-ranging discussion on what we believe are some of the more important historical insights that students should come away with after having read, thought about, and discussed these sources.

Al-Bakri's *The Book of Routes and Realms* and, to a lesser extent, al-Masudi's *Meadows of Gold* allow us to see the ways in which Islam was penetrating the societies of sub-Saharan Africa during the tenth and eleventh centuries and the manner in which it was merging with the indigenous cultural traditions of the peoples among whom it was taking root. The topic of cultural-religious conversion in sub-Saharan Africa is one that we first considered in Chapter 8, source 62, where we looked at Mansa Musa's early fourteenth-century hajj, and it is one to which we shall return in Chapter 12, source 109, when we study Ibn Battuta's travels in Mali. Let us now, however, simply concentrate on evidence for West Africa supplied by al-Bakri; al-Masudi is just too vague on this issue, except for his mentioning that the important island trading center of Kanbalu has a Muslim population and royal family.

Questions 5 and 6 are the key questions for source 94. Note that by the mid-eleventh century Islam had become sufficiently established in the region called Awkar, or Ghana, that its main city, Koumbi-Saleh, was divided into two separate but connected entities, one of which was inhabited by Muslims, who had twelve mosques and salaried imams and muezzins. What percentage of these Muslims were native Ghanians, as opposed to resident Arab and Berber merchants, is anyone's guess, but surely some were. Al-Bakri tells us that the majority of the royal ministers were Muslims; undoubtedly their literacy in Arabic served the monarch well, especially in his dealings with merchants from North Africa. Although the monarch, Tunka Manin, remained faithful to the old religion, he was sufficiently respectful of Islam to have a mosque near his court of justice for the use of Muslims visiting al-Ghaba, or the sacred grove, where he resided.

As al-Bakri informs us, most of the indigenous population of Ghana was still pagan (more precisely, they were animists), but the rising importance of Islam in this region of West Africa can be inferred from several clues. As we have seen, the Muslims had their own separate town and a number of mosques, most of the king's officials were Muslims, and Tunka Manin maintained a mosque near his law court. What is more, if al-Bakri is correct, the monarch allowed Muslims to deviate from traditional forms of obeisance. According to our source, whereas followers of the old religion fell on their knees before the king and sprinkled their heads with dust, Muslims were allowed to greet the king simply by clapping their hands. If this is true and if native Ghanian Muslims were included in this dispensation, it is significant. The reason we are less than fully satisfied that al-Bakri is correct on this point is that he never traveled to the region, and, as we shall see in Chapter 12, Ibn Battuta, who did visit Mali in the early fourteenth century, observed and reported on the same practice of sprinkling dust on one's head as a sign of respect. The difference is that Ibn Battuta seemed to imply that the Muslim subjects of Mali performed this ritual act. To be sure, Ghana was not Mali, and the monarchs of Mali were far stronger and more absolute than the earlier kings of Ghana. Moreover, Tunka Manin was obviously courting the favor of the Muslims, and it is possible he granted this dispensation as a way of showing them favor. It is also possible that only non-native Muslims were allowed this dispensation. Still, one is hesitant about accepting al-Bakri's testimony on this issue at face value. No matter the truth on that point, the evidence is otherwise compelling that Islam was becoming a major force in Ghana, despite the fact that it was a minority religion.

One reason for the growth of Islam in sub-Saharan West Africa can be found in the story of the king of Malal's conversion. This nucleus of what later became the mighty trade empire of Mali saw its monarch adopt Islam, thereby becoming *al-musulmani*, because, much like Prince Vladimir of Kiev and Duke Vajk (King Stephen) of Hungary, the king became convinced that this foreign God was far more powerful than his ancestral deities. There is, however, one significant difference between Prince Vladimir's reasons for conversion and the slow process of Islamization that took place in West Africa. Reading between the lines of the account of Vladimir's conversion in *The Russian Primary Chronicle*, it is easy to infer that the main reason the prince adopted Byzantine Christianity was that he desired the additional power, respectability, and legitimacy that conversion to the culture of mighty Tsar'grad, or Constantinople, would bring him (and the same was probably true for Duke Vajk who accepted Roman Catholicism and, with it, a royal crown). Although we can never say with certainty why one person chooses conversion and another does not, al-Bakri's account of King Tunka Manin of Ghana leaves us with the impression that Islam had little to offer this monarch in the way of splendor or increased power. To be sure, it probably gave him a literate ministry, or at least ministers who could converse with and relate to the merchants from the north. Also, as we have already seen, Tunka Manin was appropriately respectful of this faith from outside. But from what al-Bakri tells us of his power and wealth—a power and wealth based on his ability to control the traffic in salt and gold (and also slaves, but this account does not mention them)—it is reasonable to infer that the king of Ghana believed that Islam had little to offer in the way of strengthening his position. After all, he never converted, and his colleague in Malal seems to have converted for essentially religious reasons.

We will never be certain why King ʿEzana of Axum adopted Christianity in the early fourth century, but that conversion has had a profound effect on Ethiopian civilization down to our own day. In dealing with *The Glorious Victories of ʿAmda Seyon*, it is best to concentrate on questions 1 and 3 because answers to them show us some of the reasons why Ethiopia, although largely surrounded by Islam, was able to maintain its Christian culture. Probably the major reason, and it is not touched upon in our source, was geographic. Ethiopia's rugged highlands provided its people with a natural bastion from which they could defend themselves with comparative ease. The mountainous inaccessibility of the Abyssinian plateau meant that Ethiopia was largely isolated, except on its own terms, from the rest of East Africa and lands washed by the Arabian Sea and Indian Ocean. Far more isolated than Christian Nubia, Ethiopia did not succumb, as Nubia eventually would, to the pressure of Islam. Beyond a favorable topography, however, there were two other major factors, and they are revealed in our selection. First and foremost of these was Ethiopia's sense of identity. Its unique, ancient form of Christianity, as well as its accepted tradition that the Solomonid Dynasty (1270–1974) was descended from a union between King Solomon of Israel and the Queen of Sheba, were (and are) such an integral part of Ethiopian culture and the self-image of this special land and people that conversion to Islam was unimaginable. Despite their spirited resistance to Islam, however, we would be mistaken if we thought that fourteenth-century Ethiopians looked upon their Islamic neighbors as solely and simply agents of the forces of evil who were better killed than tolerated. To be sure, Sabr ad-Din, the rebel Muslim prince, is characterized in the account as the enemy of Christ and a son of the devil. But note that he was also one of the Ethiopian king's vassals and, despite his crimes of forcing Christians to convert to Islam and killing those who did not and also of burning down churches, he was shown mercy when he surrendered. Apparently, in this multicultural region of northeast Africa there was a certain amount of live-and-let-live.

When Sabr ad-Din realized that his revolt had failed, he turned to Queen Mangesa for help, hoping, not unreasonably, that she would help him secure favorable terms of surrender. The queen of Ethiopia was apparently a woman of some influence over her husband.

Our next source out of Africa shows us another woman of influence, the statue of an iyalode, which was discovered in Esie, Nigeria. This statue is one of several such items depicting powerful women among these Yoruba-speaking people. In analyzing the statue, we ask our students to address in their journals both Questions for Analysis. On more than one occasion students have offered insights that we missed.

The first question requires rather straightforward answers. Consider all of these clues: the woman is seated (the seat of authority?); she bears a ceremonial cutlass in a formal, military pose (If that cutlass is not a sign of authority, we will give up trying to analyze artifacts.); she has a rather severe (or, at least, serious) visage; she has an elaborate and exceedingly high coiffure; her face is scarred in a formal, equally elaborate manner; and her necklace appears to be more than just decoration. To our mind, she can be nothing less than an iyalode. The second question forces our students to come to grips with some of the cross-cultural ways of depicting authority—one of which was to evoke a sense of mystery and awe.

The Mochica ceramic effigy pot also conveys a sense of mystery and awe—the awe one feels in the presence of gods. Students seem to enjoy analyzing this work of religious art, and most find it not too challenging, in large part because we have been liberal with hints. Consider the following points, each of which is hinted at in the seven Questions for Analysis. The mountain cave from which the deity on the right is emerging implies to us that he is identified with the mountain, itself a divine entity, and this in turn suggests that he was a sky deity and a creator god as well. (Mountains often symbolize the sky and creative forces.) These latter inferences are strengthened when we consider his sunrise headdress (remember: the mountain lies to the east of the Moche Valley), his rather impassive expression, and the fact that four life-giving rivers (the snakes which represent water and fertility in so many different cultures) flow out of the mountain. The feline deity (or shaman who has metamorphosed into a jaguar god) on the far left is quite different. His fanged, jaguar-like features symbolize power, but it is not a remote power, nor is it a frightening power. Note that his face is much more expressive than that of the sunrise god. In fact, this cat god looks kindly, to the point of being almost a comic figure. He is certainly more earthbound than the sunrise god, for unlike that other deity, the jaguar god has a full body. With his feet in motion, firmly treading on the back of a snake (river), he seems to be descending on his own power down to the people of the valley, bringing them water and, with it, life. In short, he seems to be the beloved intermediary between the lofty sky deity and Moche people. Possibly they saw im as the incarnation or son of the creator god. Of the two gods, the fanged cat god was probably the one more prayed to in times of prosperity, crisis, and disaster.

The Tainos of the Greater Antilles and the Bahamas, led by their *bohutís*, or shamans, prayed to household and village *cemis* to assure prosperity, survive crises, and avert disasters. Despite an obvious, deep-rooted skepticism regarding the Taino spirit world based on his own religious faith and European education, we think Ramón Pane did a fine job of reporting the beliefs and magical practices of the inhabitants of Española. Consequently, we favor using this account as a means of helping students understand that reports by unsympathetic observers can be quite valuable and even factually reliable. We begin by asking them to identify Pane's perspectives or assumptions. His Christian faith, which led him to view the cult of cemis as worthless superstition at best and pernicious devil worship at worst, is easy to see. Most students will also easily see that he considered the bohutís to be medical charlatans. Although fifteenth-century European medical science had not progressed beyond the theories of ancient Greek medicine, educated people such as Pane accepted the notion that illnesses are natural phenomena with natural causes and remedies. Once students have identified the cultural prism through which Pane viewed and evaluated Taino beliefs and practices, they are asked to create a three-columned list in their journals. In the first column they list four Taino beliefs or religious practices of their choice. (Four seems to be about the right amount of items for this exercise.) In the second column they write down Pane's commentary on or evaluation of that belief or practice, if he has made one (and in this regard we caution them to be on the lookout for subtle implications). In the third column they note whether or not Pane seems to have reported the belief or practice accurately, regardless of what he might have thought or written about it, and why they think so. They are further told that these lists will provide the basis for a class discussion. On the basis of those lists we are able to address and answer quickly and easily questions 2, 3, and 4. Just as important, we are able to return again to the historian's primary question, a question that has no single, simple answer: How does one evaluate the worth of a source and use it to gain valid insight into the past?

In analyzing the selection from *The Book of the Community*, or the *Popul Vuh*, we favor addressing questions 1, 2, and 4 and doing so in an integrated fashion. As we can see from this source, Tohil, the "giver of riches," demanded from all, but especially from the Mayan rulers, pain and sacrifice. In the words of our author: "This was the price of a happy life, the price of authority." Many pictures exist from classical Mayan times depicting its monarchs and their wives committing ritual acts of painful bloodletting (such as piercing their tongues and genitalia with strings of thorns). This was done as a means of offering the gods their most precious possession—the force of life itself. Elsewhere, in a section not included in this source excerpt, the *Popul Vuh* speaks of Tohil's suckling his people. Experts on Mayan culture tell us that the metaphor does not mean he suckles milk from them. Rather, it refers to hearts that were ripped out of the chest cavities of victims offered to Tohil—giver and taker of life. Tohil's name means "obsidian," probably a reference to the razor-sharp obsidian knives used in human sacrifices, and he was quite demanding when it came to demanding blood. It is true that no blood sacrifices are specifically mentioned here (but see note 5). Nevertheless, just as Tohil sustained and nourished the Mayan rulers, who in turn sustained him by offering him their sacrificial gifts of fasting (thereby undergoing, in a ritual manner, an act of suicide), so the Mayan rulers sustained and nourished those people whom they had united through conquest and protected by their fasts. In return these people offered their rulers gifts, tribute, and sacrifices. As our author informs us: "They [the ruling class] did not squander the gifts of those whom they sustained and nourished, but they ate and drank them. Neither did they buy them; they had won and seized their empire, their power, and their sovereignty." Sacrifice, therefore, drove the Mayan cosmos and kept all of life in balance.

The Incas of South America, like the Maya and Aztecs (whom we shall see in Chapter 13), were a warlike people, but the Inca Empire differed substantially from the Aztec and Mayan states. Not only was it vastly larger and more heterogenous, the empire did not apparently exist to feed the hungry appetites of the gods of the Incas. Moreover, the Incas appear to have been guided by a desire to provide their subjects with good, and even caring, government. How have we reached this conclusion? Simply trying to answer all four Questions for Analysis that accompany León's *Chronicles* leads us to that judgment.

The Inca Empire was organized into coherent administrative units so that "there was not a village that did not know where it was to send its tribute." To keep the peace, the Inca rulers bestowed wide-ranging powers on their provincial governors, maintained large military garrisons in the provinces, and also practiced systematic resettlement of their subjects. Although each governor enjoyed a good deal of latitude in the application of his authority, each was also responsible directly to the Inca at Cuzco. From Cuzco accountants would go out into the provinces, armed with their record-keeping *quipus,* to monitor the tax accounts of these far-flung provincial governors. Hardly a year went by in which each governor was not required to render an account either in person in Cuzco or to an accountant from the capital. In addition to the accountants, the Incas also sent out circuit judges "to punish wrongdoers." In order to facilitate communication in an empire that stretched about two and a half thousand miles from north to south, the Inca rulers maintained post roads and also required every subject, no matter her or his native tongue, to learn Quechua. Despite all of these efforts, however, "there were many provinces that warred with one another, and the Incas were not wholly able to prevent this."

Thanks to the quipus, the Incas were able to keep fairly accurate census records, for the purposes of taxation. Such record-keeping and organization, however, could and apparently did serve the needs of the subjects, as well as the lords. León informs us that this well-organized empire had such plentiful and well-stocked storehouses that in times of war the government did not need to commandeer supplies from the people. Moreover, in times of peace these storehouses provided food for the poor and disabled. In years of bad harvest they provided welfare for everyone.

To be sure, there is probably some romantic tinge to León's account, but other sources agree that, on balance, the Incas managed to provide good and fairly humane government for the short while during which they had an empire.

Other Ways to Use the Sources

1. After studying sources 94–96, what can you reasonably conclude about the role and status of women in each of the three societies represented here? Are you willing (or able) to make any statements about African women in general?
2. Consider the religious cosmologies of the Moche, Tainos, and the Maya as revealed in sources 97–99. Which strike you as more significant, the differences or the similarities? What conclusions do you draw from your answer?
3. Compose Asoka's commentary on León's description of the Inca Empire (see Chapter 5, source 37).

C H A P T E R

12

Adventurers, Merchants, Diplomats, Pilgrims, and Missionaries: A Half Millennium of Travel and Encounter: 1000–1500

Chapter Theme

In Chapter 5 we looked briefly at the first grand era of Afro-Eurasian interchange. We also saw that the collapse of the Han and Roman Empires closed down many of the channels of communication between the Mediterranean and China. Nevertheless, indirect contacts between the eastern and western extremes of Eurasia were not completely severed, even during China's worst time of troubles. Several centuries before the turn of the millennium there was a decided upturn in the tempo of long-range travel and communication along an east-west axis due to a number of factors. Chief among them were the westward push of Tang China, the emergence of an Islamic Ecumene by 750 C.E., the labor of Arab, Persian, Jewish, Indian, and Southeast Asian merchants in the Indian Ocean, the development of East Africa's Swahili Coast, and the movements of various Turco-Mongol peoples. After 1000 C.E. long-distance interchanges increased dramatically in number, frequency, and significance. With the emergence of the Turks as a new force within Islam and the drive of Islam into India and beyond, the movement of Western Europe into the eastern Mediterranean in the era of the crusades, the development of regular caravan routes into sub-Saharan West Africa, the expansion of Song China's merchant marine into the South China Sea and Indian Ocean, and, most spectacular and important of all, the rise of the Mongol Empire, a new and greatly expanded Afro-Eurasian Ecumene took shape.

The opportunity for the exchange of goods, ideas, and even peoples now exceeded all previous historical levels. Although the world was still centuries away from the creation of a true global community, a process had begun that not even the fourteenth-century collapse of the Mongol Empire could bring to an end. Humanity was on its way toward a new stage of global history, a stage that the Iberian kingdoms of Portugal, Castile, and Aragon would usher in during the late-fifteenth century as they endeavored to reach East and South Asia by transoceanic routes.

Why These Sources?

We begin by looking at the ways in which informed persons within various cultures perceived the world far beyond their borders. Our three witnesses to a larger world are a late-twelfth-century Chinese customs inspector, a fourteenth-century European man of letters, and an early-fifteenth-century Korean world map.

When we studied the fictional Sinbad (Chapter 9, source 78) and when we looked at East Africa's Swahili Coast (Chapter 10, source 93), we viewed lands and peoples touched by the Indian Ocean as seen and understood by the Arab merchant-sailors who sailed those waters. Zhau Rugua's account, to the contrary, shows us far-away Arabia and its associated lands (including Egypt and southern Spain) as seen from South China. His account's mixture of information and misinformation illustrates the double face of the Afro-Eurasian Ecumene around 1200. It was a world in which peoples separated by many thousands of miles could have some indirect knowledge of one another, but it was also a world in which vast distances made direct communication and intimate knowledge of distant cultures essentially impossible.

As sources 104–108 of the chapter's second section will show, the rise of the Mongol Empire and the consequent establishment of the *Pax Mongolica* after the mid-thirteenth century finally made possible, on a level never before enjoyed, direct overland travel between the eastern and western extremes of the Afro-Eurasian World. With that direct travel came greater knowledge of the Far East by Western Europeans. Toward the middle of the fourteenth century, one European writer proceeded to set down an account of the marvelous lands and peoples of the *Indies*. The largely fictional account of the wonders that Sir John Mandeville (undoubtedly a *nom de plume*) claimed to have seen from Jerusalem to China became a bestseller, rivaling and probably even surpassing Marco Polo's work in popularity. One of the chief reasons for Mandeville's success lay in the fact that he synthesized in an especially entertaining manner the most up-to-date knowledge that Europeans had of the world and its many different peoples.

Source 102 presents Sir John's description of the people of Sumatra, a Southeast Asian island, his explanation of how the world could be circumnavigated, and the story of Prester John, the mythical Christian priest-emperor in the East whom Westerners had been seeking out since the mid-twelfth century. Although the reader might initially see these as simply fanciful and/or totally wrongheaded stories written by an obvious humbug for an undiscriminating readership (the fourteenth century's version of Elvis sightings at Roswell, New Mexico), closer examination reveals a good deal of worldly sophistication on the part of Sir John and his intended audience. His wry description of the putative customs of the people of Sumatra [Lamary] reveals not only wit but also a delight in recounting the ways of these foreign people, including sexual practices that ran counter to the teachings of the Catholic Church. Rather than condemning the practices, Mandeville slyly presents a biblical defense of them. Even when he deals with the practice of infant cannibalism, which he duly characterizes as "an evil custom," Sir John blunts his criticism by sardonically noting, "They say this is the best and sweetest flesh in all the world." Does nothing shock our author or his audience? Here truly is an author who is a multiculturalist insofar as he recognizes that there are societies around the globe whose customs, strange as they might appear to Europeans, have their own internal logic and worth. We see this cosmopolitanism also in Mandeville's description of Prester John. Although this Christian emperor's people "do not share all the articles of our faith," Mandeville portrays the emperor as a worthy and pious Christian. Such a book could not have become as popular as it was in a society that had a narrowly parochial vision of the world.

That broader vision of the world extended to the idea that the globe could be circumnavigated. It is time to lay to rest Washington Irving's humorous myth that educated Europeans of the fourteenth and fifteenth centuries believed that the world was flat. Irving had a great sense of humor; unfortunately many of the people who read him missed the joke. John Holywood's *On the Sphericity of the World*, which was largely a reworking of the writings of the ninth-century Arabic geographer al-Farghani, was produced in Paris around 1220 and became a standard textbook in the schools of the West. Mandeville might have been in error in believing that someone of his day could travel safely over both poles, but he was not wrong when he wrote that the world is a sphere that can be circumnavigated.

As is the case with Zhau Rugua's *Description of Foreign Peoples* of a century and a half earlier, Mandeville's *Travels* is a charming pastiche of information and misinformation. And it is especially heavy on the latter when dealing with lands and peoples beyond Southwest Asia. Nevertheless, it provides strong evidence that Europe, one of the most isolated regions of Eurasia so far as knowledge of a larger world was concerned before the rise of the Mongol Empire, was now fascinated with the larger world. That fascination would propel European mariners to the Americas and into the Indian Ocean before the end of the fifteenth century.

Our third source for the section "The World Perceived" is *The Kangnido,* an extraordinary Korean map that dates from 1470 but is based on a map of 1402. The map shows us the Afro-Eurasian World as seen from Korea but through an Arabic prism. The map's Chinese transcriptions of European, Southwest Asian, and African placenames clearly originate from Persianized Arabic words. Even if we did not know that, there is plenty of additional evidence that indicates this map was influenced by Islamic cartographic sources. The Arabian Peninsula, the Red Sea, and the Persian Gulf, with the Tigris and Euphrates Rivers and the delta region around Basra clearly delineated to its north, figure prominently in the map. In fact, not only are their relative sizes exaggerated, but this region of Southwest Asia, rightly called Sinbad's Route, is one of the most accurately detailed areas of the map. Note also that although the map-size of Africa is substantially smaller than its actual mass, the continent's shape is fairly accurate—suggesting, as was the case, that Arab mariners had rounded the tip of Africa and sailed both coasts long before the Portuguese accomplished this feat. Also clearly shown is the Islamicized region of the Niger River in West Africa. Moreover, in accordance with Arab geographic theory, the Niger is portrayed as a source of the Nile. Europe is rather indistinct and considerably misrepresented, but Iberia, still an outpost of Islam in the fifteenth century (until 1492), is correctly shown as separated from North Africa by the narrow Strait of Gibraltar, and even Italy and Sicily can be identified with some difficulty—but they are there. Also worth noting is the fact that India and the continental lands of Southeast Asia are molded into a single entity and dominate the center of the map. This surely was the view of both Islam and East Asia toward this rich Indian Ocean region of South Asia. This map certainly helps make clear for our student-readers that the Indian Ocean was the center of the Afro-Eurasian World at this time. The modern Western vision of the globe, centered as it is on the Atlantic Ocean, just does not make sense before 1492—or for many years thereafter. After all, Columbus stumbled across the Caribbean while trying to sail to the Indian Ocean. Moreover, the Arabo-Islamic imprint on this Korean map illustrates an important verity. During the period 1000–1500 C.E. the Islamic world served as the connecting southern link between East Asia and Europe. Da Gama would never have been able to sail directly from East Africa to India in 1498, a 2,500 mile journey across the western Indian Ocean, without the aid of an Arab navigator, Ahmed Ibn Majid, who shipped on at Malindi, located on the coast of present-day Kenya.

No survey of the Afro-Eurasian Ecumene would be complete without documents relating to the Mongols and their empire. Sources 104–108 do just that and offer us a number of different perspectives in the process.

The Franciscan missionary and envoy, William of Rubruck, traveled for two years among the Mongols, in order to "preach the work of God and to instruct men to live by His will." Not only was Brother William a courageous exponent of his faith, in the best traditions of Franciscan missionary labors, he also composed a lengthy report of his travels and observations. His eye for ethnographic detail was extraordinary, and his account of the Mongol culture that he encountered between 1253 and 1255 is one of our most valuable documentary sources for mid-thirteenth-century Mongol society.

Although the Polo brothers, Niccoló and Maffeo, journeyed to East Asia as emissaries of Pope Gregory X (r. 1271–1276), they were probably motivated to make this, their second, trek to the lands of the great khan, Kubilai, primarily out of a desire for commercial gain and adventure. They and Niccoló's son, Marco, achieved the riches and adventure they sought, as well as something else—immortality. The immortality came as a result of the happy literary collaboration of Marco Polo and Rustichello of Pisa. Polo's stories, as retold by Rustichello, became a late medieval European bestseller. One value of Marco's account of his travels was that it introduced Western Europeans to a wide variety of different Asian cultures, thereby fostering a desire on the part of many, Christopher Columbus included, to visit these exotic lands.

The primary selection we have chosen from Polo's memoirs details the hazards of travel through the eastern regions of the great Taklamakan Desert. Crossing even a relatively small portion of this wilderness was extremely dangerous for all involved, beasts as well as people. Although bookish, stay-at-home scholars might write sanguinely of the relative ease and safety of travel during the *Pax Mongolica*, we should never forget its inherent dangers nor should we cease marveling at the fortitude of those who undertook the journey. We can only guess at how many lost their lives in the endeavor.

At the same time, life along the many routes of the Silk Road was not all danger and hardship. For a young man such as Marco Polo (as well as for older men such as his father and uncle) the various oasis towns along the way did offer a number of pleasures and diversions, as he also makes clear in the excerpts presented here. Perhaps for this reason the Polos spent an entire year in one such town.

The Polos were certainly not the only Europeans who lived and worked in Mongol-dominated China. Small but significant numbers of Western missionaries and merchants not only traveled to but took up residence in Yuan China's cities. Friar John of Monte Corvino, the most celebrated of the Roman Church's medieval missionaries to China, shows us in his letter not only the admirable courage and faith that drove the handful of Western Christian priests who labored in East Asia but also the difficulties and frustrations that beset them, cut off as they were from their homeland and working in a civilization that distrusted foreign cultures. John's cry for help underscores the fact that the Roman Church's thirteenth- and fourteenth-century oriental missions were too understaffed and ill-supported to accomplish any significant number of conversions among the Mongols or Chinese. Most of Friar John's Catholic flock appears to have been Turkish converts from Nestorian Christianity and the one hundred five Chinese (?) boys whom he purchased and educated. Still, insofar as these missions opened the West to direct contact with India and China, they proved to be a first act with a great sequel.

Marco Polo's Chinese contemporary Zhou Daguan, like Polo and Rubruck, had an eye for ethnographic details, and his *Recollections of the Customs of Cambodia* is the best extant account of late-thirteenth-century Khmer civilization. Here we see a society deeply influenced by its great neighbors, India and China, but retaining at its core its own ancient culture.

Francesco Pegolotti was neither a student of foreign cultures nor a person providing a first-hand account of foreign adventures. He was an exceedingly able commercial employee of the Bardi house of merchants and bankers, a person whom some might ungenerously characterize as a "bean counter." Although he had traveled and worked from London to the Levant, his *The Practice of Commerce* is, as its title suggests, a handbook of advice for Italian international merchants drawn from the wide-ranging experiences of the whole Bardi establishment and his own contacts—merchants who had traveled far beyond Pegolotti's own limited sphere of activity. As such, it represents the best compilation of information concerning foreign markets as far away as China that was available to fourteenth-century European commercial travelers. (One of our students renamed it "Travel to Cathay for Dummies.") The fact that this work exists suggests that there were hundreds, perhaps thousands, of now unknown Western merchants who in the thirteenth and fourteenth centuries braved the hazards and discomforts of long overland journeys across the steppes, mountains, and deserts of Inner Asia to travel to China.

Long-distance travel between the years 1000 and 1492 was not confined to either the lands or period of Mongol domination. The known world-champion record holder for fourteenth-century travel is Ibn Battuta. Like Polo, Ibn Battuta narrated his travels after the fact to a professional storyteller, and, like Polo's account, Ibn Battuta's *rihla* contains a number of confusing and controversial elements. Both Ibn Juzayy, Ibn Battuta's literary collaborator, and Rustichello appear to have sacrificed, at times, veracity for readability. Notwithstanding this, both travelogues are invaluable sources. Without them we would know substantially less about the Afro-Eurasian cultural mosaic and the opportunities for world travel in the centuries preceding Europe's great transoceanic explorations.

We chose Ibn Battuta's account of his trip to Mali as source 109 for several reasons. It is simply the best pre-sixteenth-century description of the Sudanese trading societies of West Africa in any language and provides a privileged insight into the culture of this sub-Saharan people. This story also dramatically illustrates the extent of the Islamic Ecumene, itself possibly the single most important factor contributing to long-distance communication across Eurasia and Africa during these five centuries. At the same time, it shows us the significant diversities that existed within the worldwide community of Islam. Continuing a theme raised in our analysis of al-Bakri's description of eleventh-century Ghana, Ibn Battuta's description of the Mandike people of mid-fourteenth-century Mali suggests how these people wedded the ways of Islam to native, pre-Islamic traditions.

Both the Moroccan Ibn Battuta and the Chinese Ma Huan were Muslims and, by that fact alone, members of a multiethnic world community. Yet their travelogues betray quite different attitudes toward the world beyond their immediate frontiers. For all of his ethnocentrism, narrow-minded devotion to his own branch of qur'anic jurisprudence, and even racism when it came to the populations of sub-Saharan Africa, Ibn Battuta exhibited an awareness of and appreciation for the *umma*, or world family of Muslims. He traveled and made his fortune almost exclusively within the boundaries of that community. His travels, in fact, largely consisted of pilgrimages, searches for employment as a religious judge, and missions for various Muslim princes. Ma Huan, on the other hand, was preeminently the Chinese official in the employ of the Son of Heaven. He traveled to foreign shores as a member of three great fleets sent out to awe the barbarians on the fringes of the civilization with the majesty and power of the Middle Kingdom, and his account carries the flavor of a sense of Chinese superiority.

The voyages of Admiral Zheng He deserve a special niche in any chapter devoted to pre-sixteenth-century travel. They illustrate several important verities, some of which we have emphasized in earlier chapters: the technological superiority of China in the era prior to 1500; the wealth and power of the Ming imperial establishment, despite the great blows that China had endured in the Mongol period; and China's supreme confidence that it was the only true civilization on the face of the Earth, and the outside world had nothing to offer except tribute. When steppe border problems, a severely stretched imperial treasury, and Confucian ascendancy shifted China's gaze away from the Indian Ocean, it was probably done without too much anguish or soul searching.

The Indian Ocean was, however, a compelling magnet for Western Europeans during this pre-Columbian era of Afro-Eurasian linkage. When Vasco da Gama arrived at Calicut on the southwest Indian coast on May 20, 1498, he sent ashore a one-man landing party to scout out local sentiment toward European merchants. Instead of finding a local population in awe of these strangers from the West, da Gama's hand-picked, and probably unhappy, envoy was surprised to be greeted by a merchant who asked of him, *in an Italian dialect.* "What the devil are you doing here?" Long before the Portuguese began sailing the waters of the Indian Ocean, Western merchants and adventurers were traveling and trading in the region. Prominent among the handful of Westerners who visited India and its environs from the thirteenth century onward were Italian entrepreneurs such as the Venetian Nicolo de Conti, who set out for the East around 1420 and was back home by 1441. As early as 1291, two Genoese, the Vivaldi brothers, tried sailing to India by way of the Atlantic Ocean, apparently by following the African coast. They were never heard of again.

About fifty years after the disappearance of the Vivaldi brothers, Mandeville wrote in his *Travels:* "I say with certainty that people can encircle the entire world, below the equator as well as above, and return to their homelands provided they have good company, a ship, and health." By the mid-fifteenth century, Western Europe had its ship—the caravel, and this first-rate craft made it possible for Europeans to reasonably dream of sailing directly to the Indian Ocean and the lands that were washed by this great body of water. Good health and good company were harder to come by, but some nations, most notably Portugal, decided to give it a try, anyway. Tiny Portugal's ventures along the western coast of Africa seem timid and puny by comparison with the massive fleets of Admiral Zheng He, but they ultimately would result in a major reshuffling of power in the Indian Ocean and the dawning of a new era of global history. Gomes Eannes de Azurara's biography of Prince Henry shows us that the crusader spirit, forged in Iberia's case in the centuries-long *Reconquista*, was alive, well, and continuing to serve as a driving force in European affairs. Added to this were a sense of curiosity, a search for new commercial outlets, and a sincere desire to convert the many different peoples of Africa and distant Asia to Christianity. Moreover, this excerpt also hints at an aspect of long-distance trade probably as old as civilization itself—the trade in human cargo. European involvement in West African slaves would play a profound role in the history of three continents for four centuries.

Analyzing the Sources

For this chapter we ask our students to write a lengthy journal entry describing and evaluating, in turn, William of Rubruck, Marco Polo, John of Monte Corvino, Zhou Daguan, Ibn Battuta, and Ma Huan as travelers. In this exercise they must try to identify, if possible, each person's reason(s) for the trip and the expectations he had upon embarking on his journey. We warn them that they will have to make quite a few educated guesses, but there are sufficient clues, in the introductions and in the documents themselves, to enable them to make some good guesses—in most cases. Finally, we ask the students to end their entry with a subjective evaluation of each man as a traveler, addressing such issues as: Was he open to new experiences? Was he culture-bound? Did he seem to learn and grow from his experiences? We warn them the evidence might not allow them to answer these last questions in every instance.

During class discussion we ask several volunteers to read their entries to the group. Class members then discuss their reactions to these entries and are encouraged to raise additional insights and judgments, perhaps points they have touched upon in their own journals.

When we have finished with this portion of the class period, we turn to two other issues. First we look at our four armchair, or stay-at-home, travelers: Zhau Rugua, Mandeville (although he claimed otherwise), Pegolotti, and Prince Henry. We ask the class to consider each one's place in this age of expanded travel. How did each see his role? What does each man's writings or work tell us about this age? Did any or all of these four men make a significant contribution to long-range travel? What were those contributions? Then we ask the class to look again at the six travelers they have written about and to see if they can discover anything they all have in common. The answer we are looking for is that each of them enjoyed some official status. Even the Polos traveled as emissaries of both the papacy and the khan of khans.

We hope that students will begin to realize, through pondering all the questions in these two exercises, that trans- and intercontinental travel in the late thirteenth, fourteenth, and fifteenth centuries was much more than simply a hit-or-miss enterprise undertaken by a few heroic adventurers. It was often a business or a state function. As such, it demanded serious planning. A second conclusion is that, as a business and an extension of statecraft, long-distance travel had become too important for merchants, monarchs, and missionaries ever to allow their civilizations to retreat to regional insularity. Even later Ming China was open to controlled foreign trade. If circumstances closed down one interregional route, another would have to be found. World history had now reached a new plane.

Other Ways to Use the Sources

1. Compose a commentary on *The Kangnido* by either Zhau Rugua or Ma Huan.
2. Compose a description of Ibn Battuta and his visit to Mali by one of Mansa Sulayman's court members.
3. Religion, trade, statecraft, and curiosity were four of the chief factors driving long-distance travel in the period 1000–1500. Where do you find evidence of any or all of these motives in these sources? Do some of the sources suggest other motives? Be specific in your answer.
4. It has been said that the early Portuguese and Spanish explorations of the world were driven by six C's—crusade, conversion, conquest, commerce, curiosity, and chivalry. Other historians list the three G-motives—God, gold, and glory. Choose either list of motives. How many of them can you find in Gomes Eannes de Azurara's account? Can you discover any motives not contained in these lists? Be specific.
5. Compose Ma Huan's commentary on Gomes Eannes de Azurara's *Chronicle of Guinea.*

C H A P T E R
13

Trans-Oceanic Encounters: 1500–1700

Chapter Theme

Between 1500 and 1700 C.E. the tempo and direction of global history changed dramatically as a single culture, Western Europe, opened up for itself new frontiers in Africa, South and East Asia, and the Americas. This assault was largely one way. With the exception of the Ottoman Turks' advance into southeast Europe, Europe was the aggressor. Only Europeans regularly and systematically traveled to lands as widely separated geographically and culturally as China and Brazil, and it was Europeans who first circumnavigated the world.

It would be wrong, however, to term these two centuries an Age of European World Hegemony. Australasia, most of North America, large portions of interior South America, and inner Africa were still *terrae incognitae* to European explorers, merchants, and colonists. More significantly, the well-established civilizations of East and South Asia, as well as Southwest Asia, most of North Africa, and Africa's other coastal regions were able generally to deal on their own terms with Europeans. At the same time, European merchants and colonial powers connected the continents of Europe, Asia, Africa, and the Americas in ways never before realized or even dreamt of, making this the dawn of a new period of global interchange.

European presence around the world occasioned a variety of responses and consequences during these two centuries. Large areas of the Americas were permanently transformed culturally and demographically, due to substantial influxes of both European colonial masters and their African slaves. The source of this human chattel, the west coast of Africa, was affected but not metamorphosed by the European trade in slaves. Similarly, European enclaves elsewhere along Africa's coastline influenced but did not substantially change local cultures. The well-rooted civilizations of North Africa and Asia were even more resistant to European influences—at least during these two centuries.

Why These Sources?

Although Sahagún was a Spaniard, he based major portions of his history of New Spain upon available Amerindian sources, thereby preserving for us a view of the Spanish invasion of Mexico from the perspective of the invaded. Even when we take into account Sahagún's own cultural blinders, which inevitably affected his use of the evidence, we still must admit that he wrote a story that has the ring of truth. Sahagún's dramatic and compelling account is as close as we are going to get to a true picture of the Aztec view of the Spanish invaders.

Espinosa's descriptions of the mercury mine and processing facility at Huancavelica and of the silver mine at Potosí graphically bring home to the student-user of this textbook the tremendous human cost involved in the Spanish pursuit of riches in the New World. Here we see in vivid detail the enforced labor system (a system modeled on the Incan *corvée*) that made it possible for Spanish colonists to extract and process huge amounts of precious ore and the inhumane conditions under which the virtually enslaved Amerindian workers labored.

The letters of King Nzinga Mbemba (Afonso I) to the king of Portugal provide evidence of other forms of exploitation and cultural displacement. The leaders of the West African kingdom of Kongo accepted Christianity, the Portuguese language, and Portuguese court etiquette and welcomed European medicine, but wished to restrict other Portuguese activities, especially the trade in slaves. These letters show us the frustration of King Afonso in his attempts to limit the slave trade and also, ironically, his complicity in that trade. What upset him was the unwarranted enslavement of his free subjects, especially young nobles and even royal relatives. He assumed that the enslavement of captives, presumably from other tribes and kingdoms, was licit. After all, it had been part of the fabric of West African history for uncounted centuries. The tone of the first two letters is that Portuguese merchants had violated the trading privileges extended to them and must be restrained. There was little chance of that. The profits to be made guaranteed an upward spiral in the volume of the West African slave trade over the next several centuries.

James Barbot's account of slaving negotiations at Ibani almost two centuries later shows that various West Africans cooperated with the European slavers to create a regular system of exchange and also illustrates the cheap price both placed on the life and freedom of one human being. The value of a mature female slave was roughly that of a cow or nine goats. Another reason we selected this particular document is because of its tone. Barbot's barely disguised contempt for King William and his retinue, as well as the cold-blooded manner in which he described these negotiations, conveys a strong flavor of the attitudes that enabled European slave traders to carry on their business.

If some European visitors to West Africa held the Africans in contempt, the attitude was reciprocated. The two pieces of Benin art that combine to make up source 115 present several images of Europeans, none of them especially flattering. The Afro-Portuguese saltcellar speaks eloquently both of how many Africans viewed these visitors from the sea and, ironically, how many Portuguese saw themselves. After all, this work of decorative art was produced for a Portuguese market and possibly was commissioned directly by the buyer. Whatever the reason for his creating the piece, the artist has given the Portuguese officials fierce and formidable countenances. (We see only one of the officials in this photo; the other is on the reverse side of the saltcellar.) Their scowling faces, the massive weapons they hold, and the crucifixes around their necks appear to be constituent elements of the crusader from Iberia rapaciously laboring for God, gold, and glory. The soldier-assistants who flank the officials are no less fierce. The only relief in this grim tableau is the comic sailor in the crow's nest—a Kilroy-Was-Here type of figure peering out of his basket at the top of the mast. One wonders what message the Portuguese purchaser extracted from this magnificent work of art. We are willing to bet it was not the same message envisioned by the sculptor. To the contrary, the message of the copper plate is not the least bit ambiguous. The two Portuguese merchants in the background are grotesque caricatures (the are made to look monkey-like) dwarfed into insignificance by the heroic *oba* who dominates the foreground. The message is clear enough, as was the reality. The kings of Benin managed to keep the Portuguese at bay. It was not until the eighteenth century that Benin, then wracked by civil war, finally began to lose ground in its struggle to ward off European pressures.

When we turn to Asia we receive a somewhat similar picture of European relations with indigenous, well-established cultures. Matteo Ricci's journals show us the frustration of well-meaning and even selfless European missionaries, some of whom even had a deep appreciation of Chinese civilization. Their inability to overcome basic Chinese contempt for the religion they preached and the culture it represented shines through in this account of the trials of the Jesuits at Nanchang, despite Ricci's optimistic evaluation of the Jesuits' achievements. Ricci's upbeat tone suggests that he was a seventeenth-century spin-doctor.

The Jesuits faced even greater resistance in Japan, but only after a half century of initial success. The Japanese Catholic Church experienced spectacular growth during the latter half of the sixteenth century. This fact, combined with the foreign and native-born Christians' intolerance to other religions, particularly Buddhism, led the Tokugawa shoguns to conclude that Christianity was subversive to Japan's new national unity. As early as 1587 Toyotomi Hideyoshi officially banned Christianity, but the Japanese Christian movement was not crushed until the late 1630s.

The shoguns' suppression of Christianity stood at the center of an overall program of isolating Japan from pernicious foreign influences and severely regulating trade with the outside world. The two edicts presented here as source 118 are representative of a substantial number of similar prohibitions issued during a period of over half a century. As both documents show, Japan's Tokugawa rulers did not ban all contact with foreign merchants, but they did manage to isolate the country effectively from subversive foreign ideas, particularly those of the West, for the next two centuries.

The Mughals themselves were sixteenth-century invaders of India, and for over a century effectively blocked the European newcomers—initially this meant largely the Portuguese—from penetrating deeply into the fabric of Indian life. Although the Portuguese controlled Goa on the west coast as early as 1510, their sixteenth-century impact on Indian civilization was minimal.

Source 119, a collection of short excerpts from the *Akbarnama*, underscores the relatively small place of the *Faringis* in Mughal consciousness and court policy in the days of Akbar (r. 1556–1605). Tavernier's account, to the contrary, written several generations later, shows cracks beginning to appear in the Mughal defenses. English, Dutch, French, and even Danish factories (trade centers—not places of industrial production as the word is understood today) proliferated along both coasts during the seventeenth century, and along with them grew the influence of Europeans on the course of Indian history. Tavernier is a witness to the growing presence and power of the various East India companies and the lure of profit that India held for those engaged in this trade—factors that would result in a Franco-British struggle for control of India in the eighteenth century.

Ways to Use the Sources

We deal with this material either toward the end of fall semester, when everyone feels the pressure of papers and other work that has piled up, or at the beginning of spring semester, when newcomers, who were not enrolled in the first half of the course, have barely begun to learn what it means to analyze a primary source. In both cases we find it desirable to turn our discussion period for this week into a history lab. Although students are still responsible for reading and comprehending all of the sources in the chapter, the laboratory does relieve them of some burden and, we hope, also introduces an element of fun.

A week or so before holding the laboratory, we inform the class that the assignment for this chapter will be to produce a group report on three related issues: (1) How did Europeans view the world and the different peoples beyond their shores during the period 1500–1700?; (2) How did various other peoples view Europeans during that same period?; and (3) What was the range of impact that Europe had on the rest of the world from 1500 to 1700? We then divide each discussion section into laboratory units of four or five persons and name one member of each unit as laboratory leader. That person is responsible for organizing the laboratory into a research unit. The leader assigns each member the task of becoming the lab's expert on one of the four chapter divisions and of drawing from the sources within that division all information and inferences relevant to the three research questions. Each of these experts is expected to jot down all of her or his insights and to bring those notes to the lab meeting.

When the day arrives for class discussion, we send each lab unit off to its own corner of the room. There, under the direction of the laboratory leader, each unit prepares a two- or three-page journal entry on the topic within twenty-five minutes—exactly one half of the class period. We ask them, in that short amount of time, to synthesize each lab member's insights and to arrive at some articulated conclusion, or general statement. The laboratories then reassemble into the normal fifteen- to twenty-student discussion section, where they read their reports in turn and discuss their findings and conclusions. A variation on this is to require each laboratory unit to meet independently before the class meeting and to draft its report then. This allows us to devote the full fifty minutes of class time to plenary group discussion. Personal schedules, however, often make it impossible for all of our many students to arrange such out-of-class meetings.

As long as the instructor clearly sets out the ground rules and objectives of this exercise and stresses beforehand that each lab unit will be strictly limited to twenty-five minutes of class consultation time (if one chooses that option), then a fifty-minute class period is enough time in which to conduct successfully this experiment in group research. Students will know that they have to come to class prepared, and lab leaders will be motivated to organize and oversee their units properly. As an added incentive for taking this laboratory seriously, the instructor can announce that each unit is to hand in its report at the end of class. Those reports that adequately answer the research question and show a mastery of the sources will earn their lab members a bit of extra credit. We have also been known to award prizes— usually books—to members of the lab unit that have produced the best report.

Other Ways to Use the Sources

1. Compose in your journal an account of initial Spanish contacts with the Amerindians of Mexico written by a Spaniard in the service of Cortes.
2. Compose in your journal an Amerindian account of life at either Huancavelica or Potosí.
3. Compose a journal account in which one of the leaders of Ibani society describes the negotiations of 1699 that Barbot has written about. Be sure to show his attitude toward the Europeans and his evaluation of trade with them.
4. Study the two works of art in source 115 and then compose explanations by the two Benin artists of the messages behind their sculptures.
5. Compose the Shah-bander's report on the incident at Tatta that Tavernier relates. His report should contain recommendations for dealing with these European sailors and merchants.

VOLUME II
Since 1500

C H A P T E R

1

Europe in an Age of Conflict and Expansion

Chapter Theme

This chapter's title characterizes Europe's experience in the sixteenth and seventeenth centuries as one of conflict and expansion, and if anything, the sources we have chosen emphasize the former more than the latter. By highlighting Europe's internal conflicts and tensions, we hope that students can avoid some of the errors that frequently distort their perceptions of early modern Europe and its place in the world.

Students frequently draw false conclusions about the significance and meaning of Europe's transoceanic explorations and expansion. Because the stories of Europe's explorers, conquistadors, and colonists are so well known, and because the importance of their exploits is self-evident, many students assume that expansionist Europe must have been a society experiencing an upsurge of post-medieval "progress." Many also assume that Europe's expansion reveals its superiority over other contemporary states and societies. Such views are inaccurate, and the readings and editorial material in this chapter seek to show why.

Europe was neither the strongest nor the most successful society during the sixteenth and seventeenth centuries. It was militarily weaker than the Ottoman Empire, poorer than Mughal India, and less well governed than China (at least until the Ming dynasty went into a tailspin at the end of the sixteenth century). Furthermore, if one were to list the major developments in Europe during the sixteenth and seventeenth centuries, they would hardly add up to what most people would consider to be a "successful" society. Such a list would include the following: religious schism and religious wars; rampant religious persecution; widespread urban and rural violence; increasing use of torture; civil war and revolt in France, England, the Netherlands, central Europe, and elsewhere; inflation followed by an economic slump in the first half of the seventeenth century; military defeat and territorial losses at the hands of the Ottoman Turks; a decline in the legal and economic standing of women; and a growing fear of satanism and witchcraft that led to the arrest, trial, and execution of thousands of mostly female "witches." Europe, in other words, was full of disorder and seemed to be heading toward breakdown and disintegration, not world dominance.

This chapter cannot possibly provide sources to illustrate all the events and movements that contributed to Europe's conflicts and tensions, but those chosen all center on these themes. It also seeks to show that many of the events and developments in Europe that later generations viewed as "progressive" and "modern" were deeply unsettling and disturbing to the people who actually experienced them. Europe's overseas discoveries are in this category. Conquests in the Americas and increased trade with Africa and Asia brought new wealth to Spain and Portugal and created new commercial opportunities for small numbers of merchants in other parts of Europe, but they damaged trade in the Mediterranean and created new sources of conflict among states. The influx of gold and silver from the New World also was a major contributor to the sixteenth century's price inflation, which caused hardship for artisans and landowners and growing fiscal problems for governments. Furthermore, Europe's discoveries were unsettling to many intellectuals. For some, acquaintance with the customs of the peoples outside of Europe caused them to question their society's own institutions and values. For others, (along with some political leaders and churchmen) conquests in the Americas led to a troubling debate over how newly encountered peoples should be treated.

The Scientific Revolution in its early stages was also disturbing to many Europeans. Copernicus, Brahe, Kepler, Galileo, and others called into question a centuries-old cosmology and undermined a view of nature that had prevailed among intellectuals during the Middle Ages and Renaissance. For most of the sixteenth and seventeenth centuries, however, astronomers were unable to achieve any agreement about how a sun-centered universe worked, and this fostered confusion and doubt about humanity's intellectual capacities. We know the story ends happily in 1687 when Isaac Newton in his *Principia* provides a new and satisfactory model for understanding the universe. But until then, one certainty after another gave way to doubt and confusion. John Donne's poem, "An Anatomy of the World," captured the mood of many Europeans when he wrote the following words in 1611:

'Tis all in pieces, all coherence gone,
All just supply and all relation.

Why These Sources?

The choice of Martin Luther to represent mainstream sixteenth-century Protestantism needs no justification. Luther sparked the Protestant movement when he attacked indulgences and papal authority in the Ninety-Five Theses of 1517, and he provided leadership and theological guidance for Protestantism until his death in 1547. Some, however, might question our decision to represent Luther with excerpts from his *Tischreden*, or *Table Talk*. After all, this is not a work actually written by Luther but a transcription of his sayings written down by his followers some time after they had been spoken. Undoubtedly, at least some of the phrases in the *Tischreden* (a work of several hundred pages) are not literal, and some may even be apocryphal.

Despite these weaknesses, *Table Talk* has enough strengths to justify its inclusion in *The Human Record*. One of its advantages is that it is all encompassing, including such topics as theology, politics, child rearing, marriage, music, and pets. In addition, Luther's sayings are more colloquial, less technical, and hence, more understandable, than the content of many of his formal theological treatises. Luther's words in *Table Talk* also reveal the folksy, informal side of the reformer's personality.

Sixteenth-century reformed Catholicism, represented in the next selection, is drawn from decrees of the Council of Trent, one of the most important such councils in the Church's history. It discusses theological issues such as salvation, saint worship, and indulgences, giving students an opportunity to compare Catholic and Lutheran doctrines. The council's decrees also shed light on another dimension of the Catholic Reformation, namely the Church's efforts to address the abuses that Protestants and pre-Reformation reformers had roundly denounced.

This section concludes with two woodcuts, Lucas Cranach's *Two Kinds of Preaching* and Mattias Gerung's *The Chariot of the Pope and the Turk*. Cranach's woodcut, which was printed many thousands of times and distributed throughout Lutheran Germany, drives home the point that the Reformation was Europe's first major historical movement in which the *printed* word was significant. The choice of these pro-Lutheran woodcuts illustrates another important point, namely that Protestants made greater use of printed material than Catholics. Cranach's woodcut gives students an opportunity to visualize many of the doctrinal differences between Catholics and Protestants (even though these differences are being caricatured by a Lutheran artist). Gerung's woodcut is less well known and less complex than Cranach's. It is of interest because it reveals the depth of anti-papal feeling on the part of the German Lutherans. It also links up nicely with the comments on the Ottoman Turks made by Luther in *Table Talk* (source 1) and by Ogier de Busbecq in his *Turkish Letters* (source 21).

The next section, "Women's Places," introduces the topic of women's roles in sixteenth- and seventeenth-century Europe. We have dropped Anna Bijns' poem, "Unyoked is Best! Happy is a Woman without a Man." Although students found the poem clever and engaging, we concluded that Bijns' disparagement of marriage and her praise of life as a single woman were too atypical and too idiosyncratic to justify keeping her poem. We also concluded that a more balanced picture of women's role in early modern Europe would be provided by including a source dealing with women's work. Bijns' poem has been replaced, therefore, with excerpts from Nuremberg city ordinances dealing with midwifery, one of the few exclusively female professions in sixteenth-century Europe.

The other selections in this section center on marriage and the family. Two of them express what might be called the orthodox (that is, male) perception of the ideal woman. In the first selection, an Anglican priest, John Mayer, eulogizes a pious English woman, Lucy Thornton. Although he praises her Christian virtues, his words confirm the notion that women are inferior to men and should be subservient to them. In the second selection, the German artist Anton Woensam expresses many of the same ideas about women but with a Catholic twist. The last source in the section, Erhard Schön's woodcut, *No More Precious Treasure*, presents differing perspectives on marriage, not all of them flattering.

The next section, "Perspectives on the New World," illustrates how from the very beginning of Europe's era of expansion, Europeans disagreed on how the peoples they encountered should be treated. Sepúlveda, who claims that the "superior" Spaniards have the right to enslave and exploit the Americans, and Las Casas, who pleads for brotherly love and the humane treatment of Native Americans, represent opposite poles of a debate that continued until the very end of European colonialism in the twentieth century. Furthermore, the image of these two learned scholars offering up arguments to influence their king in the Valladolid debate provides a dramatic element that intrigues our students.

The concluding section on "intellectual ferment" introduces students to dimensions of "the crisis of European thought" during the sixteenth and seventeenth centuries. Both sources illustrate how traditional ways of viewing the world came under attack during these years. Montaigne was chosen because, more than any thinker, he illustrates the disquiet experienced by many European intellectuals as a result of the sixteenth century's conflicts and changes. With a moral vision shaped as much by the classics as Christianity, Montaigne was deeply troubled by Europe's religious divisions,

France's civil wars, and the era's endless intellectual debates. His decision to abandon the law and retreat to his country estate to think and read reveals his frustration with the inability of human beings to maintain civilized and humane institutions and relationships.

Of Montaigne's more than one hundred essays, "On Barbarians" seemed the best choice for *The Human Record*. It shows, first of all, that the discovery of the Americas was not a one-way street, with influence exerted only by Europeans on the Americas. Montaigne is an example of a European intellectual whose disillusionment with Europe increased after he learned about the customs and values of New World peoples.

Chapter 1 concludes with Galileo's Letter to the Grand Duchess Christina. It too illustrates the conflict between explosive new ideas (represented by the new science) and traditional intellectual assumptions (defended by the Roman Catholic Church). Although many other leading figures in the Scientific Revolution—Copernicus, Descartes, and Newton—worried about religious opposition to their theories, Galileo's clash with the Catholic Church in the early 1600s remains the classic conflict between science and religion. Only the debate between evolutionists and creationists in the last century and a half can rival it. Galileo's letter addresses the issue of science versus religion with force and clarity. It gives students an opportunity to see what was at stake for both him and his opponents. It is also an important statement of the principle that scientists need to carry on their research and draw conclusions without interference from religious authority. Galileo's struggle with the Church and his ultimate vindication contributed to the secularization of European thought.

Analyzing the Sources

What do the excerpts from *Table Talk* reveal about Luther's basic beliefs? They show, first of all, that two concepts—the absolute majesty and sovereignty of God and the lowliness of humanity—stand at the center of his theology of salvation. From the concept of God's majesty two corollaries follow: first, human beings can never fully understand God's designs and judgments, and second, because of their innate weaknesses (original sin) they can never *earn* their salvation *by their own actions*. "Good works," such as striving to live according to God's commands (the law) and acts of devotion such as partaking of the sacraments, prayer, fasting, and other penitential acts are, according to Luther, worthless as far as bringing about a person's salvation. One is saved or "made righteous" in God's eyes only through faith in God, a faith that God freely and mysteriously gives to those He predestines for salvation and withholds from those He predestines for damnation. In Luther's view, to believe in the efficacy of good works is tantamount to idolatry—abandonment of true worship of God for the worship of a false image or heathen deity. No greater sin against God's majesty is imaginable.

The medium for receiving this faith is the Word of God as revealed in the Bible. By scripture alone—*sola scriptura*—one receives the pure and untarnished Word that saves. To Luther, the teachings of Roman Catholicism had obscured and perverted the pure gospel and had led Christians to false beliefs and false practices and the ultimate damnation of countless misguided Christians. People had sought salvation by following the false path of good works, believing they could be absolved from their sins through the sacrament of penance or the purchase of indulgences. Luther taught that humans remain sinners even after receiving the gift of faith, but that their sins are covered over by the gift of God's grace, and one is made righteous, or justified, in God's sight. Thus faith is mightier than even the most heroic good works.

Luther also teaches that each individual is responsible for nurturing his or her own faith (and hence one's salvation) through personal introspection and reading of the Bible. Salvation no longer depends on the intercessionary powers of the Church or on a specially ordained priesthood that alone is capable of administering the sacraments. Each person serves as his or her own priest.

In these doctrines, all spelled out in the excerpts from *Table Talk*, Luther seems to encourage individualism. Students should be cautioned, however, that neither Luther, nor any other sixteenth-century religious leader gave the individual free reign to draw his or her own conclusions about the Scriptures' meaning. Luther had strong convictions about what was theologically acceptable and believed that those who stubbornly embraced erroneous beliefs deserved to be punished and, in extreme cases, executed.

Luther, in addition to challenging the theology of Catholicism also harshly criticized the Catholic clergy. As Luther's words under the heading "The Reform of the Church" clearly show, he placed more value on his doctrine of justification by faith than piecemeal reforms of specific clerical abuses. Yet Luther rarely missed an opportunity to condemn the papacy, the church's hierarchy (cardinals and bishops), and members of the clergy. He was especially severe in condemnation of monks and friars, who to Luther epitomized hypocrisy and false Christianity.

Luther's willingness to stand up for his beliefs and defy the authority of the Church made him a heroic symbol of German resistance to a Church that many Germans considered rapacious. The former friar became a lightning rod for discontented groups, especially the peasants, who saw his revolt against Rome as a justification for rebellion against lords and princes. The socially conservative Luther would have none of this. While in the mid-1520s the peasants used the gospel to justify their revolt, he sided with the German princes who forcefully suppressed their revolt.

Two new subsections, one containing Luther's comments on marriage and one his comments on the Turks, have been added to the excerpts from Luther's *Table Talk* for the fourth edition. Both link up with themes developed in other parts of *The Human Record*. Luther, who abandoned clerical celibacy in 1525 when he married a former nun, Katherine von Bora, became a spirited defender of the institution of marriage…for reasons clearly spelled out in the excerpted passage. Marriage, he argues, is the foundation for society and the Church. He feels compelled to defend it against those who oppose it because of misguided (Catholic) religious principles or try to avoid it because of the "difficulties and troubles" it may cause. He also endorses the standard view of the age about women's role in marriage. They are to carry out their household chores with a "merry disposition," and strive to be a "pleasure, joy, and solace" to their husbands. Luther's comments can be compared with the perspectives of Mayer, Schön, and Woensam which are presented later in the chapter.

In Luther's comments on the Turks, several points are worth noting. First, like most central Europeans, Luther views the Turks as a cruel and powerful enemy, more than a match for the ill-trained armies the Europeans can field against them. These sentiments are echoed in Ogier de Busbecq's Turkish Letters in Chapter 3. Second, Luther interprets the Turkish onslaught in two ways. In the first part of the passage, he interprets it as divine punishment for Europe's sins. In the second, he suggests a darker and more sinister interpretation: the Turks and the Catholics have joined a secret conspiracy to obliterate the German Lutherans. A similar view is expressed in another source that comes later in the chapter, Mattias Gerung's woodcut, *The Chariot of the Pope and Turk.*

The first section of the excerpts from the decrees of the Council of Trent reveals the theological divide separating Protestants and Catholics, especially on the issue of salvation. It is important, first of all, to have our students see that Luther and the Catholic theologians at Trent agree that no human being can be saved *solely* through his or her own efforts. God's grace, freely given, is necessary for salvation according to both camps. For Luther, this grace is the beginning and end of the process, but for Catholics, God's grace must be augmented and perfected by each individual Christian through partaking of the sacraments, living according to God's commands, and performing other good works. Behind this difference in theology is a disagreement over interpreting the scripture: Luther emphasizes certain passages in Paul's epistles where it is stated that faith, not works, makes a person justified; Catholics downplay such statements and emphasize the assertion in the Epistle of James that "Faith without works is dead." Even more fundamentally, the Lutheran and Catholic doctrines of salvation rest on different views of human nature. Luther believes that all human efforts to live up to the moral teachings of Jesus and perform truly selfless good works are doomed to failure. The requirements of the "law" exist to reveal human weakness and the need for Christians to rely on faith in God's grace as the only means of salvation. Catholics believe that humans, despite their weaknesses and shortcomings, must strive with God's help to fulfill the letter of the law.

The excerpts from the Council of Trent highlight differences between Protestants and Catholics on several other significant issues. Indulgences, which are rejected completely by Lutherans, are retained in the Council of Trent's decrees, but "abuses" in connection with their use are to be corrected. In the same vein, the decrees of Trent retain the veneration of saints and saints' images, another practice rejected by Luther. According to the theologians at Trent, saints "can offer their prayers to God for man" and thus obtain favors for believers. For Luther, such practices smack of idolatry, detract from the majesty of God, and undermine what should be a personal relationship between God and the individual.

In the sections on reform of the clergy, it can be seen that the Council of Trent adopted an approach similar to its stance on indulgences and saint veneration: key Protestant demands are rejected, traditional Catholic practices are retained, but more rigorous standards are demanded. Bishops and cardinals, for example, retain their places in the Church hierarchy but are expected to avoid scandalous behavior. The priesthood remains a special order within the Church, and priests retain their roles as intermediaries between God and the individual Christian layperson. Because they stand apart from laypersons, priests are expected to live according to more demanding moral standards, including celibacy.

The council's pronouncement on the founding of seminaries is worth noting. Many students are surprised to learn that at this late date in its history the Catholic Church had no seminaries or any other special educational institutions for training priests. A few years of schooling and some haphazard training with an experienced priest sufficed. Why the change? With literacy among the laity and competition from Protestants both growing, a better-educated clergy was now deemed necessary.

An effective way of highlighting the differences between Lutheranism and Catholicism would be to raise the issue of how Luther might have responded to the Council's reform proposals (as opposed to the decrees on theological issues). A quick response might be, "Luther would approve; after all these were attempts on the part of the Church to deal with at least some of the abuses he (Luther) was condemning." A better answer would be, "For

Luther all these 'reforms' would be nothing but window dressing unless the Church changed its theology." This second response is more accurate because it shows an understanding that Luther's priorities were *theological* issues of faith and salvation. Reforming abuses was an important, but secondary concern.

Two woodcuts conclude this section on religious developments. Lucas Cranach's popular woodcut, *Two Kinds of Preaching*, presents in caricature form an early Protestant view of Roman Catholic, or papal, "perversions" of Christianity, and simultaneously, an image of the ways in which Protestants imagined themselves to have revived the pure spirit of faith. Gerung's *The Chariot of the Pope and the Turk* is a bitter depiction of the pope as an enemy of true faith, in league with the Ottoman sultan, a Muslim, whose armies were threatening southeastern Europe. The sixteenth century was not a time of moderation or tolerance for either Protestants or Catholics. Both woodcuts exude the passions of heated controversy, thereby providing a sense of the animosity between Protestants and the Church of Rome.

There is no mistaking the message of Cranach's woodcut. The preacher on the left (who *is* Martin Luther) is preaching to a crowd of earnest laypeople and is gathering inspiration directly and *solely* from the Bible that rests on the lectern before him. The friar on the right, who is addressing a rather inattentive group made up mostly of clerics, is drawing inspiration from a demon that blows empty air into his head. Luther, inspired by God the Holy Spirit, who appears in dovelike form above him, instructs the people before him that heaven, or salvation, is to be reached only through Jesus Christ, who has redeemed sinners through his suffering and death. Empty good works such as those represented on the right side of the woodcut cannot justify, or make one righteous, in God's sight. The key text, "If we sin, we have an advocate before God, so let us turn in consolation to this means of grace," clearly delineates Luther's message of salvation—one is saved only by faith in Jesus Christ. The friar on the right, in contrast, draws his listeners' attention to the sale of indulgences behind them.

Other key Lutheran ideas, including the absolute power and majesty of God (spelled out in the opening passages of Luther's *Table Talk*) and the sufficiency of Christ's death and resurrection as a means of ensuring man's salvation, also are illustrated in Cranach's woodcut. God, who appears on both sides of the panel, is represented as an all-powerful God, holding in his hand the orb that symbolizes the created order. On the left panel God holds up his hand in a blessing, while in the right he extends it in disgust as he observes Catholic perversions of Christianity. Also, whereas Christ is shown prominently on the left, he does not appear at all in the scene on the right.

Also, because Luther's theology was based on *sola scriptura* (scripture alone, not the teachings and traditions of the Roman church) and *sola fide* (by faith alone), Luther and other Protestant reformers rejected the Church's sacramental system and its definition of the priesthood. In contrast to the Catholic concept of a celibate, tonsured, and privileged clergy that possessed, by virtue of its ordination, unique religious powers, Protestants taught that all true believers are equally priests. Therefore, unlike the Catholic clergy depicted in the right panel, the Protestant pastors who are administering the sacraments of baptism and the Eucharist (according to Luther, the only two sacraments created by Christ and mentioned in the Bible) wear the same garb as the laity and are untonsured. They are, in other words, members of a community of Christians, chosen by that community to minister to its religious needs.

The grotesque chariot that holds the pope and sultan in Gerung's woodcut, *The Chariot of the Pope and Turk*, sits astride a narrow channel, blocking a ship from entering the safe and placid harbor in the background. The ship, a common image in Gerung's works, undoubtedly symbolizes the "ship of faith," while the harbor beyond represents God's grace or salvation. The sultan's side of the chariot is pulled by three demonic beasts, while the pope's side is pulled a bear, a lion, and a goat, all three of which are animals associated with the devil. The sultan, who appears to be fused to the pope at the waist, admonishes his soldiers on the left, whose swords and pikes carry the heads and limbs of slaughtered Christians. The "weapons" of the papal army on the right are an indulgence proclamation, papal flags, and a monstrance (a vessel in which the consecrated host is displayed for veneration by the faithful). The implication is that the Turk's weapons kill the body, but the pope's weapons kill the spirit. The sword of judgment at the top of the woodcut represents divine wrath and divine judgment and lends an apocalyptic overtone to Gerung's work.

* * *

The debate between Sepúlveda and Las Casas on Spanish policy toward the Indians ended with no decision. But students inevitably are interested in deciding who "really won the debate." If asked, 99 percent of them will respond that Las Casas won. He may well have, but we should be sure that our students make their decision on the basis of the strengths and weaknesses of each man's arguments, not on Las Casas's political correctness.

Sepúlveda begins his argument by stating a given—a self-evident truth—that is the foundation for all that follows. This truth, which he believes all reasonable men will accept, is that "the dominion of prudent, good, and humane men over those of contrary disposition is just and natural." This doctrine, derived from Aristotle, is buttressed by citing other authorities—Aquinas and Augustine—who support it. This approach, which begins with a general statement and then proceeds to particulars, is, of course, an example of the deductive method used by generations of medieval scholastic philosophers and theologians.

Assuming that his readers will accept his major premise, Sepúlveda then must prove that the Spaniards are indeed superior beings and the Amerindians barbarians. He begins by citing examples of Spaniards who achieved prominence in literature and philosophy. These are unquestionably impressive names, but the last person he lists, King Alfonso, died in 1284. Should it be inferred that no Spaniard has produced anything of note since then? Most of his arguments about the frugality, sobriety, courage, etc., of the Spaniards cannot be proved one way or another. Knowing what we do about sixteenth-century armies, however, it must be said that Sepúlveda's claims about the gentlemanly and humane behavior of Spanish soldiers must be taken with a large grain of salt. Certainly his point that Spanish soldiers demonstrated their religious dedication by making provision in their wills to return the goods *they had stolen* from civilians is not the strongest of arguments to prove the saintliness of Spanish fighting men.

What about his proofs of the Amerindians' barbarism? One point worth noting is that his examples overwhelmingly come from the Aztecs. He adopts this strategy because if the barbarism of these, the most advanced and powerful Amerindians can be proved, then his case is made. This, however, is a dubious strategy, since in many ways the Aztecs were exceptional. Few other native American people were as warlike as the Aztecs or practiced human sacrifice on so large a scale. Sepúlveda had no way of knowing about the accomplishments of the Mayans in astronomy and architecture, but if he had, it would have made it difficult for him to sustain his claims that the Amerindians were barbarians.

Sepúlveda tries to prove his point about the Amerindians' servility by pointing out that despite the Aztecs' incessant wars, they mounted only a pathetic, "woman-like" resistance to the Spaniards. If and when students read the account of the battle of Tenochtitlan by Sahagun in Chapter 2, they will be able to see the flaws in Sepúlveda's argument. The Aztecs and their leader Montezuma did, it is true, panic when they first encountered the Spaniards. But this passed once they got used to their invaders' firearms, horses, war dogs, armor, and appearance. Sepúlveda also fails to mention that the "few hundred" Spaniards had plenty of help in their fight with the Aztecs from thousands of Amerindian allies. Nor does Sepúlveda mention how smallpox devastated the Aztecs during the Spaniards' campaign. Finally, and most importantly, Sepúlveda distorts what happened during the battle. Rather than capitulating in terror, the Aztecs mounted and sustained an ingenious and heroic defense of their city against an enemy with many military advantages.

Las Casas rejects all of Sepúlveda's premises, arguments, and examples, although he does concede that in certain respects the Native Americans can be considered barbarians. Most fundamentally, he refuses to accept Sepúlveda's assertion that a superior people have the right to exploit and enslave inferiors; broad acceptance of such a notion would create international anarchy. He also rejects Sepúlveda's contention that "inferiors" have no right to resist. He refuses to accept Sepúlveda's characterization of the Amerindians as only slightly above the level of beasts. He points to their sophisticated governments, humane laws, commerce, architecture, painting, and needlework. They are capable of self-government and have no need of Spanish rule.

Las Casas brings another perspective to the debate when at the end of our excerpt he introduces the elements of Christian ethics and values. He reminds his listeners that "Christ wanted love to be called his single commandment. " Torturing and exploiting other human beings, even when their culture is uncivilized in certain respects cannot be justified. This is a point Sepúlveda does not even consider.

*   *   *

In discussing the sources in the section, "Women's Places," some students might wonder why of the four sources we have included only one is the work of a woman. This is a valid question, one worth discussing before moving on to the sources themselves. The fact is that historians studying the role of women in medieval and early modern Europe have little choice but to rely on sources written by men. Until the nineteenth century, extant writings by women were far too rare to provide a complete picture of women's views and roles in society.

Students may want to consider why so few sources written by medieval and early modern European women are available. One explanation is that few female authors existed because of women's higher illiteracy rates and their exclusion from universities and scholarly careers. In addition, their letters and diaries, were deemed insignificant by family members, archivists, and historians, and hence less likely to be preserved. Raising this issue could lead to further class discussion about the reasons why individual families and society as a whole were unwilling to invest energy and resources in female education.

John Mayer's eulogy of Lucy Thornton, "A Pattern for Women," read superficially, seems to present a favorable view of women. This particular wife and mother, Lucy Thornton, was charitable, devout, and courageous in the face of sickness and imminent death—a woman of admirable spiritual and moral accomplishment. She was literate and knowledgeable in the scriptures. Mayer tells his listeners that as a model for society, especially her family and immediate neighbors, she had an important social function to fulfil.

For all of Mayer's praise, however, his eulogy reveals his low estimate of women and his opinion that women should be subservient to men. He praises Lucy's qualities of humility, meekness, obedience to her husband, and "childlike" fear of God. Mayer states that she had her share of faults, including a "naturally sharp disposition." Furthermore, in her piety and humility she was an exception among women, most of whom were given to "vanity" and "unruliness." Women who indeed followed the "pattern" of Lucy Thornton would be subservient to their fathers, husbands, and pastors and their lives would have revolved around family and church.

Anton Woensam's woodcut, *Allegory of a Wise Woman*, has a similar message. Woensam's wise woman is pious, virtuous, chaste, charitable to neighbors, and obedient to her husband "no matter what his faults." But there are aspects of Woensam's woodcut that give it a particular Catholic flavor. The key that opens the wise woman's ears to God's word is also the symbol of the papacy, and the turtledove that stands for obedience to her husband is the symbol of the Holy Spirit in Catholic iconography. The woodcut also emphasizes good works as a means of attaining salvation (see the section of the text on serving the poor and the message of the last paragraph). The pillow she carries is used to kneel on during Catholic ceremonies.

It is also worth noting what Woensam has left out of his woodcut. There is no Bible or a book of any kind, which sends a strong message that "wisdom" for women does not include book learning or even literacy. Lucy Thornton, on the other hand, a Protestant living in the early seventeenth century, has "much understanding" of the Holy Scriptures, which she is able to quote during her final illness. Woensam's woman comes across as dull and joyless, plodding along on her horse's hooves while passively serving others.

Erhard Schön's woodcut, *No Greater Treasure*, along with the accompanying poem, are meant to be humorous and thus contain a strong element of exaggeration. Taken together, however, they provide important insights into the status of women and the realities of matrimony. Schon's work appeared at a time when for reasons that are not altogether clear marriage patterns in Europe were changing significantly. The age of first marriage was increasing for men and women, and more individuals were remaining single. Furthermore, convents no longer served as socially acceptable institutions where unmarried women could live out their lives. In Protestant Europe convents were closed entirely, and in reformed Catholic lands they were restricted ideally to women with sincere religious callings. Is there a connection between these demographic developments and the sour views of marriage expressed by the woman fool, wife, and husband in Schön's woodcut? Are these characters providing a justification or rationale for the increasing number of European men and women who were remaining single? Certainly it is an intriguing possibility.

The portrayal and commentary by the wife, husband, and woman fool in Schön's woodcut certainly present an unflattering view of matrimony. The wife has rebelled against the authority of her shiftless, carousing husband, whose failure to provide support has reduced her to begging. She has in her hands his breeches, sword, and money purse, symbols of his maleness, authority, and role as a breadwinner. The husband has been reduced to a position of abject subservience, pulling a cart with a pail of dirty diapers. Washing them was seen as the most demeaning and menial of tasks. The woman fool warns the prospective bridegroom that such will be his fate if he marries. She recommends the socially irresponsible course of resorting to the brothel rather than marriage. The young girl holds out the prospect of a marriage based on mutual respect and her obedience, while the old man, wearing a hat suggesting a position of political authority, reminds the young man that marriage is a civic and religious duty. His words echo the sentiments of Luther in his *Table Talk*.

The Nuremberg ordinances on midwives remind us that on top of the their responsibilities as wives and mothers, most women in early modern Europe worked outside the home both before and after marriage. The ordinances also provide information about the training and practices of midwives, and more interestingly, about social attitudes and relations. The ordinances were written by the wealthy, male members of the "high honorable" Nuremberg city council; they were administered by upper-class women who made up the *Ehrbare Frauen*. The midwives themselves were drawn from the lower ranks of Nuremberg society, but their services were needed by women of all classes.

What were the values and concerns of the Nuremberg councilors? Clearly, they were interested in the welfare of all Nuremberg women. The ordinances are designed to guarantee that women during childbirth can expect to receive care from midwives who are responsible, well trained, experienced, and sober at the time of delivery. They express special concern for the needs of poor women. The council has set aside a fund to pay the labor and delivery costs of poor women, and it strictly prohibits midwives from demanding anything over and above the salary provided by the overseer of the poor. The ordinances clearly state in the first paragraph that midwives should make no distinction in carrying out their responsibilities to rich and poor women.

What do the ordinances tell us about the midwives themselves and their duties? They tell us that the ideal midwife is an older, single woman "living alone." They will be more responsible than "flighty" young women who might be distracted by family responsibilities or who as apprentices might abandon their training for matrimony. The ordinances also imply that older single women will be more diligent because of their economic needs. Dependent on their own income, they will be less likely to turn down a job. Midwives, the ordinances tell us, have other functions besides helping mothers through labor. They are responsible for carrying newborns to their baptism and for enforcing the city council's policies designed to curb abortions and infanticide.

Midwifery was a demanding and difficult profession, sufficiently so that maintaining a sufficient number of midwives was a worry for the city council. At the end of the selection, experienced midwives are urged to take on new trainees no more than a year after previous apprentices have completed their training. Students may wish to discuss why it was difficult to keep the ranks full. At least some answers are provided in the ordinances themselves. First, if indeed midwives were to be limited to "older, single women living alone," the pool of potential apprentices was limited from the outset. Second, the physical and emotional demands of the profession were enormous. The ordinances in the second paragraph specifically discuss how midwives must ask for relief during long and difficult labors. Thirdly, the income from the profession was not high, especially, so it seems, when midwives were attending poorer women. Finally, although this is not stated in the document itself, the potential for failure for midwives was high. Many children and mothers died in childbirth or shortly thereafter, and midwives were often blamed for these deaths. Several studies suggest that midwives made up a disproportionately high percentage of women accused of witchcraft. It is not surprising that male physicians were more than willing to leave this particular medical specialty to female midwives.

* * *

Montaigne draws upon his own observations of human behavior and his broad reading of the classics to challenge his readers' assumptions. Challenging the religious and intellectual dogmatism of his age, he approaches his topics with a well-honed sense of irony and skepticism and a belief in the relativity of morality and philosophical truth.

In his essay "On Cannibals" Montaigne blurs the distinction between "civilized" Europeans and the "barbarian" inhabitants of the Americas. He uses the term "barbarian" in several different senses. As a student of ancient languages and literature, Montaigne certainly knew that *barbarian* to the Greeks simply meant "different" or "foreign." Thus from their own perspectives, the Europeans and the Amerindians are equally "barbarians" in each other's eyes; both consider the other's customs strange and bizarre. The reactions of the Amerindian visitors to France cited by Montaigne at the end of our excerpt confirm this point. Montaigne also uses the term barbarian in the sense of "uncivilized," or as he puts it, "fashioned very little by the human mind." This applies to the Amerindians only. They live simple, unexamined lives, have only a few uncomplicated rules, and for the most part act and live according to their natural instincts. Montaigne seems to approve some of their practices and habits—daily dancing, sobriety, conjugal devotion, and an absence of greed. He condemns others—battles to the death, killing of prisoners, and cannibalism.

Montaigne also uses the term barbarian in the sense of cruel and inhumane. According to this definition, the Europeans are the greater barbarians. In a famous passage he compares the cruelties of Amerindian cannibalism with the even worse cruelties of the European torture chambers and battlefields. The Amerindians, he concedes, "don't wear breeches," confirming their barbarism in the sense of Montaigne's second use of the term, but in the end his conclusion is clear—Europeans, not the inhabitants of the Americas, are the true barbarians.

Would Montaigne's arguments have supported Sepúlveda or Las Casas in the debate about Spanish policy in the Americas? The answer, we believe, is neither. Montaigne's assessment of Europeans as barbarians undercuts the very foundation of Sepúlveda's defense of the Europeans' enslavement of the Amerindians—their claim to moral superiority. Nor is there any justification for the kind of altruistic intervention on behalf of the Amerindians that Las Casas championed. According to Montaigne, contact with the "civilized" Europeans would only result in the destruction of the Amerindians' simplicity and innocence.

Tension between the pioneers of the new science and Europe's religious establishment did not begin with Galileo's clash with the Catholic Church. Copernicus, a Catholic clergyman, worried that his heliocentric theories would inspire religious opposition, and as a result, he refused to have his works published until the very end of his life. Then he dedicated *On the Revolutions of the Heavenly Spheres* to Pope Paul III and in the preface defended his theories against the claim that they were unscriptural.

Unlike the deferential Copernicus, the confident Galileo is contemptuous of his opponents. Afraid that their erroneous ideas will be rejected, his enemies, claims Galileo, have launched a vendetta against him and rely on poorly formulated religious and biblical arguments. He asserts that the Bible's authority should be strictly limited to the realm of faith; reason and the senses must have primacy in the study of nature. He further dismisses the "authority" of the scriptures by arguing that much in the Bible is unclear and, if taken literally, false. Galileo advances the radical argument that nature more clearly and accurately reveals God than the scriptures, which use figures of speech and simplified expressions that are not literally true but are necessary to accommodate the limited understanding of the rude and unlearned. Thus Galileo demands freedom for natural philosophers—the scientist of his day—to seek knowledge and draw conclusions without fear of religious interference.

Galileo's letter is not only a defense against charges of religious error but also a classic expression of the idea that science and religion had their own legitimate and *separate* spheres of inquiry. Just as Machiavelli had demanded the separation of politics from the realm of Christian morality in his Renaissance classic, *The Prince*, Galileo argued that a similar separation should apply to the study of nature. There were, he claimed, two realms of truth: religious and scientific.

Other Ways to Use the Sources

1. Many of the sources in this chapter have something to say about the nature of *authority* in religious and intellectual matters. Basing your essay on insights drawn from the authors represented in this chapter, write an essay that speaks to the issue of what sixteenth- and seventeenth-century Europeans thought about *authority*. You should think about what authorities they accepted and which ones they rejected. What significance do your conclusions have for understanding sixteenth-century thought? (Our students should be able to see that the idea of "authority" was in shambles during the sixteenth century. Antiquity, the scriptures, personal conscience, and observation of nature all had support as authorities, but all of them also had detractors. Intellectual consensus was breaking down. Similar comparative essays could be written on a number of other topics such as *human nature* and *change*.)
2. Compose a response to Galileo's arguments by a conservative seventeenth-century Catholic theologian.
3. Imagine that you have been commissioned by the Catholic Church to design a woodcut to counter the message of Cranach's *Two Kinds of Preaching* or Gerung's *The Chariot of the Pope and the Turk*. What details would you have included?
4. Compose a refutation of the decrees of the Council of Trent by Luther.
5. How might Sepúlveda have responded to the point of view expressed in Montaigne's "On Cannibals"?

6. Write an essay in which you evaluate the role of religion in early modern Europe based on the sources in Chapter 1 of *The Human Record*. What information in the sources suggests the continuing importance of religion? What passages in the sources suggest that religion was a weakening force?

C H A P T E R
2

Africa and the Americas

Chapter Theme

The sources in this chapter are evenly divided between Africa and the Americas, with most of them concentrating on the ramifications of the arrival of Europeans, the most important single event in the history of each region during the early modern era. This chapter sheds light on the following questions, among others. How did Europeans and the people of Africa and the Americas perceive one another? How did these perceptions affect their actions in dealing with the other? How were the experiences of Africa and the Americas similar and different? How did the results of interaction in the 1500s and 1600s differ from the expectations the various parties had at the outset?

For Africa, European impact was mainly limited to its coasts, where the Portuguese established and maintained fortified trading stations and purchased slaves, ivory, and gold in exchange for iron bars, weapons, textiles, hardware, and other manufactured goods. European penetration into the interior was virtually non-existent, and Africans maintained their political independence and distinctive religions and cultures. Europeans became involved in the slave trade during the fifteenth through seventeenth centuries, and there is no denying the anguish and pain of the many Africans who were sold into slavery in Europe or the Americas. But for a few exceptions, however, such as the kingdom of Kongo (see source 13), which disintegrated in part because of Portuguese slaving, the slave trade's overall impact on Africa during the sixteenth and seventeenth centuries was relatively slight compared to the eighteenth century, when six million Africans were sold into slavery in the Americas alone.

European expansion had more far-reaching ramifications for the Americas. For several reasons—geographic, biological, political, economic, and demographic—Native Americans were less able to resist European encroachment and exploitation. They were either driven off their lands, as was ultimately the case in most of North America, or subjected to European political control and economic exploitation, as was the case in Mexico and Central and South America.

Why These Sources?

Although it would take dozens of sources to portray fully the complexity and variety of African societies, we hope the two sources in this section, when combined with those in the following section, will give students an idea of the continent's great diversity. The sources in the first section represent two different and distinctive geographical regions of Africa—the Western Sudan and the East Coast from Sofala in the south to Brava in the north. They also represent two different types of society.

The Sudanic kingdoms described by Leo Africanus in the first selection—Songhai and the nearby kingdoms of Mali and Borno—exist in a region where some of Africa's most significant historical developments had taken place. An important area of trade linking regions to the south with Trans-Saharan caravan routes, the region had been dominated by several large empires going back to Ghana in the tenth and eleventh centuries C.E. It was also an area where Islam had penetrated beginning in the tenth century.

The second selection, an excerpt from the writings of a Portuguese official, Duarte Barbosa, describes seven city-states on Africa's east coast, a region somewhat ignored by historians because of their preoccupation with the transatlantic slave trade. Barbosa's descriptions add to our picture of Africa's diversity and reveal the many connections between east Africa and the outside world.

Our next section deals with European (mainly Portuguese) impact on Africa in the sixteenth and seventeenth centuries. It begins with excerpts from letters written by the king of Kongo, Nzinge Mbemba (Afonso I), to the king of Portugal in the early 1500s. Few other sources better illustrate the tendency of early African-Portuguese relationships to degenerate from optimistic expectations and idealism to disaster and disillusionment. Afonso and many of his courtiers converted to Christianity and began to learn Portuguese, hoping that European technology and medical knowledge would strengthen their state and improve their subjects' lives. Instead, rampant Portuguese slaving caused chaos and undermined Afonso's authority. The letters express more, however, than Afonso's disappointment and anger. They also reveal his continuing hope that he and his subjects will benefit from the Portuguese presence. (Afonso's letters are also included in Volume I of *The Human Record*. For further comments on this source, see p. 156 of *Using The Human Record*.)

The excerpt from João dos Santos's *Eastern Ethiopia* was chosen for several reasons. Most importantly, it shows that despite the advantage provided by their firearms, steel swords, and armor, the Portuguese were on some occasions no match for Africans in battle. This selection (along with

Afonso's letters) also complements the material in the chapter's first section by further illustrating Africa's diversity.

This section concludes with two pieces of Benin art from the sixteenth century: a saltcellar and a wall plaque. Both works are included in Volume I of *The Human Record*. For a discussion of the significance and message of these two works, please consult p. 157 of *Using The Human Record*.

Our next section, on early European-Amerindian encounters, begins with Sahagún's *General History of the Things of New Spain*. It too is included in Volume I of *The Human Record*. It provides a dramatic and compelling description of some of the events connected with the battle of Tenochtitlan. A retelling of Cortés's conquest from the perspective of the Aztecs and its powerful evocation of the Aztecs' response to Cortés's invasion is unrivalled.

The second source in this section is new to the fourth edition of *The Human Record*. A speech delivered to an audience of French settlers and missionaries by an elder of the Mi'kmaqs, a native American people who inhabited eastern Canada, replaces David Pieterzen Devries' *Voyages from Holland to America*. Although the Devries source provided valuable insights into relations between the Algonquins and the Dutch settlers of New Netherlands, we were attracted to this new source for a number of reasons. First of all, it gives a voice to a native American rather than to another European, whose writings already fill up many pages in Volume II of *The Human Record*. It also provides an excellent complement to Montaigne's essay "on Cannibals" in Chapter 1. Montaigne asks the question, "Who is the true barbarian?" and answers, "the Europeans." This Amerindian elder asks the question, "Who is truly civilized?" and answers "the Mi'kmaqs." Comparing each man's logic and line of argument should make an interesting student exercise.

Chapter 2 concludes with three selections that deal with the economic relationships between Amerindians and their Spanish overlords during the early colonial period. The first two sources in the section shed light on the two major systems of labor exploitation utilized by the Spaniards in the Americas. The first is a list of regulations pertaining to the encomienda system in Paraguay. We chose to include this particular document even though Paraguay was a thinly populated region on the periphery of the Spanish Empire. The document's strength is that it clearly portrays the efforts of Spanish officials to balance the interests of the Spanish settlers and the Native Americans. It is as if they were trying to integrate the views of Las Casas and Sepulveda.

The second source in the section (also included in Volume I of *The Human Record*) is an excerpt from Antonio Vazquez de Espinosa's description of the silver and mercury mines in the region of the famous Potosi mine of modern Bolivia. It describes the condition of the Amerindian laborers who were part of the *mita* system of forced labor, widely used by Spaniards in areas formerly under Incan control.

The last source in the section, from the records of the municipal council of Tlaxcala in modern Mexico, is new to the fourth edition of *The Human Record*. It makes the point that economic relations between Europeans and Native Americans did not always mean forced labor and exploitation. For some, including the Tlaxcalans who cornered the market on cochineal, a brilliant red dye produced from the bodies of cochineal insects, the arrival of Europeans meant new opportunities, new wealth, and unsettling social changes.

Analyzing the Sources

Leo Africanus and Duarte Barbosa describe two strikingly different political systems. From Leo Africanus's description of the governments of the Sudanese kingdoms, we learn that all three, Mali, Songhai, and Borno, are ruled by all-powerful kings with armies and great quantities of gold. Leo's reference to the Songhai king's "secretaries, treasurers, stewards, and auditors" suggests that the administration of this Sudanese kingdom was more sophisticated and developed than that of Mali and Borno. Since these Sudanic kingdoms all existed in a region that was officially Muslim, their rulers could not claim divinity, although we do know that many of them continued to participate in non-Muslim rites and ceremonies long after their official conversion to Islam.

The states Duarte describes on Africa's East Coast were much smaller than Songhai, and in fact are often referred to as city-states. Barbosa tells us little about the details of their governments. All we learn is that they all were governed by rulers Barbosa describes as kings, except Brava, which was ruled by a council of elders.

Both authors are impressed by the economic vitality of the areas they describe. Although Leo describes rural regions where the people support themselves at a rather meager level through pastoralism, generally speaking the authors depict diversified economies capable of maintaining a high level of prosperity. The economies of the Sudanic kingdoms and the east African coastal states all rest on an agricultural base that produces a wide variety of grain crops and fruits. Trade is important to both regions, however. Leo Africanus makes numerous references to commercial contacts between the Western Sudan and the Mediterranean coast, Italy, and Asia Minor. Similarly, Duarte Barbosa is much impressed with the business savvy of east African merchants.

The Sudanic kingdoms and the cities of the East Coast were officially Muslim. The descriptions by Leo Africanus of mosques and Qur'anic schools show that Islam had taken root in the cities of Songhai and Mali, where Islamic merchants had introduced the faith several centuries before. It may be significant that he fails to mention any signs of Islam in the predominantly rural and less-developed kingdom of Borno, where animist religions were still widely practiced. Duarte Barbosa has little to say about the religious life of the cities he describes.

Many other aspects of these three societies could be analyzed and compared. Slavery is prevalent in the Sudan, and slaves are a key item of trade. Barbosa, however, makes no mention of slavery. Both the Sudanic kingdoms and the East Coast cities have impressive palaces and mosques. The Portuguese have made contact with the coastal cities, often with devastating results when the leaders refused to cooperate with the Portuguese. The Sudanic kingdoms, however, have had no significant contact with Europeans except indirectly through trade. Borno and Songhai appear to have strong military traditions, something lacking in the commercial cities on the East Coast. Those cities were unable to mount any sort of effective defense against the Portuguese, whose naval guns reduced several of them to ruin.

* * *

The letters of King Afonso to the King of Portugal were written by a desperate man. What he had hoped would be a beneficial working relationship with the Portuguese had turned into a disaster. He had co-operated with Portuguese officials, accepted Christianity, sent his sons to Europe to be educated, made Portuguese the language of the court, and tolerated the activities of Portuguese merchants. In return he hoped to profit from trade, benefit from European medicine, and enhance his prestige among his subjects.

Instead, he was losing control of his vassals and feared that his kingdom was on the brink of disintegration. The roots of these problems were twofold. First, there was an unanticipated high demand for Portuguese merchandise. Afonso does not specify what this merchandise is, but if the pattern of Portuguese trade in other parts of Africa was being followed in Kongo, it consisted mainly of woolen and cotton textiles, probably of North African origin, and also items such as iron knives, glass mirrors, Venetian beads, and even Chinese porcelain. Portuguese merchants sold these goods directly to provincial and local chiefs, thereby upsetting the system of carefully regulated and centrally directed trade and tribute the Kongo kings had established. Such a system had not only provided the king with income, but it had also enabled him to assure his vassals' loyalty by controlling the flow of goods to them. In a passage in the first paragraph, Afonso complains that as a result of Portuguese sales, his vassals have withdrawn their allegiance to him because they have goods in such abundance that their supply exceeds that of the king. He adds, "...it was with these things that we had them content and subjected under our vassalage and jurisdiction."

The demand for these Portuguese goods in turn led to a second problem for Afonso, a dramatic increase in the slave trade. The letters reveal that slavery already existed in the Kongo, and that Afonso has no objection to it. But in order to pay for the European goods they coveted, Afonso's subjects have resorted to kidnapping free men, some even nobles, and selling them to the Portuguese. Although in Afonso's view the Portuguese are primarily at fault, clearly, without the participation of his subjects, the slave trade would have faltered. Afonso himself is inconsistent in his statements about his wishes concerning the slave trade. In the first letter he states he wants it to end altogether; in the second he merely wants it regulated so that only captives, but no free men, are sold to the Portuguese.

Despite his disillusionment, Afonso still believes both sides can benefit from cooperation. Thus he does not demand the expulsion of the Europeans; instead he petitions the Portuguese king to send physicians and priests to his kingdom. What Afonso did not realize was that the attentions of the Portuguese royal court had shifted from Africa to Asia and that the early plan of turning the Kongo into a prosperous, profitable trading partner and a model of successful missionary activity no longer generated much interest in Lisbon. Instead the Kongo came to viewed as a source of cheap slave labor for the plantations on Sao Tome and later Brazil.

It should be noted in conclusion that Afonso undoubtedly was overstating the depredations caused by Portuguese traders. After all, he was trying to make an impression on the Portuguese king. At this early point in the history of the slave trade it is highly doubtful that the Kongo was coming anywhere close to being "depopulated" as a result of slave trade. And the political crisis was probably less severe than Afonso suggested. Actually the kingdom held together until the seventeenth century, even surviving the devastating military raids instigated by the Jaga in the 1560s. (For further commentary on these letters, see p. 156 of *Using the Human Record*.)

João dos Santos' description of the military campaigns fought by the Portuguese and their allies against the Zimba in the 1590s provides a valuable corrective to the notion that the Portuguese met little or no effective military resistance in Africa. It also allows students to make comparisons between the successful military campaign fought by the Zimba in the 1590s and the failed defense of Tenochtitlan by the Aztecs between 1519 and 1521.

Current scholarship suggests that the Zimba attacks on the Portuguese had economic motives, specifically, frustration over their loss of a market for ivory as a result of Portuguese indifference to this particular product. Dos Santos does not mention this theory, but his account does offer a few hints about possible reasons for their attack. The Zimba were, he tells us, interested in extending their territory. He tells us at the outset that the Zimba took land from a chieftain who appealed to a Portuguese official, Andre de Santiago, for help. He also relates that after each of their victories they carried off booty from the camp of their defeated opponents. Another clue is provided by Dos Santos's explanation of Pedro de Sousa's decision to attack the Zimba: he feared they would prey on Portuguese river traffic unless pushed back. Thus according to Dos Santos, land, booty, and damaging Portuguese trade all were goals of the Zimba.

Another intriguing issue is the Zimba's motives for cannibalism. Unless they are near starvation, societies that practice cannibalism rarely do so simply to augment their food supply. Usually the consumption of human flesh has some magico-ritual significance that might range from placating the gods to drawing strength or power from the dead person. The Zimba flaunted their cannibalism, marching off with legs and arms of their dead opponents so their enemies would be sure to see them and hear their taunts. Their macabre procession after the ambush of the Portuguese and the torture/execution of Father Nicolau seem to have been designed mainly to terrorize Andre de Santiago and his troops. It worked. The Portuguese attempted to retreat but were ambushed and suffered heavy losses.

The Zimba were able to withstand the attacks of the Portuguese in part because of their success in cancelling out the potential advantages of Portuguese firearms and artillery. Before encountering the troops of Andre de Santiago and Dom Pedro de Sousa, they were ready to defend themselves behind an earthen rampart and a double palisade of wood. As a result, Portuguese artillery had little or no effect. Furthermore, none of the Portuguese commanders distinguished himself. André de Santiago underestimated his enemy's strength, and Pedro Fernandes de Chaves was unprepared for the Zimba's ambush. Dom Pedro de Sousa's idea of building tall earth-filled wood frames from which his soldiers could fire down on the Zimba's palisade had promise, but when he naively believed his African troops' story about a rebel attack on Sena, it was never implemented. This episode provides another clue about the reasons for Portuguese military problems. Their allies were traders without a strong military tradition and had little interest in fighting battles for the Portuguese.

[The Portuguese/Benin saltcellar and the Benin wall plaque both appear in Volume I. They are discussed in this instructor's manual on p. 157.]

* * *

Few events in world history match the drama and significance of the Battle of Tenochtitlan, which lasted more than two years between 1519 and 1521 and resulted in the destruction of the Aztec empire at the hands of the Spanish conquistador Cortés and his Amerindian allies. Our selection that recounts this battle is an early example of oral history. Bernardino de Sahagún's *General History of New Spain* is based on interviews of Aztec survivors of the conquest some twenty-five years after the events themselves took place.

Discussions of this document always seem to end up focusing on the question, "Why did the Aztecs lose?" Most students assume Spanish artillery and firearms were the decisive factors. But as is clear from Sahagun's account, much more was involved.

We have found that an effective method of discussing the reasons for the Spanish victory is to compare the Aztec defeat in 1519–1521 with the Portuguese defeat at the hands of the Zimba in the 1580s. Obviously, there were huge differences between the two encounters. The battle between the Zimba and the Portuguese involved comparatively small numbers of troops and lasted only several weeks. Cortés's campaign lasted more than two years, involved hundreds of thousands of soldiers, and was fought on land and water. At stake in Mexico was one of the world's most impressive cities. Tenochtitlan had magnificent buildings, botanical gardens, zoos, and a population estimated from 80,000 to over 200,000. Despite these differences, a comparison of the two encounters can be instructive.

Some of the reasons for the Portuguese defeat at the hands of the Zimba have already been discussed. The following points explain the Spanish victory over the Aztecs.

- Firearms were important, but not decisive. The noise, smoke, and destructiveness of the Spaniards' guns terrified the Aztecs at first, and in the final stages of the battle were effective in knocking down walls the Aztecs had erected on the main roads to the city. But in the actual fighting, much of which took place in the close confines of the city, the heavy, slow-firing Spanish guns were less lethal than the Spaniards' steel swords, daggers, and pikes. Of the 900 Spaniards who made up Cortes's army in 1521, only 118 carried harqebuses and crossbows.

- Just as the Portuguese defeat in east Africa resulted in part from poor generalship, Aztec resistance was weakened by the indecisiveness of Montezuma. The Zimba knew their enemy well, but to Montezuma and the Aztecs everything about the Spaniards was strange—their appearance, their weapons, their horses and dogs, and their strange fascination with gold. Montezuma's early efforts to counter the

Spaniards by buying them off with gold and using priests and wizards both failed.

- A key factor was the enormous number of Amerindians who fought with Cortés against the Aztecs. In the final assault on Tenochtitlan, as many as 100,000 Amerindians were under Cortés's command.

- Tenochtitlan, an island city that could be supplied only by three main causeways, was vulnerable to siege. The city finally capitulated because of mass starvation.

- The smallpox epidemic that struck in 1520 was decisive. Nothing analogous befell the Zimba.

- The Aztec method of fighting was ill suited to a long campaign involving large numbers of fighting men. As is shown in Sahagún's account, Aztec warfare was based on individual combat, with the goal of capturing the enemy for sacrifice rather than killing him.

One thing is clear. Nothing in Sahagún's account confirms Sepulveda's assertion (see source 4) that the Aztecs showed servility and cowardice in their defeat by Cortes. If anything, the battle for Tenochtitlan reveals their bravery and ingenuity.

The next document in this section, a speech by an elder of the Mi'kmaq people delivered around 1660, resembles Sahagún's *A General History of New Spain* in one important respect. Just as Sahagún's description of the Battle of Tenochtitlan is a transcription and translation of the words of Native Americans by Europeans, this Mi'kmaq elder's speech was recorded and translated by a French missionary, Chrétien LeClerq. Otherwise the context and meaning of the two documents are far different. Unlike the Aztecs, who knew nothing about the Spaniards before their fateful confrontation in 1519, the Mi'kmaqs had been familiar with the French since the early 1600s through contacts with merchants and missionaries. Furthermore, the French were interested in trade and missionary work, not conquest and plunder.

The elder who made the speech recorded by LeClerq knew of the French only from his personal observations of the French settlers and missionaries and from the descriptions of France these settlers had offered. He had been told, of course, that the French were more advanced, more enlightened, and happier than the primitive Mi'kmaqs. France so it was claimed, lived in an "earthly paradise." The Amerindian speaker rejects such assertions with arguments that might strike student readers as unsophisticated, and almost childlike. Why, he asks, do humans who are only five or six feet in height need houses that are sixty or eighty feet tall? Why build a new house every time you move when you could, like the Mi'kmaqs, carry your dwelling on your back as you moved from place to place? Why do so many Frenchmen leave France for the New World if their native land is the paradise they claim it is?

But the Mi'kmaq elder also raises some fundamental issues. To him, life has value because of simple pleasures… "resting, drinking, sleeping, eating, and amusing ourselves with friends." These things the Mi'kmaqs have in abundance, so why change? Why imitate the French, who abandon their homes and undergo enormous hardships to seek cod and animal skins, things on which the Mi'kmaqs place little value? Another thing the Mi'kmaq have is freedom and independence. As the elder points out, "we find all our riches and all our conveniences among ourselves;" they live where they want, "independently of any lord whatsoever." Finally, the life of the Mi'kmaqs offers opportunities for leisure and repose that are lacking for the French farmers and traders. Who is "wiser and happier—he who labors without ceasing and only obtains… enough to live on, or he who rests in comfort and finds all he needs in the pleasure of hunting and fishing?"

Not all students will find these arguments convincing, but the translator, LeClerq, found them so. He admits that in many respects the simple life of the Mi'kmaqs is superior to the vexatious and annoyance-filled lives of most Europeans. Like another Frenchman, Montaigne, who wrote his essay "On Cannibals," some one hundred years earlier, LeClerq questions the presumption of European superiority to the native peoples of the Americas.

* * *

The first two documents in the section "Land and Labor in Spanish America" deal with methods used by the Spaniards to exploit native American labor, the encomienda, and mita systems. A comparison of the two documents reveals that the mita system was more oppressive and dangerous.

Although practice often fell far short of the ideal, the encomienda system was designed by the Spaniards to balance two seemingly contradictory goals of the Spanish conquest of the Americas: the Spaniards wanted to utilize native American labor to generate wealth from mining and agriculture, but they also wanted to make the Amerindians good Christians and docile work-ers. This meant protecting them from extreme exploitation. The result on paper was a system of what might be called "regulated," or, if there is such a thing, "benign exploitation."

Indeed, the regulations for the Paraguayan encomiendas provide evidence of concern for the welfare of Amerindians on the part of Spanish colonial administrators. True, the regulations restrict the Indians' ability to move from place to place and they require that the Indians provide labor to the encomenderos in the form of "repairing their houses, in farming, stock raising, hunting, fishing and other enterprises." There is no pay for these services, and there are unspecified penalties if the labor is not carried out as ordered. The rest of the document, however, focuses on protecting the Indians from excessive demands and unfair treatment. To make sure its provisions are followed, it spells out penalties for encomenderos who abuse their Indians, establishes a grievance procedure for Indians who have complaints, and provides for annual visits by colonial officials called visitadores who enforce regulations so that "justice may be done in everything, and the relief, welfare, benefit, conservation, and pacification of the Indians may be obtained."

The Paraguayan encomienda regulations raise two questions. How sincere were the Spaniards in their stated concern for the Indians' welfare, and how well were the regulations enforced? Both questions are difficult to answer. The document itself suggests that abuses did occur. Why else would the document establish punishments for offending encomenderos, set up grievance procedures, and mandate annual visits by colonial officials? As far as the sincerity of the Spaniards is concerned, there is no doubt that the Spanish government and thousands of Spanish priests and friars were devoted to the Indians' spiritual and physical welfare. It is just as certain that many landowners took advantage of their Indian charges and drove them to the limit and beyond. Sepúlveda and Las Casas both had their supporters among the Spaniards who administered and settled the New World.

The spirit of Sepúlveda was stronger in the silver and mercury mines of Bolivia and Peru. This is clearly the impression left by Antonio Vazquez de Espinosa's descriptions of the mining operations at Huancavelica in his *Compendium and Description of the West Indies.*

[This document is included in Volume I of *The Human Record.* It is also discussed in this resource guide on p. 156.]

Workers were required to leave their homes to work in the mines for two months a year at Huancavelica and four months a year at Potosí. As a result, as de Espinosa reports, villages were depopulated, local chieftains faced stiff punishments when they failed to achieve their quotas of workers, and, since many wives accompanied their husbands to the mines, family life was disrupted. Disease and injury levels (from the cold climate, long hours, mercury poisoning, and exhausting labor) must have been high.

It is true that Spanish officials provided for a hospital and a chapel. It is also true that the mita workers were paid. But with a little calculation, one can see that the pay was paltry. The 3,000 to 4,000 workers at Huancavelica divide up 60,000 pesos provided by the Spanish government. This means they received around fifteen pesos for their work. Workers at Potosí are paid at a comparable level. For four months' work they receive four *reals*. With each real equal in value to eight pesos, these workers would only be receiving about eight pesos a month for their work. *Mingados*, or non-mita laborers, are paid much better, anywhere from 12 to 24 reals a year. In comparison, the curate at the Huancavelica hospital receives an annual salary of 800 pesos, or 100 reals. But the worth of the silver extracted from the mines was almost beyond calculation. De Espinosa estimates its value at 1,800 million pesos.

The final selection in this section is a petition from the municipal council of the Mexican state of Tlaxcala to the Spanish viceroy, who resided in Mexico City. It contains the following words: "Things are no longer the way they were long ago...." Such sentiments, if not the exact words, have appeared in a number of other sources in this chapter. King Afonso of Kongo deplored the effects of Portuguese slaving and complained that Portuguese trade had weakened his authority and upset traditional social relationships. The Mi'kmaq elder described how his people's health and life expectancy had both declined after the French introduced them to wine and wheat. And in this document, the Tlaxcalan nobles who dominated the municipal council lamented the rapid changes that came in the wake of the Spaniards' arrival.

Specifically, they deplored the cochineal dye boom, caused by new export opportunities to Europe. Although many Tlaxcalans were getting rich by raising the nopal cactus, collecting and drying the bodies of cochineal insects, and selling the brilliant red dye to Spaniards, the council members believed that damages outweighed the benefits. They came to this conclusion for several stated and unstated reasons. They raised the specter of famine now that farmers were growing the nopal cactus rather than beans and chilis. They deplored the negative effects upon religion. The nouveaux riches cochineal growers and merchants were ignoring their religious duties on Sundays and Holy Days and flouting old standards of morality. Drunkenness and sexual profligacy are rife among the newly wealthy.

What most bothers the nobles is their loss of dominance within Tlaxcalan society. Before the arrival of the Spaniards and the boom in cochineal, no other group rivalled their political power or their wealth. Everyone knew his or her own place. Now all was in turmoil. Cochineal producers had more money than they knew what to do with; women were involved in commerce; and people no longer respected the old ways. Truly, things were no longer as they had been.

Other Ways to Use the Sources

1. The sources in this chapter provide an excellent opportunity for our students to do some thinking and writing about the use of historical evidence and the evaluation of historical sources. In an exercise we have found to work well, we pick four or five sources and ask students first to find in them three statements of fact and three statements of opinion. Then we ask them to decide which of the sources is the most factual and which is the least factual. They are also expected to write a brief justification of their choices.

   We then center our class discussion around some important issues that confront every student of history: what do we mean by a historical fact? How can we be reasonably certain that what we consider historical knowledge matches historical reality? What criteria can we use to judge the reliability of historical sources? In answering the latter question, students should be able to come up with some of the following points: consideration of the author's background, the author's audience, the author's reasons for writing, the type of document, the document's congruence with other known facts, the document's internal coherence, the author's method of securing information (first hand or second hand), etc. We then try to apply some of these criteria to a specific document.

2. Using information contained in the documents written by Leo Africanus, Afonso I, Dos Santos, and Barbosa, write an essay on the "diversity of African societies." Economics, politics, and religion are topics that should be considered.

   [Students occasionally question assignments like this, claiming that reading three or four brief documents does not give them enough information. Of course, they are correct. They cannot hope to cover the topic with any degree of thoroughness. Admit that this is in certain respects an artificial exercise, but at the same time point out that historians are *always* trying to recreate the past with only incomplete evidence.]

3. Using information contained in King Afonso's letters and the writings of Barbosa and Dos Santos, write an essay describing ways in which the Portuguese affected Africa.

4. What do the encomienda regulations, the records and writings of Sahagun, the Mi'kmaq elder's speech, and Espinosa's description of mining operations at Potosí and Huancavelica reveal about European attitudes toward Native Americans in the sixteenth and seventeenth centuries?

5. Amerindians living on an encomienda in Paraguay are given the opportunity to draw up a list of complaints about their treatment by their

encomendero before the visit of a Spanish colonial official. What might they have included on their list? Workers in the mercury and silver mines of the Potosi region are given the same opportunity. What might they have included on their list?

6. Compare the military success of the Zimba in their battles with the Portuguese to the failure of the Aztecs in their conflict with the Spaniards.

7. Compare the economic effects of the Europeans' arrival on the kingdom of Kongo (source 13) and the Mexican state of Tlaxcala (source 20).

C H A P T E R
3

The Islamic Heartland and India

Chapter Theme

The first section of this chapter sheds light on what is unquestionably the most important development in Southwest Asia and India during the sixteenth and seventeenth centuries, the emergence of three large, powerful states—the Ottoman Empire centered in Asia Minor, the Safavid Empire in Persia, and the Mughal Empire in India. It does so by focusing on three of the most illustrious rulers of the age, the Ottoman sultan Suleiman I (r. 1520–1566), the Persian shah Abbas I (r. 1587–1629), and the Mughal emperor Jahangir (r. 1605–1627).

While the chapter's first section illustrates the dynamics of political change in South and Southwest Asia, the second section focuses on religion and society. The sources have been chosen to present basic Islamic and Hindu beliefs (a review for students who have had world history to 1500) and to highlight certain religious and cultural developments that took place in the sixteenth and seventeenth centuries, most importantly the emergence of Sikhism in India. The first selection, a letter from Sultan Selim I to Shah Ismail dating from 1514, shows how the emergence of a strong Shi'ite state in Persia contributed to Shi'ite-Sunni tensions and eventually war. The second selection, a brief excerpt from Busbecq's *Turkish Letters*, provides information about the status of women in Ottoman Turkey. The third, from Abu'l Fazl's *Akbarnama*, is an effort by an open-minded Muslim to describe and explain Hinduism to other Muslim readers. In doing so Abu'l Fazl hopes to win support for the tolerant religious policy of his patron and friend, Emperor Akbar. The selection from the *Akbarnama* also provides insights into Hindu attitudes toward women. The chapter concludes with excerpts from poems and hymns written by Nanak, the founder of Sikhism, from Sikhism's holy book, the *Adi-Granth*.

Why These Sources?

The first three sources have been chosen to illustrate some of the personal attributes and policies of three of the most illustrious rulers of their age, Suleiman the Magnificent, Abbas I, and Jahangir. Taken together, the three sources provide plenty of material for writing assignments and class discussions on the exercise of political power.

The letters of Ogier de Busbecq to his fellow diplomat Nicholas Michault, written while Busbecq was on diplomatic missions to the Ottoman court in Istanbul (Constantinople), provide a wealth of information about Ottoman government and society. That Busbecq exaggerates Ottoman military strength and the efficiency of the Ottoman state does not negate the letters' value.

Father Simon's account of his visit to Safavid Persia is less well known than Busbecq's letters. In fact, it was filed away and forgotten in the Vatican archives until it was translated into English and published in the 1930s. Father Simon, a Carmelite friar, not a diplomatic luminary, lacked access to the inner circles of the Persian court and stayed in Persia only briefly. This might explain why his report fails to mention certain important aspects of Abbas's reign, notably his encouragement of commerce and his recruitment of foreigners to bolster Persia's economy and army. Nonetheless, his sketch of Abbas and his descriptions of Persian society contain valuable information about Abbas and the country he ruled. For the fourth edition of *The Human Record*, the section on Abbas's religious views and policies has been expanded. It contains insights into his views of Europe and what he expected to gain by encouraging the hopes of Catholic missionaries.

Jahangir's memoirs, in addition to providing insights into the sources of Mughal power, are a delightful self-description of a ruler who fully indulged his love of palaces, jewels, servants, poets, wine, and music but also took his responsibilities seriously and thought deeply about the principles of effective rule. In this edition of *The Human Record*, Jahangir's memoirs have been modified to include the twelve decrees he issued at the beginning of his reign. They show how Jahangir's general philosophy translated into actual policy.

In the chapter's second section, Selim I's letter to his Safavid rival, Ismail, and the excerpt from Abu'l Fazl's *Akbarnama* have been chosen in part to overcome one of the difficulties encountered at the beginning of the second semester of two-semester global history courses. Some of our students have had the first semester of global history and presumably know something about Islam and Hinduism, while others are beginning their first semester of global history and are spectacularly uninformed about the two religions. These two sources give the instructor an opportunity to teach something about Islam and Hinduism (valuable to new students) while simultaneously introducing new themes specific to the sixteenth and seventeenth centuries (thus preventing our continuing students' eyes from glazing over too quickly).

Selim I's letter to Shah Ismail, for example, can be used to introduce students to Islam's core beliefs *and* to show the bitterness between Ottoman Sunnis and Persian Shi'ites in the early 1500s. It also can be used as the basis for discussions of Ismail's meteoric rise and the political disputes that led to the Ottoman attack on the Safavids in 1514. In addition, the excerpts from the *Akbarnama* can be used to introduce certain basic Hindu beliefs or to serve as a starting point for a discussion of the intellectual and cultural milieu of Akbar's court.

The next selection in this section, also from Busbecq's *Turkish Letters*, further develops an ongoing theme in *The Human Record*, namely the status of women in different cultures and eras. Since Abu'l Fazl's *Akbarnama* also contains many references to women in Hindu society, the two sources together provide material for what should be a successful discussion of this topic.

The final source in this chapter consists of excerpts from sacred hymns written by Guru Nanak (1469–1539), which, along with writings of other gurus, make up the holy book of Sikhism, the *Adi Granth*. Sikhism is an example of India's ability to adopt changes in the light of tradition and a sign of religion's continuing vitality in Indian life in the 1500s and 1600s. Continuous tension between Hindus and Muslims had been a curse to Indian society ever since the first Muslim conquerors arrived in the subcontinent around 1000 C.E., and the first Muslim empire, the Delhi Sultanate, was founded in 1206. Until the mid-seventeenth century India's Mughal rulers attempted to defuse this tension by following a policy of religious toleration and equal treatment of Muslims and Hindus. In the religious sphere, an effort to reconcile Hinduism and Islam is represented by the emergence of Sikhism, a religion that drew on both traditions but was explicitly neither Hindu nor Muslim. Centered in the Indian state of Punjab, Sikhism became the faith of millions in the sixteenth and seventeenth centuries, and from that time to the present Sikhs have played an important role in India's political and economic life.

Analyzing the Sources

What kind of man was Suleiman I, and how did he wield the almost unlimited power that was his as Ottoman sultan? The information contained in Busbecq's *Turkish Letters* provides some answers. In his sketch of

Suleiman, Busbecq captures the sultan's seriousness, strong sense of duty, and rather dour manner. That he also had a fierce and frightening temper is revealed by the episode toward the end of his life when he glowered into the tent to motivate the assassins of his son, Mustafa.

Several of Busbecq's observations reveal the extent of the sultan's autocratic power. On Busbecq's arrival at the Ottoman court, Suleiman was absent, so Busbecq began to negotiate with his prominent advisors, who warned Busbecq, however, that in the end only the sultan's opinion would matter. And at the close of his first audience with Suleiman, Busbecq concluded that the sultan's impatience and abrupt dismissal of his European visitors resulted from the resentment of someone "who deemed his wish was law" having to hear things that did not please him.

Busbecq then goes on to describe what he believes to be one of the Ottoman state's most admirable features, namely its merit-based system for making government appointments. According to Busbecq, advancement and honors in government go to those with merit and merit alone. Because birth means nothing, those who receive high office are "for the most part sons of shepherds or herdsmen." Here Busbecq is undoubtedly exaggerating. We know, for example, that promotion within the Ottoman administration was to a great extent merit-based, but that sons of court officials had advantages in the competition for appointments. It is certainly doubtful that sons of shepherds predominated.

Busbecq also has much to say about the formidable Ottoman army. He is awed by the army's size and its disciplined soldiers. He is particularly impressed by reports of how troops conserve their limited food rations while on long campaigns in Persia. He also is impressed by the Ottomans' skill as bowmen and their effective utilization of European artillery.

The Ottoman army was undoubtedly impressive. But here again, Busbecq's account might well contain an element of exaggeration. Why would he exaggerate? His letters were directed to another high-ranking Hapsburg diplomat, and Busbecq must have realized that at least some of what he wrote would be communicated to other key Hapsburg officials. Busbecq, so it seems, was trying to discourage the Hapsburgs from launching an ill-considered and premature attack on the Turks in Hungary, an undertaking that Busbecq believed would be catastrophic. He also was trying to convince the Hapsburgs that military and political reforms were in order.

Busbecq's letters also provide insights into why the empire began its slow decline soon after Suleiman's death. His description of the Turkish soldiers' reaction to the introduction of firearms (as opposed to artillery) is instructive. Because the new weapons broke frequently, were difficult to repair, and dirtied their users' hands, soldiers bitterly complained about having to use them. Significantly, Rustem, the chief vizier, on hearing their complaints quickly gave into their demands and withdrew the new weapons. This was a dangerous precedent. Over time the Ottoman army was slow to adopt new and improved weapons developed in the West, in part because of the prejudices described in this episode.

The dispute over the succession which led to the murder of Suleiman's popular and capable son Mustafa also did not bode well for the Ottoman state. Such disputes became a regular feature of Ottoman politics, distracting sultans and officials and poisoning relations between sultans and their sons. As a result of his actions, Suleiman was succeeded not by the capable Mustafa but by the drunkard Selim II, known to history as Selim the Sot.

The author of the next source, Father Paul Simon, differed markedly from Busbecq. While Busbecq was a widely traveled diplomat from an aristocratic family sent to the Ottoman court to negotiate a treaty, Father Simon was a comparatively unworldly and inexperienced Carmelite father sent to Persia for missionary work. Thus while Busbecq's position might have led him to exaggerate Ottoman strength, Father Simon's background helps explain the occasional examples of credulity and naivete we find in his report.

Father Simon presents Abbas I as a robust, image-conscious, serious, hard-working, and rather frightening authoritarian ruler. Heeding Machiavelli's advice that a successful prince should always strive to *appear* to have the various virtues his subjects esteem (even when he does not have them), Abbas eats frugally *while in public*, mixes freely with his subjects, and wears plain, unadorned clothes to show how different he is from his lavishly dressed predecessors. Such displays of humility, affability, and simplicity are for the public only, however. In private he eats what he wants, has no close friends, and without blinking orders the execution of people who have insulted him. We know from other accounts that the lavishness and opulence of Abbas's court was almost unrivalled. Machiavelli also would have approved other qualities of Abbas: his decisiveness, his frugality in giving gifts, his preoccupation with warfare, and his harsh treatment of potential rivals. Abbas executed or ruined princely and noble rivals and filled many administrative posts with slaves and people from the lower classes.

Abbas's approach to religion was also Machiavellian. Although Father Simon does not mention it, Abbas created many religious endowments and built numerous mosques to show his dedication to Islam. Yet Father Simon records that Abbas failed to "observe the Muslim law in many things." Furthermore, Abbas had an intellectual interest in Christianity, tolerated Christian worship (especially among the Christian women of his harem), and even allowed preaching by the Carmelites.

Although Father Simon expresses bewilderment over Abbas's religious beliefs, it seems clear from his account that his attitude toward Christianity was dictated more by politics than conviction. His favorable treatment of the Augustinian missionaries before Father Simon's arrival was undoubtedly motivated by his hopes that such treatment would encourage Spanish/Portuguese cooperation in his struggle against the Turks. When such cooperation was not forthcoming, Abbas's public ardor for Christianity cooled. It would appear that Abbas was a man without strong religious beliefs.

The opening passage from Jahangir's memoirs gives the impression that this powerful ruler/author was very different from his Persian contemporary, Abbas. Whereas Abbas in public ate rice and water and dressed in simple linen robes, Jahangir began his reign with a public coronation ceremony that with its display of jewels, throne, crowns, carpets, gold censers, musicians, and gem-clad youthful dancers was lavish beyond belief. Jahangir reveled in pomp and splendor and made no effort to hide his enjoyment of life as an emperor. It is as if Jahangir sought to secure his subjects' obedience by astounding them with his opulence and god-like magnificence.

Jahangir, however, resembles Abbas in a number of ways. Like Abbas, he wore his Muslim faith lightly and tolerated other faiths. For reasons he explains in this excerpt, he continued to tolerate Hinduism, as had his father, Akbar. Except for widow burning *(sati)*, which he sought to curtail, he allowed his Hindu subjects to continue their "superstitions." The policies set forth in his Twelve Decrees are meant to benefit Hindus and Muslims alike, and he utilized and richly rewarded capable Hindus such as Rai Rayan in his administration.

Both Abbas and Jahangir realized that a successful ruler must rigorously enforce laws and use force, even in ways that seem cruel, to preserve his power and maintain order. Jahangir states that without "severity and occasional extinction of human life" human beings would behave "like wild beasts." Unlike Abbas, who meted out "justice" without much forethought or afterthought, Jahangir agonized over some of his judgments. Even the battle deaths of seventeen thousand (!) Afghan bandits caused him no little pain, and he decided to spare the lives of the Afghan prisoners taken in battle.

Another pillar of Jahanigir's administration was his concern for public works, the fair treatment of his subjects, and the honesty of his officials. All these issues are addressed in the Twelve Decrees Jahangir issued at the beginning of his reign. How well his decrees were implemented is a good question. One would imagine that the fifth decree, which banned the making and selling of wine, was not rigorously enforced. Jahangir never lost his taste for wine and opium, and their use undoubtedly contributed to his death at the relatively early age of 58.

* * *

As discussed in the section, "Why These Sources," one of the values of Selim I's letter to Shah Ismail is that it illuminates both a contemporary event (the political/religious conflict between the Safavids and Ottomans that erupted into war in 1514) *and* some fundamental tenets of Islam. Students can discover references to several Islamic beliefs, especially in the first paragraph of the letter: the existence of a single supreme being, Allah; the authority of the Muslim holy book, the Qur'an; the prophetic role of Muhammad; the existence of Heaven and Hell; the reality of an afterlife; the need to earn Allah's blessing to gain salvation; Allah's punishment of those who go against his word; and Islam's claim to be the one true religion.

Selim's thunderous denunciation of Ismail at the end of the long second paragraph generates more heat than light about the Shi'ite-Sunni feud, but the reference to "the cursing of the legitimate caliphs" does touch upon one of the main sources of dissension between the two parties, namely the issue of the necessary qualifications and exact function of the successors of Muhammad, or caliphs (with Shi'ites insisting that only members of the Prophet's clan, specifically the descendants of Muhammad's daughter, Fatima, and her husband, Ali, could qualify). Selim, who in this letter never claims to be caliph, nonetheless depicts himself as the defender of Islam against nonbelievers and heretics.

Was Selim motivated entirely by religion? Several passages show he also had territory and power on his mind. Ismail, according to Selim's letter, is guilty not just of grievous religious crimes but also of the political sins of territorial usurpation, tyranny, and self-glorification. Furthermore, at the conclusion of the letter, when he urges Ismail to reconsider his actions, Selim demands that the Shi'ite prince return the territory he has "violently" and "illegitimately" seized. Selim's demands resulted from the fact that when the charismatic Ismail became shah, he won many followers in eastern Anatolia, some of whom opposed Selim 's accession and were in revolt against local and provincial Ottoman officials. So when Selim's forces smashed Ismail's army at Chaldiran in August 1514, it was every bit as much a political as a religious victory.

Students should also consider the timing of the letter. When he composed it, Selim already was preparing his troops for an invasion of Ismail's territory. Furthermore, Selim assuredly knew that the likelihood of Ismail's acceptance of Selim's demands was essentially nil. So why send the letter? There are several possible explanations, but the most likely is that he needed to convince his troops of the justice of his cause despite the fact he was attacking another Muslim ruler.

The next selection, another excerpt from Busbecq's *Turkish Letters,* provides a brief but revealing look at the position of women in Turkish society. In agreement with the view of some Catholic clergy during the European Middle Ages, Muslims considered women a threat to male virtue. The Muslims' reasoning behind this assumption was quite different, however. In Europe, women tended to be the temptresses whose carnality lures men into sin. In the Muslim view of things, men, who desire every woman they see, are the cause of the problem. Nonetheless, even though women in Turkish society were not the problem, they became the basis of the solution. The solution was that wives must be veiled and live in seclusion, especially wives from the upper classes. And concubines, who have been purchased or won as booty, serve as added outlets for male sexual urges until they are discarded and replaced by other women.

Ottoman Turkish women were not completely without rights. The children of concubines had full legal equality with children of legal wives, and bearing children for their owner was a way slave/concubines could win their freedom. Wives exercise authority within the confines of their homes, and a wife is guaranteed the return of her dowry if she is divorced from her husband and she is not at fault. It is also possible for women to divorce their husbands, although with "more difficulty."

Before reading and discussing Abu'l Fazl's description of Hindu beliefs and practices, we should remind our students of two points. First, Abu'l Fazl was a close friend and advisor of Emperor Akbar, and he heartily supported Akbar's efforts to harmonize Hinduism and Islam. Thus in these passages from the *Akbarnama* he clearly is interested in highlighting the *similarities* between the two faiths, not the differences. Second, although Abu'l Fazl was an intelligent and learned individual, even he could not possibly have grasped the almost limitless diversity of Hinduism's cults, doctrines, and ways of life during his years in India. Thus his account gives an impression of more unity in Hindu beliefs than actually existed.

If Abu'l Fazl found it difficult to grasp the complexities of Hinduism even after his discussions with "many learned and upright men," our students also can be expected to encounter some problems on reading these excerpts from the *Akbarnama*. Nonetheless, they should be able to gain important insights from the selection. Abu'l Fazl, for example, presents an accurate summation of basic Hindu belief in Brahman, the uncreated, eternal, infinite, and transcendent principle that is the sole reality and the ultimate cause, source, and goal of existence. Because Hindus believe that Brahman causes the universe and all beings to emanate from itself, Abu'l Fazl would like his Muslim readers to believe there is a kernel of monotheism in Hinduism. Brahma, Vishnu, and Rudra (more commonly known as Shiva) constituted in one form the three aspects of Brahman, and thus resemble the trinitarian beliefs of Christianity, like Islam, a monotheistic faith. Similarly, Abu'l Fazl claims that the idols of the Hindus were not true objects of worship but merely means to draw the mind toward the contemplation of ultimate reality.

Abu'l Fazl's descriptions of caste and *karma* both show how Hindus believed that nothing in a person's life was accidental; everything was ordained by the caste status of one's parents, and more broadly, by one's behavior in previous incarnations. His description also reveals why the seeming simplicity of the four basic varna groups quickly became extraordinarily complicated when individuals from different groups intermarried. His description also shows the low regard for women in traditional Hinduism. Improper behavior in a previous life by a male result-ed in rebirth into a lower caste or *as a female*. Conversely, a life of special virtue might result in woman's reincarnation as a man.

Before finishing with Abu'l Fazl's account of these Hindu practices, students should be given an opportunity to discuss some broader implications of Hinduism for India's historical development. How, for example, might the caste system have affected the Indians' approach to education? How might the Hindu belief in the physical world as an illusion have affected the development of science as a field of study? How might the belief in reincarnation have encouraged what many perceive as a "fatalism" among its followers? Students usually achieve a number of excellent insights while discussing these questions.

After having been introduced to some of the characteristics of Hinduism and Islam, our students have the opportunity in the last section to analyze some of the key doctrines of yet another Asian religion, Sikhism, whose founder, Nanak, lived between 1469 and 1539. Nanak's message of salvation through total and uncompromising devotion to God was not unique. Mendicant Hindu *sants* (saints) of India's Punjab region, most notably Kabir (1440–1518), a poet and religious reformer, had already sung the praises of the all-encompassing and merciful Divine Name and had equally denounced the empty externals of religion such as sectarianism, caste, pilgrimages, fasting, idol worship, and ritual. Likewise, within Islam, Sufi mystics of the Punjab had preached and lived a strikingly similar religious vision. The legend that Hindus and Muslims alike claimed Kabir's corpse as the mortal remains of one of their holymen tells us much about the rich religious syncretism of the Punjab, homeland of Sikh monotheism.

Nanak's claim to greatness and religious originality is not vitiated by our realization that his mystical vision and teachings grew out of a fertile Hindu-Sufi religious environment. Nanak's genius lay in his ability to articulate coherently, clearly and with compelling beauty the way to mystical union with God, or, put another way, the path of salvation. Through his poetry, from which we draw our selections, Nanak became the father of a new Indian monotheistic faith.

With some professorial guidance, students should be able to discern elements of Islamic and Hindu beliefs in Nanak's hymns. A bigger challenge for them would be to compare and contrast the religious messages on Nanak and one of his contemporaries, the European religious reformer and founder of Protestantism, Martin Luther, whose major ideas are set forth in Chapter 1, sources #1 and #2.

The similarities between Luther's and Nanak's religious visions are as follows. Both had a vision of a single, absolutely sovereign deity. Compare each man's notion of God's unique majesty. Both also rejected rituals and other "good works" as a means of salvation, believing that faith alone saves. Each also emphasized the personal, internal relationship between the believer and God. For Nanak it was a faith and devotion very close to classic bhaktism, a late development in Hinduism that emphasized personal reverence for and worship of a Hindu deity such as Krishna, Shiva, or Rama. For Luther it was total faith in Jesus Christ the Savior along the lines spelled out in Paul's Letter to the Romans. Both men were also predestinationist. Luther taught it was God's choice who should be saved and damned, while Nanak wrote, "By his (the Divine Name's) order some are pardoned, some are by his order always caused to wander about in transmigration."

The differences between the two theologies are just as significant. Luther, obviously, was a Christian, who began from the position that Jesus Christ was humanity's God-incarnate savior. His vision of divine reality was shaped by 1,500 years of Christian tradition. At the same time he preached a narrowly sectarian message, violently attacking other Christian interpretations of God's relationship to humanity, and he especially excoriated the traditions of Roman Catholicism. Such sectarianism is, as we have seen, fairly common within the Judaeo-Christian-Islamic tradition of ethical monotheism, where the notion of absolute right and wrong predominates.

Nanak, as someone working largely within a Hindu tradition, was broadly tolerant. He retained many Hindu beliefs, such as the concepts of dharma (Hindu moral law), moksha (the separation of self from the physical world and the merging of the soul with Brahman), and the notion of innumerable worlds and countless intermediate deities between humanity and the Divine One. He also accepted the Hindu insight that there are limitless paths to the truth. Even though he claimed to have special revelation of the Divine Name, he acknowledged that others, Hindus and Muslim alike, served the Name.

Both Luther and Nanak claimed that there exists a special medium through which the human can know and believe in God. For Luther it was the divinely inspired Bible; for Nanak it was himself, the divinely inspired Guru. Finally, Nanak taught in true Indian fashion that the Name, like Brahman, is contained in every living creature ("You, O Hari! The one Supreme Being, are unintermittingly contained in every body."). In Luther's theology there is no hint of pantheism, a notion deemed heretical throughout the history of Christianity.

Other Ways to Use the Sources

1. Compare and contrast the religious issues facing Jahangir and Abbas I and their respective religious policies.
2. Compose an imaginary letter written by Shah Ismail in response to the letter he received from Selim I.
3. What qualities of leadership did Suleiman, Abbas I, and Jahangir have in common? How did their leadership styles differ?
4. By now your students have had the opportunity to study a fair number of sources that shed light on the status of women in early modern societies (Mayer, Woensam, Schön, the Nuremberg ordinances, Busbecq, Abu'l Fazl). Using these sources and material such as lectures or other course readings, we have used the following assignment with some success:

   You are on the staff of a major museum that has decided to set up an exhibit on the subject of women in the sixteenth and seventeenth centuries. You have been given the job of planning the exhibit, and, as a first step, must develop a proposal for the display. Your proposal should consist of the following parts:

   a. A slogan or title for the display. It should express the central theme of the exhibit.
   b. An explanation (about one paragraph in length) of why that theme is appropriate and historically justifiable.
   c. A description of the contents of your display room. Which aspects of women's lives will you include? Remember, your space is limited, although you can divide it up as you like. How will you present the history you choose to include? What kinds of artifacts, documents, or scenarios will you use? (Assume the museum has just received a huge grant, and you have an unlimited budget.) This should be the longest section of your proposal.

d. A defense of your selections for the display. Why do you consider the choices you made to be appropriate and historically justifiable?

Your proposal should be about three pages long.

5. Compose a commentary on Nanak's religious vision by an orthodox Muslim teacher.

C H A P T E R

4

Continuity and Change in East and Southeast Asia

Chapter Theme

This chapter has three sections, each emphasizing a different theme in the history of Southeast and East Asia in the sixteenth and seventeenth centuries. The first section, on Confucianism, has the same goal as the section on Hinduism and Islam in Chapter 3. For students just beginning their study of global history in the post-1500 era, it provides information on basic Confucian concepts, while for continuing students it offers fresh perspectives on a subject that should already be familiar to them.

The second section focuses on the political problems of sixteenth- and early-seventeenth-century China and Japan. For Japan, aristocratic rebellion and the breakdown of central authority caused a century-long civil war that lasted until the early 1600s. The selection we have included on Japan, "The Laws of Military Households," reveals some of the strategies used by the victors in the civil war—the Tokugawa clan— to stabilize Japan after interminable decades of turmoil. For China a period of stability and responsible government gave way in the late 1500s to an era characterized by inept emperors, military slackness, peasant rebellion, and bureaucratic in-fighting, all signs that the Ming dynasty was declining rapidly. China's political recovery under the Manchu (Qing) dynasty, which succeeded the Ming in 1644, comes only at the end of the seventeenth century and is taken up in Chapter 7.

The third and last section introduces another ongoing theme of Part I of *The Human Record's* second volume, namely the impact of Europeans on the world, in this case, of course, East and Southeast Asia. The two sources we have chosen illustrate the exclusion of Europeans from Japan and some of the difficulties Europeans faced as they sought to establish a commercial presence in Southeast Asia. Chinese reactions to Westerners are dealt with in Chapter 7.

Why These Sources?

Our section on Confucianism begins with a new selection to the fourth edition of *The Human Record*, excerpts from the seventeenth-century morality book, *Meritorious Deeds at no Cost*. It replaces the excerpts from the Italian Jesuit Matteo Ricci's *Memoirs* in which he describes some basic features of Confucianism and the Chinese Civil Service Examination system. We believe this new selection is livelier and better reveals how Confucianism affected Chinese notions of class and gender. It also is in keeping with a long-term goal of *The Human Record*, that of keeping the number of "European observer" sources to a minimum.

Selections from two works by Kaiberra Ekiken, an important seventeenth-century writer, represent Confucianism in Japan. These educational treatises clearly state Confucian educational principles, and in the sections devoted to raising girls, they provide insights into the status of women in Japan.

The next selection, consisting of two brief biographies of Ming era merchants by Wang Daokun, brings together the worlds of Confucianism and commerce. By showing how merchants themselves were influenced by Confucian ethical teachings, and by giving examples of friction between merchants and Confucian scholar-officials, we are able to see how Confucian values permeated Chinese life at many levels, and how they influenced China's commercial development.

This section on Confucian culture in China and Japan concludes with two Chinese paintings, Zhang Hung's *Landscape of Shixie Hill* and Sheng Maoye's *Scholars Contemplating a Waterfall*. They introduce students to one of the glories of Chinese culture, landscape painting, and reveal how China's learned elite viewed nature and humanity's place in it. Using these paintings with material provided in Chapter 5, students should also be able to make some comparisons between Chinese and European views of the natural world.

The next section, on politics in Japan and China, begins with The Laws Governing Military Households, issued by Tokugawa Hidetada 1615. With its outline of the key points in the Tokugawa political program, it is an obvious choice to illustrate Japan's political recovery in the early seventeenth century. Also, by examining the "solutions" it proposes, students can infer what were the root causes of Japan's political breakdown during the 1500s.

In this edition, Yang Lien's "Memorial to Emperor Ming Xizong Concerning Eunuch Wei Zhongxian" replaces Zhang Tingyu's *History of the Ming*. Both writings express the dismay of scholar-officials over the rise of eunuch power during the late Ming Era. This new source has the advantage of having been written during the Ming Era itself rather than a century after the fact, as was the case with Zhang's history.

This chapter's concluding section focuses on the West's impact on East Asia. At least two other sources would have been needed to present a reasonably thorough picture of the different ways the West affected the region—one on the Philippines and another on China. The Philippines was the one area in the region that succumbed to Spanish political domination, and as a result its population largely was converted to Christianity. The Chinese permitted small amounts of closely regulated trade with Europeans and tolerated the presence of Jesuit missionaries in Beijing because of their knowledge of science, mathematics, clocks, and guns, but in general they viewed Europeans and their religion with disdain and condescension. Several sources on the Chinese reaction to the West are included in Chapters 7 and 10.

The two sources that make up this chapter's last section shed light on the problems encountered by Europeans in Japan and Southeast Asia. The Japanese Closed Country Edict of 1639 includes the provisions of the exclusion policy and provides insight into why the Tokugawa leaders instituted it. The letter written to the Board of Directors of the Dutch East India Company by one of its agents in 1635 illustrates how even the aggressive and well-armed Dutch had to make special efforts to avoid provoking their trading partners in the region.

Analyzing the Sources

The excerpts from *Meritorious Deeds at No Cost* consists of no less than 157 recommendations for "meritorious deeds," touching on situations and human relationships that range from farm etiquette to treatment of a faithful dog. The challenge for students will be to discover the underlying themes of the recommendations in order to gain a sense of Confucianism's general principles.

It is significant, first of all, that various social groups discussed in *Meritorious Deeds* all have their own special codes of ethics. Doing "good deeds" means one thing for a member of the landed gentry and something quite different for a merchant or a peasant. This is in keeping with one of Confucius's basic teachings—that a healthy society depends on members of various social groups knowing their proper place in society and behaving accordingly. The focus on a "healthy society" is also worth noting. Students should be able to see that overwhelmingly the precepts listed in this selection encourage behavior and attitudes that will lead to harmony and peace in society. They deal with friendships, family, and relations among friends and neighbors and between children and parents, rich and the poor, merchants and customers, students and teachers, landlords and peasants, and subjects and rulers. Its orientation is this-worldly, not other-worldly.

Along the same lines, students should also keep in mind that the popularity of "morality books" in seventeenth-century China resulted from their promise that if people conscientiously and dutifully performed the recommended good deeds they would be rewarded with *worldly* success. Again, this contrasts with Christianity, Islam, Hinduism, Buddhism, and other major religions, in which a spiritual reward *after death* was the major incentive to behave according to a prescribed moral code.

Before focusing on the underlying Confucian principles in *Meritorious Deeds*, let us first examine the differences in the expectations and demands for the various social groups. One of the things that sets the local gentry and students apart from the other groups is that they, as members of China's elite, have a responsibility to teach, correct, and inspire those below them on the social scale. Gentry are urged to "rectify your own conduct and transform the common people," and "influence other families to cherish good deeds," while scholars should "instruct the common people in the virtues of loyalty and filial piety." Members of these groups are expected to encourage their social inferiors to read and study, respect their parents, settle disputes without recourse to lawsuits, and admonish them when they have committed misdeeds. Most importantly, scholars and members of the gentry should serve as models of morality for the lower orders and children. The common people and the young learn by imitating the deeds and attitudes of their social betters and their elders. Thus scholars and members of the gentry should center their lives on self-examination and self-improvement.

The author has different, and somewhat lower, expectations for merchants, craftsmen, and peasants. Peasants are expected to show up for work, respect property lines, and avoid petty disputes and feuds that would disrupt the village community. Similarly, craftsmen should take pride in their work and treat their customers honestly. Both peasants and craftsmen should respect their masters and not complain, even when they believe they have been treated poorly. This is an expression of the Confucian doctrine that common people owe deference to their social betters. The author has rather low expectations for merchants. For them, most of the recommended good deeds involve restraining themselves from cheating or taking advantage of their customers.

Another point worth noting is that these recommendations seem to be mainly directed toward individuals who are in charge of households, are involved in trade, are studying for the civil service examinations, and have concubines. In other words, the author seems definitely to have *men* in mind when compiling his list of "meritorious deeds." Women are not disparaged.

To the contrary, meritorious men will not gossip about women, comment on their "sexiness," or think lewd thoughts about them. Chaste women are to be respected. Nonetheless, for this author striving for morality is essentially a male activity.

The last part of the selection, "People in General," summarizes general precepts that are scattered throughout the previous sections. Significantly, the section begins with a number of good deeds related to the key Confucian concept of filial piety, the need to be obey one's parents and to treat them with patience, respect, and honor. Another key Confucian principle finds expression in the various "good deeds" that pertain to the general welfare of society, something that will be achieved when all members of society treat one another with mutual respect. It is especially important for those who are well off and powerful not to be condescending to the poor, or neglectful of their needs. An essential teaching of Confucius is expressed in the last line, "In all undertakings, think of others."

The selections by Kaiberra Ekiken provide numerous insights into Confucianism and family and gender relationships in Japan. A good place to start would be to ask students about specific Confucian qualities of Ekiken's educational system. This is not a particularly difficult question because both treatises are full of Confucian principles and values. Notable examples of Confucian influence would be the choice of books for boys once they reach the age of ten. Confucian texts are used exclusively. In addition, the content of the schooling Ekiken recommends is designed to shape the young peoples' values and behavior, rather than to hone their intellects or fill their minds with lots of information. The degree to which Ekiken emphasizes obedience and conformity is also noteworthy. Young people are to revere and obey their parents and above all be discouraged from "doing their own thing."

This emphasis on conformity and obedience in Ekiken's treatises explains why the Tokugawa shoguns found Confucianism so attractive. Another appeal is that for boys, especially the aristocratic boys Ekiken has in mind, the sole purpose of education is to prepare them for careers as just and responsible rulers and administrators. This fits in with the Tokugawa goal of transforming the contentious and rebellion-prone Japanese aristocrats into pliant, obedient and high-minded public servants. The shoguns also would have approved Ekiken's interest in preserving Japan's class structure and in assuring that his students know their place in Japanese society. His aristocratic students, both boys and girls, learn that they must adhere to higher standards than people from the lower classes. When they reached adulthood and assumed their duties as domain rulers and administrators, boys were to be conscious of their role as models for their social inferiors.

In their comparison of boys and girls' education, our students will have little difficulty coming up with plenty of differences. Once they reach the age of seven, boys and girls go their separate ways. Boys come under the tutelage of a teacher, while girls continue to be educated by their parents; boys are taught to read so they can study the Confucian Classics, while girls remain illiterate. In addition to the qualities of filial piety and obedience, important for both boys and girls, passivity is a attribute that girls in particular must cultivate.

But in the most general sense Ekiken's goals for boys and girls are quite similar. Education for both is centered on inculcating attitudes and principles of behavior suitable for their roles as adults. The roles of boys and girls are of course far different. Boys become public servants and heads of households. Girls, who have been taught to be obedient daughters, leave their natal homes after marriage and become obedient wives and daughters-in-law. Their role is to bear children and manage servants. Their obedience to their husbands and fathers-in-law and their tolerance of their servants' failings (after all, not much can be expected from the lower classes) will ensure harmonious families, which in turn provide the foundation for a stable society.

If students have been assigned the material in Chapter 1 on women in European society (sources 6–8), they should be encouraged to make some comparisons between European and Japanese attitudes toward women. There are of course major similarities. Women in both societies are expected to be obedient to fathers and husbands. In Japan, there is more emphasis on obedience to in-laws, reflecting the fact that in Japan a newly married couple moves into the household of the groom, while in Europe it was becoming increasingly common for new couples to establish themselves in separate households. There are other differences. In Europe more emphasis is placed on the mutual responsibilities of husbands and wives, and as several sources reveal, it was more likely that women would be taught to read and write.

Before discussing Wang Daokung's biographical sketches it would be a good idea to point out that the author was a rarity in sixteenth-century Chinese society. He was an official in the imperial bureaucracy who came from a family of merchants rather than the gentry. Thus, although he was familiar with Confucianism and its anti-business bias, his background made him sympathetic to the interests and activities of merchants.

As presented by Wang, both Zhu Jiefu and Gentleman Wang lived according to the teachings of Confucius. Zhu was studious, fair, and dutiful, saw virtue as its own reward (he refused payment after saving his fellow merchants from the false accusations of "two scoundrels" who took them to court), revered his ancestors, and was respectful of government authority (accepting without complaint his banishment to the frontier army at the end of his life). Gentleman Wang's outstanding characteristics were concern for the welfare of the poor and his ability to mediate disputes. His life also shows that one did not have to abandon moral principles to prosper: because he treated his customers fairly, they thronged to him; the 1000 taels he paid on behalf of Magistrate Xu ultimately was repaid.

In addition to revealing the importance of ancestor worship and the proper burial of the dead in Chinese society, these two biographies also provide insights into the status of women. Note how both Zhu Jiefu and his father have concubines in addition to their wives. It is also revealing that when the author summarizes the fruits of Gentleman Wang's virtuous life, he mentions wealth, a long life, and the presence of thirty *sons* and *grandsons* living in his home. The laws of probability suggest he also had daughters and granddaughters, but they were not considered as rewards for his virtuous behavior.

The most important point to be derived from this source is the adversarial relationship between merchants and government officials. The officials did little to encourage or support business activity and instead subjected merchants to arbitrary decisions, extraordinary demands for taxes, and unfavorable court decisions. This reflects in part the social background of the scholar-officials, most of whom came from the landed gentry, and in part the low status of merchants in the Confucian scheme of things. This is in distinct contrast to the policies of most European governments, which especially in this the age of European mercantilism considered the encouragement of commerce a priority.

Our section on Confucianism concludes with two paintings, Zhang Hung's *Landscape of Shixie Hill* and Sheng Maoye's *Scholars Contemplating a Waterfall*. They fit into a section on Confucianism in part because painting along with calligraphy was valued and cultivated by many Chinese scholars. In addition, Confucianism along with Daoism and several other currents in Chinese intellectual and spiritual life had an important influence on the themes and subject matter of Chinese landscape painting.

There is always a great deal of subjectivity involved in interpreting paintings, so we can expect that different students will see different things as they attempt to analyze the "inner spirit" of nature and "humanity's relationship to the natural world" in each painting. Most should be able to see that the two paintings present two quite different views of nature. In Zhang's painting the overall impression is of nature's fullness and vitality. Trees cover every bit of space with the exception of the very top of the mountain peak. The forest meshes with the stream and the outcropping of rocks to impart a feeling of harmonious beauty. In Sheng's painting, on the other hand, the craggy, dark, moss-covered, and thorny trees that appear in the foreground against desolate and barren hills convey a sense of melancholy, even dread. Waterfalls, which figure prominently in both paintings, reveal nature's power and suggest at the same time both change and permanence.

Nature is not something for human beings to dominate, alter, or control. Rather, in its contemplation, human beings can gain insight into the meaning of existence. There are several man-made huts and a bridge in Zhang's painting, but they are tiny structures dwarfed by the grandeur and magnificence of their natural surroundings. Each has been built to fit harmoniously and unobtrusively into the surrounding forest. But the contemplation of nature is not for everyone. In each painting, the servants look away, disinterested, leaving the learned and sensitive scholar-gentlemen to seek meaning in what they view.

* * *

The "Laws Governing the Military Households," when read in conjunction with the Japanese exclusion edicts, which appear in the next section, outline the Tokugawa strategy to bring order to Japan after its tumultuous sixteenth century. The regulations for military (aristocratic) households reveal the Tokugawa belief that Japan's political disintegration had resulted from lawlessness, the blurring of class lines, feuding aristocrats, and the breakdown of central government. These rules, handed down by Tokugawa Ieyasu and guided by Confucian principles, offer solutions to each of these problems.

Articles 1–4 and 12 direct the samurai and daimyo to lead lives of military service, frugality, sobriety, and obedience to the law. Such discipline will create an effective ruling class and inspire the lower classes to adhere to the moral code suitable for their station in life. To acquire these qualities, military training is not enough. The study of literature, that is, Confucian literature, is also necessary to produce high-minded and dutiful aristocrats who can provide effective service to their lords and serve as models for their social inferiors. Articles 6–9 are intended to subordinate the daimyo to the shogun in Edo. Castle building, any kind of "innovation," and even marriages must now be approved by the shogun. In addition, regular daimyo visits to Edo, usually lasting a year, are to be required. These edicts preserve the daimyo's power within their domains (see articles 4 and 13) but limit their ability to challenge the shogun's authority or foment rebellion.

Several articles show Confucian influence. Articles 5, 10, and 11 are all intended to ensure the stability of Japanese society by preventing geographical mobility and the blurring of class distinctions. The proclamation concludes by urging daimyo to appoint "able men" to subordinate offices and to exercise moderation and self-control. All of these are statements of time-honored Confucian principles.

While Japan was on its way to political recovery in the early seventeenth century, as is revealed in the next document, Yang Lien's "Memorial to Emperor Ming Xizong," late Ming China was suffering from court intrigue and misrule, or, in the case of the emperor, no rule at all. Yang's decision to write and send this memorandum to the emperor was an act of great courage or great stupidity, depending on one's point of view. He probably knew that the emperor, who was more dedicated to carpentry than government, would do nothing about eunuch Wei. And he also knew that Wei would not tolerate his disloyalty. Indeed in 1625 Yang was accused of treason, tortured, and executed on Wei's orders.

One question to consider, therefore, is why, given the political circumstances at the imperial court, did Yang write and send the memorandum. One can only guess at what finally drove him to take this step, but the memorandum itself provides some clues. His sense of honesty, duty to the state, and personal responsibility seem to have played a role. He also felt bound by a promise he had made to the emperor's father to do all he could to make his son a sage and an honest ruler. Most of all, however, as a high official of state whose view of the world was shaped by the high standards of Confucian morality, Yang was outraged by Wei's power and behavior. Yang seems to have reached a point where "he couldn't take it anymore."

What was there about Wei that drove Yang beyond the point of tolerance? He was the antithesis of everything a dedicated disciple of Confucius would value and respect. Confucianism valued erudition won through long years of study; Wei was illiterate. Confucianism viewed harmonious families as the foundation for society; Wei had himself castrated as an adult to advance his political career. Confucianism taught the virtue of decorum and restraint; Wei was uninhibited. Confucianism taught the importance of etiquette; Wei rode his horse in the palace grounds and ignored court protocol. Confucianism taught that good government rested on the shoulders of the emperor; Wei bypassed the emperor to increase his own power. In addition to these general characteristics, Wei was guilty of innumerable acts of treachery, greed, and cruelty. As a result, the government was in shambles.

But was it all Wei's fault? Certainly the emperor must share much of the blame. After all, this was the young man who after eunuch Wei made a travesty of court etiquette by riding his horse in the palace grounds shot the horse but did nothing to the rider! Yang pulls out all the stops to make the emperor behave responsibly. He cites examples of previous emperors who had cracked down on wayward eunuchs; he draws a grim picture of the state of the government; he appeals to the emperor's sense of pride and the memory of his father; and he promises adulation and acclaim if he punishes Wei. Nothing worked, and Yang paid with his life.

Yang was correct in warning the emperor of the dangers he faced. The conflict between scholar-officials and the eunuchs paralyzed the government, and Wei and his entourage certainly lacked the inclination and expertise to deal with the host of diplomatic and internal problems China was facing. Just seventeen years after Wei committed suicide, revolt and foreign invasion brought the Ming Era to an end.

* * *

The Closed Country Edict of 1635 and the Edict for the Exclusion of the Portuguese (1639) are key steps in the near total isolation of Japan from the outside world that was established under the Tokugawa. Clearly, what mainly worried the Tokugawa was Christianity, which in the sixteenth century had made approximately a half a million devotees, some of them from powerful daimyo families. Convinced that Christianity was a potential source of rebellion, in 1612 the shoguns ordered an end to missionary activity and commanded all Christians in shogunal domains to renounce their faith. Despite subsequent persecutions, Christianity still had enough followers in 1635 to be addressed once more in the Closed Country Edict. The requirement that Japanese no longer travel abroad and that Japanese returning from abroad would be put to death were both aimed at the suppression of Christianity rather than trade.

The remaining regulations in the edict show that the shoguns did not oppose trade as such, but only trade they could not control. As long as foreign merchants brought in no priests and followed the rules set down by the government, they could trade in Japan. But the English found the Japanese market unprofitable and withdrew in 1623; a year later the Spanish were excluded because of their involvement in missionary activity. Then, following the suppression of a major Christian revolt in western Kyushu, the edict banning the Portuguese was promulgated. For the next century and a half foreign commerce was limited to one Dutch ship per year and an insignificant amount of trade with China and Korea.

Even in those places in East Asia where Europeans were free to trade, life was not easy, as the 1655 letter written by the harried agent of the Dutch East India Company to his bosses clearly shows. His main worry was the king of Siam who was peeved because the Dutch had reneged on their promise to support his efforts to suppress a local rebellion and because the Dutch had blockaded the port of Tennasserim to keep out foreign competition. What is interesting about this episode is the timid response of the Dutch, a response that shows their limited options and their tenuous position. The agent at the Siamese court, Westerwoldt, found himself in the awkward position of first denying the existence of the Tennasserim blockade, and then after learning that it had indeed taken place, meekly listening to the dressing down he received from the Siamese king and his councilors. He feared for his life and considered escaping, but abandoned the plan when he was warned that this would only make the Siamese king even angrier. Westerwoldt concluded that the Dutch could save themselves only by making good their promise of sending aid to the king.

The idea of the Dutch desperately trying to stay in the good graces of this Southeast Asian king and passively suffering his insults may seem strange to readers who imagine episodes of well-armed, aggressive Europeans having their way with African and Asian rulers. Instead, these events show some of the somber realities facing the Dutch in Southeast Asia at this point. Although they were clearly on their way to becoming the preponderant European power in southeast Asian waters, they were still facing competition from the English and the once dominant Portuguese. They lacked the naval strength and manpower to coerce rulers, such as the king of Siam, who were able to play off one European power from the others. With war being fought against Portugal and England, the probable end of trade with Japan, and an unsure future in Siam, it is no wonder this letter has a gloomy tone.

Other Ways to Use the Sources

1. Suppose Wang Daokun wrote another series of biographies in which he describes the lives of "bad merchants." In two pages write the biography of such a merchant: "Gentleman Wu."
2. Using Kaiberra Ekiken's educational writings as a source for your ideas, compose a list of "meritorious deeds" that would be appropriate for women in Confucian society.
3. Compose a memoir written by a Japanese daimyo in which he describes how his life and his family's lives changed after the takeover of the Tokugawa.
4. Compose a position paper written in the early seventeenth century by a high official in the service of the Tokugawa clan in which he defends the position, "Japan should follow a rigid policy of isolation." Compose a position paper written by an official given the job of defending the opposite position: "Japan would be ill-served by isolating itself from the outside world."

C H A P T E R
5

Europe and the Americas in an Age of Science, Economic Growth, and Revolution

Chapter Theme

Change and innovation, as had been the case in the Middle Ages, the Renaissance, and the Reformation era remain the key themes in European history from the mid-seventeenth to the early nineteenth century. The changes that took place in these centuries, however, were more rapid and profound, more destructive to tradition, and influenced people over a wider geographical area. They affected not just Europe itself, but also Europe's giant neighbor to the east, Russia, and Europe's offshoots in the American colonies.

The most striking changes took place in the spheres of politics and ideas. The Scientific Revolution reached its climax in 1687 with the publication of Isaac Newton's *On the Mathematical Principles of Natural Philosophy*. After Newton, intellectuals and educated Europeans increasingly came to grasp science's enormous implications for religion, philosophy, social thought, and the future of humanity. During the eighteenth-century Enlightenment, intellectuals inspired by the methodology and promise of science advanced an agenda characterized by rationalism, secularism, social criticism, and a belief in human progress.

Political changes in Europe were just as momentous. During the seventeenth century, England experienced two revolutions, the English (or Puritan) Revolution between 1642 and 1660 and the Glorious Revolution of 1688–1689. Together they spelled defeat for the principle of divine right absolutism, established a government controlled by an elected parliament, and guaranteed basic individual liberties. Revolution erupted in France in 1789 with even greater force. The ideals of political and social equality, nationalism, and the very concept of revolution as an instrument of change all were products of France's revolution.

In eastern Europe and across the Atlantic, important political changes also took place. Beginning with the reforms of Peter the Great (r.1689–1725), the Russians became the first people to confront the issue of Westernization. And, between the 1780s and 1810s, the thirteen colonies on North America's Atlantic coast and the Spanish and Portuguese colonies in Latin America all won their independence through armed struggle.

In economics Europe's commercial center continued to shift to the north and west, until by the late 1700s, Great Britain moved ahead of its rivals, France and the Netherlands, to become the world's leading commercial power. New markets in the Americas and growing European commercial activity in Africa and Asia meant that world trade reached its highest level in history during the eighteenth century. In much of Europe, especially Great Britain, the Netherlands, and France, that complex mixture of attitudes, institutions, and practices we know as capitalism increasingly came to dominate agriculture, manufacturing, and trade. Elements of Europe's command economy, represented by mercantilism, came under attack, and its traditional economy, represented by guilds and vestiges of manorialism, weakened. Most importantly, with the increased mechanization of England's textile industry in the 1760s, one of the most profound transformations in human history, the Industrial Revolution, was underway.

Why These Sources?

The impact of science on European thought is the subject of the first section in Chapter 5. The Scientific Revolution has already been introduced in Chapter 1 with Galileo's letter to Grand Duchess Christina. Galileo's letter was included there because the controversies surrounding Galileo's ideas fit into one of that chapter's central themes, namely Europe's unsettled intellectual climate in the sixteenth and early seventeenth centuries. Returning to the topic of European science in Chapter 5, we begin with a selection from Francis Bacon's *New Organon*. Of the many important scientific writings from the seventeenth century, we chose this one because it so clearly enunciates what became an article of faith for Europeans—that science has the power to provide human beings with the knowledge and methodology to understand and control nature for their benefit. Bacon's writings also represent another important aspect of the Scientific Revolution, namely the weakening hold of ancient authorities on European thought. Bacon argues that human reason with its ability to collect and analyze data through observation and experiment is a better guide to truth than the writings of the ancients.

Two engravings by Sébastien Le Clerc, *The Royal Academy and its Protectors* and *Dissection at the Jardin des Plantes*, comprise our next selection. These engravings effectively communicate important features of the Scientific Revolution such as the formation of scientific academies, the role of royal and aristocratic patronage, and the significance of experimentation. Le Clerc's engravings also convey a view of nature quite different from that seen in the Chinese paintings in the previous chapter.

We chose the Marquis of Condorcet's *Sketch of the Progress of the Human Mind* to illustrate Europe's growing belief in the idea of human progress—another hallmark of Western thought that grew out of the Scientific Revolution. Condorcet is the best-known figure in a group of eighteenth-century thinkers who came to believe that change was positive and possible.

The chapter's second section deals with economic change. The first selection depicts the assumptions, goals, and policies of seventeenth-century mercantilism; the second represents the ideas of mercantilism's critics. Our choices, Colbert and Adam Smith, should surprise no one. Colbert was the leading advocate of mercantilism during the seventeenth century, and as Louis XIV's controller general was in a position to put many of his ideas into practice. The excerpts from his two memoranda to Louis XIV provide insights into mercantilism's theoretical assumptions and its economic results.

Just as Colbert is the best representative of seventeenth-century mercantilism, the Scot, Adam Smith, is the best-known eighteenth-century advocate of laissez-faire and free markets. The excerpts from Adam Smith's classic, *The Wealth of Nations* (1776), introduce students to a thinker whose importance transcends his critique of mercantilism: he is also the founder of the modern discipline of economics. Smith's doctrine of free trade, based on his theory that an "invisible hand" directs the individual's pursuit of his or her economic self-interest so that it contributes to society's welfare, also will serve as a counterpoint to the socialism of Marx and Engels in *The Communist Manifesto* (source 63).

For the fourth edition the excerpt from the *Wealth of Nations* has been modified to include a longer passage dealing with Smith's theories of prices and markets.

The next section, on the westernization of Russia under Peter the Great, begins with excerpts from seven of the thousands of decrees the ambitious tsar issued during his reign. They reveal Peter's motives and goals and show some of the ways his reforms affected his subjects. This is followed by excerpts from Mikhail Shcherbatov's *On the Corruption of Morals in Russia*. He was an aristocrat of the late 1700s who had deep reservations about the moral and political results of Russia's headlong rush to imitate the West.

The two concluding sections of this chapter, which deal with political revolutions in Europe and the Americas, have been somewhat modified in this edition of *The Human Record*. The English Bill of Rights, the petition of the Parisian women to King Louis XVI, and Bolívar's Jamaica Letter remain, but the Declaration of Independence of the thirteen colonies and the Declaration of the Rights of Man and of the Citizen have been dropped. There is no denying that both declarations—the American and French are landmarks in political history. We have found, however, that neither has been especially effective as a means of encouraging class discussion. Many students are already familiar with the two documents and for this reason take their revolutionary ideas for granted. We have replaced the Declaration of Independence with excerpts from Thomas Paine's *Common Sense,* a revolutionary best seller that communicates the depth of anti-British feeling in the colonies with a passion that will catch the attention of our student readers. The Declaration of the Rights of Man and of the Citizen has been re-placed by excerpts from the statement of grievances, or cahier, drawn up on the eve of the revolution by the bourgeoisie of the city of Paris. It was one of thousands of such cahiers sent to Versailles for consideration by the delegates to the Estates General when they convened in 1789. The Parisian cahier reveals the sources of discontent among the Parisian bourgeoisie and serves as an excellent companion piece to source 45, the petition sent to King Louis XVI in 1788 by a group of Parisian women.

Analyzing the Sources

Bacon's thoughts on science resemble and differ from those of Galileo, whose letter to Grand Duchess Christina can be found in Chapter 1. As Bacon states in Aphorism I, he affirms, like Galileo, that reason and the senses provide the sole path to the understanding of nature. Thus without explicitly saying so, he rejects biblical authority as a source of scientific truth just as Galileo had done. In this passage, however, Bacon is much more concerned with defi-ciencies in the *methodologies* of contemporary science, not the damage caused by religious interference in scientific inquiry. To understand Bacon's views, Aphorisms XIX, XXII, XXXI, and XXXVI are of special importance. Without specifically mentioning Aristotle or contemporary scholastic philosophers (who represent the traditional science still taught in Europe's universities), Bacon sees them as the main impediments to the advancement of knowledge. Aristotelianism, he argues, is flawed because it is based on the insufficient observation of nature. It "just glances at experiment and particulars in passing," and then jumps to broad generalizations and theo-rems; these in turn are further analyzed to form explanations of specific phenomena which he calls "middle axioms" (Aphorisms XIX and XXII). Bacon argues that with this method knowledge cannot grow; it can only rehash and reformulate what is already known. Bacon's method, which is limited by its disregard of mathematics and its neglect of hypothesis formation as the first step in effective experiment, calls for extensive observation and "fact-gathering" before making generalizations. In this process, using available technology, or "instruments and helps," is essential.

Bacon's importance rests not only in his rejection of traditional scientific methodologies but more importantly in his optimism concerning the power of science to improve the human condition. For Bacon, the underlying patterns of nature are not beyond human understanding but can be known and *controlled* (Aphorism III). Thus at a time when Europe was burdened by political conflict, war, religious divisions, and intellectual discord, Bacon offered a philosophy of "hope through the dismissal or rectification of the errors of past time" (Aphorism CVIII). Much, argues Bacon, had been discovered in the past through accident but if his methods were applied systematically the possibilities would be beyond the human imagination.

The two engravings by Sébastien Le Clerc show that only a few decades after Bacon's death Europeans had gone far in achieving the goals the English prophet of science had outlined. The founding of the French Academy of Sciences, along with similar organizations founded in England, Prussia, and Tuscany, meant that science was no longer a semi-esoteric undertaking of individual scholars but had become an endeavor carried on by a community of researchers and experimenters who drew inspiration and knowledge from one another and disseminated their ideas to the public. His engravings also show the degree to which science had attracted the interest of the highborn and the powerful. Kings and aristocrats are interested in being identified with the emerging scientific community as patrons and supporters.

Le Clerc's engravings reveal other things about the scientific activity of the seventeenth century. In *The Royal Academy and it Protectors* the room in which the scene is staged is filled with scientific instruments of all kinds for measuring, weighing, and analyzing. In the other engraving, instruments are being used for dissection and are scattered throughout the room. This too is the fulfillment of Bacon's dream that scientists should avail themselves to all available "helps" in their studies of nature. Both engravings also show how much the practice of science in the seventeenth century differs from the science of the Middle Ages and Renaissance, when natural philosophers did their work in a library or study where they analyzed and compared ancient texts, especially those of Aristotle.

The last question for analysis in the text raises the issue of how the representation of nature in Le Clerc's engravings differs from the views of nature seen in the Chinese paintings in Chapter 4. Clearly there are significant differences. Whatever "inner spirit" of nature the Chinese painters are attempting to convey, nature is, for lack of a better word, "natural." It follows its own inner dynamic and shows its own inner power.

Human beings quietly contemplate the clouds, waterfalls, and trees, but they they make no effort to control nature, alter it, or bend it to their wills. The tiny human figures in Zhang Hung's *Landscape of Shixie Hill* are hardly perceptible; the manmade structures in the painting are built to fit into the environment without disturbing its fundamental character. In Sheng Maoye's *Scholars Contemplating a Waterfall,* the thorny and gnarled trees have attained their menacing appearance by following their own inner laws of growth without human intervention.

Le Clerc's engravings are quite different. They show human beings aggressively assaulting nature to probe its secrets and controlling nature to make it conform to human standards of rationality. Animals are dissected, and their skeletons displayed on the wall like trophies. The formal gardens that can be seen through the windows in Le Clerc's engravings are examples of human beings imposing their own standards of reason and order on the natural world.

Condorcet's *Sketch of the Progress of the Human Mind* gives students an opportunity to explore some of the Enlightenment's beliefs about humankind's past and future. It allows us as instructors to emphasize just how revolutionary many of the philosophes' ideas were in the context of European and world history. In contrast to most societies, which have revered tradition and lacked any conception of progress, Condorcet and other Enlightenment thinkers reject the past, which in their view was a time when superstition reigned supreme and when "respect for authority and the imagination" impeded the exercise of reason. According to Condorcet's view of history, in the Ninth Stage of humanity's development, reason broke the hold of superstition in France, England, and the Americas, and in the Tenth Stage, the future, reliance on reason will spread around the world.

Condorcet's ideas are a culmination of earlier ideas about science expressed by Galileo, Bacon, and many others. Galileo had called for the liberation of science from the shackles of biblical literalism and religious authority, and in Condorcet's view this had been achieved in humankind's Ninth Stage. Bacon had proclaimed that science as an instrument for understanding and controlling nature held out the prospect of improving the human condition, and now Condorcet makes even more extravagant claims about its potential. When Bacon thought of progress, he imagined specific inventions such as gunpowder, printing, and new manufacturing techniques. Condorcet has a similar vision of "new tools, machines, and looms" that will increase human productivity and create more durable products with less waste and in a safer working environment. But Condorcet, writing at the end of an era of profound intellectual and cultural change, perceives that values and morality will also be transformed by science. Slavery, oppression, war, bigotry, sexism, and other afflictions that have plagued humanity will no longer be tolerated once science and reason sweep aside the veil of superstition and supernatural religion.

Several points in this excerpt are, we believe, especially noteworthy. One such point is Condorcet's strong endorsement of the concept of women's full equality with men. Along with the ideals of the French Revolution, the Enlightenment was a major inspiration for the efforts of nineteenth-century women to achieve legal and political equality with men. Another is the early formulation of what Rudyard Kipling would later call the "white man's burden" during the heyday of European imperialism around 1900. Condorcet believes it will be the mission of Europeans to extend the reign of reason to the New World, Asia, and Africa, despite the Europeans' previous dreary record of political and economic exploitation. "Savage people," he writes, will either be civilized, or, in what sounds closer to the later doctrine of manifest destiny, "made to disappear." Finally, Condorcet's theory of progress has certain affinities with nineteenth-century ideas of evolution. Future humans will not just have better ideas and higher standards of morality. They will also have better brains and bodies. They will surpass late-eighteenth-century humans in "physical abilities, strength, dexterity, and sharpness of the senses."

*   *   *

Colbert's writings to Louis XIV should dispel the commonly held assumption that mercantilism pertained only to trade and, even more specifically, trade with colonies. Trade, of course, was a major concern for governments inspired by mercantilist doctrines. Colbert states to Louis XIV that commerce is the "most important matter in the world." He also enunciates a fundamental principle of mercantilism when he states that the amount of wealth and trade in the world is fixed and, for this reason, any increase in France's wealth must be at the expense of its competitors. Trade, in his view, is a "perpetual battle in peace and war."

It must be realized, however, that for mercantilists trade was only a means to other ends. Colbert's economic philosophy might more accurately be called "bullionism" than "mercantilism," because of his conviction that what ultimately determines the wealth of societies and the fiscal health of states is their money supply, specifically their supply of gold and silver. Colbert's goal is to maximize France's supply of bullion. Achieving this goal provides the rationale for the imposition of high tariffs on foreign goods, the abolition of internal customs duties in France, and the establishment of hundreds of new manufacturing concerns and agricultural enterprises. Colbert argues that poverty in France can be attributed to a depletion of its money supply, which results from France's unfavorable balance of trade and creates an adverse ratio between taxes paid and the amount of money that circulates.

Probing further, it can be seen that Colbert's concerns go beyond economics to politics, specifically issues relating to military power. His ultimate goal is a strong French state, with its strength measured by a strong army and navy supported by a full treasury. The list of state-sponsored manufacturing and agricultural enterprises shows a disproportionate emphasis on undertakings with military or naval applications. Thus to Colbert the welfare of Louis XIV's subjects was incidental except to the degree the king's subjects had enough money to pay their taxes to the crown.

At the beginning of our excerpt from *The Wealth of Nations,* Adam Smith outlines two basic tenets of capitalism: first, that the pursuit of individual self-interest is beneficial to society, and second, that prices and wages should be determined by the free market, not by government or privileged organizations such as guilds. In the first section of the excerpt, Smith urges the reader to face the fact that no human being can survive on his own: economic specialization, and therefore, economic dependence are facts of life. This results in trade and bartering, activities that are based on the pursuit of personal advantage by the parties involved. The baker, butcher, and brewer can never be expected to supply us with the essentials of life out of benevolence or concern for the general welfare. They will give us what we want only if we in turn can give them something they require or covet. Self-love, says Smith, determines our economic behavior, and without acknowledging this fact, our understanding of economics will be blurred.

Smith offers a concrete example of how the principle of self-interest works in the next section on prices and the free market. How does it happen, Smith asks, that society gets the products and goods it needs at a cost it is willing to pay and the producer of the commodity and the merchant are wiling to accept? The answer, of course, is the law of supply and demand. Shortages of a product society wants will drive up its price, but only temporarily. The high price will attract new producers, and their increased production will drive down prices by erasing the shortages. Similarly, low prices caused by overproduction or declining demand will drive out producers; production and availability will fall, causing prices to rise. Thus by allowing humans to consider their self-interest and act accordingly, prices will always have a tendency to return to their "natural level." Competition is healthy for society, and anything that unnaturally discourages it— monopolies, guilds, wage and price controls—is harmful.

In the next section Smith criticizes the fundamental assumption behind mercantilism, namely that a nation's wealth is based on the amount of gold and silver it controls. Smith downplays the importance of having large gold and silver reserves. Although precious metals comprise part of a nation's riches, they are only a small percentage of a country's true wealth, which consists of its "lands, houses, and consumable goods of all different kinds." Without goods to purchase, Smith argues, gold and silver have comparatively little value.

Smith goes on to outline his famous theory that governments should abandon economic regulation and allow individuals to employ their capital however they wish. Smith argues once more that allowing individuals to pursue their economic self-interest will promote the general welfare even though each individual is thinking only of his/her own profit. This optimism is based in part on Smith's belief that an individual will always prefer to invest "as near home as he can," and that he will direct his energies to increase the value of his enterprise. Thus by pursuing one's self-interest the individual augments the nation's wealth, produces the goods society needs, and provides employment.

Smith also rejects government monopolies and efforts to protect domestic industries through high tariffs. He defends his position not through hard facts and figures but through common-sense arguments and analogies. Individuals, he asserts, can make better economic decisions than bureaucrats because they are familiar with local conditions. Furthermore, he argues, it is foolish to subsidize domestic industries when it is possible to buy what they produce more cheaply from foreigners. Nations should be specialists just like farmers, tailors, and shoemakers, all of whom make and sell products for which their training, background, and resources are suitable. They purchase everything else from other "specialists."

Smith concedes, in the last paragraph, that the abandonment of protection will cause economic hardship for some, and that complete free trade will never be attained because of negative public opinion and the opposition of powerful interests. Nonetheless, cautiously, and with a "very long warning," the establishment of free trade is the only reasonable option for societies wishing to augment their wealth. The reign of free markets will never result in equality, but in the long run everyone from the top to bottom of the economic order will benefit.

* * *

The best place to start a discussion of Peter the Great's westernization campaign is probably his invitation to foreigners, even though it came three years after the decree on the new calendar and one year later than his decree on Western dress. In this appeal to foreigners (Western Europeans), Peter spells out his motives for the momentous changes he is demanding in Russia. He speaks of the tsar's responsibility to increase his subjects' prosperity (and hence their ability to pay taxes) and to provide internal order and security. He admits at the end, however, that his main concern is protecting Russia's security through bolstering the military. Clearly, Russia's recent military setbacks at the hands of the Swedes, Poles, and Ottomans are the inspiration for his westernization campaign.

Peter's concern with military preparedness is also evident in the instructions issued to Russians studying abroad. Their training is to be strictly practical and utilitarian, focused entirely on learning the skills and techniques needed by the new Russian navy Peter hoped to create. One also can safely assume that the factories referred to in the Statute for the College of Manufacturers would mainly be producers of weapons, ammunition, and uniforms.

Students are sometimes puzzled by Peter's decrees on dress and shaving, wondering why he sought to impose these changes on his subjects despite their lack of enthusiasm for them (why else the draconian fines mandated in the decree on shaving?). Within the ranks of westernizing reformers, Peter was not unique in his concern for outward appearances. In the twentieth century Mustafa Kemal ordered Turkish men to abandon the fez, their traditional brimless hat, to symbolize their break from Turkey's past (source 98). And after the Meiji Restoration in Japan, Western business suits replaced traditional Japanese dress for the same reasons (source 85). Peter viewed his mandates on dress and shaving (in addition to his abandonment of Moscow for his new "Western" capital, St. Petersburg) in much the same light. He was convinced rightly or wrongly that externals were important. Thinking and behaving like Western Europeans would be easier if one looked the part.

The reasons for the unpopularity of Peter's decrees become clear if students are asked how they would react if the United States government suddenly mandated that all males wear kilts or all females wear their hair in sausage curls. In addition, for Russian males shaving had religious connotations. Wearing a long beard confirmed the biblical statement that man was made in the image of God, who was uniformly represented in Russian art as having a long flowing beard.

Westernization, especially when it comes quickly and is imposed from above by government fiat, is never without its critics and opponents. This was the case in eighteenth-century Russia, where Peter's reforms uprooted the nobility, dramatically altered cultural mores, resulted in higher taxes for almost everyone, and insulted the religious sensibilities of countless devotees of the Orthodox Church. Even while Peter was alive, opponents to his reforms—known as "long beards"—rallied around his son Alexis in the hope that when the tsarovich took power he would reverse his father's policies. These hopes were dashed when a ferocious and inebriated Peter murdered Alexis, but critics of Russia's Westernization remained a force both during and long after Peter's reign.

Mikhail Shcherbatov is a good example of a cultured Russian aristocrat of the late eighteenth century who had strong reservations about the results of Peter's policies. He approved some of the things Peter had done. He appreciated the fact that Peter introduced Russia to "a knowledge of sciences, arts and crafts, a proper military system, trade, and the most suitable forms of legislation." He approved Peter's efforts to curb the superstitious excesses of popular religion. He also admired Peter's commitment to Russia's well-being and the simplicity of his morals and his dress.

Shcherbatov is convinced, however, that Peter's policies had unexpected and disastrous results. This was most apparent in the area of religion. In Shcherbatov's view, Peter's goal of eradicating gross superstition and credulity from Russian religion was a worthy endeavor. But Peter did not realize that for most Russians empty rituals and superstitious practices comprised the totality of their religion, and that when these practices ended religion itself would die. The Russian people, Shcherbatov lamented, had lost their love of God and their respect for his holy decrees, and as a result morality had deteriorated.

Westernization also introduced a new love of luxury among the Russians. According to Shcherbatov, Peter mandated the wearing of Western European clothes in the hope it would create a demand for products that native Russian industries could provide. This had not occurred, and tastes became ever more lavish. Now that men and women had opportunities to interact with one another at the theater and balls they were driven to adorn themselves in the latest luxurious fashions, most of which were imported from western Europe. Outward display became more important than one's inner being. Making a social impression became more important than one's family. And as their expenses grew, Russia's impoverished nobles cast aside their self-respect and dignity to grovel for favors from the tsar and high aristocrats to help cover expenses.

What, in Shcherbatov's view, might Peter have done differently to stave off Russia's moral decline? In his discussion of religion, Shcherbatov suggests that Peter had gone too fast and attempted too much. He overwhelmed the uncultured and unenlightened Russians, and as a result, religious beliefs died. Otherwise, however, Shcherbatov seems to believe that moral decay was inevitable once the Russians abandoned their old customs and developed a taste for Western fashion and behavior. Even the example of Peter, who lived a simple life himself, could not halt his subjects' rash embrace of the new ways. Given the inability of Peter to stave off his subjects' degeneration, one must be skeptical about Shcherbatov's hope stated at the end of the excerpt that the example of an inspiring and morally upright ruler could bring about Russia's regeneration. This hope, however,

...ep aversion for Catherine the Great, the German-born tsarina notorious for her extravagant tastes and numerous lovers.

* * *

The English Bill of Rights, the major document of England's Glorious Revolution of 1688, was written by men concerned with limiting royal authority, preserving Protestantism, and protecting the rights of Parliament. In contrast to the American Declaration of Independence and the French Declaration of the Rights of Man and of the Citizen, the English Bill of Rights does not attempt to justify the steps it prescribes on the basis of natural law or on political principles that pertain to all of humanity. Instead, it justifies its action by citing specific abuses of royal power in England's recent political history, most of them acts by King James II that deprived Parliament and its members of their rights.

Relying on the Bill of Rights only, it is difficult to decide whether political, economic, or religious abuses most disturbed its authors. We do know that general grumbling about the king coalesced into a revolutionary plot only after the Catholic king and queen produced an infant son, thus threatening English Protestantism. The actual provisions that the new sovereigns, William and Mary, were forced to accept were designed to protect the Protestant religion as represented by the Church of England and the rights and privileges of Parliament. This in turn meant protecting the political power of England's wealthy and influential families, most of whom were drawn from the ranks of the landed aristocracy. Few provisions would have much relevance to the lives of common men and women unless they were dedicated Anglicans.

There is a world of difference between the English Bill of Rights and the cahier the Paris Third Estate drew up a century later on the eve of the French Revolution. Inspired by the natural law philosophy of the Enlightenment, the writings of Montesquieu and Rousseau, and the successful revolt of the thirteen colonies, the lawyers and businessmen who wrote the French cahier in 1789 used a new political vocabulary and had political aspirations that went well beyond the Bill of Rights.

The English Bill of Rights focused almost exclusively on the issue of royal power, especially the abuses of that power by James II. "Rights" were for the most part rights of Parliament or rights of the propertied classes. When it mentions freedom of speech, for example, it means freedom of speech *in debates and proceedings in Parliament.* "Freedom" means free elections to Parliament.

In contrast, in its proposals for a declaration of rights, the Parisian cahier states in its opening words that "in every political society all men are equal in rights." Rights are universal to all men, not limited to the wealthy and powerful. Rights also involve more than political rights. Human beings also have the right to be protected from torture, cruel punishments, and the death penalty, except for the most atrocious crimes. The French cahier also raised the issue of slavery, although it made no concrete proposals.

Another important difference between the two documents is that for the authors of the Parisian cahier, the key issue was not monarchy, as it was for the writers of the English Bill of Rights. True, the king in the new constitutional order outlined by the authors will no longer be "sovereign" or "absolute." He will be subject to the law and will exercise less authority than in the past. The "nation" will be the source of all power, and the "general will" will make the law. A centralized bureaucracy under royal control will give way to a decentralized system in which elected provincial and municipal assemblies will be responsible for tax collection, "agriculture, education, commerce, manufacturing, communications, public works projects, construction, and public morals." But the document affirms that the "sacred and inviolable" monarchy will remain a fundamental part of the government.

The main issue for the bourgeoisie authors of the cahier is not monarchy, but equality, a natural byproduct of their belief in universal rights. In specific terms the Parisian cahier sought to remove the legal distinctions between the privileged and nonprivileged orders of French society. Before the law, the clergy, who made up the First Estate, and the nobles, who made up the Second Estate, were to be treated no differently from the unprivileged commoners, who made up the Third Estate. Tax exemptions and tax privileges for the clergy and nobles will end. The complicated and inequitable tax structure will be scrapped in favor of "general taxes payable by all citizens of every order." The object of laws will be to "protect every people of every order and every class equally." Those convicted of crimes will all be subject to the same penalties, "no matter what order of society they are from." Noble hunting privileges will be brought to an end.

The last Question for Analysis asked students to identify what ideas and proposals in the cahier might later have proved controversial or divisive once the actual revolution began. Of course it is true that almost everything mentioned in the cahier was potentially the subject of acrimonious debate. But several matters proved especially contentious. These included the issues of slavery and the legal status of the French Catholic Church. The cahier mentions them both but provides no solutions. One also wonders how practical it was for the authors of the cahier to endorse doctrines of equality and popular sovereignty and at the same time accept the continuation of the monarchy (which somehow will be a part of the legislative power) and the division of society into orders. Most fundamentally, in their proposal for a declaration of rights, the authors used words such as "the nation," the "general will," and "citizens." But who makes up the nation? How is the general will to be determined? Who qualifies for citizenship? Were the unpropertied to have voting rights? When they spoke of the "equality of men," did they literally mean men, or did they include women too? The debates that accompanied the drawing up of the cahiers were just a preview of the controversies that would divide the French people in the years that followed.

The Petition of the Parisian women to King Louis XVI highlights another major difference between the French Revolution of the 1790s and the English revolutions of the seventeenth century. To a much greater degree, the French Revolution raised political expectations and inspired political involvement among groups of people who previously had been uninvolved in politics. There is no better example of this phenomenon than the involvement of French women in the events of the revolution.

The beginning of the Parisian women's petition shows that its authors were not lacking in political sophistication. The first paragraph shows a grasp of the political issues facing France, while the second shows an understanding of the realities of French politics. The authors concede that gaining representation in the Estates General is an impossible dream, given the prevailing legal and cultural environment. This explains why they are addressing the king directly.

The next section of the petition paints a bleak picture for Parisian middle class women. They receive at best a deficient education. The less attractive women are consigned to unfulfilling marriages while those with beauty are seduced and corrupted. Women who manage to maintain a sense of honor and have higher ambitions for themselves can enter a cloister or try to support themselves through honorable work. The latter course is fraught with difficulties, however. Parents are unlikely to support their daughters' efforts to embark on a career, and competition from men excludes women from many vocations for which they are suited.

Jobs, therefore, are a major concern for the petition's authors. They ask the king to allocate certain types of jobs—dressmaking, embroidery, hat-making—to women and women alone. This will allow them to support themselves as respected workers, not as prostitutes whose career brings dishonor and shame on all women.

In the last analysis, the most important thing for the petition's authors was women's dignity and honor. Prostitutes should be forced to wear some sort of special garb so that decent women's reputations will be protected. The education they seek would also be centered on moral, religious, and ethical training.

* * *

Thomas Paine's best-selling pamphlet *Common Sense* is not in any classic sense a work of political philosophy. True, it expresses a deep aversion for monarchy, affirms the rule of law, and outlines a plan for the government of an independent American state. But Paine will never be mentioned in same breath as Rousseau, Locke, or Hobbes. His was more a work of persuasion and a call to action. Its goal was to destroy whatever sentimental attachment the colonists still felt for Great Britain and the British crown. To his many thousands of readers he seems to have achieved his goal.

Paine's pamphlet does share some ideas in common with the English Bill of Rights and the cahier drawn up by the Parisian Third Estate. The most important of these similarities is the idea that in a well-ordered state, the law must be supreme. It, rather than any individual, is truly sovereign. This is the message of the English Bill of Rights when it spells out the various limitations on royal power. The same message is communicated in the Parisian cahier when it describes how the nation's charter should be engraved on a monument, sworn to by the king at the time of his coronation, and celebrated in a solemn national holiday. In *Common Sense*, Paine makes a similar proposal. Since "in America THE LAW IS KING," the nation's charter should be celebrated annually, with the highlight being a ceremony in which the charter is placed on a Bible and literally crowned!

In contrast to the other revolutionary documents, however, Paine rejects the idea of monarchy completely. He is a devoted republican willing to make no compromises with an institution he despises. In the new American government he proposes that executive power be exercised by a president elected by the national congress with the office rotating among the thirteen former colonies.

Paine's ideas are not difficult to grasp. And this is one of the reasons for the pamphlet's enormous popularity. One did not have to be a graduate of Harvard or of William and Mary to understand Paine's message. He takes a few common sense ideas (the principle of hereditary succession is flawed because it might raise a rogue or fool to power), blends in a bit of history (the English monarchy is of "rascally origin" because it was founded by the ruffian French bastard, William the Conqueror), and sprinkles the treatise liberally with colorful language (alluding to George III as the "hardened, sullentempered Pharaoh"). Most importantly, Paine characterizes the American struggle with Great Britain as more than a squabble over taxes. "The sun never shined," he writes, "on a cause of greater worth." It will affect the whole continent, and not just the present, but the future of humanity "to the end of time." Herein is expressed the idea of America's special destiny and its unique role in human history.

The main value of Simón Bolívar's Jamaica Letter is its clear, though hyperbolic, statement of the conditions in colonial Spanish America that inspired the wars of independence. The sources of resentment were twofold: political and economic. Politically, Spanish administration had reduced the people of the Americas to a position "lower than slavery" by retaining ultimate decisionmaking power *and* by excluding Americans from all important posts in royal, administration, the military, and the Catholic Church. According to Bolívar, this made the Spanish Americans' position even worse than that of the Turks and Persians, who at least got to carry out the tyrannous decisions of their rulers.

The other main source of conflict was economic. While Spanish America's political subservience reduced the people to "less than slaves," Spain's economic policies reduced them to "less than serfs." Bolívar resented the many restrictions Spain imposed on the colonies' economic activities: control of trade; restriction of manufactures; and preservation of monopolies beneficial to Spaniards. Because Spain saw the colonies as nothing but a source of raw materials, Bolívar saw no economic future for the Americas unless they gained their independence.

If Bolívar characterized the condition of Latin American creoles as "lower than slavery and serfdom," it is hard to imagine what he thought of the condition of Latin America's Amerindians. One can only guess, because Bolívar himself says little about the poverty, illiteracy, and political impotence of Latin America's masses. He analyzes Latin America's past and future from the perspective of a Spanish American aristocrat and shows no inclination to apply the "principles of justice, liberty, and equality" to anyone but the creole elite.

Thus Bolívar's vision of Latin America's future contains no bold plans for social and economic reform. Even his political hopes are modest. Bolívar, who as a young man came under the spell of Rousseau, would have preferred a single republican government for all of Latin America. But he realized this was improbable. He had a keen sense of how difficult it would be for Latin Americans to maintain free institutions after years of authoritarian Spanish rule. Nor does he believe that a single government for all of Latin America is feasible in the near future. Instead, Latin America after independence will consist of several states, some monarchies, some republics, until the region is ready to move on to its next stage of development.

Other Ways to Use the Sources

1. This is an assignment we have used in connection with the topics of Europe's Scientific Revolution and early modern economic development; it goes back and picks up Galileo's Letter to Arch Duchess Christina (Chapter 1), which might have already been assigned:

    Did a distinctive Western worldview emerge in the seventeenth and eighteenth centuries? This assignment should help you draw some conclusions about this issue. Base your answers on the following writers: Galileo, Bacon, Smith, and Condorcet.

    a. Quote a sentence or two from each of the three men you chose that you believe expresses in a nutshell their central idea(s). Explain briefly why you chose those particular sentences.

    b. Write a paragraph in which you identify an underlying assumption that you believe is shared by all three of the writers you chose. An underlying assumption might be a belief about human nature, the accessibility of knowledge, the role of religion in the world, the possibility of progress, the path to truth, or similar important concepts. Explain what convinced you that each writer holds this assumption and describe why the assumption is significant.

    c. Write down your thoughts on the following issue: Many historians argue that a distinctly Western, modern worldview crystallized out of the discoveries, breakthroughs, and departures of the seventeenth and eighteenth centuries. Does your reading of the sources in this assignment bear out this claim?

2. A similar assignment can be formulated using the documents in the sections on revolution in Europe and the Americas:

    What values and assumptions did the revolutionary movements that swept across the Western world from the seventeenth to early eighteenth centuries have in common? This assignment will help you draw some conclusions about this issue. The documents to be used are the English Bill of Rights; the Parisian cahier; Paine's *Common Sense*; the petition of the Paris women; and Bolívar's Jamaica Letter (optional).

    a. For each document, quote a sentence or two that expresses its central idea(s) in a nutshell.

    b. Write a paragraph or two in which you identify an underlying assumption shared by all the documents. The assumption should have to do with a "big issue," such as human nature, the characteristics of a just society, the ends of government, the idea of freedom, and the meaning of right.

   c. Write a paragraph in which you explain how the political concepts you discussed in this assignment relate to the underlying assumptions of Galileo, Bacon, Smith, Voltaire, and Condorcet.

3. Make a brief list of Condorcet's predictions about the future. To what degree have his prophesies been fulfilled?

4. Compose a proclamation by Peter the Great in which he justifies to his subjects his reasons for making them dress like foreigners and shave off their beards.

5. Compose a brief essay in which you discuss the meaning of "rights" in the English Bill of Rights and the cahier drawn up by the Parisian bourgeoisie on the eve of the French Revolution.

6. Compare the proposals made in the Parisian cahier and the actual events of the revolution. How many of the cahier's proposals actually were achieved?

CHAPTER

6

Africa, Southwest Asia, and India in the Seventeenth and Eighteenth Centuries

Chapter Theme

This chapter reveals that although the histories of Africa, Southwest Asia, and India in the seventeenth and eighteenth centuries differed in many respects, they also shared a good deal in common. Political decline provides one unifying theme. This was most apparent in the Mughal and Safavid empires, both of which collapsed in the eighteenth century. The Ottoman Empire survived, but its territory shrunk, its sultans' authority declined, and its once formidable army fell further behind the armies of the West. From the seventeenth century onward reforming ministers and sultans tried in vain to halt the empire's decline. African political history presents a mixed picture, but here too, the weakening of older kingdoms rather than the emergence of new, stronger political entities stands out.

Increasing Western pressure provides a second common theme in the histories of these regions. In India, the beginnings of direct British rule in the eighteenth century is the most conspicuous example of foreign encroachment. In Africa, Western pressure is best represented by the dramatic increase in the transatlantic slave trade and the first European efforts to explore the "dark continent" at the end of the 1700s. Western impact on the Ottoman Empire and Persia was less direct, but military pressures and economic competition exacerbated internal problems.

A third theme focuses on religious movements in the Islamic world. Despite the political weakness of the major Islamic empires, Islam itself lost none of its influence among the people of the region. In West Africa and Arabia it inspired vigorous reform movements.

Why These Sources?

The transatlantic slave trade peaked in the eighteenth century, and for this reason we have included more sources on this subject here, in Part II, rather than earlier in the volume. The first selection, by Olaudah Equiano, describes the slave trade from its point of origin in an African village, to a coastal trading post, to the stinking, disease-infested hold of the slave ship, and finally to America. Equiano's graphic first-hand account of his experiences cannot help but deeply move our students. No other eighteenth-century antislavery tract, most of which were written by whites, has the power of Equiano's memoir.

Olaudah's memoir is followed by an excerpt from *A Voyage to the New Calabar River*, a description of the experiences of James Barbot, a French-born slave trader who moved to England, during a slave trading expedition to Africa's Guinea Coast in 1699. It offers insights into the economics of the slave trade on the African coast and the role played in the slave trade by Africans.

The section on slavery is rounded out by a new selection to this edition of *The Human Record*. The *Code Noir*, or Black Code, was a set of rules issued by the French government in 1685 to regulate the slave system in France's West Indian possessions. The editors are fully aware of the limitations of law codes such as the Code Noir as historical sources. A list of rules on how people ought to behave should not be confused with how they really behaved. Nevertheless, we believe the French code can provide significant insights into French racial and religious attitudes, the economics of West Indian slavery, and slave culture.

The next section, which focuses on the military, economic, and financial problems of the Ottoman and Mughal empires, consists of two sources. The first selection, from Mehmed Pasha's *The Book of Counsel for Viziers and Governors*, was composed in the early years of the 1700s by an Ottoman government official. It provides many insights into the financial and military morass into which the Ottoman state had fallen. It also should help students understand why, despite the sincere efforts of many ministers and sultans, meaningful reforms in the Ottoman Empire proved difficult to achieve. The section continues with excerpts from Francois Bernier's Letter to Colbert on the Mughal Empire, written in 1670. This is a new source for Volume II of *The Human Record*, replacing the excerpt from Bakhta'war Khan's *History of the World* in which he describes the values and convictions of Emperor Aurangzeb. Bernier's letter, we believe, presents a more balanced analysis of the reasons for the problems of the late Mughal Empire. Bakhta'war Khan's brief biographical sketch of Aurangzeb essentially makes one point only, namely that Aurangzeb's intense devotion to Islam alienated his Hindu subjects.

The final section of the chapter deals with the phenomenon of religious revival in two parts of the Islamic world. Abdullah Wahhab's *The History and Doctrines of the Wahhabis* introduces students to the Wahhabi movement, whose disciples sought to purify Islam by banishing all rites and practices that, in their view, deviated from the duty of Muslims to worship God alone. Their dedication and fervor, no less than the opposition they inspired from other Muslims, are similar in many ways to the impact of fundamentalist movements within Islam today. This is followed by excerpts from various works by Usman dan Fodio, the reformer whose campaigns for Islamic renewal redrew the political and religious map of Western Africa in the early 1800s.

Analyzing the Sources

The opening paragraphs of Equiano's account reveal the effect of the transatlantic slave trade on the interior of Africa and also offer insights into the institution of slavery in Africa itself. Equiano's village is on constant alert against African raiders who kidnap children and sell them into slavery. These kidnappers, it would appear, were not in the business of selling their captives directly to Europeans on the coast. Equiano and his sister were sold to other Africans and passed through the hands of several other African owners before they reached the coast. Equiano's description of his kidnappers' roughness and their indifference to his separation from his sister shows that Africans as well as Europeans were insensitive to human suffering in their quest for profit from slaving.

The words of Equiano's description of conditions on the slave ship are understood easily enough, but the brutal treatment of slaves during the "middle passage" is difficult to comprehend. Students sometime raise the question whether Equiano, a spokesperson for the English anti-slavery movement, might have exaggerated the horrors in his account. The answer is no. His description agrees with a mountain of written testimony and is confirmed by what we know of casualty rates on slave ships, which might have been as high as 55 percent on average.

Other students have raised questions about the reasons for the crew's cruelty to the captured blacks, and in a few instances, to their fellow crewmen. There are no simple explanations for their behavior, although economic motives (getting as many live blacks to the Americas as possible), fear of insurrection, and the harsh discipline routinely practiced by Europeans everywhere on the high seas all must be taken into account.

[James Barbot's *A Voyage to the New Calabar River* is analyzed earlier in this volume on pp. 156–157.]

Our section on slavery continues with excerpts from the *Code Noir* (Black Code), promulgated in 1685 by King Louis XIV of France for the regulation of slavery on France's West Indian possessions. It provides depressing testimony about the fate of millions of human beings that labored and died under appalling conditions so that Europeans could satisfy their ever-greater appetite for sugar.

Just as the Spaniards justified their exploitation of the Amerindians in the encomienda system by teaching them Christianity, the French in the *Code Noir* pay scrupulous attention to the religious life of their slaves. All slaves are to be baptized as Christians, all overseers of slaves are to be Catholics, and no work is to be demanded of slaves on Sundays and Holy Days. Dead slaves who had been baptized as Christians were to be buried in hallowed ground (the unbaptized, however, were to be buried at night in any convenient field).

To the French such provisions were just a few of the examples of their concern for the welfare of the slaves. Article 11 prevented slave owners from coercing their slaves into marriage. Article 26 gave slaves the right to complain to the judicial officer, the Procurator General, if their masters were withholding provisions or subjecting them to "barbarous and inhumane treatment." Article 27 required slave owners to provide sustenance and medical care for old and sick slaves. Article 47 made it illegal for slaveowners to break up slave families by selling husbands, wives, and children to different owners.

Even if these "enlightened" provisions had been rigorously enforced, they do little to diminish the depressing reality of the slave's life. Although slaves could not be made to work on Sundays or Holy Days, the *Code Noir* places no other restrictions on the type or extent of labor that could be demanded of them. For their labor they receive two outfits and a weekly provision of cassava flour and salted beef or fish. They were permitted to have absolutely no property of their own. Social gatherings and consumption of alcoholic beverages were strictly regulated. As Article 9 reveals, female slaves experienced another form of abuse—sexual exploitation by overseers and masters.

The *Code Noir* gives chilling evidence of the mutual fears that pervaded slave societies. Numerous articles provide evidence of the owners' fears of rebellious and runaway slaves. Slaves are prohibited from carrying clubs or weapons, and nocturnal gatherings are banned. Masters are expected to keep their slaves under tight control, and if they fail, they will be fined and forced to "make reparations" for any damage their slaves have caused. The slaveowners' fears also find expression in the harsh penalties imposed on disobedient slaves. True, Article 42 prohibits masters from mutilating or torturing slaves, but they can have their slaves bound in chains and beaten with rods when they feel their slaves merit it. Branding, beatings with rods, and executions are prescribed for other crimes. Article 37 provides a clear insight into how the French perceived their slaves. It stated that if a slave committed a robbery, he could make reparations by making a payment in money or in kind, or he could simply "give away the slave to the party who is owed damages." Human beings had been reduced to the level of a commodity.

* * *

Before analyzing Mehmed Pasha's *The Book of Counsel for Viziers and Governors,* students should be encouraged to review the observations of Ogier de Busbecq, the sixteenth-century Hapsburg diplomat who visited Ottoman territories and the Ottoman court in the sixteenth century (source 21). Even after having taken into account Busbecq's exaggerations of Ottoman strength and the likelihood that Mehmed Pasha was overstating the extent of Ottoman problems, comparisons with Busbecq will show the extent of Ottoman decline from the days of Suleiman I to the late seventeenth century.

The first part of the selection from Mehmed Pasha's *The Book of Counsel for Viziers and Governors* provides immediate opportunities to note the differences between the Ottoman government in the sixteenth century and in the years around 1700. According to Busbecq, Suleiman I named men to posts in his administration solely on merit, with neither favoritism nor a person's birth playing a role. By the end of the seventeenth century, according to Mehmed Pasha, bribery was routine. Mehmed Pasha, who achieved high office in government after working his way through the ranks, objected to bribery for two main reasons. First, it provides offices for "unfit and tyrannical oppressors." Second, it encourages the financial exploitation of the sultan's subjects, especially peasants. The people suffer because office-holders feel compelled quickly to recoup the money they spent on bribes so they can begin to reap profits. As a result, peasants are demoralized and any incentive to increase production is destroyed. Additionally, since potential revenues end up in the pockets of corrupt officials rather than the treasury, bribery compounds the government's financial woes.

The other reason for the government's financial straits is runaway expenditures, an issue discussed in the next section. Government, according to Mehmed Pasha, has come to be viewed as a source of handouts and financial favors and is a target for unscrupulous contractors and officials. Part of the solution, in his view, is to have a determined, savvy, and honest chief treasurer (presumably like himself) who, with the sultan's help, can prevent fraud and say no to those demanding financial favors. Beyond that, revenues should be collected by government officials, not tax farmers. Most importantly, efforts must be made to control expenditures for the military and superfluous government offices. The janissary corps, once the pride of the Ottoman army, comes under special criticism. Their lists are filled with nonexistent troops whose salaries end up in the pockets of corrupt officers and other janissary corps members. They are more skillful in robbing peasants than fighting the enemy.

The last section addresses the issue of inflation. Prices are rising because of the venality of merchants, whom the author clearly despises, in part because many of them were Christians. Soldiers and common people alike are victimized. According to the author, the sultan needs to be more attentive to market prices and prevent merchants from overcharging.

Overall, Mehmed Pasha's treatise is more effective in delineating problems than in providing solutions. He expresses hope that the sultan himself will become involved in solving some of the problems confronting the state, but as the title of his treatise implies, viziers and governors will have to do most of the work. Even in the unlikely circumstance that these officials all prove to be dedicated and honest men, it is difficult to imagine they could make much headway against massive inertia and venality without the support of a committed and unwavering sultan. Even then, opposition from those who benefit from the status quo might well be too powerful to overcome. Abandoning tax farming and all its attendant opportunities for exploiting the sultan's subjects and skimming government revenue sounds reasonable, but how would the government recruit and pay the thousands of new officials necessary to collect taxes? Would price controls provide a long-term solution to inflation? Shortages of goods and the declining value of money were the root causes of this problem.

Just as a quick review of Busbecq's *Turkish Letters* prepares students to better appreciate Mehmed Pasha's *The Book of Counsel*, a rereading of Jahangir's *Memoirs* (source 23) provides useful background for an analysis of Bernier's letter to Colbert on Mughal India. Jahangir's memoir gives the impression of a secure and enlightened government under a free-spending and powerful ruler with unlimited resources. Bernier, writing only a few decades after Jahangir's death, presents a far different picture. Although impressed by Mughal India's wealth, he is struck more by the weaknesses of the Mughal state and the oppression of the Indian people under Mughal rule.

To Bernier, the outstanding symptom of Mughal weakness is in the area of finance. Although India is rich in precious metals, the government has a chronic shortage of funds. [Here, it should be noted, Bernier is writing to Europe's greatest proponent of mercantilism, Colbert (see source 39), and Bernier is thinking like a mercantilist himself. Fiscal health and prosperity are measured in terms of the amount of gold and silver a government or society has at its disposal.] After reading of Jahangir's extravagance, it should not surprise us to learn that Bernier cites excessive spending by the

Mughal court as a major cause of the government's financial problems. But to the French observer, other more fundamental political flaws are also at work. He points out that although the extent of the territories claimed by the Mughals is impressive, many Indian states, although technically under Mughal authority, are more or less independent and pay little in the way of tribute or taxes to the central government. The Mughal's political situation keeps expenses high. Not only are large military expenditures needed to keep enemies in Persia and Uzbek at bay, they are also required to keep order within the empire itself. Bernier points out that religious tension between Muslims and Hindus and the existence of powerful states within the empire make rebellion a constant threat.

Bernier also paints a depressing picture of poverty and oppression among the Indian people, much of it caused by the abuse of power by jagirdars, military men given grants of land to provide for their expenses. In Jahangir's Twelve Decrees, issued at the beginning of his reign, the emperor required his jagirdars to treat the peasants and artisans in his territories fairly and to use state funds for beneficial projects such as infirmaries. Bernier sees no sign of restraint or responsibility on the part of the jagirdars. Their sole concern is extracting as much as they can from their peasants, whose condition Bernier equates with slavery.

Bernier proved to be an astute observer. The Mughal Empire began to disintegrate in the closing decades of the seventeenth century under the pressures of war and rebellion. By the mid-eighteenth century it had virtually ceased to exist, and Great Britain and France were competing for territories it had once controlled.

* * *

The selections in the concluding section of this chapter provide an opportunity to compare the beliefs of two Islamic reform movements that emerged in the late eighteenth century. Although the beliefs of the Wahhabis resemble those of Usman dan Fodio and his followers in certain respects, the two movements had distinct priorities and goals. These dissimilarities, in turn, can be explained by the differences in the religious and political environments in which the two movements took root.

The key Wahhabi doctrine was unitarianism—an insistence that God and God alone was worthy of a Muslim's worship, prayers, and highest devotion. Thus the greatest threats to Islam were any and all beliefs and practices that seemed to suggest that a mortal human being, no matter how saintly, shared in God's power or divinity. Thus the Wahhabis denounced cults of saints and destroyed the tombs of holy men where acts of worship and prayers took place. This also explains their aversion for Shi'ism, whose followers believed that Muhammad's son-in-law, Ali, Ali's son, Husayn, and the imams who followed them were recipients of God's revelation and were worthy of special veneration.

A good deal of insight into the Wahhabi vision can be gained by examining the events that followed their conquest of Mecca. By taking Mecca, the holiest city in Islam and the destination of pilgrims from all over the Muslim world, the Wahhabis wished to make the city and its people a model Islamic community that would inspire Muslims everywhere to follow their doctrines. Thus after the conquest, Wahhabi leaders required the Meccans to accept their teachings (which, in view of the military situation, most did), destroyed tombs where people had worshipped, and outlawed the use of tobacco and hashish. They also tried to restrict sectarian divisions within the ranks of Islam by prohibiting the practice of praying in separate groups dedicated to different imams.

But the Wahhabis also attempted to assure the Meccans that their only concerns were practices that had a direct bearing on religion and pious works. Smoking tobacco and playing musical instruments in a mosque would be included in this category but not "drinking coffee, reciting poetry, (and) praising kings." In any case, the Meccans did not have long to worry about the Wahhabi reformers. Within a few years the armies of Ibrahim Ali, Muhammad Ali's son, put an end to their reign over Islam's holy city, but the Wahhabi movement continued to have followers in other parts of the Arabian Peninsula.

The concerns of Usman dan Fodio and his followers grew out of a religious and political situation far different from the environment of the Arabian Peninsula, where Wahhabism took root. Islam in Western Africa had still not struck deep roots among rulers and the general population. Thus when Usman denounced certain religious rites and rituals, he was referring to non-Muslim, or pagan, practices. In contrast, what the Wahhabis condemned were *heresies,* that is, erroneous beliefs and rituals among professed Muslims such as worshiping at shrines of holy men. The Wahhabis were also interested in purifying Islam of the philosophical subtleties that had grown within Islam as a result of efforts to apply ancient Greek logic to an understanding of God. This was not an issue for Usman dan Fodio.

In addition, Usman's message had a much stronger political component than that of the Wahhabis. For the Wahhabis military support from the Sa'ud chieftains enabled them to survive and spread their doctrines throughout much of the Arabian Peninsula. But to them, even the capture of Mecca had more religious than political significance. Usman, on the other hand, attracted many of his followers by denouncing the region's corrupt and tyrannical rulers. That these rulers were Hausa while Usman and his followers were largely Fulani added another dimension to his movement that was lacking for the Wahhabis.

Finally, Usman's message shows a concern for social justice that is lacking among the Wahhabis. His alienation from the Hausa rulers resulted partly from his anger over their indifference to the well being of their subjects. Usman is also sensitive to the plight of women in West African society. He objects to the fact that harem women, who rulers recruit by the thousands, are treated no differently than slaves. Similarly, wives are treated like slaves by their husbands and denied even rudimentary religious instruction. Usman calls on his male followers to provide religious instruction for their wives and treat them equitably. Women, for their part, should resist their husbands' demands if they are expected to act against the teachings of the faith.

Other Ways to Use the Sources

1. Write an account of James Barbot's slaving expedition to the New Calabar River from the point of view of one of the Africans in "King Williams" entourage.
2. What similarities and differences do you see between the weaknesses of the Ottoman and Mughal empires in the seventeenth century?
3. You have been commissioned by the Ottoman sultan to devise a plan for strengthening the Ottoman army. What would you propose?
4. What similarities do you see between the religious ideas of the Islamic reformers, the Wahhabis and the followers of Usman dan Fodio, and the Christian reformer, Luther? [An emphasis on the majesty of God, a concern over "idolatry," and a strong sense of conviction are all areas where one can speak of certain similarities between Luther and the Wahhabis. Usman is more concerned with social and political issues than was Luther. Obviously there were also a lot of differences too.]

CHAPTER

7

Change and Continuity in East Asia and Oceania

Chapter Theme

On the surface, the societies of East Asia, Southeast Asia, and Oceania were a picture of peace and stability from the late seventeenth to the early nineteenth century. In reality, however, these Asian societies were neither static nor lacking tensions. Eighteenth-century Japan and China saw the beginning of social and economic changes that in the 1800s grew into serious problems for both societies. In China's case the major change was its rapidly growing population, while for Japan it was urbanization and increased social mobility, which weakened the aristocrats, who traditionally had been at the top of the Japanese social order, and enriched the merchants, who tradition-ally had been at the bottom. Eighteenth-century Japan also experienced intellectual ferment as a result of the Dutch Studies and National Learning movements, both of which competed with state-sponsored Confucianism.

In addition, Western pressures on the region were growing at the end of the eighteenth century. In China this meant increased sales of opium by the British and British pressures on the Qing government to open the country to more trade. In the East Indies it meant the expansion of Dutch rule; in Australia and New Zealand, the first European settlements; and in the islands of the South Pacific, increased European exploration. All these devel-opments prepared the way for the even greater changes that swept across the region during the nineteenth century.

Why These Sources?

The first section of the chapter focuses on developments in China during the first century and a half of Qing rule. It begins with Kangxi's "Self-Portrait," a creation of the U.S. historian Jonathan Spence, who took excerpts from the emperor's various writings and arranged them to resemble a memoir written by Kangxi toward the end of his life. Despite the source's artificiality, it is still valuable. It provides another portrait of an all-powerful ruler from the early modern period, making it possible to create a number of assignments comparing Kangxi, Suleiman I, Abbas I, and Jahangir. It also offers insights into the challenges facing the early Qing rulers and their policies. For the fourth edition of *The Human Record*, the selection has been modified to include extensive material on Kangxi's views of Europeans, especially European Catholics.

Emperor Qianlong's letter to George III from the 1790s is a well-known and frequently quoted source. It is evidence of British interest in increasing trade with China, but its main value is what it reveals about Chinese views of the outside world, in particular, the Western "barbarians." It reveals some of the reasons why such views made it difficult for the Chinese to respond effectively to increased Western pressures during the nineteenth century.

The next section focuses on eighteenth-century Japan. The two sources, Mitsui Takafusa's *Some Observations on Merchants* and Honda Toshiaki's *A Secret Plan for Government* illustrate some of the social, economic, and intellectual changes that were beginning to disturb the placid surface of Tokugawa society. They also provide opportunities to draw some comparisons between Japan and China and offer insights into the reasons for Japan's successful transformation following the Meiji Restoration of 1868. Mitsui Takafusa's *Some Observations on Merchants*, written in the early eighteenth century, provides insights into merchants and their views. Honda Toshiaki's *A Secret Plan for Government* describes the social ills of late eighteenth-century Japan, in particular the problems of peasants and samurai. It also illustrates how as early as the late eighteenth century some Japanese were being drawn to Western ideas and technology while becoming disenchanted with China as a model for Japan.

Although Oceania is one of those areas that instructors of global history often bypass in their rush to cover "more important" regions, we feel that the history of the arrival of Westerners in Oceania is sufficiently important and revealing to be included in our text. The memorandum of the Church of England Missionary Society on its activities in New Zealand and the report of George A. Robinson on his dealings with the native Tasmanians provide material for discussion of two central themes in recent world history— the complex motives behind Western expansion and the West's impact on native peoples. These two sources also contain material that can be used for a number of effective student exercises comparing the British impact on Australia and New Zealand with the European impact on the Americas.

Analyzing the Sources

Any discussion of Kangxi's memoirs will inevitably end up as some sort of comparative analysis. A good place to start might be to raise the question of how things had changed in China since the closing decades of the Ming dynasty, the era that produced Yang Lien's Memorial to Emperor Ming Xizong (source 32). A notable difference between the two eras is the change in the emperors' work ethic. Kangxi is an energetic, attentive ruler who spends long hours pouring over memoranda, reviewing judicial decisions, consulting with his advisors, meting out punishments to corrupt or abusive officials, and studying Western mathematics and music. This is a far cry from late Ming rulers like the Ming Xizong, who withdrew from state affairs and turned the government over to eunuchs. Kangxi, in contrast, has nothing but contempt for the eunuchs. He keeps their numbers to a minimum and excludes them from important state business.

Many insightful comparisons can also be made between Kangxi and several rulers previously encountered in *The Human Record*. Kangxi, for example, is similar in several respects to the Mughal emperor, Jahangir. Both were powerful, conscientious rulers who faced many of the same problems. Both wrestled with the issue of where the line should be drawn between justice and mercy. They accepted the necessity of harsh punishments for those who break the law, especially if they are government officials. But they also realized that at times leniency was the right course.

Kangxi also resembled Abbas I of Persia in certain respects. Both rulers had a "common touch," and made a point of meeting their subjects in person to hear their concerns. Another similarity between Abbas and Kangxi is their response to Europeans. Abbas encouraged the hopes of Catholic missionaries when it suited his foreign policy goal of drawing Catholic Spain into an alliance against the Ottoman Empire. He turned against the missionaries when hopes for the Spanish alliance faded. Kangxi had no need for European military aid, but he was certainly interested in Western mathematics and science. He too turned against the missionaries when the pope required Chinese Christian converts to abandon ancestor worship and their veneration for Confucius.

Another topic worth considering is Kangxi's views of the Chinese civil service examination system. His comments show that in practice the system often fell short of the ideal. The emperor, as a result of his close attention to the functioning of his administration, realized the system was weakened by favoritism and corruption. Significantly, however, the Qing emperor does not consider abandoning the system. Instead, he seeks to rid the system of abuses by more rigorous monitoring of the examinations and more personal oversight on his part.

Emperor Qianlong's dismissive letter to King George III is a product of China's long-standing lack of interest in the cultural and intellectual developments in the outside world. Unaware of both the potential threats posed by the British and of China's own internal problems, the emperor begins his letter by summarizing the underlying principles of China's foreign policy. The world, in the emperor's view, is divided between China, the hub of the world and its one true civilized state, and everyone else, who are all to a greater or lesser degree barbarians. China tolerates trade and diplomacy with these barbarians not because of anticipated benefits or China's needs, but because of the emperor's benevolence. Foreigners, conversely, are expected to recognize China's superiority and obey the emperor and his officials.

Qianlong then goes on to explain (in simple language even the English can understand) why he cannot agree to any of the ambassador's requests. First, he is committed to treating all foreigners equally and fairly; thus to accede to the British would open the floodgates to other requests. (In this respect Qianlong was correct. Concessions to the British after the Opium War of 1839 to 1842 were soon followed by similar concessions to other Western powers and Japan.) Second, he seeks to minimize contacts between foreigners and Chinese. His reason is that friction between Chinese and "barbarians" would inevitably follow, thereby threatening to diminish the emperor's benevolence.

In case the British were unconvinced by his reasoning, the emperor also warns them against disregarding his decree or trying to cheat. Nothing escapes the emperor's officials, he claims. Indeed they watch over every inch of Chinese territory. Any attempt to disregard his decree will result in instant expulsion.

The last question for analysis asks students to consider what the British could have done to convince the Chinese to change their minds about trade. In reality, the answer to this question is probably "nothing." Given the deeply ingrained Chinese view of the world, it is unlikely that the British could have come up with any arguments or actions that would have persuaded the Chinese.

Let's say, however, that the British had given it a try. They might have tried to impress the Chinese with the durability and low price of the cotton goods that were now being manufacturing in the first stages of England's industrial revolution. They might have groveled before the emperor and promised to behave if only the emperor made a few concessions. They might have threatened to pack up and leave, thus depriving the Chinese treasury of the silver that British merchants regularly exchanged for the Chinese products they sought. They might have tried bribes. They might have sent some warships to China's coast to give Chinese officials a demonstration of the firepower and accuracy of European naval armaments. Such a list could be easily expanded.

* * *

Our two sources on Japan, Mitsui Takafusa's *Some Observations on Merchants* and Honda Toshiaki's *A Secret Plan for Government*, both provide evidence of the social and economic changes that took place during the Tokugawa era. Both documents attest to the growing wealth and influence of merchants, while Honda's treatise discusses the problems confronting certain segments of the peasantry and samurai. Honda's treatise also is an example of the eighteenth-century Japan's growing interest in the West.

The business philosophy of Mitsui Takahira and Mitsui Takafusa, the father and son team that contributed to *Some Observations on Merchants*, can be reduced to a few maxims: work hard; don't spend lavishly; beware of schemes to promise easy profits; don't be gullible; know your place in society; resist making loans to daimyo. If a merchant follows these simple rules he will achieve what should be his one goal in life—to make lots of money and hold on to it.

This wholehearted endorsement of personal wealth as a worthy goal is quite different from the attitude expressed in Wang Daokun's biographies of the Ming era Chinese merchants in Chapter Four (source 31). What distinguishes the Chinese merchants, Zhu Jiefu and Gentleman Wang, is not their wealth but their ethical values. Both men are remembered for devotion to their families, integrity, filial piety, and concern for the poor. In his final words, Zhu urges his son not to build up the family fortune but to behave righteously. It is almost as if each man's selflessness and good sense was the cause of whatever business success he had. This would appear to be the point of the last paragraph of Wang's biography where it is implied that his "pursuit of excellence" was the cause of his long life and his many sons and grandsons.

Morality and ethics play hardly any role at all in the business vision of the Mitsui. The closest they come to endorsing a moral principle is their devotion to the doctrine of filial piety. They admonish merchants not to squander wealth that their parents and grandparents have accumulated. There is no sense that successful merchants have a responsibility to share their wealth with the poor or those in need.

The Mitsui do endorse a traditional view of the merchant's place in Japanese society, at least in regard to their relationship to the daimyo and samurai. They seem to be in awe of the samurai's power and social standing, both of which put merchants at a disadvantage when they are trying to force an aristocrat to repay loans. Under no circumstances should the successful merchant ape the manners and spending habits of the samurai or show off his wealth through conspicuous consumption. This is the lesson taught in many of the biographical sketches in the book, including those of Juemon I and II and Ishikawa Rokubei. All three failed because of their extravagance and lack of restraint.

Honda Toshiaki wrote his *Secret Plan for Government* in 1798, some eight decades after the completion of Mitsui's *Some Observations on Merchants*. This explains in part why his views of social and economic relationships in Japan differ from those of the Mitsui. In addition, Honda is a disciple of Confucius, even though his admiration of Western science and government is distinctly "un-Confucian."

As a disciple of Confucius, Honda yearns for a Japan in which the common people are obedient and content, rulers benevolent and honest, the aristocracy dedicated to self-cultivation, frugality, and good government, and merchants know their place. The blame for Japan's failure in all these areas is not limited to any one group. The daimyo have allowed themselves to fall deeper and deeper into debt; the merchants have been quick to take advantage of the daimyo's plight; and the shoguns have failed to solve these problems or show compassion for the lower classes. The lower classes have committed heinous crimes, such as infanticide, but in Honda's view, they are innocent victims. Their prospects have been ruined by high taxes paid to the daimyo but which ultimately find their way into the hands of the merchants. By his somewhat dubious calculations, 15/16s of Japan's total income goes to merchants, a trend that if it continues, will completely distort the proper relationships in Japanese society.

In Honda's view, if Japan is to be saved, its political leaders—the daimyo and shoguns—must take the initiative. The daimyo must end their massive indebtedness through discipline and self-control, while the shoguns must rededicate themselves to the principles of Tokugawa Ieyasu, who "used his power to control the strong and give succor to the weak." Specifically, the shoguns should rule according to the "four imperative needs."

These four needs, which are not discussed in this excerpt in *The Human Record*, break down into three categories. In the area of technology, the Japanese must master the manufacture and use of firearms (imperative need #1), and to accomplish this, they must develop their skills in metallurgy (imperative need #2). They should abandon their isolation and strive to increase trade (imperative need #3), and finally they should expand and colonize nearby islands and even areas on the Asian mainland (imperative need #4).

Honda is asking the Japanese to perform a difficult task. On the one hand he is calling for renewed commitment to the essentially conservative social and political values of Confucianism. On the other hand he is calling for commercial expansion, colonization, imitation of the West, and technological innovation, developments that would undermine the traditional class relationships he values. Honda is unaware of the many difficulties that would result from attempting to graft Western ways to Eastern values, but subsequent Japanese thinkers continued to wrestle with the problem, and in the end, the Japanese accomplished much of what Honda proposed.

* * *

The two sources we have included on early relations between the English and the native peoples of New Zealand and Tasmania give us an opportunity to return to an issue that was raised earlier in this volume, namely the motives and goals of European expansion and the Europeans' attitudes toward the "backward" and "primitive" people they encountered. Sepulveda thought that the Europeans' "superiority" justified their enslavement of the Native Americans (source 4); Las Casas and others, however, defended the God-given rights of the Amerindians and urged his fellow-Europeans to work with the native peoples so that all parties benefited from their interactions (source 5). Now, in the early nineteenth century the English once more were facing these issues as they began to explore and settle Australia, New Zealand, and Tasmania.

Many English settlers, whalers, sealers, and government officials were motivated by self-interest and gave not even the slightest thought to the welfare of the native peoples they encountered. The settlers of Tasmania did not hesitate to take over the island, establish large sheep herds, introduce Western notions of private property, and either kill the native peoples or resettle them in special reserves. George Robinson, the director of the Flinders Island settlement, concedes that the hostility of the native Tasmanians toward the settlers was justified. The memorandum from the Church of England Missionary Society to the Earl of Bathurst is filled with lurid reports of English sailors massacring and beating natives (including women and children) and settlers robbing the native peoples' lands and crops. Even if one accepts the probability that the authors of the memorandum might have exaggerated English cruelties to make an impression on government officials, the urgency of their appeal suggests that the incidents they described were not fabricated.

Yet there was another side to English involvement in the region. Samuel Marsden and like-minded missionaries were idealists who left secure and comfortable lives in Europe for a precarious life of service thousands of miles away. George Robinson, although he went to Tasmania as a carpenter not a missionary, was deeply committed to making the Flinders Island colony work for the benefit of the Tasmanian people. By the standards of their day, and perhaps even our own, they were humanitarians.

The views of Marsden, Robinson, and like-minded individuals are well worth considering. The memorial to Lord Bathurst describes the Maoris as "active and intelligent," and in retelling the episodes of mistreatment by the English, characterizes them as guileless, amiable, and prone to violence only when provoked. Robinson, who is interested in defending the native Tasmanians against assertions that they were a primitive human sub-species (it had been suggested that they were the missing link between apes and human beings), also emphasizes the positive qualities of his charges. At the close of his letter he speaks of their "aptitude to acquire knowledge" and "precocity of intelligence." Their "wildness" resulted from their circumstances and mistreatment, not any defect of character.

When Robinson and the missionaries thought of helping the island people, their priority was religious instruction. In their view, as long as the native peoples lacked knowledge of Christianity and an opportunity to develop faith, as pagans they would forever be excluded from heaven in the afterlife. Furthermore, teaching and enforcing the moral precepts of Christianity would enable the native peoples to escape from the "savage customs by which they are now degraded." Christianity was viewed as a civilizing force and a source of moral enlightenment. Robinson proudly reports that under the regimen of Christian instruction at Flinders Island, the Tasmanians have developed a sense of modesty, cleanliness, and personal hygiene, and abandoned their "nocturnal orgies."

Robinson and the authors of the memorandum to Lord Bathurst also speak of efforts to improve the material life of the native populations by teaching them useful skills. Such efforts, however, are secondary to their main mission of converting them. In describing their "successes" the New Zealand missionaries speak first of "diffusing the knowledge of Christianity," and mention only later "ameliorating the condition of the islanders." Robinson describes how the inhabitants of Flinders Island have increased their "proficiency in the useful arts" such as knitting, but admits that such activities are economically insignificant. Even he cannot decide whether their activities should be classified as "useful industry or amusement."

Robinson's upbeat comments have a hollow ring in view of what we know about the Tasmanians' imminent demise. One has the feeling that their abandonment of "savage" customs resulted as much from resigned despondency as it did from moral enlightenment and Christian inspiration.

An objective observer would have to conclude that in the short run even the best-intentioned Europeans did more harm than good to the people they encountered. And the thought of just leaving these people alone never seems to have crossed their minds.

Other Ways to Use the Sources

1. Kangxi could be included in a written exercise in which students compare his ruling style with that of several other early modern rulers, for example, Suleiman, Jahangir, and Abbas I. Or more specific comparisons could be made, for example, between Abbas I's and Kangxi's views of Europeans.

2. Honda Toshiaki and Mitsui Takafusa are given the opportunity to discuss "the role of the merchant in Japanese society." About what would they agree and disagree?

3. Compare the views of merchants expressed in Mitsui Takafusa's *Some Observations of Merchants* and Wang Daokun's biographies of Ming Era merchants (source 31).

4. The New Zealand missionaries and George Robinson both believed that the native peoples of New Zealand and Tasmania were educable and capable of self-improvement and religious understanding. These convictions motivated their efforts to help the Maori and Tasmanians. Consider, on the other hand, the behavior of the sailors denounced by the missionaries and the majority of Tasmania's European settlers, who thought nothing of driving the Tasmanians off their land. What conceptions of the native peoples were behind their behavior?

5. Compose a letter by George III (or one of his advisors) in which he responds to the letter he has just received from Emperor Qianlong.

CHAPTER
8

The West in the Age of Industrialization and Imperialism

Chapter Theme

This chapter's documents illustrate some of the momentous changes that took place in the Western world during the nineteenth and early twentieth centuries. These changes include the spread of industrialization from England to much of the continent and the United States, the broad acceptance of liberalism and democracy, the growth of nationalism, spectacular scientific and technological achievements, a profusion of new intellectual and artistic movements, and the emergence of new classes and class relationships.

These changes had an effect well beyond the geographical boundaries of Europe. They widened the already existing gap in power and wealth between the West and the rest of the world. They enabled the West to establish political control over Africa and much of Asia; led to the emigration of millions of Europeans to the Americas, Australia, New Zealand, and parts of Africa; and were responsible for extending Europe's economic influence throughout the world.

Why These Sources?

The history of the industrial revolution is so complex and its impact so far-reaching that the sources chosen for inclusion in *The Human Record* could have approached the topic from any number of different angles. We have chosen to concentrate on three aspects of industrialization. Our first source, which deals with the effect of early industrialization on workers in England, is drawn from testimony on conditions of factory workers and coal miners in England from hearings before parliamentary committees in the 1830s and 1840s. The excerpts we have chosen depict the working conditions and attitudes of the workers themselves and also the views of capitalists, clergy, overseers, and parents of child workers.

For the fourth edition of *The Human Record,* Otto von Leixner's *Letters from Berlin* has been replaced by excerpts from Samuel Smiles' two best sellers, *Self-Help* and *Thrift.* Although Von Leixner's description of the situation of a late nineteenth-century German working-class family enabled students to make some valid comparisons about working-class life in the early and later stages of the industrial revolution, we concluded that students would benefit more from reading Smiles. Smiles' glorification of individualism, self-reliance, thrift, and hard work provides insights into the values of the middle class, whose rise to economic and social prominence in the nineteenth century is every bit as important as the emergence of the proletariat.

The last topic in this section is socialism, and, not surprisingly, we have chosen *The Communist Manifesto* by Karl Marx and Friedrich Engels to represent it. The excerpts we have included introduce students to such basic Marxist concepts as dialectical materialism, the class struggle, the state as an instrument of class suppression, the flaws of capitalism, the role of revolution, and the inevitability of capitalism's demise.

Our next section seeks to provide insights into the wide-ranging debate on women and their role in the emerging industrial society. Our first selection, new to the fourth edition of *The Human Record,* is excerpted from *The Wives of England* by Sarah Stickney Ellis, an English woman who wrote several books on women's issues in the late 1830s and 1840s. She represents a traditional view of women's role in society. She accepts the notion that women are emotionally and intellectually different from men and ill-suited for the rigors of politics, business, and advanced education. Their proper place was in the home, and their proper role was to provide a calm, comfortable, and well-run household for their husbands, who, if not perfect, could do very little wrong.

Our next selection, resolutions adopted at the Ohio Women's Convention in 1850, expresses markedly different aspirations for women. Calling for complete equality between men and women in the areas of politics, education, and professional opportunities, it describes an agenda for feminists on both sides of the Atlantic for the rest of the nineteenth century.

The next section of this chapter deals with two subjects, late nineteenth century nationalism and imperialism. The two topics are related in that nationalist fervor was an important cause of Europe's imperialist thrust into Africa and Asia from the 1870s to 1900. Nationalism is represented by Heinrich von Treitschke, the German historian and politician whose nationalism was strongly colored by militarism, racism, and opposition to democracy. Familiarity with his views will make the outbreak of World War I and the triumph of Hitler more understandable.

Nationalism is clearly evident in Jules Ferry's pro-imperialist speech to the French Chamber of Deputies in 1883. But the speech succinctly expresses several other pro-imperialist arguments. Ferry describes imperialism's economic benefits, and proclaims France's responsibility to take the benefits of civilization to the world's "inferior races." His speech also shows that late nineteenth century imperialism was controversial, with both socialists and conservatives opposing it.

Ferry's speech is supplemented by several visual sources relating to British imperialism—a newspaper advertisement, excerpts from a children's book, the masthead of a missionary newspaper, and an illustration from a collection of Rudyard Kipling's short stories. They convey the perceptions, values, and expectations of the British public during the heyday of imperialism.

The chapter ends with a section on nineteenth-century European migration, by any standard of measure one of the era's most important developments. This new section to the fourth edition of *The Human Record* is made up of two sources, both of which deal with migration to the United States, the destination of a vast majority of Europe's emigrants. We chose to include Gottfried Menzel's *The United States of America, with Special Reference to German Emigration* because it provides insights into both the motives and risks of emigration. We chose Henry Cabot Lodge's senate speech of 1896 because it expresses the beliefs and values of the many Americans at the end of the nineteenth century who feared that massive immigration threatened American prosperity and democracy.

Analyzing the Sources

The testimony taken by the English parliamentary committees about working class conditions in the 1830s and 1840s provides students an opportunity to consider the issue of the reliability and accuracy of historical evidence. In this connection, it would be helpful to mention that the main advocates of these hearings and sponsors of most factory legislation were members of the Tory party, which represented the nation's landed interests and was the rival of the Liberals, who had strong support from businessmen. It is altogether possible, therefore, that witnesses were chosen and questions posed in ways to strengthen the Tory position and embarrass the Tories' rivals. Certainly anyone familiar with congressional hearings in the United States today is aware that such proceedings are often used for political purposes.

One must also consider the reliability of specific witnesses. Were they recalling events and conditions that happened in the distant past or recently?

Does their testimony present fact or opinion? How are their opinions affected by their own personal experiences and situations? Are they responding to leading questions? One way of sparking discussion on this subject is to ask class members to choose the witnesses they consider the *most* and *least* reliable. We begin class by polling the class, and then provide an opportunity for class members to defend their opinions. It usually works.

Elizabeth Bentley, the first witness in our selection, seems to be describing her experiences as a doffer in a textile mill in a factual, straight-forward way. Note however, that she is led through her testimony by a series of queries from the examiner, many of which are leading questions. Twenty three years old at the time of the inquiry, she is also being asked to recall events and experiences that took place seventeen years earlier when she was only six years old. Edward Potter, the manager of a coal mine, Hannah Richardson, the mother of a boy who works in the coal mines, George Armitage, a local school teacher, and Robert Willan, a clergyman, all might have had reasons to slant their testimony.

Despite the likelihood that details of each individual's testimony were distorted or exaggerated, the general picture is clear enough. Students should be encouraged, however, to go beyond the horror stories of physically abused children working fourteen-hour days for a pittance. The point of view of the businessmen and the workers themselves should also be considered.

The testimony of William Harter and Thomas Wilson reveals the thinking of the middle-class entrepreneurs who risked their capital to build new factories and open new mines. Both men embrace the ideas found in Adam Smith's *The Wealth of Nations* and the premise of nineteenth century English liberalism that individuals, not the government, should make decisions about how to use their capital. Harter, after explaining what he believes will be the economic consequences of the proposed ten-hour workday, concludes that it would result in his loss of 3,000 or 4,000 pounds, or one-sixth of his investment. Wilson opposes government regulation "on general principles" and objects to the proposal to make the education of child-miners the responsibility of the mine owners.

It is also worth considering what the sources reveal about the impact of industrialization on family life, and how the families themselves view their condition. Clearly, economic survival demanded that the whole family, including wives and young children, work. One can infer that the long hours, the pre-dawn start of the workday, exhaustion, and poor health prevented workers from having a "normal" family life as defined by the middle class. The testimony of George Armitage and Thomas Wilson confirms the common sense assumption that young workers had next to no opportunities for schooling. Nonetheless, parents were anxious to have their children begin work at an early age, and at least, according to Hannah Richardson, her son liked working in the mine "pretty well." Such attitudes were rooted in economic necessity and the attitudes of many workers who were displaced agricultural laborers accustomed to putting farm children to work at the age of six or seven. Furthermore, at this early stage of industrialization, without unions or political representation, most workers never considered the possibility that their lot could be improved as a result of their own or others' efforts.

As shown by the enormous success of his books, no nineteenth century author better captured the values, hopes, and expectations of the emerging middle class than the Scottish writer Samuel Smiles. To his many readers, Smith's formula of hard work, frugality, sobriety, and punctuality guaranteed success and respectability. People, he taught, controlled their own destiny. An hour a day spent on self-improvement will make an ignorant man wise "in a few years" and ensure a fruitful and satisfying life. Even fifteen minutes a day devoted to self-improvement will make a difference. Smiles' formula became a major part of a distinctive middle class identity that set its members apart from their social betters, the idle and extravagant aristocrats, and those below them, the shiftless and irresponsible workers.

Smiles' philosophy also had significant political implications. It strengthened the cult of individualism and reinforced the key doctrine of nineteenth-century liberalism that society was best served when government activity was minimal, and its members were free to make decisions for themselves. Smiles' ideas, in other words, reinforced the laissez-faire economic theories of Adam Smith and the point of view of businessmen like William Harter and Thomas Wilson, who testified before parliamentary committees against government intervention in their business affairs (see source 61).

Smiles had no sympathy for England's working poor. In his view, defects in character, not the factory owners or unfair laws, explained their plight. The English poor are hard workers but lack restraint, discipline, and self-control. They live for the moment and provide nothing for the future. Thus their misery is "voluntary and self-imposed." They are "entirely uncivi-lized," and resemble "savage tribes" like the Indians of North America. Government can do nothing to change this. Only through the "gradual diffusion of education" will the working class learn habits of thrift, economy, and frugality. But this will take generations. As Smiles states, "Social improvement is always very slow."

Karl Marx and Friedrich Engels, the authors of the *Communist Manifesto*, had a decidedly different view of the causes and future of poverty. Poverty, they argued, resulted not from defects of the working poor, but from the defects of a capitalist economic system that enriched the few and impoverished everyone else. Capitalism and the poverty it caused will not gradually fade away, but end in violent revolution, a revolution that will usher in a new stage in human history.

An effective way of initiating discussion of Marxism is to encourage consideration of the issue raised in the sixth question for analysis: Why did Marx's "scientific" socialism become so popular and replace so thoroughly earlier forms of "utopian" socialism connected with men such as St. Simon, Fourier, and Owen (all of whom are probably discussed in the course text book)? Part of the explanation for Marx's appeal lies in the two adjectives, "utopian" and "scientific." In Marx's view, Fourier, St. Simon, and Owen were "utopian" because they had no philosophical underpinning for their ideas and no practical plan for achieving their goals. Marx and Engels, on the other hand, claim to be "scientific" in that their ideas are grounded on a coherent and supposedly objective interpretation of history and human nature. Such an approach had wide appeal in an age when people believed science was the surest way to truth and history provided the key to understanding the present.

Marx and Engels also presented workers with the comforting prospect that as bad as their present situation might be, history was on their side and the future would be theirs. The destruction of capitalism, the triumph of the proletariat, and the establishment of a classless society all were inevitable, so claimed Marx and Engels.

To understand this conviction, it is necessary to review their theories of dialectical materialism and class struggle. Taking the idea from George Wilhelm Friedrich Hegel (d. 1831), the dominant voice in German philosophy when Marx studied at the University of Berlin, Marx saw reality as a process of unending, patterned change, leading to a specific end or goal. Marx also accepted the Hegelian principle that change resulted from conflict (the dialectical process). To Hegel this was a conflict of ideas, but to Marx, it was a conflict between classes, the characteristics of which are determined by the prevailing economic system. Because the "material basis" of society determines its class structure and other characteristics, Marx's theory is known as *dialectical materialism.*

In the *Manifesto,* the authors spend a good deal of time describing the historical developments that led to the "simplified" class conflict of the nineteenth century between the proletariat, the propertyless factory workers, and the bourgeoisie, the owners of the "means of production and exchange." They trace the origins of the bourgeoisie to the burghers, or citizens, of Europe's medieval towns, who provided the first challenge to the feudal system and the dominant, landed aristocracy. It should be noted that for Marx and Engels "feudalism" is defined broadly to include not just the political/military relationship between lord and vassal but also the *economic* domination of rural workers by the aristocracy and the control of industrial production by the "closed guilds" of the cities.

According to Marx and Engels, with new markets opening up because of European commercial expansion and colonization, the feudal system of agriculture and manufacturing no longer sufficed to meet demand. As a result, factories and machines were introduced. This change in the "modes of production" caused the destruction of feudalism and the emergence of the bourgeoisie, characterized by the authors as merciless, single-minded exploiters of their class rival, the proletariat.

In one of Marxism's most important theories, however, and indeed one which certainly contributed to its appeal among workers, Marx and Engels claimed that the bourgeoisie were doomed, and that they, the bourgeoisie, would be the cause of their own destruction. Their insatiable greed, which prevents them from paying workers anything above subsistence wages, leads to recurring crises of overproduction. This throws workers out of their jobs, thereby worsening their misery, but more importantly, it ruins the weaker capitalists, who fall into the ranks of the proletariat.

Meanwhile, factory work molds the ever-increasing proletariat into a true class with a distinctive consciousness, bent on the destruction of capitalism. As the forces of history drive capitalism to the brink of destruction, a "small section of the ruling class" (like Marx and Engels) abandons its class to join the proletariat. The violent revolution that follows ends capitalism and class conflict. The dialectic of history ceases. Like Condorcet, Marx saw human history in terms of progress, not as a result of the ever-greater application of human reason to human affairs, but rather as a result of the inexorable working of economic laws.

What follows the revolution? Marx and Engels did not make this clear. Private property will be abolished, national rivalries will disappear, and the state (historically nothing more than an instrument of class oppression) will "whither away." Marx did not get much more specific than this, thus leaving the field open for debates about the nature of socialist society among his disciples.

Once having discussed the basic principles of Marx, students should be encouraged to critique some of his ideas. Was nineteenth-century European society truly characterized by a simple class conflict between bourgeoisie and proletariat? Is human behavior determined solely by class and economic considerations? Are states indeed nothing more than instruments by which one class dominates the others? Why did the two major Marxist revolutions take place in Russia and China, two "feudal" societies by Marx's definition?

* * *

The writings of Sarah Stickney Ellis and the propositions of the Ohio Women's Convention clearly highlight the divisions and disagreements among nineteenth-century women concerning their proper role in society. The authors of the Ohio propositions, like other feminists on both sides of the Atlantic, sought full legal equality with men and demanded places in schools and professions from which they had been excluded. Sarah Stickney Ellis rejected the feminists' agenda, arguing that women's proper place was the home, and that their proper role was keeping their husbands happy. The brisk sales of her books show that many women subscribed to her views.

Defenders of patriarchy in Europe's past had argued that men had the right and duty to dominate women because of males' innate superiority. Men were physically stronger than women, more intelligent, and more capable of moral action. Ellis's view of the sexes is different. Indeed, her depiction of middle-class English men is quite unflattering. They tend to be preoccupied with business, inconsiderate, self-centered, and used to having their own way. They are easily disturbed by meals that fall short of expectations, household disturbances such as those that attend washing day, and perceived flaws in their wives. Such behavior, says Ellis, results in some cases from being raised by "silly mothers," but mostly it is simply the way men are.

Women, according to Ellis, are not necessarily intellectually or morally inferior to men. But they are different. Their natures make them indulgent, forbearing, and patient, which is fortunate because it enables them to put up with the "trials of patience arising out of the conduct of men." Since men are essentially incorrigible, women are ultimately responsible for maintaining domestic tranquility. They must accept their husbands' faults and cater to their wishes, since "it is the inalienable right of all men, whether ill or well, rich or poor, wise or foolish, to be treated with deference and made much of in their own homes." In other words, even when married to a fool, a woman is expected to honor and obey him. According to Ellis, "she has voluntarily placed herself in such a position that she must necessarily be his inferior."

Not surprisingly, intellectual attainment and political activity have no part in Ellis's conception of the ideal English woman. Planning a good meal and having a clean parlor will more likely contribute to domestic harmony than spending the day preparing a "treatise on morals." Attachment to a political party and making political speeches (even in private) are out of the question for women. Their political "involvement" is limited to making innocuous and frivolous comments during polite conversations about candidates' manners and the color of their banners. "Small talk," not discussion of serious matters is in keeping with women's natures.

While Sarah Stickney Ellis's ideas about female subservience to males have a pedigree dating back to the Middle Ages, the ideals of the Resolutions of the Ohio Women's Convention are of more recent vintage. Specifically, they were generated during the Enlightenment and the French Revolution. The authors of the Ohio resolutions justify many of their demands by referring to the doctrines of natural rights and human equality, principles that had wide support among eighteenth-century intellectuals. They refer to iniquitous laws that deprive women of control of their property and children, keep them politically powerless, and prevent them from receiving education's to prepare them for careers in male-dominated professions. These were all issues that first emerged during the French Revolution. Particularly galling, in the view of the document's authors, is male conde-scension and scorn, especially for independent women who state their rights and seek to expand their professional opportunities. This is not dissimilar from the concerns of the women who petitioned King Louis XVI before the French Revolution (source 45). They too resented men's presumption that any independent woman was probably a prostitute.

It is important to emphasize that the authors of the Ohio resolutions are aware that women's struggle in society was more than just a matter of gaining the right to vote and achieving legal equality with men. What was needed was a fundamental change in attitudes about women's capabilities and social roles. They state, "while we deprecate thus earnestly the political oppression of Woman, we see in her social condition, the regard in which she is held as a moral and intellectual being, the fundamental cause of the oppression." Women's history in the twentieth century confirms the truth of this statement: although women in the United States received full political rights by the 1920s, they continue to lag behind men in terms of educational and professional opportunities even after the gains they have made since the 1970s.

The authors concede that some women lead "idle and aimless" lives and that some are indifferent to the many indignities they suffer. Borrowing a concept straight from the Enlightenment, they argue that this was not the result of any inherent inferiority on their part but rather was the fruit "of ignorance or degradation, both resulting legitimately from the action of... laws." Clearly, there was very little agreement between the ideas of Sarah Stickney Ellis and those of the women who attended the Ohio Women's Convention in 1848.

* * *

In introducing the excerpts from von Treitschke's works, we should make sure our students realize that this German writer represented just one aspect of nineteenth century nationalism. To early nineteenth-century nationalists such as the Italian Giuseppe Mazzini, nationalism was a blend of revolutionary egalitarianism, romantic republicanism, Christian purposefulness, and Enlightenment optimism. All peoples, according to Mazzini, had a valid claim to an independent national life. The nationalism of Treitschke, on the other hand, was shaped by Bismarckian *realpolitik*, social Darwinism, militarism, and authoritarianism. It focused on the special attributes of Germany, a state he believed was destined for greatness at the expense of its neighbors.

Early nineteenth century nationalists believed that despite differences in language, religion, and culture, all human beings were essentially one. All peoples aspire to freedom, and all are subject to the same universal, God-given moral laws. Two of these moral laws were to treat other peoples with respect and to strive for a system of peaceful, co-operating states. Treitschke, on the other hand, sees fundamental differences among the world's peoples. In his view, the world is divided into a multiplicity of nations ("nation" in his case is used in the sense of a distinctive ethnic or racial group, not a government or state), all unique and different from one another. If the nation is fortunate, it has a strong state to protect its interests and give it an oppor-tunity to fully develop its unique character. Such states, says Treitschke, will most likely be achieved under monarchies, the form of government best suited to keep a nation unified and powerful.

For Treitschke nationalism meant both love of Germany and also disdain for other nations and peoples. The English and the Jews were Treitshcke's main targets. England, which in the late nineteenth century was the world's greatest economic and colonial power, especially excited the jealousy of aristocratic German nationalists such as Treitschke. He denounced the English as materialistic, cowardly, and hypocritical; they lacked the depth of thought, idealism, courage, and honor that made the Germans great. His comments on the Jews might very well have been taken from the pages of Hitler's *Mein Kampf* (source 93). He speaks of the "international Jew" as the "disintegrator" of nations, and even asserts that the Jews "can be of no further use to the world."

Applying Darwin's concept of the struggle for existence to international politics, Treitschke sees the world in terms of constant struggle. Small, weak states unable to protect their people or foster true civilization do not deserve to exist. Strong states are defined by their power, that is, military power, and war is a glorious opportunity for individual self-sacrifice and the promotion of national honor.

Promotion of national power and the achievement or maintenance of great power status was an important incentive for the states that participated in Europe's dramatic overseas expansion during the era of imperialism. But as the remaining two documents in this chapter seeks to show, other factors also were involved.

The section begins with Jules Ferry's speech to the French Chamber of Deputies in 1883. In trying to convince the French Chamber of Deputies to support his plans for French expansion in Southeast Asia, Ferry's main pitch is economics. Other wealthy nations, he points out, have adopted protectionism—the policy of establishing high tariffs for imports—thereby weakening the market for French goods. As a result, France must have colonies or else face commercial stagnation. Ferry also advances the "nobler" pro-imperialist argument that superior races have the duty *and the right* to civilize "inferior" races. And, finally, he argues that because modern naval warfare requires stations for refueling and repairing ships, France needs to control territories in Southeast Asia, Madagascar, and Tunisia.

Ferry's efforts to defend himself against his critics give us a glimpse of the arguments of imperialism's opponents. French political parties on the left opposed it because it violated the basic principle of the French Revolution that all human beings have rights to freedom and dignity; those on the right opposed it because they would have preferred that France bolster its position in Europe and concentrate on winning back Alsace-Lorraine from the Germans, who had taken it after the Franco-Prussian War. Although not mentioned in Ferry's speech, socialists also opposed it because of their conviction that it took money away from domestic programs and mainly benefited big business and the military.

Our section on imperialism concludes with a number of illustrations from late-nineteenth- and early-twentieth-century British books and periodicals. Taken together they provide insights into imperialism's appeal to the British public and a sense of what the British thought they were up to as they extended their colonial empire.

What images do the illustrations present of the African and Asian subjects of the British? Exotic. Technologically backward. Unenlightened. Clown-like. Dependent. These are all impressions of Africans and Asians that might easily be derived from these illustrations. The most unflattering image is that of the African chieftain in *An ABC for Baby Patriots*. The spears, shield, and tiger skin rug emphasize the unsophisticated technology of Africans (even though Africans had been using firearms for centuries); the chieftain's nudity and foolish hat reinforce the notion that he represents humanity at its most primitive level; his gesture and facial expression both suggest simple-mindedness and gullibility. The images in the other illustrations are only somewhat less flattering. The picture of the starving children from the Kipling book portrays the Indians as helpless and dependent on the English for their survival. The rather exotic figures in *The Missionary News* masthead are all in the process of being liberated from the oppression, ignorance, and despair that characterized their existence before they saw the light of the Gospel. Finally the message of the Lipton tea advertisement is that the main role of the colonial peoples is to provide the sweat and muscle to make sure that European enterprises run efficiently and profitably.

How are the British depicted? In the illustrations from Mrs. Ames's book for children, it is certainly possible to detect an element of self-mockery in the drawings of the stiff, proper, and somewhat dandified Englishmen. There is also more than just a touch of arrogance in the English hunter as he looks down from his elephant to shoot the tiger and lion (how the lion got to India is unclear). But even here the message is one of the Englishmen's honesty, authority, and fitness to rule. The same impression is conveyed in the Lipton tea advertisement by the British overseer who has organized and controls the growing, processing, and shipping of Ceylonese tea. The railway train and the steamship highlight England's superior technology. The most impressive image of English colonialism is provided by the illustration from Kipling's book. Here we see the personification of ideal young English manhood. Neatly dressed with his hair perfectly combed (despite the fact he's been herding sheep in sweltering heat), he strides forward with a clear sense of purpose and mission. The shining light behind his head makes him appear god-like.

Taken as a whole, it is not difficult to see how illustrations such as these strengthened the British public's support for imperialism and reinforced their convictions about imperialism's benefit for all concerned. There is no hint in any of the illustrations of imperialism's darker side—the bloody battles that were fought, the exploitation of native workers, and the upheavals that colonial rule entailed. Instead, imperialism's supposed benefits—economic development and the spread of civilization and Christianity—are emphasized. The illustrations also express the notion that the British have a right by virtue of their higher level of civilization to rule and exploit their colonies. This is perhaps best communicated in the illustration from *An ABC for Baby Patriots* having to do with India. The British hunter seated on an elephant while being fanned by a dutiful native servant, looks down on the innocent-looking and defenseless animals that soon will adorn the walls of his trophy room. They are his for the taking. India indeed is a "land in the East where everyone goes to shoot tigers and feast."

* * *

Why did emigrants leave Europe by the millions for the Americas during the nineteenth and early twentieth centuries? At least for German emigrants of the mid-nineteenth century, Gottfried Wenzel's *The United States of North America* provides some answers. Politics and poverty, according to

Wenzel, were the major incentives to migrate. Wenzel states at the very beginning of our excerpt that many Germans were dissatisfied with their "state organizations and institutions," and sought greater freedom. (The approximately 38 German states that made up the German Confederation were hereditary monarchies; efforts during the Revolution of 1848 to establish parliamentary governments failed.) Wenzel returns to political issues again in the section, "What Does North America Offer that is Good?" Here he speaks of the appeal of lower taxes in America and the lack of conscription and the need to billet troops.

Economic motives play a greater role than politics in emigration, according to Wenzel. He states, "much greater is the number of those who leave the fatherland because of poverty of its material conditions and in order to better their condition in America." Pay is higher in the Americas, land is cheaper, and the cost of living less. Furthermore, in America, a land without guilds, there is complete freedom in the "trades and professions."

Two other factors also played a role according to Wenzel. Some Germans, who lived in a society where landed aristocrats and urban patricians lorded over everyone else, looked forward to living in a society where birth and rank mattered little. Others, says Wenzel, were lured to America because of the pleas of friends who had already emigrated or because of the false portrayal of America as "a land of paradise" by speculators and authors of guidebooks.

Wenzel's main purpose in writing his book was to set the record straight on what really faced the emigrant when he or she reached the United States. Wenzel's message is that America is not for everyone. Many emigrants have failed and returned to Germany; others have stayed and are miserable, despite what they write home in their letters to friends and relatives. To succeed in a new country requires a strong back, discipline, and more money than emigrants think. Interestingly, Wenzel warns his German readers that schools in the United States do not compare with those of Germany. Providing a truly valuable education for one's children will be expensive. The worst aspect of life in the United States is being "despised as an alien" and hearing the taunts of Americans and newly arrived English and Irish. Life, he says, will be unbearable unless the German immigrant can live in a community of fellow German-Americans.

Native opposition to newly arrived immigrants, hinted at in Wenzel's treatise, became more pronounced in the 1890s when most immigrants were Poles, Italians, Hungarians, Greeks, Russians, and Jews, not English, Irish, and Germans. This shift in migration patterns from northwestern Europe to eastern and southern Europe was particularly disturbing to Americans who believed that such people could never be assimilated into American life. Indeed, they threatened the very fabric of American democracy.

In his speech before the senate in 1896, Henry Cabot Lodge, the patrician Republican from Massachusetts, gives the impression that he is smugly satisfied with the work of his committee that has been looking into the "immigrant problem." Its members had come up with a plan to require a literacy test for all new immigrants, a step he believed would "fall most heavily upon the Italians, Russians, Poles, Hungarians, Greeks, and Asiatics, and very lightly, or not at all, upon English-speaking emigrants or Germans." This is just what the country needs, implies Lodge. Immigrants from southern and Eastern Europe, whose numbers have swelled to "enormous proportions," just don't belong in the United States. They will forever remain aliens incapable of assimilating into American society.

The economic arguments in favor of limiting migration had been made by many others before Lodge, and they continue to be made in the United States today by those who favor tightening our borders. Waves of immigrants drive down wages by flooding the market with workers willing to accept minimal pay for the labor. What is new and striking about Lodge's case against immigration is its appeal to blatant racism. Race to Lodge means differences in moral and intellectual capacities among the various peoples of the world, differences that are the result of long historical development. They are the products of "all its past, the inheritance of all its ancestors," and essentially are "indestructible."

Lodge believes that the United States has been shaped by the English people with the help of other closely related racial groups from northern Europe such as the Germans, French, and Dutch. As he told the senate, "it is on the moral qualities of the English-speaking race that our history, our victories, and all our future rest." He imagines a dark future for the United States if the nation is flooded with "lower races." He fears they will mix with the "higher races," meaning a deterioration in intellectual and moral capacities of its citizens, and indeed, an overall decline in civilization. In Lodge's words, we are not far from the racist ideas of Adolf Hitler in *Mein Kampf* (source 93).

Other Ways to Use the Sources

1. Elizabeth Bentley (the 23-year-old textile factory worker from the parliamentary testimony), William Harter (the textile factory owner from the parliamentary hearings), and Samuel Smiles get together to discuss Marx's ideas. What would the dialogue have sounded like?
2. In *The Wealth of Nations*, Adam Smith describes the promise of liberal economics with its emphasis on free trade and free enterprise (source 40). Imagine that Adam Smith returns to England in the early nineteenth

century. What would be his response to the social and economic consequences of early industrialization?

3. The Ohio constitutional convention to which the Ohio women directed their petition in 1850 failed to act on any of the women's demands. Write a statement composed by one of the delegates in which she gives her explanation of why they rejected the women's demands.

4. One of the authors of the resolutions of the Ohio Women's Convention has the opportunity to critique Sarah Stickney Ellis's ideas about marriage and women's role in society. What would she write?

5. Write an essay on the topic of "Continuity and Change in Ideas about Marriage." Use as your sources Luther, *Table Talk* (source 1); Mayer, "A Pattern for Women" (source 6); Woensam, *Allegory of a Wise Woman* and Schön, *No More Precious Treasure* (source 7); Busbecq, *Turkish Letters* (source 26); Kaibara Ekiken, *Common Sense Teachings* (source 29).

6. Discuss the ways that the images of imperialism from late nineteenth-century England distort the realities of imperialism.

7. A well-educated Vietnamese has the opportunity to respond to Jules Ferry's speech in the French Chamber of Deputies. What might he have said?

8. To what extent are nineteenth-century historical developments reflected in the chapter's sources a fulfillment of or a departure from the dreams of Condorcet (source 38) and others in human progress?

C H A P T E R
9

Western Pressures, Nationalism, and Reform in Africa, Southwest Asia, and India in the 1800s

Chapter Theme

The unifying theme in the history of Africa, India, and Southwest Asia in the 1800s is the escalation of Western influence in all three regions. In the case of India this meant the extension of British rule from its eighteenth-century base in Bengal, in the northeast, to virtually the whole subcontinent. In Africa, it meant the continent's sudden and dramatic reduction to colonial status after the arrival of European imperialists in the 1880s. In the case of Persia and the Ottoman Empire, it meant grudging acceptance of Western economic penetration and diplomatic influence and painful recognition of their political weakness and economic backwardness in comparison to the West.

The documents on Africa emphasize the nature and human impact of European imperialism in Africa, while those on the Ottoman Empire and Persia focus on the growth of nationalism and efforts to revive the political fortunes of these states through reform and revolution. The documents on India are intended to reveal the range of the Indians' reaction to British rule. Rammohun Roy, in a letter written in 1823, expresses hope that India will benefit from Western science and education. G. V. Joshi, on the other hand, in his essay written in 1884, harshly criticizes the British for lavishing huge sums of money on public works projects that benefit European investors, but not the Indian people.

Why These Sources?

The section on Africa begins with the Royal Niger Company's Standard Treaty, used to establish the company's authority in the Niger River region. The European takeover of Africa was not always as easy as this document suggests. As the next two documents show, many Africans offered staunch resistance to the imperialists. Nevertheless, this short treaty is a valuable document because of the way it reveals certain unique features of European imperialism in Africa—the urgency and rapidity of the Europeans' take-over; the Europeans' tendency to see all Africans as essentially the same (one treaty fits all); and the one-sided nature of the European-African colonial relationship.

While the standard treaty reveals the impersonal nature of European colonialism in Africa, the next two documents show how imperialism affected real people. Ndanski Kumalo's recollections are interesting for a number of reasons: they describe African efforts to resist European encroachment; they reveal how European firepower doomed these efforts to failure; they shed light on the effects of European rule; and with their description of Ndanski's film career and trip to England, they make a remarkable story. The final source in the section on Africa, various records relating to the Maji-Maji Rebellion of 1905, is new to the fourth edition of *The Human Record*. It portrays the brutality and exploitation that attended the European takeover of Africa.

The documents in the sections on the Ottoman Empire and Persia were chosen to reveal various facets of Western penetration in the region and the range of responses to that penetration. The edict from the Tanzimat era—Sultan Abdul Mejid's Imperial Rescript (1856)—is a prime example of efforts to reform the Ottoman Empire while maintaining authoritarian rule by the sultan and the empire's religious, ethnic, and cultural diversity. The proclamation of the Young Turks, drawn up a half century later, expresses Turkish nationalism and a greater commitment to Western liberal ideas.

The letter of Sayyid Jamal ad-Din to the Persian religious leader Hasan Shirazi sheds light on an extraordinary event in the region's history during the late-nineteenth century—the nationwide Persian tobacco boycott of 1891 directed against the recently granted tobacco concession to a British firm. This is a rich document, one that reveals a good deal about Persian society, the religious values of the Persians, and the depth of anti-government feeling generated by the shah's willingness to sacrifice the nation's long-term economic welfare for short-term fiscal gains.

This section concludes with a source that is new to the fourth edition of *The Human Record*. "The Announcement to the Arabs, Sons of Qathan," is an early expression of Arab nationalism, and adds balance to the section.

The two sources on India show how Indian opinion about British rule shifted in the course of the nineteenth century. British colonialism inspired a wide range of responses among the Indian people, and hundreds of books, essays, and speeches exist on the subject. We chose Rammohun Roy and G. V. Joshi because they represent two poles of Indian opinion. Rammohun Roy's letter to Lord Amherst expresses the views of Indians from the educated Hindu elite who thought the British presence afforded an opportunity to lift India out of its backwardness and bring it into a new age of science and Western enlightenment. G. V. Joshi's essay on Indian railway construction examines one of the fundamental questions concerning the effects of British imperialism in India: Did the economic development planned and sponsored by the British benefit the Indian people as a whole?

Analyzing the Sources

The sample contract from the Royal Niger Company should not unduly tax our students. Clearly the African chieftains "were being had." In return for vague promises that they would be "bettering" the condition of their "country and people," they ceded to the company territory, control over resources and commerce, and what in Western terms would be called their political sovereignty—their right to control relations with other African peoples and unnamed "strangers and foreigners," i.e., other Europeans.

In our discussions of this document we try to move quickly from the actual provisions of the treaty to its deeper implications. What, for example, might be significant about having just one treaty for all the various groups of Africans the company would deal with? (*Answer*: The British failed to appreciate the differences among Africans and assumed that one treaty could be used for all of them). How did the language of the treaty give the company broad leeway to do what it wanted to do? (*Answer*: Much of the language of the treaty is vague to an extreme. The company undoubtedly will be the contracting party deciding what "native laws and customs [are] consistent with the maintenance of order and good government;" what a "reasonable" payment for any land acquired will be; and what "protection" against "neighboring aggressive tribes" will consist of.) How reasonable is it to assume that the chieftains really "understood the meaning" of the treaty? (*Answer*: Not very. Many of its concepts such as boundaries and "chartered and limited" companies were unfamiliar to them, even more so when translators tried to render them into an African language.) In the most general sense, what is the underlying assumption of the treaty? [*Answer*: We see here an expression of the thinking exemplified by Jules Ferry in his speech to the French Chamber of Deputies (source 71)]. "Superior races" have the right to dominate the "inferior races" of the world.)

We pick up Ndanski Kumalo's story with the events that led to war between the Ndebele and the British in 1893. The Ndebele had recently established themselves as farmers and cattle-raisers in the region north of the Transvaal after fleeing from the Zulu. But in 1890 English settlers began to arrive, and war broke out in 1893. In Ndanski's account, blame for the hostilities rested partly on the shoulders of the Ndebele commander, Gandani, who did not follow his king's instructions, but even more so on the shoulders of the white settlers. They gave Gandani an impossible ultimatum, and his failure to meet their demands gave them an excuse to attack King Logunbula's kraal and confiscate Ndebele cattle.

The rebellion four years later resulted from Ndbele grievances over abuses of the Ndebele by native (African) police and over cattle stealing. The Ndebele, armed with breech-loading rifles, fought hard but were no match for the English and their rapid-fire Maxim guns.

After their defeat, the Ndebele were relegated to a reservation where they felt the full force of British colonial rule. Ndanski summarizes the effects of British colonialism in the closing paragraphs of this excerpt. On the positive side, conditions are more peaceful and young people have new educational opportunities. The negatives seem to weigh much more heavily on the scale. The Ndebele are stuck on a dry, unproductive reservation. Before the Europeans arrived and introduced concepts such as property lines and legal boundaries, the Ndebele could "pick their own country" and migrate, but this was now impossible. The Ndebele's economic prospects are bleak: agricultural prices are low except during shortages, and taxes (to support the colonial administration and perhaps also to force Ndebele men off their land and into wage paying jobs in the mines) are high. In Ndanski's view, the greatest change has been the erosion of old religious beliefs and practices as a result of conversions to Christianity. Ndanski Kumalo mourns the passing of ancient ways, but he accepts it with a sense of resignation.

Ndanski Kumalo, when asked about the effects of European imperialism, was able to think of some positive features, although in his mind the harm certainly outweighed the benefits. As the next source shows, however, for the rural inhabitants of German East Africa, the experience of colonial rule had no redeeming features, especially after the Germans embarked on their campaign to turn their colony into a producer of cotton.

It is not hard to see why the Matumbi were driven to rebellion against the Germans. They hated the new tax that was imposed to coerce the Africans to take wage-paying jobs. As is shown by the comments of Ambrose Ngombale Mwiru, it made no sense for Africans, the "hosts," to make payments to the German visitors, especially after the Germans had taken land and built houses on it.

Africans were used in two ways to help the Germans grow cotton. Ndundule Mangaya and Nduli Njimbwi both describe a system of forced labor in which people were requisitioned to work a certain number of days a year on farms owned by Germans or by native colonial officials, the jumbe and the akidas. Discipline was harsh, with whippings and beatings common. Pay was non-existent. According to Ndundule Mangaya, German officials did occasionally make payments to the akidas and jumbe for distribution to the workers, but for the most part the akidas and jumbe simply kept the money themselves. Meanwhile, with labor conscriptions taking place at key times in the agricultural year, tasks in the home village were neglected. Not surprisingly, Ndundule Mangaya reports that men avoided labor by fleeing or by sending slaves in their place. If a husband fled, however, his wife was obligated to take his place.

The Germans also required each village to establish communal plots where the villagers would be required to work a few times a week to grow crops for German export. In 1904–1905, it was ordered that all such plots be given over to cotton growing. Once more there is evidence of non-cooperation. Von Geibler, a German official, reported that in 1904–1905, many headmen were placed in chains or solitary confinement because they had been unable to make their people work on the communal plots. Again, their resistance is understandable. After 1902–1903, they received no wages for their work, so their situation was not far removed from slavery.

The events in German East Africa give us a glimpse of the harsh reality of colonialism: a small number of Europeans, with the help of co-opted native police and administrators, try to squeeze some small economic benefit from their newly won colony. The result is forced labor, brutal discipline, a disruption of village life, and in the last analysis, very meager economic gains for the Europeans.

* * *

For students to understand the significance of Sultan Abdul Mejid's Imperial Rescript, it may be necessary to remind them of the cultural and religious diversity of the Ottoman Empire's population, which consisted of Turkish, Kurdish, Arab Muslims, Jews, and Christians. It is also important to point out the circumstances under which this document (and its earlier companion the Noble Rescript of 1839) was issued. The Noble Rescript was drawn up against a background of increasing diplomatic cooperation between the Ottoman Empire, Great Britain, and France, all three of which were interested in halting Russian expansion toward the Mediterranean. The Imperial Rescript was written after the close of the Crimean War (1853–1856), in which the Ottoman Empire joined France, Britain, Austria, and Sardinia in defeating Russia. The victors were about to meet in Paris to draw up a treaty, which, among other things, would guarantee the territorial integrity of the Ottoman Empire. To "sell" the idea of making an alliance with the Ottoman Empire and later guaranteeing its boundaries (even in Europe), European diplomats urged Abdul Mejid to show his commitment to reform by issuing the Imperial Rescript.

A key aspect of the Imperial rescript is its concern with protecting the rights of the sultan's non-Muslim subjects. According to its provisions, no longer would the Ottoman government interfere with elections of religious officials or prevent the construction and repair of non-Muslim religious buildings in areas where Jews or Christians predominated. It calls for complete equality among all the sultan's subjects irrespective of their "religion, language, or race," and outlaws the verbal abuse of any Ottoman subject by private individuals or government officials. The edict affirms the principle of religious liberty and ensures that non-Muslims will have equal access to all professions and schools. Legal cases that involve non-Muslims and Muslims, or Muslims of two different sects, were now to be determined by mixed tribunals, with their deliberations open to the public. Taxes and military service are to fall equally on the shoulders of all subjects irrespective of their religious beliefs.

Although the Imperial Rescript fully accepted the doctrine of religious, ethnic, and linguistic equality within the empire, it made few other concessions to liberalism and democracy. Through self-chosen assemblies each community is to control its own local administration and has the right to send representatives to the Supreme Council of Justice, a body to be convened to consider issues "which might interest the generality" of the sultan's subjects. Otherwise, nothing in this document hints of limiting the absolute power of the sultan. In fact it specifically mentions that all government appointments will be made according to the sultan's "sovereign will."

The rescript also sheds some light on economic conditions within the empire. Only now, as a result of the proclamation, can foreigners own land and religious minorities freely "purchase, sell and dispose" of property. Only now are taxes to be levied equally among all religious groups, government budgets made public, and bank formation encouraged. The need for such provisions reveals some of the reasons for the weakness of the nineteenth-century Ottoman economy.

Another characteristic of the rescript is its concern with improving the state of the Ottoman government's finances. One of the things the Imperial Rescript recommends is the end of tax farming and the direct collection of taxes by government officials. This had been a step recommended by Mehmed Pasha in *The Book of Counsel for Viziers and Governors*, written in 1703 or 1704 (source 51). This says something about the slow pace of change in the Ottoman Empire.

The history of the Ottoman Empire in the nineteenth and early twentieth centuries provides an example of how European powers influenced the diplomacy and internal politics of a sovereign nation. As is revealed in the next document, Jamal ad-Din's letter to Hasan Shirazi on the Persian tobacco concession, the history of Persia in the same years provides an equally good example of economic imperialism.

The mass involvement of the Persian people in their opposition to the tobacco concession granted to British businessmen was a new phenomenon in the politics of the region. Previously, advocates of political change were mainly drawn from the ranks of government officials and the military, and their causes rarely generated enthusiasm or support from the largely illiterate masses. An exception took place in 1891, when large numbers of Persians participated in a nationwide tobacco boycott that forced the government to abandon an unpopular policy. The letter of Sayyid Jamal ad-Din to the Islamic religious leader, Hasan Shirazi, played an important role in this episode.

A reasonable place to begin analyzing this document is to ask our students why Sayyid Jamal ad-Din makes his appeal to Persia's highest *religious* leader. This should enable us to make a number of points: the prestige of Islamic religious leaders in Persia; the ability of religious leaders to get across a message to a largely illiterate population through the network of local mosques; and finally, the absence in Islam of any sharp division between the religious and the secular spheres of life.

Jamal ad-Din's letter is a masterpiece of persuasion. After reminding Hasan Shirazi of his high standing among the people and the grave responsibilities attached to his office, the author goes on to denounce the personal and public failings of the shah. These failings are easy enough to understand but are worth reviewing quickly.

Close attention should be given to some of the nuances of the letter. It is interesting to note, for example, that although Jamal ad-Din himself advocated selective borrowing from Western science and technology, his letter has a strong anti-Western tone. Westerners are described as "foes of our faith" and the "enemy of Islam." He states that the worst excesses of the shah began after his return from a trip to Europe. And he warns that unless the shah's disastrous policies are ended, an unthinkable calamity would occur—that "the realms of Islam will soon be under the control of foreigners, who will rule as they please and do what they will."

What is Jamal ad-Din's vision of Persia's future? It emphasizes anti-Westernism and holds out the prospect of a Persia free of all foreign influence and economic control. Without such a foreign presence, he argues, the authority of the shahs will be strengthened, the Islamic community as a whole will be protected, and Persia's humiliations will end. The letter fails to mention, however, anything about Jamal ad-Din's convictions concerning Islam's need to selectively borrow from the West. In a letter addressed to a prominent Islamic religious leader, expressing such ideas would not have been prudent.

The last question for analysis asks students to consider what the letter reveals about the prospects and progress of reform in Persia as compared to the Ottoman Empire. Of course, the answer to this question is determined by how one defines "reform." If it is construed in the sense of reform according to the Western model, then one might conclude that prospects were more favorable in Ottoman lands. Both the imperial rescript and the proclamation of the Young Turks reveal the influence of Western-inspired political ideas— equality before the law, a regularized system of justice, and legal, administrative, and constitutional reform. Persian reformers in the 1890s were still concentrating of the personal failings of a specific shah and the evils of foreign influence. If, on the other hand, one defines "reform" in terms of purifying Islam and protecting it from foreigners, then one might arrive at a different conclusion. The subjects of the shah were unified in their adherence to Shi'ite Islam and, as their support for the tobacco boycott reveals, were capable of united political action. The Ottoman sultan's subjects were divided among Christians, Jews, and a number of different Muslim groups (with a strong majority as Sunnis). Devising policies that would satisfy all these groups proved difficult and ultimately impossible.

The Young Turks' Resolution of 1908 breathes a spirit quite different from that of Abdul Mejid's rescripts. The resolution resembles the sultan's early proclamations in that it calls for complete equality among the empire's subjects irrespective of their religion. The Young Turks go further, however. For example, they seek to limit the power of the sultan by reviving the 1876 constitution that had been repressed by Sultan Abdul Hamid II. They proclaim that every Ottoman over the age of twenty will have the right to vote, and furthermore, that the Prime Minister will need a parliamentary majority in order to rule. In addition, all Ottoman subjects will have the right to form political organizations.

The most striking feature of the Young Turks' proclamation is its strong Turkish nationalism. It demands the exclusive use of the Turkish language in all official correspondence and the mandatory teaching of Turkish in all primary and secondary schools. When steps were taken by the Young Turks to implement this "Turkification" policy, many of the empire's millions of Arab subjects were incensed, and Arab nationalism with a strong anti-Ottoman bias became an important force in the region.

An example of Arab nationalist sentiment is provided by the final document in this section, "Announcement to the Arabs, Sons of Qathan." It is an interesting document in many respects. Firstly, it defines "Arab" almost exclusively in terms of language. The author is clearly a Muslim, and clearly is concerned about Islam's future. But as a nationalist he hopes to enlist all Arabic-speakers, whether they are Muslims, Jews, or Christians, in his cause. He admits that many Arab Jews and Christians hesitate to join forces with

Arab Muslims, because they identify the Muslims with religious fanaticism and superstition. He goes on to argue, however, that Christians and Jews have less to fear from fellow Arabs who speak their language than from Turks with whom they have nothing in common. More importantly, the author dreams of the day when fanaticism and intolerance among Arabs will disappear altogether and that all Arabs, irrespective of their religion, will live together harmoniously in an independent Arab state.

Unquestionably, the author has no love for the West. He bitterly complains that Arab lands have been sold off to the English, French, and Germans, who reap profits while the Arabs starve. But the Turks are the real enemy. They are usurpers, degenerates, second-rate Muslims, and oppressors of the Arabs. Referring specifically to one of the policies instituted by the Young Turks, the author states that the Turks' worst crime was their campaign to suppress the use of Arabic in the schools, courts, government offices, and even in Muslim prayers. This, he feels not only insults the Arabs, but also threatens the very basis of Islam.

For all these calamities the Arabs themselves are partly to blame. Internally divided and passive under Turkish rule, they need to assert themselves and fight for what is theirs—freedom from tyranny and political independence. The Armenians, Christian subjects of the sultan, have been rewarded for having stood up for themselves. They have won provincial autonomy, and in his view, will soon be independent.

*   *   *

Rammohun Roy's letter to Lord Amherst is an example of the optimism of some Indians in the early 1800s about the prospects of British rule in their country. Such optimism was not uncommon among other African and Asian peoples after their first contacts with Europeans. As shown in Chapter Two of *The Human Record*, King Afonso I of Congo dreamed of taking advantage of Portuguese technology and agricultural techniques to improve the lot of his subjects, only to be bitterly disappointed.

In his letter Roy adopts a tone of humility, noting at the beginning how extraordinary it was for "the natives of India" to express an opinion to the English government and expect it to be considered. For a man who was well aware of his impressive intellectual achievements and professional accomplishments, in all likelihood this modesty was as much a rhetorical devise as an expression of any real sense of personal inferiority. In the first paragraph he quickly shifts his tone from that of a humble supplicant to that of a teacher who will try to instruct the newly arrived British on the realities of India's needs.

Roy, despite his interest in the ethical teachings of Christianity, is more interested in drawing on Western science and mathematics for India's benefit. He has little use for traditional Hindu learning and scholarship, which he equates with the supposed obscurantism of the medieval European scholastics. In his view, like medieval European theologians and philosophers, Hindu pandits rehash and redefine ancient "grammatical niceties and metaphysical distinctions" to no practical purpose. To have young Indians spend years learning Sanskrit and then pondering the "foolish" questions Roy lists would add up to a worthless education for the students and for Indian society as a whole. Withholding the teaching of Baconian philosophy from India and maintaining old standards will, he predicts, "perpetuate ignorance" and "keep the country in darkness." If the British are sincere in their expressed intent to help the Indians, then they are obligated to promote "a more liberal and enlightened system of instruction."

While Rammohun Roy was mainly interested in the effects English rule had on Indian education, G. V. Joshi, some five decades later, explored the ramifications of English economic policies. He was convinced that despite impressive statistics showing railway construction, bank foundations, and increased imports, English economic policy was catastrophic for the Indian people.

As Joshi states at the beginning of his article, railroads were not all bad for India. He writes, "They are good in their own way as providing cheap transit, and promoting national solidarity, and facilitating trade-movements." But viewed in a broad sense, railways symbolize the selfishness of English economic practices and the subordination of Indian interests to the profits of the colonial master. To Joshi, a major villain was the Marquis of Dalhousie, who as governor general of India between 1848 and 1856 initiated the ambitious program of public works and railway construction with the purpose of getting Indian agricultural products as cheaply as possible to coastal ports and ultimately to England, where they could be turned into manufactured products. Another villain was the doctrine of free trade, which enabled the British in the absence of tariffs to flood the Indian market with manufactured goods.

Why were such policies damaging to India's interests? The reasons, according to Joshi, are almost too numerous to count. First of all, the mania for railroad construction has made it impossible to attain any balance in India's economic development. Altogether too many resources were being allocated to this one undertaking. It has also opened the door to foreign control of newly established enterprises. Not only railroads, but banks and factories are also under foreign management and ownership. Furthermore, because management positions and positions requiring technical knowledge are monopolized by Europeans, Indians get what's left—menial, low paying jobs which require no skill or training.

Joshi also objects to railroads because they symbolize the worst features of English economic thinking. Basically the English are applying to India the mercantilist principles that had guided their colonial policy since the 1700s: colonies exist to produce raw materials that are sent to England, where they are turned into manufactured goods that are then sold back to the colonies. Joshi believes that railroad lines had been designed and built mainly to transport agricultural products, especially cotton, cheaply to Indian ports from which they could be shipped on to England and turned into finished cotton cloth. These textiles and other goods were then sold to India. With the disciples of free trade making sure that tariffs on English exports were low to nonexistent, native industries were ruined by the flood of cheap, machine-made products.

What needs to be done? Joshi believes, first of all, that tariffs should be established to limit English imports and protect Indian manufacturers and artisans from rapid and total collapse. Second, India's educational system should be revamped to meet the demands of India's new economy. It now concentrates on history, literature, and modern languages to prepare young Indians for careers in the lower echelons of the Indian civil service. Joshi recommends that the schools also teach finance, science, and technical subjects so that Indians would be qualified for responsible, high-grade jobs in banks, railroads, and factories. Otherwise, English policy will continue to be "financially burdensome and economically ruinous" for the Indian people.

Other Ways to Use the Sources

1. When asked about the impact of British colonialism on his people, Ndanski Kumalo observed that it had both good and bad effects. After reviewing the documents in this chapter, do you agree with his assessment? On balance, did the benefits of colonialism outweigh its damage?
2. What do the sources in this chapter reveal about European attitudes toward their colonies and the people who lived in them?
3. Based on your knowledge of society and politics in the late Ottoman Empire, explain some of the reasons why it was difficult to effectively implement the Tanzimat reforms and the decrees of the Young Turks.
4. Compare and contrast the proposals for reform of the Ottoman empire offered by Mehmed Pasha in *The Book of Counsel for Viziers and Governors* (source 51) and those of the nineteenth-century reformers.

5. Although Rammohun Roy rejected the idea of having the British establish Sanskrit schools, other Indians disagreed with his position. What arguments might they have offered to support their views?
6. What do the documents in this chapter reveal about the differences and similarities between European imperialism in Africa, India, and Southwest Asia?

C H A P T E R
10

East Asia Confronts the West

Chapter Theme

Chapter 10, like Chapter 9, deals with the impact of the expanding West, in this case, on East and Southeast Asia. It does not neglect, however, important internal developments in the region. The first section focuses on the overwhelming problems of nineteenth-century China, which as late as the eighteenth century was still viewed with awe by all who were familiar with its size, government, and culture. In the 1800s, however, China reeled under the impact of foreign pressures, military defeat, a worsening economy, rural discontent, political paralysis, and growing self-doubt. China's leaders were unable to solve these many problems, and after the Revolution of 1911, China's imperial regime collapsed. This chapter explores the fundamental questions of why China failed to respond more effectively to its problems and why its failure had such disastrous consequences.

The chapter then goes on to examine the counter-example of Japan. Japan, like China, faced severe problems in the nineteenth century but responded quite differently. In 1867, a small group of Japanese aristocrats overthrew the Tokugawa shogunate and instituted a government that successfully plotted a new course for the nation by promoting Western science, technology, industry, and military reorganization. As a result, Japan became a major economic and military power within a few decades. Our documents shed light on the factors that made Japan's rapid transformation possible.

The chapter concludes with a section on Southeast Asia, a region that also experienced increased pressure from the West, but because of its diversity, had widely varying experiences. Burma, Cambodia, Malaya, Vietnam, and many parts of the East Indies became new European colonies. The Philippines and parts of the East Indies, however, had been under Spanish or Dutch rule as early as the sixteenth and seventeenth centuries, while Thailand, although it lost territory to the French and English, remained independent.

Why These Sources?

The documents on China are intended to illustrate both the severe problems faced by late Qing China and also some of the reactions and proposed solutions to these problems. The section begins with a document relating to the first major crisis faced by China in the nineteenth century—widespread Chinese opium addiction caused by a flood of British imports. We chose to illustrate China's response to British opium sales with a letter written by the Confucian scholar-official Lin Zexu to Queen Victoria. The letter shows a more realistic understanding of world relationships than Qianlong's letter to George III (see source 56), but it still reveals some of the reasons why China's Confucian-trained officials had such difficulty formulating effective policies to deal with the West. Lin overestimates Queen Victoria's power, and is naively convinced that she will be won over by his appeal to ethical principles.

The next document, Zeng Guofan's memorial (memorandum) to Emperor Xiangfeng, is included to make sure students do not erroneously conclude that China's problems all resulted from foreign meddling. As this document reveals, China faced severe internal problems, the most devastating of which was the deterioration of life for the rural masses. Zeng's report provides a clear and balanced assessment of China's internal problems at mid-century.

The last selection, from Sun Yat-sen's *The Three People's Principles and the Future of the Chinese Revolution* shows how, by the end of the nineteenth century, some Chinese had concluded that revolution, not reform under the Qing, was China's only hope. In this selection, Sun Yat-sen, China's leading revolutionary and the founder of the Goumindang, or Nationalist Party, discusses his "three people's principles"—nationalism, democracy, and livelihood—and how they are to be attained.

The section on Japan focuses on the decisive turning point of modern Japanese history, the Meiji Restoration of 1867/1868. Sakuma Shozan's *Reflections on My Errors* presents one side of the debate among the Japanese after Commodore Perry ended their nation's isolation in 1853. Sakuma's position, that Japan should somehow combine Eastern ethics and Western science became a major inspiration for the Meiji reformers.

The next document sheds light on Japan's economic development during the Meiji Era. The letter of Iwasaki Yataro, founder of the Mitsubishi business conglomerate, reveals how patriotic sentiment contributed to Japan's rapid and successful economic transformation.

The section concludes with a series of illustrations covering the period from the 1850s to the 1880s. They show how Japanese views of the West evolved from fear and revulsion in the years immediately following Perry's arrival to extreme adulation in the early Meiji period to a more balanced view by the 1880s. These written and visual documents on Japan, used in conjunction with the three preceding documents on China, provide material for the analysis of a wide range of issues relating to the histories of these two East Asian nations.

Representing the diverse historical experiences of the peoples of Southeast Asia during the nineteenth century with only a few documents is difficult. Phan Thanh Gian's letter to the Vietnamese emperor and his "Last Message to his Administrators" were included because they poignantly express the frustration and pain occasioned by French colonialism in the region. The selections from the Thai king, Chulalongkorn, were chosen because they suggest a possible scenario of how Southeast Asian societies might have developed without colonialism. Thailand was the one Southeast Asian country to preserve its independence, and even without "enlightened" Western guidance, it gradually began to reshape its traditional institutions under royal leadership.

Analyzing the Sources

Lin Zexu's letter to Queen Victoria, in which he implores the queen to halt England's sale of opium to China, is based on some of the same conceptions we saw in Qianlong's letter to George III in the 1790s (source 56): since the Chinese emperor is the world's premier ruler, all foreigners should be subservient to him; the emperor tolerates trade and diplomatic relations with foreigners only because of his benevolence; China has no need of foreign goods, but the outside world cannot live without goods produced in China. Unlike Qianlong, however, Lin has seen first hand the strength of the British navy, and despite his boasting at the end of the letter about China's "great and awesome" power, he seems to realize more clearly than Qianlong just how grave a threat the British were to China.

Thus his letter lacks the bravado of Qianlong's contemptuous dismissal of British requests for increased trade. He speaks favorably of previous Anglo-Chinese relations, flatters Victoria for her kindness and compassion, and helpfully suggests that opium traders make up only a small, unscrupulous minority of all English merchants. Lin first attempts to convince Victoria (whose power he seems to equate with the power of the Chinese emperor) to end the opium trade by appealing to her conscience. Surely, he writes, she does not understand opium's disastrous effects on China or else she would have acted already. Then he attempts to convince her that ending the opium trade will result in rewards from Heaven—a long life and many descendants. Only at the end does he make the threat that foreign opium merchants will be executed unless they abandon their trade in opium. For Lin, whose Confucian training discouraged the use of force, this would be a last resort, and a step, he probably realized, that would lead to further conflicts with the foreign devils.

Zeng Guofan's memorial to Emperor Xianfeng is the anguished plea of a serious-minded statesman who realizes that China is slipping into a morass of corruption, disorder, and injustice that is making a mockery of the Confucian ideals to which he was devoted. He begins his memorandum with a restatement of the Confucian tenet that the people's contentment depends not simply on prosperity, but also on their respect for their rulers. Rulers, in turn, earn this respect by making sure their decisions and policies are guided by ethical principles and love of their subjects. Zeng Guofan courteously dismisses the possibility that Xianfeng himself lacks love for his subjects; instead he blames local officials for their apathy and their failure to communicate the emperor's "compassionate sentiments" to the people.

Does Zeng honestly believe that the people would be content if they respected the emperor and were fully informed of his devotion to them? After reading the rest of his memorandum, one has doubts. His memorandum paints a grim picture of rural China's miseries and calls for action to deal with a long list of abuses.

Once one carefully reads Zeng's (perhaps exaggerated) analysis of the rents and taxes paid by Chinese peasants, it is easy to understand why peasant revolts plagued nineteenth-century China. With peasants having to pay 50 percent of their harvest in rent and almost 40 percent in taxes and requisitions, their plight sounds bad enough. But having to pay most of their taxes in copper or silver coins made things worse. Rice had to be sold for overvalued copper coins and then had to be exchanged for even more expensive silver. Once these transactions had been completed, the rural population's plight is no longer bad, but impossible. It comes as no surprise that according to Zeng tax delinquency is rife, and that government officials, themselves under pressure to reach their quotas, threaten and brutalize the people who cannot pay.

Zeng's descriptions of the methods officials use to deal with rural law-lessness and banditry puts local government in an even worse light. The officials' collusion with bandits, their bribe-taking, their reckless abuse of power, and their brutality all deepen the people's misery. Anyone who appeals his case at the Ministry of Justice in Beijing can expect further mistreatment and abuse. Claiming to have reviewed over one hundred such appeals, Zeng has found case after case of collusion between judges and local officials. Invariably, some reason is discovered to deny the plaintiff's petition, and in most cases the plaintiff, not the official, is penalized.

How practical were Zeng's solutions to China's problems? It is unlikely they would have done much good. We have no idea whether Zeng ever drew up his plan for stabilizing the price of silver. But his request that the emperor issue a "strict" order to high provincial officials requiring them to "think carefully" about China's problems and devise a cure was not the kind of bold action the solution to China's problems required.

Writing some fifty years later, Sun Yat-sen outlined a program for China's future that went far beyond Zeng's appeal to the emperor's benevolence and his call for "serious thought." By the late nineteenth century, China's internal problems had become more desperate and foreign interference more pervasive. Having lost all faith in the monarchy, Sun calls for a revolution that will implement his three people's principles of *nationalism, democracy*, and *livelihood*. Although inspired by Western ideologies and shaped by his understanding of recent world developments, his political vision is also shaped by Confucianism and China's unique circumstances.

In 1905, when Sun presented the speech from which this excerpt was taken, the principle of nationalism was directed almost entirely against the authority of the Manchus, the northern invaders who had established their control of China and established the Qing Dynasty in the mid-seventeenth century. Only later, especially after the Revolution of 1911, would the principle be expanded to include opposition to Western and Japanese interference in China's affairs. At this stage the nationalist struggle involves Han Chinese against their Manchu overlords, a struggle comparable, in Sun's view, to the recent struggles of the Boers of Transvaal against the British and of the Filipinos against the United States.

The principle of democracy means a commitment to a "constitutional, democratic political system." Only a government with such a system will be capable of protecting China from foreign conquest. Sun does not provide a detailed description of how China's democratic government will work, other than that it will embody the principle of the separation of powers. Sun derived this doctrine from the writings of the eighteenth-century French *philosophe*, Montesquieu, who had argued in his *Spirit of the Laws*, that freedom can best be protected when power in a government is divided among three branches; the judicial, executive, and legislative. Sun, however, adds a Chinese twist to Montesquieu's theory by increasing the number of powers from three to five. The examinative power will be responsible for administering civil service examinations, which will be mandatory even for the highest officials. Such a system will "eliminate such evils as blind obedience, electoral abuses, and favoritism." Ironically, Sun was calling for the continuation of the civil service examination system in the very year it was abolished by the Manchu government. Sun also adds a fifth branch of government, the supervisory power, or Censorate, which like the civil service examinations, had been part of the Chinese system of government for centuries. It offers criticism of government policies and recommends discipline or impeachment for derelict officials.

Sun's principle of livelihood later came to mean state ownership of property, i.e., socialism, but at this point it meant a general commitment to alleviating poverty among the rural masses. The root of poverty, according to Sun, was high taxation. His plan was to eliminate taxation for China's people altogether, except for the small number of wealthy people who were landowners. These wealthy Chinese would be obligated to pay what amounted to a capital gains tax of close to 100 percent on the sale of any land that had gone up in price. Sun, on the basis of his observations of developments in Hong Kong and Shanghai, was convinced that "with the advance of civilization and the development of communications" (in other words, economic modernization), land prices would skyrocket. Owners would be allowed a small profit, but anything above that would go to the state. In Sun's rather unlikely scenario, no other taxes would be needed, and a huge burden would be lifted from the shoulders of the Chinese people.

Sun undoubtedly had an excellent point in his recommendation that the state should tax the enormous profits some Chinese were making from land sales. But his assumption that such a tax could solve China's financial problems shows a naivete and lack of experience. This was a major problem for Chinese reformers and officials after the Revolution of 1911.

His efforts to apply lessons learned from the experiences of European nations and the United States also are based on hazy notions and inaccurate assumptions. Although he is aware that electricity and steam power are transforming economic life in the West, he seems to believe that the economic activity most affected is agriculture, not manufacturing. He also has an inaccurate conception of the impact of these economic changes. He states that in England poverty has undergone a "several thousandfold increase" in the course of one generation. He also asserts that the United States government's laxity and corruption are "unparalleled among the nations of the world" and that the U.S. Congress is dominated by foolish and ignorant politicians because elections are won by the eloquent, not the intelligent. The U.S. government lacked neither corruption nor fools, but Sun's depiction is nonetheless a caricature.

* * *

Sakuma Shozan's "Reflection on my Errors" begins with the parable of the vassal or son who is obliged to save the life of his sick lord or father even though his master wants no medicine and will be angry if help is given. Japan, according to Sakuma, is the sick lord, and it must be saved from its mortal sickness even if the medicine is unpleasant and unwanted. The solution is his famous formula to combine Eastern ethics and Western science.

For Sakuma, Eastern ethics basically means the Confucian values of decorum, righteousness, duty, and the pursuit of ancient learning. When he discusses the five pleasures of a gentleman in section 20, the first three pleasures express Confucian values. He equates Eastern ethics with the maintenance of a harmonious family, devotion to the Way of the Sages, and the cultivation of one's inner virtue and sense of duty. He equates Western science with understanding the external, material basis of existence. The East and the West can thus be combined without conflict in the service of the nation.

Like the Chinese scholar-official, Zeng Guofan, Sakuma blames his country's problems on defective leadership, especially among military men and intellectuals. Japan's generals are not corrupt or venal but simply incompetent and oblivious to modern (i.e., Western) strategies and weapons. He demands a clean sweep of Japan's military leadership, replacing it with officers who can create and maintain an army of dedicated, courageous, and talented volunteers capable of "driving the enemy away."

Sakuma also calls for changes within the ranks of Japan's intellectuals, who are responsible for guiding and educating the nations' leaders. Their traditional studies of "rites and music, punishment and administration, the classics and the government system" should not be abandoned, but new subjects and disciplines need to be mastered. These new subjects include military strategy, geography, mathematics, and science, all based on Western models. Beyond their achievements in science, however, in Sakuma's view, Westerners have nothing else to offer Japan. They are still barbarians whose defeat and humiliation is Sakuma's ultimate goal.

Although Iwasaki Yataro, the founder of the Mitsubishi combine, was a businessman, not a soldier, his motivation was not much different from that of the military men who were engineering Japan's military transformation. Both the generals and Iwasaki wanted to end their nation's humiliating subservience to foreigners. Thus Iwasaki tries to persuade his employees that winning control of coastal trade from foreign competitors is a national crusade, not just a means to increase Mitsubishi profits.

His appeal to his employees, who face the prospect of layoffs and smaller salaries, is similar to a speech a general might give before sending his troops into combat. Mitsubishi workers must prepare for battle against a foreign Goliath—"backed by its massive capital, its large fleet of ships, and by its experiences of operations." Sacrifice will be inevitable but the purpose is noble. Winning control of coastal trade will be a "glorious event for our Japanese Empire, which shall let its light shine to all four corners of the earth."

These two sources will, in most cases, be assigned together so naturally students should be encouraged to look for common themes in them. Everyone should quickly see that both writers are intense patriots. But we should encourage them to look more closely at some of the characteristics of their patriotism. It was more than simply loving one's country. Sakuma and Iwasaki are convinced that Japan has a mission (never precisely defined) that will bring it honor and glory. This patriotism was accompanied by a large dose of disdain for foreigners. The Westerners' temporary ascendancy had nothing to do with intellectual or moral qualities. Japan must utilize the Westerners' weapons and strategies to preserve itself, but Japan's superiority to the Western barbarians is never in doubt.

Our section concludes with a selection of prints and engravings from late Tokugawa and Meiji Japan. The first two prints, which show one of Perry's ships and one of his lieutenants, convey the shock and apprehension the arrival of the Americans at first caused among the Japanese. Perry's ship was like nothing the Japanese had seen. Since the construction of any ship larger than a small coastal vessel had been prohibited in Japan since the beginning of the Tokugawa period, the very size of the ship was awe-inspiring. The black clouds that belched from its smokestacks, the noise of its engines, its weapons, and its large side wheel all added to the ship's unsettling impression. It is no wonder that the artist added details to make the ship resemble a monster. The portrait of Adams with his scowling expression, wild eyes, bushy hair and eyebrows, menacing mouth, tiny ears, and long nose depicts a human being, but one lacking cultivation, refinement, and restraint. Adams is barbarism personified, thus confirming long-held Japanese views of Westerners.

By the 1870s, with the changes mandated by Meiji leaders well underway, and a mania of things that the West is beginning to build, quite a change has taken place. The illustration from Robun's *Seiyo dochu hizakurige* shows an enlightened man, a half-enlightened man, and an old-fashioned man, all three of whom can be identified easily by their appearance. It would appear that the illustration's message is that "enlightenment" cannot be a halfway thing. In a way the most ridiculous figure is the one in the middle who has tried to add a few Western items to his essentially traditional garb. The superiority of the "fully enlightened man" with his confident stance and bold, forward-looking gaze is unmistakable.

The triumph of the new "Western man" is also evident in the portrait of Fukuchi Gen'ichiro. From hat to boots he exemplifies the new Japanese ideal. So too does his biography. The caption to the illustration highlights his travel to Europe, his success in business and journalism, his "respectful reporting" to the emperor, and his "logic, force, and lucidity." It is also significant that

Fukuchi is shown reporting on the Satsuma Rebellion, in which anti-Meiji forces were crushed.

The final two illustrations, one a cartoon from the late 70s and the other from the early 90s, exemplify the reaction against the idealization of the West in the early Meiji period. In the first cartoon, inspired by a recent lecture on Darwinism, the cartoonist equates the Japanese with monkeys. They mindlessly abandon their samurai swords (visible on the wall) for western clothes. The second cartoon has more bite and a sharper anti-Western message. The message is that the Japanese and Westerners were basically mismatched, as exemplified by the two couples in the foreground. In the background, Japanese men are oafishly dancing with the awkward, oversized Western women while the abandoned Japanese women look on sourly from the rear. Feet may be stomping, but the scene is really nothing to shout "hurrah" about.

These sources on Japan provide an opportunity to discuss the ways Japanese attitudes toward the West differed from those we have seen in other parts of the world. The Japanese view is in one way close to that of the Chinese. Both the Japanese and the Chinese believed that their values, customs, culture, and refinement made them superior to Westerners. In China, however, this led to complacency and overconfidence, and prevented its leaders from appreciating the threat from the West or seeing much value in any of the West's achievements. The Japanese view, well expressed by Sakuma Shozun, was that the Japanese must concede the West's military and technological superiority and imitate the West in these spheres. But in the last analysis, as exemplified by the final two Japanese illustrations, the Japanese maintained a moral and spiritual superiority to the long-nosed barbarians from beyond the sea.

Most Muslims in Southwest Asia during the seventeenth and eighteenth centuries had developed quite a different view of the West. The early Ottomans had freely borrowed Western artillery and imitated certain Western military tactics. Such borrowing gradually came to be viewed with disfavor because it was considered demeaning to rely on foreign ideas and technology, especially when they came from Islam's traditional enemy, Christian Europe. In addition, many Muslim religious leaders came to view the West as the arch-representative of secularism and materialism, qualities that tainted its entire people and everything they produced. They came to believe that anything from the West, especially its science and politics, was abhorrent and dangerous to Islam and should be avoided at all costs.

From the nineteenth century onward, many Indians enthusiastically embraced Western education and philosophy, but as British subjects they lacked the freedom to pick and choose from the West. Furthermore, the Indian people had nothing in their tradition that would have led them to claim, like the Chinese and Japanese, that they were a superior people surrounded by barbarians. Many Indians were convinced that they had much to learn from the West and thus needed to take advantage of whatever tutoring they could receive from Great Britain. Thus, for many decades, Indians from the middle and upper classes were deferential to their British masters and thankful for the tutelage they offered. Such views became less common as India's colonial experience went on.

*   *   *

Our final section, on Southeast Asia, begins with Phan Thanh Duc's letter to Emperor Tu Duc of Vietnam and the final message he sent to his mandarins (Confucian scholar-officials). Both are poignant expressions of this conscientious official's shame and despair after he realized that French military made his people's cause hopeless. Having failed his emperor, he informs Tu Duc of his imminent suicide even while expressing hope that the ruler will find a way to thwart the French. He orders his mandarins to accept defeat and accept what cannot be avoided, submission to the French. But Phan Thanh Gian himself cannot bear to live under the French flag.

Two things are especially worth noting in this document. First, it gives us an opportunity to remind students that Vietnam was the sole society in Southeast Asia to be influenced strongly by Confucianism. Phan Thanh Gian's devotion to his emperor, his references to mandarins, his strong sense of duty, and his frequent appeals to the will of Heaven all underscore this point. His view of the French is also worth noting. Rule by the French cannot be tolerated. But the French have overwhelming military power, which he describes in words that are reminiscent of the fears of the Aztecs when they first saw and heard Cortes's guns.

King Chulalongkorn's writings on slavery and education give us an opportunity to evaluate the policies and ruling style of an absolute monarch who sought to change certain aspects of traditional Thai society. During his long reign he accomplished most of his goals and died a popular ruler. Why did he succeed when so many other absolute rulers who attempted to reform through decree fail?

Certainly one quality that helps explain his success was his cautious moderation, which is revealed in his approach to slavery. Chulalongkorn had no use for slavery. His opposition does not seem to have been based on the Western notions of equality rooted in natural law. Instead, it resulted from his conviction that slavery damaged Thai society. Slaves do not pay their share in taxes and are not obligated to work. They are uneducated and fritter away their time in pastimes such as gambling. But to abolish slavery with one stroke of the pen would not work. Chulalongkorn states this clearly in the opening lines of the edicts on slavery. His plan is for gradual change and no change at all unless some preconditions are met. Chulalongkorn's approach to reform differs markedly from that of the impatient Russian tsar, Peter the Great (source 41), who tried to accomplish everything at once.

In discussing his views on educational reforms, however, Chulalongkorn does resemble Peter the Great to a degree. Both rulers believed that educational change was necessary because of the clear technological superiority of the West. For Peter, the need to catch up with the West justified a crash program to transform Russians into Europeans and introduce Western schools and learning to Russia. To a much greater degree, Chulalongkorn seeks to blend Western innovations with Thai traditions. He is not convinced that Western education is perfect or even particularly suitable for all Thais. This is shown in the letter he wrote to the Thai Minster of Education in 1910.

Other Ways to Use the Sources

1. Given Zeng Guofan's description of the abuses in Chinese government and society, what plan of action might you have devised to deal with China's problems?
2. Between 1850 and 1864 China was convulsed by a massive peasant revolt, the Taiping Rebellion. Basing your ideas on Zeng Guofan's memorandum to the emperor, what can you guess were the major causes of the revolt?
3. You are a Chinese scholar-official given the task of refuting the "three people's principles" of Sun Yat-sen. What might you have said against them?
4. Taken as a group, what do the documents in the section on Japan reveal about the primary inspiration of the Meiji Restoration and its success?
5. Taking all the sources in this chapter, write an essay that describes the variety of Asian attitudes toward the West in the nineteenth century.
6. Let's say that at some point in the future all written sources about "the West" have been destroyed (admittedly, a rather extreme scenario), and our only information about its characteristics were the writings contained in this chapter of *The Human Record*. What might we conclude about the nature of "the West?" Would it be easy to draw a precise picture of its characteristics? Why or why not?

CHAPTER
11

The Industrialized World in Crisis

Chapter Theme

At the beginning of the twentieth century a huge gap existed between the industrialized world of Europe, the United States, Japan, and everyone else. A small number of industrialized nations had more powerful armies and navies, greater wealth, more schools and universities, populations made up of persons with higher standards of living, better medical care, and longer lives than those of people in the rest of the world. These disparities, among others, explain why the industrialized nations had been able to establish their political authority over much of Africa and Asia and why they controlled and reaped most of the benefits from the world's economy.

How and why this relatively small number of nations came to control so much of the world's wealth and achieve so much power has been a focus of many of the documents that have appeared in this volume to this point. The documents in this chapter show how these same nations experienced three decades of crisis between 1914 to 1945. In these three decades, the states of Europe were drawn into two major wars, experienced severe economic setbacks, saw the defeat of democracy in dozens of nations, and entered the post-World War II era so weak that they no longer had the means or will to maintain their overseas colonies or dominate international politics. Outside of Europe, industrialized societies that were offshoots or successful imitators of Europe also experienced economic difficulties and political turmoil. The Great Depression of the 1930s devastated the Japanese and U.S. economies, and in the case of Japan, promoted the expansionist agenda of right wing, ultranationalist generals and politicians. Russia experienced military defeat in World War I, revolution in 1917, and civil war between 1918 and 1921. Following these upheavals, the Russians and other peoples in their empire created the first Marxist State, the Soviet Union, and sought economic development, not through free enterprise, but rather through rigorous, centralized planning. Everywhere the old order was being challenged and foundations laid for new economic and political relationships that would dominate the second half of the twentieth century.

Why These Sources?

The sources in the section on World War I seek to show through art and poetry how and why the four years of fighting had such a devastating impact on the belligerents' morale and expectations. The section begins with a magazine illustration and three posters, all of which glamorized and romanticized the war by depicting it as an opportunity for gallantry, excitement, and camaraderie. The reality of the fighting, which included trench warfare, suicidal charges, poison gas, massive casualties, and endless stalemate are captured in the poetry of Wilfrid Owen and the art work of C. R. N. Nevinson and Otto Dix.

An excerpt from Lenin begins our section on the Russian revolution and the making of the Soviet State. Lenin certainly belongs in an anthology of world history sources. He was a major interpreter of Marx, the mastermind of the Russian Revolution and the founder of the Soviet Union. Among his hundreds of books, pamphlets, and articles, "What is to be Done" provides an excellent introduction to his basic ideas. In it Lenin states his views on a number of key issues, including divisions within Marxism, the importance of ideology, the revolutionary potential of the workers, and the role of party leadership in revolutions.

Stalin's importance in recent world history rivals Lenin's. It was not just that he was the architect of Soviet totalitarianism and the Soviet leader in World War II. Equally important was his implementation of a plan for achieving the Soviet Union's rapid industrialization through centralized government planning, an approach that inspired many imitators throughout the world. His speech, "The Results of the First Five-Year Plan" reveals his motives for launching the Five-Year Plans and describes the basic features of the Soviet Union's state-controlled economy in both industry and agriculture.

The section on ultranationalism in Germany and Japan provides insight into the political crisis of the interwar years and reveals the thinking of the leaders who were responsible for launching World War II. In *Mein Kampf*, Hitler expresses the ideas, hatreds, and fantasies that drove him and ultimately millions of Germans down the path of conquest and destruction. *The Way of Subjects* summarizes the major doctrines of Japanese ultranationalism and the interpretation of Japanese and world history that was used to justify it.

Our readings on World War II focus on the Holocaust and the dropping of atomic bombs on Hiroshima and Nagasaki. Excerpts from the memoirs of the Aushchwitz commandant Rudolf Höss provide a chilling description of the extermination camps and disquieting insights into the mind of a mass killer. Hoss raises important questions about Nazi ideology, totalitarianism, and moral responsibility.

Two new sources on the use of the atomic bomb have been introduced to this edition of *The Human Record*. They replace Iwao Nakamura's and Atsuko Tsujioka's recollections of their experiences in Hiroshima on August 6, 1945. Although this source never failed to arouse a strong emotional response among students, it did not provide them an opportunity to explore the profound moral issues involved in the decision to drop the bomb. To give students such an opportunity, we have introduced to this edition the Franck Report, a plea to President Truman not to use the bomb from a group of scientists who had worked on the Manhattan Project, and an essay by Secretary of State Henry Stimson, who explains how the decision was made to go ahead with the attack on Hiroshima and Nagasaki.

Analyzing the Sources

The four illustrations that make up the first part of the section on World War I all had specific purposes: the first, "The Departure," was designed to encourage patriotic support for the war among German readers of the magazine *Simplicissimus;* the second was meant to stimulate sales of Golden Dawn cigarettes; the third was meant to encourage young men to volunteer for the Australian army; and the fourth, "*On les aura!* "promoted the sale of war bonds in France. All of them encouraged false expectations about the war that made its horrors even more difficult to bear.

What is the message of each of the illustrations? Hennerberg's *The Departure* depicts war as an opportunity for festive celebration and a chance for young heroes to bask in the adulation of the smiling, pretty girls who have come to send them off. The card promoting Golden Dawn cigarettes sends a message that war is an opportunity for camaraderie and is not much different from performing a routine job in civilian life. The soldiers' uniforms are neatly pressed, and the enemy is far away and not very threatening. There's plenty of time to enjoy the smoke offered by the sergeant. The message of the Australian recruitment poster is that war is sport; the rifle held by the soldier has its analog in the lacrosse stick, rugby ball, tennis racket, racing oar, golf clubs, and shotgun held by the sportsmen in the background. War also is an opportunity to stay close to buddies, who will "join, train, embark, and fight" together. Finally, the French poster promoting the sale of war bonds in 1916 gives the impression that the war is really accomplishing something. The young French soldier is moving forward on the attack, looking back and encouraging his fellow soldiers to follow. "We'll get them" is his promise. Of course, at the time the poster appeared, the stalemate on the western front had lasted two years, and heroic charges like this one (by a soldier without a gas mask or helmet) had become exercises in suicide or mass murder, depending on a soldier's perspective.

Wilfrid Owen's two poems, the engraving by Dix, and the painting by Nevinson all express the war's horrors and the disillusionment it engendered. In Owen's "Dulce et decorum est," he describes a war of sludge-covered soldiers, "bent double," "coughing like hags," "lame, blind, and drunk with fatigue." The death agonies of the soldier who fails to affix his gas mask in time becomes the subject of the author's nightmare, and an affirmation that in this war, death for one's country is neither sweet nor fitting.

Owen's poem "Disabled" is a direct response to the false promises of recruiters. For the young Scot, handsome, athletic, and virile, everything about the war is a lie. At the very outset he lies about his age so he can volunteer. The knowing recruiters cynically let it pass with a smile. Without any understanding of the war, he becomes a soldier with dreams of wearing a handsome uniform, making money, and most of all, impressing the girls of the village. Instead, the war brings his ruination when blood from the wound that destroys his legs and manhood spurts from his thigh like an ejaculation. The slim waists and warm hands of the girls are now memories. Emasculated and cold, touched now only as if he were a disease, he waits helplessly for the women who once longingly glanced at him to put him to bed.

The engraving by Dix and the painting by Nevinson are quite different in their composition and subject matter, but they carry similar messages. For Dix, the war has destroyed the storm trooper's humanity, turning him into an insect-like monster bent only on killing. Nevinson sees the war profaning even the earth itself.

* * *

Our section on the Russian Revolution and the founding of the Soviet Union begins with excerpts from Lenin's famous essay, "What is to be Done." Lenin starts with an attack on "revisionism," which he feels is personified by two contemporary socialists, Eduard Bernstein and Alexandre Millerand. Claiming that the revisionists have abandoned the goal of social revolution for the attainment of mere piecemeal social reforms, Lenin reaffirms his belief in basic Marxist tenets—the materialist conception of history, the impoverishment of the proletariat, the inevitable demise of capitalism, the need for revolution, and the dictatorship of the proletariat. In Lenin's view, by ignoring these theoretical foundations of Marxism and by chasing short-term gains, the Social Democrats, just beginning their struggle to free the Russians from autocracy, will lose their sense of identity, purpose, and direction.

Especially important, argues Lenin, is the task of arousing and maintaining the workers' revolutionary consciousness. More so than Marx, Lenin deplores trade unionism, because it encourages workers to set their goals far short of the revolutionary overhaul of society. Without proper leadership, workers will never attain "Social-Democratic consciousness"— the ability to see how the economic oppression they are experiencing is only a part of a broad pattern of oppression suffered not just by workers but also by peasants, intellectuals, and soldiers.

To educate workers politically is thus a primary responsibility of the party, along with the actual planning of the revolution itself. Lenin's conception of the party's role was his most original contribution to Marxist theory. He envisions a party with broad membership but led by a small core, or vanguard, of dedicated intellectuals and activists who make revolution their profession. If leadership were extended beyond this small group, or if open deliberation and democratic votes were to determine policy, the danger of being discovered by the tsar's secret police and of failing because of amateurish execution would both increase.

In a sense, Lenin envisions the dedicated intellectuals providing the "brains" of the movement and the workers the "muscle." This was a new interpretation of Marxism that reflected unique features of the Russian experience—the conspiratorial tendencies of nineteenth-century revolutionary movements, the self-conscious importance of intellectuals or the "intelligentsia," and an oppressed working class lacking education and political experience.

The most important task we have in teaching Leninism is to make sure students are aware of how it differs from Marxism. Students should be able to derive the following points from "What is to be Done" (other distinctive Leninist ideas such as his theory of imperialism are not mentioned in "What is to be Done," and hence are not discussed here):

- Marx and Lenin both believed that the final destruction of capitalism would result from revolution. Marx believed such a revolution was inevitable but could not be hurried. It would result from the unfolding of history's inner laws (the dialectic) and would require little human planning. When the conditions were right, revolution would occur. Lenin thought revolutions needed to be planned and organized by the party vanguard. Revolutions do not just happen; they need to be created.

- As explained above, Lenin did not share Marx's faith in the workers' revolutionary potential. If left to their own devices, thought Lenin, workers will be happy with bigger pay packets and better working conditions. Thus educating the workers in the principles of revolution and planning the revolution itself are the primary responsibilities of the party leadership. Marx also ascribed a role to intellectuals. During the closing stages of capitalism, a few intellectuals from the middle-class would abandon their class, join the proletariat's cause, and become revolutionaries. But by this time most of the work of revolutionary preparation will have already taken place.

- Marx believed that the proletarian revolution would take place only in mature industrialized societies. Only in such societies would the class conflict have an opportunity to fully evolve and the contradictions of capitalism fully reveal themselves. Lenin believed that revolution was possible even in Russia, a state that according to Marx's analysis was just beginning to evolve from its feudal-agrarian stage of social development.

Stalin's speech of January, 1933, "The Results of the Five-Year Plan" is a justification of past decisions and a pep talk, but more than anything else, a celebration of the first Five-Year Plan's successes. What had Stalin hoped to achieve through the Five-Year Plan? In the second paragraph he mentions several goals: to convert the Soviet Union into an industrial power; to eliminate capitalist elements in the economy; to broaden the base of socialism; and to create the economic foundation for a true socialist, i.e., classless, society. But it is clear from the speech that Stalin has an even more important goal, namely to provide the economic foundation for a strong Soviet military. In this respect, Stalin's motives in instituting this crash program of industrialization and agricultural modernization were similar to those of Peter the Great when he sought to Westernize Russia more than two centuries earlier. Both leaders sought security and military strength through change imposed from above.

In the speech, Stalin touches upon the key aspects of the first Five-Year Plan: an emphasis on heavy industry rather than consumer goods; collectivization of agriculture; suppression of the kulaks; state control and co-ordination of both industry and farming. Stalin is somewhat defensive about the emphasis on heavy industry. He admits that resources could have been allocated differently so "we would have more cotton cloth, shoes, and clothing." That would have meant fewer gains in heavy industry, and without those gains progress in agriculture and transportation would have been held back. Worse, it would have prevented the Soviet Union from building up its military, making it weak like China, "which has no heavy industry and no war industry of her own and is pecked at by everybody who cares to do so." Collectivization was necessary to create the large agricultural units capable of efficiently using the tractors and other agricultural machinery being manufactured in factories. Collectivization also was necessary to remove the class that represented capitalism and exploitation in the countryside, namely the kulaks. Stalin admits that "certain excesses were committed" in the process of ridding the Soviet Union of kulaks. But their elimination was necessary. There could be no half-measures, Stalin states, when destroying the "kulak nests."

Stalin claims that the results of the first Five-Year Plan benefited Soviet workers and farmers while proving once more the superiority of socialism to capitalism. Workers in capitalist countries are facing mass unemployment, homelessness, and hunger, while "vast quantities of goods and products are wasted to satisfy the caprices" of capitalists and landlords. In the Soviet Union, however, the worker is free from unemployment; peasants who are no longer exploited by the kulaks have access to the tools of modern agriculture. Most importantly, however, the Soviet Union is strong enough to defend itself.

* * *

As *Mein Kampf* reveals, Adolf Hitler believed in human progress. But it was a conception of progress far different from the hopes of Condorcet and other representatives of Europe's Age of Enlightenment (see source 38). Condorcet believed that progress, based on science and rationalism, would at first take place mainly in Europe and North America, but that ultimately it would encompass all people in every corner of the globe. His hopes for the future include the realization of universal human rights, dignity for all human beings, and peace. Hitler's faith in progress was essentially racial and biological. In his view, the main purpose of human existence was to create conditions in which gifted individuals and superior races could multiply and fully exercise their creative powers and genius. His future was one of free-dom, power, and authority for the strong and the subjugation and elimination of the weak. It was a future shaped by the reality of constant struggle in human affairs.

The application of Darwin's theories to human society and international relations pervades *Mein Kampf.* Hitler believes that the struggle for existence is a constant in human life, just as it is in nature. In human affairs the struggle takes place among individuals and among races. The fittest individuals and races survive and the weak perish. Nothing should be done to hinder this process, either by artificially helping the weak or by allowing superior humans to breed with their inferiors. The survival of the fittest is the "means for improving a species' health and power of resistance, and therefore, a cause of its higher development."

Hitler goes on to describe the master race of Aryans. At first in Nazi ideology the term Aryan was restricted to only a small number of pure Nordic Germans who lived in tiny islets of racially uncontaminated communities between the Elbe and Weser rivers. By the time Hitler wrote *Mein Kampf* he was beginning to use the term in a broader sense of all Germans. According to Hitler, the Aryans were responsible for all of humankind's cultural and scientific progress, and their continuing evolution and growth in numbers are the key to further human progress.

The Aryans' great enemy is the Jews. Hitler offers grudging praise for the Jews' ability to survive and maintain their identity over thousands of years despite the "mighty catastrophes" they have endured. This, Hitler argues, results from the Jews' dogged instinct for self-preservation, which causes them to unite and protect themselves when threatened. Without a threat, however, Jews revert to selfishness and egoism. They lack idealism, a sense of self-sacrifice, and creativity, and if left to themselves will annihilate one another through continual strife and struggle.

Despite their supposed inferiority, the Jews, claims Hitler, in an alliance with the Bolsheviks, are on the verge of destroying the "superior" races of the West. They have accomplished this by polluting the blood of non-Jews, undermining their economies, and gaining a stranglehold on governments. Out of this shallow and perverted reading of history and natural science came the horrors of the Holocaust.

At some point in our discussion, some effort should be made to explore the reasons why Jews and Bolsheviks were the main object of Hitler's hates. Among the points that merit consideration are these:

- In Hitler's view, both Jews and Bolsheviks were "stateless" and incapable of devotion to a nation. The Jews, scattered across the continents, had ties of faith and culture that cut across state boundaries. Their loyalties were focused on Judaism, not a single state or government. Similarly, the Bolsheviks claimed that a worker's true loyalty should be to the proletariat rather than the state. States, according to Marxists, were simply instruments of class oppression and would wither away after the workers' revolution.

- Bolshevism, with its encouragement of class conflict, its goal of social equality, and its opposition to militarism, was anathema to Hitler.

- Jews played an important role in the history of Marxism, with Marx himself the son of a recent convert from Judaism to Christianity. Jews figured prominently in social-democratic parties in Germany and Russia, and also in the administration of the new Soviet State.

- The Soviet Union, the political embodiment of judeobolshevism, had the territory in Eastern Europe that Hitler sought for Germany according to his goal of achieving *Lebensraum,* or living space.

- The Soviet Union was a Slavic state, and in Hitler's racial hierarchy, the Slavs ranked only slightly above the Jews.

The next section of *Mein Kampf* deals with Hitler's political views and clearly reveals his loathing of democracy. Democracy is flawed because it confers power on the common (i.e., inferior) man and because it is disruptive and divisive. Supreme power should be exercised by a single individual, whose decisions are carried out by society's elite. His model of authority, discipline, and responsibility is the old Prussian army.

The last section of the excerpt from *Mein Kampf* deals with another of Hitler's fundamental beliefs, the German people's need for *Lebensraum,* or living space. The concept is simple enough. Germany is cramped into "an impossible area," and unless it finds room to expand it will collapse. Furthermore, because the Germans are "the guardians of the highest humanity on earth," they have the right to redraw national boundaries as they wish. The attainment of Lebensraum means a fundamental reorientation of Germany's foreign policy—less emphasis on sea power and concern with Germany's western rivals, France and Great Britain, and a new focus on expansion to the east. Russia and its "vassal border states" will be the Germans' victims.

The Japanese Ministry of Education's *The Way of Subjects* is similar in certain respects to Hitler's *Mein Kampf.* Like Hitler, the authors reject the ideological foundations of Western civilization—liberalism, individualism, and materialism. In the place of these decadent and failed ideologies, the authors value duty, militarism, authoritarian government, and selfless devotion to the state and emperor. Interestingly, in the view of the authors, the appearance of Hitler (and Mussolini) is a sign that the West is drawing closer to the values of East Asia. The West, they argue, will become more like the east and a "new culture" will be created.

According to the authors, the ethical underpinnings of Japanese culture can be protected only by maintaining unstinting devotion to the imperial family, the source of the nation and all its virtues. In much the same spirit as Hitler, the authors reject the pursuit of self-interest and individualism and call for the careful regulation of one's life to serve the emperor and nation.

If anything, *The Way of the Subjects'* vision of Japan's historical mission is even more grandiose than Hitler's. In the short run, Japan must save East Asia from the political control and materialism of the West by creating its Great East Asia Coprosperity Sphere. In the long run, however, Japan will be the leader of a New World order. This will result from the collapse of the West, the signs of which are confirmed by the authors' reading of recent world history, and the expansion of Japan. Materialism and individualism will be banished in a world guided by the "moral principles" that have been a part of the Japanese spirit.

* * *

The three documents in the section on World War II are close to a "sure thing" as far as their ability to inspire animated class discussion. Students inevitably have strong opinions about Rudolf Höss's "I was just following orders" defense and the assertion that the German people as a whole should not be held accountable for the Holocaust because "they never knew what was going on in the camps." Students usually have equally strong views about the dropping of the atomic bombs. If past experience is any indicator, most will argue that a detonation of the bomb over open water or over a deserted island would have been a better solution than attacking Hiroshima and Nagasaki. Others will offer the counter-argument that given the reality of a war that had already claimed millions of civilians' lives and the high probability of a tenacious Japanese defense of their islands, dropping the bombs was the only reasonable choice.

In his memoir Rudolf Höss claims he had no personal hatred of the Jews. He was, as a good Nazi, convinced they were enemies of Germany, but so too were the Russians, and presumably the British and Americans. As a concentration camp commander he seems to have made no distinction between exterminating Russian prisoners of war and Jewish civilians. Both tasks were simply part of his job. Höss implies that he opposed the mass annihilation of the Jews, and he was pleased when it was decided that some would be spared to work in factories. If he is to be believed, he admired the bravery and defiance of some of the Jews as they approached the moment of their death in the gas chambers, and he was "heartbroken" over the execution of mothers and children. He and his family had the best of relationships with the prisoners who worked in their household as gardeners and servants. Of course, he adds in the same paragraph that his family also had a deep love of horses and dogs.

He characterizes the order for the Jews' mass annihilation as "extraordinary" and "monstrous." And he claims that most of the Germans who were involved in the systematic killings were racked by secret doubts and reservations. But disobedience was out of the question. Submission to the orders of one's superiors, especially when those orders come from men such as Himmler, the head of the SS, and Hitler himself. Orders were simply to be carried out with no questions asked. In this respect, says Höss, the Germans were no different from the Japanese or even the British, whose motto was "Our Country, Right or Wrong." Höss, in other words, is a perfect embodiment of the Hitler's political views in *Mein Kampf*: absolute authority combined with absolute responsibility.

His views on how the mass extermination of the Jews was to be carried out is worth considering. He was disturbed by reports of what had happened when special troops, the *Einsatzgruppe*, attempted mass executions with firearms. It was difficult, so claims Höss, for both the victims and the German troops. Those who were wounded but not killed attempted to flee and had to be killed individually. Chaos reigned. High suicide rates and alcoholism were rife among the Germans. This is why he was excited about the possibilities of poison gas. Death could be better organized, and it would be quick.

The scientists who signed the Franck Report knew by the spring of 1945 that they had created a weapon of monstrous destructive power. In the opening paragraphs of their memorandum they describe the consequences of nuclear warfare: the destruction of Europe and the United States, and the bare survival of China and Russia. There are, they believe, only two ways to prevent such a catastrophe. The first is the establishment of some sort of international organization to protect the peace; the second is an international agreement barring a nuclear arms race. Whether or not such goals can be achieved depends greatly on how the United States introduces its new weapon to the world. To use it on Japan with no warning would be a disaster. No nation would be willing to enter into an agreement with the United States after it secretly developed such a weapon and unleashed it with no warning and no consultation with its allies.

The scientists' hope is that the United States will demonstrate the weapon's power by detonating it over a remote Pacific Island and then announce to the world that it was willing "to renounce its use in the future if other nations join us in this renunciation." It would be justifiable to use the weapon against Japan only after three conditions had been fulfilled: approval by the United Nations (Although the United Nations charter was not officially ratified by fifty one member states until October 1945, the term had been used during the war to refer to the coalition of states fighting Italy, Germany, and Japan); approval by American public opinion; refusal of Japan to either surrender or at least "evacuate certain regions." Such a strategy would offer the best hope that nuclear weapons can be controlled by international agreements and organization.

The scientists argue further that even if an international agreement proves impossible and an arms race ensues, it would be in the best interest of the United States not to use the weapon immediately. By keeping it a secret, the United States would delay the onset of a nuclear arms race, and while other nations were still unaware of its power, could improve its technology and expand its arsenal. When the arms race finally did begin, the United States would have an even greater lead.

The scientists conclude their memorandum with several other points. The all-out effort to produce the bomb had been motivated by the need to assure that Germany did not develop the bomb first. With Germany's defeat, the main reason for developing and using the bomb no longer existed. Finally, failure to use the bomb will not mean that taxpayers' money will have been wasted. All the research and manufacturing facilities that have been built can easily be reallocated to projects that will benefit the national economy, such as the generation of electrical power.

Essentially the authors of the Franck Report argued that American leaders and the American public needed to put short-term considerations aside in the interests of the future. In his discussion of the decision to use the bomb, Secretary of War Henry Stimson rejected such arguments. He relates how the Interim Committee, established by President Truman to devise a plan for using the atomic bombs, considered and rejected the idea of having a demonstration of the bomb rather than using it on an actual target in Japan. The United States did not have bombs to waste, arranging such a test was too difficult, and there was always the chance of failure.

Japan, Stimson concluded, had to be compelled to surrender by the administration of a "tremendous shock." The alternative was a deadly invasion of Japan using conventional weapons. It would cost millions of lives and, if it went as planned, would last until the end of 1946. Thus the dropping of the atomic bombs on Hiroshima and Nagasaki was "our least abhorrent choice."

Other Ways to Use the Sources

1. Compose a letter home from a soldier who has just been through his first month of fighting in the trenches on the western front.
2. If Karl Marx had an opportunity to critique Lenin's "What is to be Done?," what might he have said about the treatise's strengths and weaknesses?
3. Suppose Marx had an opportunity to critique Stalin's "The Tasks of Business Executives." What might have pleased him or displeased him? What would Adam Smith have said about the plan?
4. On the basis of your reading of Hitler's *Mein Kampf* and *The Way of Subjects,* write an essay in which you compare and contrast these two statements of ultranationalism in Germany and Japan.
5. You have been given the task of refuting the historical and philosophical premises of *Mein Kampf.* What would you include in your refutation?

6. On the basis of your reading of Rudolf Höss's memoir, write a personality sketch of Hoss in which you discuss his personality and values.
7. Who presented stronger arguments on the question of the use of the atomic bombs against Japan at the end of World War II, the authors of the Franck Report or Henry Stimson? Explain the reasons for your choice.

C H A P T E R

12

Anticolonialism, Nationalism, and Revolution in Africa, Asia, and Latin America

Chapter Theme

The title of this chapter describes its basic themes. Growing nationalist opposition to Western political, economic, and cultural dominance is a common thread in the histories of Africa, Asia, and Latin America in the first half of the twentieth century, but specific expressions of nationalism and anticolonialism varied from region to region. In Latin America, politically independent since the early 1800s, leaders in the first half of the twentieth century sought to break the hold of U.S. and European business interests on their nations' economies while trying to deal with poverty, illiteracy, and chronic political instability. In Southwest Asia, Arab nationalism took a sharp anti-Western turn, while in Turkey Mustafa Kemal sought to forge a new secular Turkish state out of the ruins of the Ottoman Empire. The region also became the focal point of a unique expression of nationalism, Zionism, which sought to establish a homeland for the world's Jews in Palestine, to the Jews, the biblical Promised Land. In Africa, nationalist movements were just beginning, while in India they were strong enough to shake the foundations of British rule.

Change was in the air, especially in China and Mexico, where revolutions took place in 1911. In that year the Chinese overthrew the Manchus, and the Mexicans toppled the corrupt dictator, Porfirio Díaz. In the aftermath, China was plunged into chaos and civil war, while Mexico struggled to attain political stability, develop its economy, and solve the problems of poverty and social inequality. The documents in this chapter shed light on all these movements and events.

Why These Sources?

The chapter's first section, which focuses on Southwest Asia, includes documents that deal with three important groups in the region. It begins with Mustafa Kemal's 1927 speech to the People's Republican Party. In it "the father of modern Turkey" recounts how he saved Turkey from dismemberment and foreign invasion after World War I by forging it into a secular, modern state. It is the most famous statement of his struggles, values, and ideology (sometimes referred to as Kemalism). For the fourth edition of *The Human Record,* this selection has been newly edited to include more detail on Kemal's early conflicts with Islamic religious conservatives.

Zionism is represented by a new addition to this edition of *The Human Record,* a speech delivered by the noted Jewish writer, Hayyim Nahman Bialik on the occasion of the inauguration of the Hebrew University of Jerusalem in 1925. In it he movingly describes the historic meaning of Zionism and expresses his hopes for its future. We believe this new source will benefit our students by providing yet another perspective on the meaning of nationalism and by introducing them to a movement that has played such an important role in the history of the region.

The section concludes with an excerpt from "Towards the Light," a pamphlet issued in 1936 by the Islamic Brotherhood, an organization founded by the Egyptian leader Hasan al-Banna in the 1920s. These excerpts, which express many of Hasan al-Banna's basic ideas, serve as a counterweight to the secularism of Mustafa Kemal. His dream is of a future for the region that is Islamic, not secular and Western. The selection provides another source on Islamic fundamentalism, a topic that was addressed with material on Wahhabism and the Sokoto jihad in Chapter Six, and will receive further attention in Chapter Thirteen.

Our next section, on anticolonialism and nationalism in India and Southeast Asia, begins with an excerpt from the writings of Mohandas Gandhi. No source collection on recent world history would be complete without something by Gandhi, the Indian leader whose ideas seem so out of step with those of most twentieth-century political figures. Among his many works, *Indian Home Rule* seemed the best choice. It is his most widely read work, and it provides an excellent summary of his views of British rule, non-violence, Hindu-Muslim co-operation, and the deficiencies of modern industrial society.

The section continues with a letter written in 1930 by Nguyen Thai Hoc, the founder of the Vietnamese Nationalist Party (VNQDD) in 1927. It is a succinct, yet moving statement of Nguyen Thai Hoc's views of French colonialism, illustrating how a moderate was transformed into a revolutionary.

Our next section concentrates on African developments during the era of colonial rule. James Aggrey's "The Parable of the Eagle" is the only carryover from previous editions of *The Human Record*. Brief and straightforward, it is a powerful statement of the psychological damage inflicted by colonialism on subject peoples. Along the same lines, the next selection, Daudi Chwa's "Education, Civilization, and Foreignization in Buganda," deplores the erosion of traditional African customs and values as a result of colonialism and the spread of Christianity. It is both a statement of African pride and a lament for all that has been lost. The final section, also new to the fourth edition of *The Human Record*, is a speech delivered by the South African activist, Charlotte Maxeke, in 1930 to a Christian youth rally attended by both whites and blacks. In it she describes how white rule in South Africa has damaged black families and has created special hardships for women and children.

The chapter continues with a section on Latin America. It begins with President Lazaro Cardenas's 1938 speech to the nation on the nationalization of Mexico's oil industry. It is a classic statement of Latin American resentment over the behavior and attitude of foreign corporations. It is followed by excerpts from speeches and interviews of the Brazilian politician Getúlio Vargas. It replaces "The Problem of the Indian," by the Peruvian Marxist José Maria Mariátegui. This was in response to the suggestions of several colleagues that the political right in Latin American should be represented in the anthology.

This chapter concludes with a section on China. It begins with a sketch of Zhang Zongchang, one of the most notorious and outrageous warlords of the 1920s and 1930s. His rise to power and his capricious and irresponsible actions are both indications of the depths to which Chinese politics had fallen. Not surprisingly, a selection from the works of Mao Zedong follows. Out of the vast amount of material that Mao wrote, we have chosen to include excerpts from two of his writings. We chose his *Strategic Problems of China's Revolutionary War* because it effectively reveals Mao's views of guerrilla warfare and of the uniqueness of China's revolutionary movement. In addition, we have also included new material from Mao's *Report on an Investigation of the Peasant Movement in Hunan*. This was the work written in 1927 in which Mao argues that the peasantry will be the driving force in China's communist revolution. From reading and analyzing these excerpts students will understand what is meant by Maoism and how it compares to orthodox Marxism and Leninism.

Analyzing the Sources

The excerpts from Mustafa Kemal's lengthy 1927 speech illustrate one of the most important developments after World War I, the end of the Ottoman Empire and the emergence of a strong Turkish nation-state under Kemal's dictatorship. It also gives us an opportunity to discuss one of the twentieth century's most extraordinary individuals and to compare his ruling style with other leaders who have sought to make rapid, fundamental changes in their societies.

The beginning of our excerpt reveals Kemal as a strong nationalist, but a nationalist who is far different from Hitler (source 93) and the authors of *The Way of Subjects* (source 94). For Hitler and the leaders of Japan it meant conquest, expansion, and the fulfillment of a national mission of world significance. Kemal's nationalism was almost the exact opposite. It was focused on building his nation's internal strength, not achieving foreign conquest and military glory.

In the beginning of the excerpt from his speech, Kemal argues that Ottoman imperialism had been a curse, not a blessing for the Turks. Conquests of non-Turkish peoples had invited counterattacks, especially from the West. In addition, the very idea of attempting to integrate various ethnic groups and nationalities under one government is flawed. Its inevitable result is political weakness and conflict. Kemal concludes that the Turks should abandon any dreams of Panislamism and concentrate instead on building a strong Turkish nation-state focused on the "real happiness and welfare of the nation."

Kemal expands this theme in the section of the speech where he explains his reasons for having opposed the elevation of Abdul Mejid, a relative of the deposed sultan, Mehmed I, to the office of caliph, or "successor" of the prophet Muhammad and religious leader of the world's Muslims. Such a step, argues Kemal, would have further embroiled Turkey in controversies throughout the Islamic world, thus preventing the Turks from solving their own problems.

Kemal's opposition to the caliphate was just one manifestation of this secular ruler's intense aversion to Islam. In the last section of our excerpt he describes the steps he took to suppress the Progressive Republicans, an opposition party that despite its name, represented the interests of Muslim conservatives. Kemal contemptuously dismisses these conservatives as muddle-headed throwbacks to an age of superstition, but he realized the threat they posed. Why else would he keep eight or nine army divisions at war strength for their suppression, and use special powers (the law for the Restoration of Order and the Courts of Independence) to deal with them?

These final passages reveal just how deeply Kemal felt about religious issues. Islam was more than a threat to his political power. More fundamentally, it symbolized centuries of superstition and obscurantism during which the Turks were viewed as less than civilized. Such views led Kemal to abolish the use of the fez and mandate the use of the hat, the "customary headdress of the civilized world." It also led to the suppression of Islamic law, Muslim titles, and many pious Muslim institutions. All these steps, Kemal believed, paved the way for progressive policies (including the liberation of women) that serve the cause of Turkey's "progress and reawakening."

In addition to our discussion of Kemal's actual words, we might also want to consider some of the reasons why Kemal succeeded in pushing through much of his reform program, and why, despite the demands he made on his people and attacks he made on Islam, he remained popular during and after his life. Among the many contributing factors, these figured prominently:

- He was a hero as a result of his leadership in World War I and the war against the Greeks.

- He did not flinch from using force against his opponents.

- He took over Turkey when its fortunes were at low ebb and rescued it from the humiliating Treaty of Sevres.

- He mixed freely with the people and convinced them that he was devoted to their welfare.

- He produced tangible results.

- He sought no personal gain from office. Toward the end of his life he donated his personal fortune to the nation.

All these factors provide a sharp contrast with the record of the Pahlevi shahs of Iran, who adopted many of his policies, but were despised by many of their subjects.

Mustafa Kemal's political battles in Turkey provide an early instance of the conflict between modernizing secularists and conservative Muslims that has been an enduring theme of twentieth century Middle Eastern history. Our next source, Hayyim Nahman Bialik's speech at the opening ceremonies of the Hebrew University of Jerusalem, provides an introduction to another source of ongoing tension in the region, Zionism.

Students should immediately sense Bialik's intensely joyous feelings as he describes the beginnings of what he hopes will become an independent

Jewish state in Palestine. After centuries of "cruel and bitter trials and tribulations, through blasted hopes and despair of soul, through innumerable humiliations," the Jewish people can at last see the prospect of living in their own state, free to nurture their ancient faith without fear of persecution. His words help us understand why the Jews in Palestine have fought so hard and sacrificed so much to establish and preserve the state of Israel.

Students should also be able to see how Zionism is part of the broad history of nationalism in recent world history. Like nationalists in Europe and colonial areas, Bialik describes a past for his people marked by glories and heroism, and most recently, the darkness of exile, persecution, and foreign rule. In addition, he warns of moral decline, intellectual ruination, and loss cultural distinctiveness unless the Jewish people can have a land of their own. As he states, "Without *Eretz Israel*—Eretz means land, literally land—there is no hope for the rehabilitation of Israel anywhere, ever."

Also, like other nationalists, Bialik considers the foundation of an independent Jewish state significant not just for the Jews themselves, but for all of humanity. The Jews, he claims, have a special mission. It was, he argues, no accident that four thousand years after the Jews arrived in the Promised Land, and after many centuries of exile, God brought back his chosen people to this land. This, he implies, is in keeping with God's plan to use the Jews to reveal the "Kingdom of the Spirit" and "the gospel of redemption to the whole of humanity."

Viewed from the perspective of the Palestinians, whose lands were being purchased by Jews and slowly settled by Jews from Europe, Zionism was just another example of European-inspired imperialism, not a movement of national liberation. Although Bialik undoubtedly would have rejected such an analogy, his language at times does resemble the rhetoric of imperialism. Just as European imperialism in Africa and the expropriation of Amerindian lands in North America were justified by claiming that unused or poorly used lands were now to be developed and made productive, Bialik is inspired by the sight of Jewish youths reviving a "wasteland" by "plowing rocks, draining swamps, and building roads amid singing and rejoicing." In addition, his assertion that the foundation of an independent Jewish state will serve the higher cause of humanity and is part of God's plan is not fundamentally different from Kipling's concept of the "white man's burden" and the American expansionist notion of Manifest Destiny.

The last source in this section returns to the subject of Islamic revival, or as it is more frequently called today, Islamic fundamentalism. Although such movements were nothing new to the Muslim world, strong pro-Islamic organizations such as the Islamic Brotherhood rapidly gained strength in the 1920s and 1930s. Anger over postwar political setbacks was one factor contributing to their widespread popularity. Apprehension over the designs of secularist rulers such as Mustafa Kemal, who was determined to narrowly restrict the role of Islam in the new Turkish state, also played a role.

What kind of future did the Islamic Brotherhood envision for Egypt, and by extension, the Arab world? It was a future far different from the one envisioned by Mustafa Kemal for Turkey. Kemal replaced Islamic law with legal codes drawn up by Western experts, and although a dictator himself, looked forward to the day when Turkey would be a constitutional republic. The Islamic Brotherhood's statement says nothing about parliaments, civil liberties, or democracy. In fact, at the outset, it calls for the abolition of political parties, and presumably, all political dialogue and debate. All that matters is whether a government acts "in conformity with Islamic law and principles." It envisions a government controlled by individuals who have won their positions through "competence and merit." But "merit" is defined in a narrowly religious sense. Graduates of Azhar University, which specializes in Islamic studies (I, #10), are to be given preference in filling government positions, and all such officials are to "understand the need for applying the principles of Islam." (I, #5) Each official's private life should be governed by Islamic principles as well, since this private life forms an indivisible whole with his "administrative life." (I, #6)

The future sought by the Islamic Brotherhood is one in which people will live by a strict moral code defined according to the principles of Islam. Part II of the brotherhood's statement, which deals with "social and everyday practical life," calls for the elimination of gambling, prostitution, drinking of alcohol, and dancing. Music, the theater, films and newspapers all are to be censored. Radio broadcasts and cafes are to be turned into instruments for spreading Islamic teachings. Anyone breaking the laws of Islam concerning prayer and fasting should be brought to trial, as well anyone who insults religion. The main purpose of education is to promote religion and morality. Memorization of the Qur'an, the learning of Arabic, and the study of Islamic history will be the core of the schools' curriculum.

As part of its efforts to bring government and private life into conformity with Islamic principles, the Islamic Brotherhood favored a wide range of initiatives to improve public health and assist the poor. The efforts they call for go beyond simply giving money to the needy. The government should undertake policies to raise wages (III, #5), create new jobs through public works (III, #7), provide technical training (III, #8), and make credit more accessible (III, #2).

Charity had always been an important part of Islam, and in fact, along with the creed, daily prayer, fasting during the month of Ramadan, and pilgrimage to Mecca, it was one of the five "pillars" of the faith. As we have seen in the case of Usman dan Fodio and his followers (see source 54), a concern for social justice had frequently been an integral part of movements for Islamic revival.

Particularly noteworthy in this document is what the Brotherhood has to say about "the problems of women" in Egyptian society. Women's lives had undergone many changes in recent Egyptian history. Patriarchal controls had loosened, educational opportunities had increased, and traditional costume had been abandoned for Western-style dress. As the statement of the Islamic Brotherhood acknowledges, all these changes have been controversial—"the subject of polemics and more or less unsupported and exaggerated opinion" (II, #2). It can be inferred that the leaders of the Brotherhood themselves were somewhat unclear about how women would fit into future Islamic society. Resolution #2 from Part II states that efforts should be made *to find* a solution to the problems of women, not *to implement* an agreed upon solution. Clearly, however, the Brotherhood was interested in preserving traditional roles for women as wives and mothers. In schools, boys and girls should be taught separately, and "any relationship" between unmarried males and females is to be considered wrong unless given some sort of approval. Although the Brotherhood approve school teaching and medicine as professions for women (II, #6), its propositions mainly promote marriage and motherhood as the female callings most valuable to the Islamic community.

What else distinguishes the Islamic Brotherhood, aside from its religious fundamentalism? Clearly it is strongly anti-Western. Western science, languages, and philosophy play no role in its schools, which instead focus on Arabic, religion, and non-Western studies. Western-inspired parliaments and constitutions have no allure. In fact, the Brotherhood's political program is close to totalitarian in its essential features. As in totalitarian states, party politics is outlawed, dissent is suppressed, and all the energies of the state are directed toward achieving a single ideological goals, in this case, society's Islamization.

* * *

In the selections from *Indian Home Rule*, Mohandas Gandhi expresses three important aspects of his philosophy: his dim view of modern civilization; his hopes for Hindu-Muslim cooperation; and his faith in passive resistance as a way to overcome the injustices of British rule.

Gandhi was a nationalist, but his nationalism was unique. Nationalists in most Asian and African colonies demanded political independence *and* economic modernization. After independence they envisioned rapid economic development through industrialization, scientific agriculture, and the adoption of Western-style education. Their societies would be free of the West's political authority, but not of its materialism and machines. Ghandhi wants independence but not at the cost of sacrificing the essentials of traditional Indian life.

When Gandhi attacks "civilization," he really means *modern civilization as represented by the West*. In his view, the worst characteristics of Westerners (and their imitators, the Japanese) are their materialism and penchant for self-indulgence. They are deluded in their belief that happiness will result from technological innovation and industrialization. Instead, argues Gandhi, modern civilization destroys the dignity of manual labor, saps humankind's health and strength, undermines the family, and reduces life to the pursuit of wealth and pleasure. Thus in his view it would be a grievous error for India to abandon its own successful civilization by mindlessly trying to become like the West.

What does Gandhi mean when he refers to India as "successful?" In part, it means India's ability to preserve its traditional ways of life over many centuries. This in turn is the result of the Indians' devotion to morality and their ability to "attain mastery" over their minds and passions. Thus both Gandhi and the Japanese authors of *The Way of Subjects* reject Western materialism and proclaim the superiority of their own morality and culture. Gandhi, the pacifist, is different in almost every other respect.

Gandhi's call for Hindu-Muslim co-operation is based partly on common sense and partly on his own religious views. Hindus and Muslims must learn to live peacefully with one another because they have no choice. It is inconceivable, writes Gandhi, that either the Hindus or Muslims could expel the other and have India for themselves. Besides, in the past the two religions have shown themselves fully capable of living side-by-side without conflict. Gandhi's tolerant attitude also reflects his personal conviction that all religions have value. All grasp some aspect of ultimate truth and all give meaning to human existence. In his own words, "Religions are different paths converging to the same point."

In the last section of our excerpt Gandhi discusses his concept of soul force, or passive resistance. He argues that individuals can combat injustices most effectively not through violence but by refusing to obey unjust laws and accepting the consequences. By doing so, the force of love, present in every human being, is released, and the oppressor is led to see the truth. Passive resistance requires no special training, says Gandhi, and is open to all persons, irrespective of their physical strength and gender.

Although Gandhi was deeply depressed about his failure to stop Hindu-Muslim violence and prevent the establishment of Muslim Pakistan at the time of independence, his life on the whole was remarkably successful. No other twentieth-century leader can match his achievement of rallying so diverse a population to the cause of anti-colonialism. What explains Gandhi's success?

Part of it undoubtedly had to do with his personality. The simplicity of his life, his voluntary poverty, and his utter lack of hypocrisy won him a devoted following. But his message was also a major source of his appeal. Ever since the British took over India, Indians had been told they were backward and needed tutoring from their colonial masters so they could become "civilized." Gandhi rejected this, and affirmed the values of the traditional Indian village, especially the dignity of human labor and a simple life. Gandhi also offered a formula for "empowering" the Indian masses even though they were weak in a conventional political sense. Their power rested in their capacity to adhere to a higher morality that would win over the enemy by love, not force. Every Indian, regardless of gender or social standing, could use this inner power to "tutor" the British about right and wrong.

Nguyen Thai Hoc, the author of our next source, is a classic example of an idealistic reformer whose futile efforts to improve his people's lot by working within the system turned him into a radical revolutionary. Embittered by French actions and despairing over the condition of his fellow Vietnamese, beginning in the mid-1920s he petitioned the French colonial administration to undertake a number of reforms—protection of Vietnamese industry, establishment of a technical school, implementation of unspecified programs to alleviate poverty, permission to publish a weekly magazine on industry and commerce, and support for public schools and libraries. (These proposals show Nguyen Thai Hoc's essentially urban perspective. His ideas for establishing technical schools and encouraging industries would not have been particularly attractive to Vietnam's peasants.)

The French ignored every one of Nguyen Thai Hoc's proposals, which led the young idealist to conclude "the French have no intention of helping my country and people." Determined that the French must leave Vietnam entirely, he turned to revolution. The result was the failed Yen Bay revolt, his imprisonment, and, shortly after he wrote this letter, his execution.

Nguyen Thai Hoc would appear to have had three major purposes in writing the letter. In the short run, he hoped to spare the lives of his followers and others that had been arrested by the French for participating in the revolt and were awaiting punishment. He also might have hoped that the members of French Chamber of Deputies, once they learned of the injustices perpetrated by colonial officials, would order a change in French Vietnamese policy (this is somewhat reminiscent of Lin Zexu's letter to Queen Victoria [see source 81]). Having been rebuffed repeatedly by the French, however, Nguyen Thai Hoc must not have been optimistic about this prospect. So he had a third purpose, that of justifying his actions to other Vietnamese. By laying bare (and probably exaggerating) the intransigence and crimes of the

French, he hoped to gain sympathy and support for the Vietnamese
nationalist movement.

* * *

James Aggrey's "Parable of the Eagle," which begins the section on
Africa, is a simple and uncomplicated story, but one with a moving message.
Colonialism, it tells us, by depriving people of their independence, by
preaching the doctrine of the West's "civilizing" mission, and by introducing
countless practices, both trivial and important, that signified the whites'
superiority, undermined colonial people's self-esteem and self-confidence. It
convinced them that perhaps they *were* incapable of self-rule. They came to
believe they were chickens when in their hearts and souls they were truly
eagles.

The point of Kabaka Daudi Chwa's essay, "Education, Civilization, and
'Foreignization' in Buganda," is in certain ways similar to a number of other
sources we have already seen in *The Human Record*. It has, for example,
much the same message as Aggrey's "The Parable of the Eagle."
Colonialism, said Aggrey, gave Africans the message that they, as human
beings, were inferior to Europeans and needed to be taken care of by their
colonial masters just as chickens needed to be fed, housed, and guarded by
farmers. Colonialism, said Daudi Chwa, sent Africans the message that their
traditional customs and beliefs were deficient and needed to be replaced by
Christian practices and European learning if the Baganda were to achieve
"civilization." In his view, too many Baganda have come to believe what the
Europeans have told them, and too many have abandoned their old ways for
a new pattern of life that neither suits nor benefits them. These are thoughts
not fundamentally dissimilar from those of the seventeenth-century
Mi'kmag elder who questioned the wisdom of French beliefs (source 17) and
those of the Russian aristocrat Mikhail Shcherbatov, who mourned the
damage Peter the Great's policy of westernization had done to Russia
(source 42).

The Baganda, says Daudi Chwa, before the advent of Europeans, lived
according to a strict code of morals similar in many respects to the Ten
Commandments. Theft, adultery, murder, indifference to one's parents, and
bearing false witness had all been considered serious offenses, and
lawbreakers were severely punished. Thieves had their right hand cut off;
adulterers were ostracized; murderers faced reprisal from the victim's
relatives; and disrespectful children could expect serious illness. In addition,
the traditional Baganda code emphasized neighborliness, sharing, and
mutual respect. Here again, claims Daudi Chwa, it taught the same things as
Christianity.

Daudi Chwa also argues that in some areas of life the advent of European "civilization" actually has led to a deterioration of morals. The example he cites relates to the suppression of polygamy by the Europeans. Polygamy had never been considered wrong by the Baganda, but now that it had been abolished, prostitution, a despised activity that had been virtually unknown before the colonial era, proliferated. Similarly, Western notions of freedom and liberty have eroded the traditional authority of families over their children. Sons and especially daughters no longer worry about offending their parents by having sexual relations before marriage, and as a result, the old morality has been undermined.

What then is Daudi Chwa's fundamental message? Simply put, he is telling his readers, especially his young readers, that borrowing from the West should be selective and modest. They should "develop and remodel" their traditions, but not abandon them completely.

Charlotte Maxeke's speech, "Social Conditions among Bantu Women and Girls," shifts the emphasis from the moral, religious, and psychological dimensions of white rule in Africa to its social impact. The speaker's main concern is women and children, but her remarks also provide much information about other aspects of life in a South Africa based on segregation, the preservation of white economic and political dominance, and a disregard for the welfare of the black-skinned Natives.

The root cause of the evils she describes is the movement of Bantus from the countryside to cities such as Johannesburg. Faced with land shortages and dwindling cattle herds as a result of epidemics, young married men have no choice but to leave their villages for wage-paying jobs in urban areas. Few return to their villages, and some simply disappear. In both cases, wives, often with young children in tow, move to the cities themselves, either to rejoin their husbands or to search for them. For those whose husbands have disappeared, this means falsely claiming marriage to a new "husband" so they can meet the requirement for housing, and then struggling to find and maintain a wage-paying job. The plight of families that remain together is not much better. Both parents must work, meaning that children are unsupervised. The alternative is for the wife to stay home and earn money illegally by brewing "Bantu beer," an activity that may cause the women to end up in jail.

Maxeke's speech reveals how many obstacles and disabilities the South African legal system created for blacks. We learn how regulations prevent unmarried black women from renting houses; how blacks must apply and reapply for passes while looking for work; how unsuccessful job-seekers are imprisoned; how blacks are allowed to travel only on all-black buses and trains; how black children have no schools to attend; how no effort has been made to ease the transition to city life for the thousands who are leaving the countryside; how women in particular have no meaningful prospects for finding work.

To encourage discussion of Maxeke's speech we might ask students to compare the circumstances she describes with those of English working-class families at the beginning of the Industrial Revolution. Like the blacks of South Africa, these English families had been driven from the countryside because of land shortages and changes in agricultural methods. They too had few marketable skills and no formal education, and arrived in cities that had neither housing nor sewerage systems to meet their needs. There were clear differences, however. The English workers, although looked down upon and even feared by their social betters, faced none of the formal legal handicaps that made life so difficult for the South African blacks. Furthermore, displaced rural English families found ready employment in the factories of the early Industrial Revolution. In some instances, whole families—husband, wife, and children—found work in a single factory or in factories that were close together. Thus family life was not completely disrupted.

* * *

Our section on Latin America begins with excerpts from the famous speech by Mexico's president Lázaro Cárdenas in 1938 in which he announced the nationalization of Mexico's foreign-controlled oil industry. Mexico's president from 1934 to 1940, Cárdenas was an ardent democrat committed to social reform and the alleviation of poverty. Limiting foreign ownership of Mexico's key industries was an important part of his strategy.

In his 1938 speech, Cárdenas rejects the oil companies' assertion that by their presence they had brought "additional capital, development, and progress" to Mexico. Profit and progress, he asserts, have come to the oil companies and their executives but not to Mexican workers or the villagers near the oil fields. The foreigners have built comfortable and secure enclaves for themselves, bribed officials, and used their influence to block social reform and oppose unfriendly politicians. Thus to Cárdenas, the oil companies' defiance of the arbitration panel's findings and the ensuing court decision was the last straw in a long history of social, economic, and political irresponsibility. Cárdenas warns at the conclusion of his speech that the decision to nationalize the oil companies might result in temporary disruption and economic hardship for the Mexican people. He hopes to win them to his side by appealing to their nationalism and sense of pride. He really had no reason to worry. Nationalization was wildly popular, and Economic Independence Day is still celebrated as a holiday in Mexico.

Our section on Latin America continues with a series of excerpts from speeches and interviews delivered by the Brazilian politician, Getúlio Vargas, whose *Estado Novo*, or New State, dominated Brazilian politics in the 1930s and early-1940s. His success in revamping the Brazilian government and his general popularity are both manifestations of the destabilizing effect of the Great Depression on Brazil.

In his interview of April 1938, Vargas offers a very traditional defense for scuttling the Brazilian constitution, based on limited democracy and federalism, and establishing a highly centralized government under the control of the president… in other words, a dictatorship. According to Vargas, the government under the old constitution had been paralyzed by plots, regional conflict, and personal rivalries. Capable and principled men had withdrawn to private life, leaving the way open for communist demagogues to further destabilize Brazilian society. Dictatorship was the answer.

Although Vargas suppressed Brazil's avowedly fascist party, the Intergralists in 1938, Vargas has often been tagged as a fascist himself. True, there are similarities between his policies and pronouncements and those of European fascist rulers such as Franco, Mussolini, and perhaps even Hitler. Like the fascists, Vargas is intensely antidemocratic. He suppressed political parties, clamped down on free speech, crippled the legislature, and brought the judiciary under the control of the president. Democracy has been limited to plebiscites on specific issues. He is also intensely nationalistic. Political power has been centralized at the expense of provincial autonomy. In addition, he is dedicated to encouraging "Brazilian traditions and sentiments," and organizing public opinion "so that there is, body and soul, one Brazilian thought." Finally, he professes to be militaristic. He speaks of the need to rearm our "brave armed forces" for internal and external defense.

In other respects Vargas differs from the European fascists. He lacks Hitler's racism and Mussolini's and Hitler's dreams of foreign military conquests. His nationalism finds expression in his denunciations of regionalism and foreign business interests. Furthermore, he is focused much more on Brazilian economic development than were the European dictators. As he explains in his speech of July 1938, agricultural and industrial diversification and general economic growth are the keys to his New State.

* * *

How far had China's political fortunes fallen during the 1920s and 1930s? Our first source in this section, an account of the career of the warlord Zhang Zongchang, will provide some useful answers, even after taking into account that it is based on after-the-fact recollections by readers of the Chinese journal *Yijing* and undoubtedly contains some exaggerations.

The story of Zhang Zongchang reveals, first of all, how the rapid disintegration of the old Confucian/imperial order created political opportunities for Chinese without social standing or formal education. No longer were positions of authority monopolized by members of the gentry with Confucian training. Zhang's father was a trumpet player, and his mother a shamaness who later lived with a cobbler, a bathhouse proprietor, and cloth-vendor. Zhang himself had been a servant in a gambling house and then joined a troop of bandits.

Zhang's rise to power also reveals the chaos that overwhelmed much of China after the death of the would-be emperor Yuan Shikai in 1916. Zhang followed opportunities that came his way with no thought to higher political principles. The end result was that in 1917 he became chief of the personal guards for China's president, Feng Guozhang, and ultimately the military chief of Shandong Province.

Finally, the account of Zhang's policies shows how the Chinese people suffered under warlord rule. True enough, at least some of the anecdotes in the magazine article may have been exaggerated to embarrass Zhang. Who knows if he actually was duped by the prescient fortuneteller, Tong Huaga, or if he fired cannons toward Heaven when the drought persevered. But even if only part of the stories of Zhang's cruelties and capriciousness is true, it is safe to conclude that life was a nightmare for the people of Shandong Province while he was in charge. Bullied by his troops (including foreign mercenaries), robbed of their money through extortion and runaway taxes, coerced to "volunteer" for his army, and subjected to beatings and execution at his whim, the people of Shandong province must have rejoiced when the "Dog-meat general" fled to Manchuria before the arrival of Guomindang troops in 1928.

Basic elements of Mao Zedong's political views are revealed in the excerpts from two of his major works, " Report on an Investigation of the Peasant Movement in Hunan," written in 1927, and his "Strategic Problems of China's Revolutionary War," presented as lectures to the Red Army College in 1936. Taken together, the two sources show how Mao adopted Marxist and Leninist principles to fit the economic and social conditions of China.

Like Lenin, Mao is convinced that China's anti-imperialist and anti-capitalist revolution must be planned and organized by officials of the Communist Party, who alone in China have the necessary experience, vision, and organizational abilities to reach such a goal. Also like Lenin, Mao is convinced that social revolution is possible in China even though capitalism and industrialization have barely taken root. Both Lenin and Mao agree that Marx's dialectic can be accelerated.

In disagreement with Marx and Lenin, however, Mao believes in the revolutionary potential of the peasantry, a class Marx and Lenin both dismissed as irrelevant to revolution. Mao first expressed his faith in the revolutionary potential of the peasantry in his report on conditions in

Hunan, a province where the peasants had already organized peasant associations to break the power of the landlords. Here, in their anger and violence he saw China's future. He imagined "several hundred million peasants" rising like "a mighty storm" to sweep away the gentry, and ultimately the state itself, the clan system, religion, and patriarchy. It would be the communist party's role to "march at their head and lead them."

At the beginning of his speech on "Strategic Problems of China's Civil War," Mao pays lip-service to the orthodox Marxist view that the proletariat will provide leadership of the revolution along with the party. Subsequently, however, he singles out the peasantry as the class with the motivation and ability to smash the Guomindang and win China's revolutionary war. The peasants, he reiterates, are the backbone of the revolution.

Mao's strategy for fighting this revolutionary war also makes his thought distinctive. When Marx and Lenin thought of revolution they had in mind Europe's urban-centered revolutions of 1789, 1792, 1848, and 1871, in which crowds took to the streets, attacked government buildings, threw up barricades, fought the army, and brought down their governments. In Mao's view, the overwhelmingly rural base of China's communist movement made such scenarios inapplicable to China, as did two other factors: the military strength of the Communists' main enemy, the Guomindang and China's semi-colonial status.

Thus the Red Army will succeed only if it wins the rural masses to its cause and fights a war based on "strategic defensive." The need to adopt a defensive strategy was dictated by the military realities facing the Communists in 1936, less than two years after their legendary long march from Jiangxi to their new headquarters in Yan'an. Given the superiority of Guomindang weaponry, an offensive strategy would be suicidal according to Mao. Instead, the communists must fight a guerrilla war, recruit the masses to their cause, and prepare for a counterattack. When they have lured the enemy into an indefensible position they will smash its "campaigns of encirclement and annihilation" and go on the offensive.

Other Ways to Use the Sources

1. Suppose you are a Palestinian Muslim intellectual opposed to Jewish settlement in Palestine. What arguments could you offer to show the injustice of Zionist claims as set forth by Bialik?
2. Kemal, Gandhi, Bialik, and Cardenas were all in some fashion nationalists. How was their nationalism similar? How was it different?

3. Many Hindus and most Muslims rejected Gandhi's dream that Muslims and Hindus could and should live peacefully in India together. What arguments might they have offered against Gandhi's position?
4. Mustafa Kemal launched Turkey on a course of rapid industrialization. How might he have justified this if confronted by Gandhi's assertions about the drawbacks of "civilization."
5. What might Marx have offered as criticisms of Mao's ideas in "Strategic Problems of China's Revolutionary War?" What criticisms might Lenin have made?
6. Compare and contrast the problems of black families in South Africa as they moved from the countryside to the cities with the problems of English working-class families at the beginning of the Industrial Revolution (see source 61).
7. Compare and contrast the ideas of Kabaka Daudi Chwa and any or all of the following: the Mi'kmaq elder (source 17); Mikhail Shcherbatov (source 42); King Chulalongkorn (source 86); Gandhi (source 101).

C H A P T E R
13

The Global Community since 1945

Chapter Theme

It is tricky business to predict what future historians will consider to be the most important themes in the history of the late-twentieth century. Thus the selections in this chapter touch on several developments, rather than focusing on one or two. Most subjects—women, racism, international relations, political change, the environment—have played a role in human history since its beginnings and have received extensive treatment in both volumes of *The Human Record*. This chapter will reveal to our students, however, that the rapid changes in the second half of the twentieth century—the end of colonialism, the break-up of the Soviet Union, accelerating technological developments, and the end of the Cold War—have put a unique twist on many of these enduring issues.

The selections in this chapter also highlight the vast distance humanity has traveled in the last five hundred years. Around 1500, the peoples of Asia, Africa, Europe, the Americas, and Oceania all existed in individual spheres with relatively little interaction. Since then isolation has given way to integration, so that we, the human beings who are making history at the beginning of the second millennium, are doing so on a stage that is truly global.

Why These Sources?

Chapter Thirteen begins with a section entitled "The End of a European Dominated World." It focuses on two developments—the Cold War, in which the Soviet Union and the United States assumed leadership in international diplomacy, and the end of colonialism in Asia and Africa. Both developments show the eclipse of Europe as a dominant force in world affairs.

The two sources we have chosen on the origins of the Cold War are classic statements of the distrust and antagonism that had come to characterize U.S.-Soviet relations by 1946, the year when many statesmen concluded that conflict between the two emerging superpowers was unavoidable. Both sources are new to the fourth edition of *The Human Record.* George Kennan's "Long Telegram" replaces National Security Council Report-68, another influential statement of U.S. Cold War attitudes and aims dating from 1950. We decided Kennan's Long Telegram was preferable for two reasons. First, it is arguably the more important document in that it came earlier and actually provided the basic framework of ideas for NSC-68. Second, it pairs nicely with the Soviet document on the origins of the Cold War, another telegram on the state of U.S.-Soviet relations written in 1946. This is the so-called Novikov telegram, written in September 1946 by the Soviet ambassador to the United States, Nikolai Novikov, to the Soviet foreign minister, Viascheslav Molotov.

A source on the break-up of Europe's colonial empires follows. It is made up of excerpts from the debates on Indian independence that took place in the House of Commons in 1947. The speeches, by both proponents and opponents of Indian independence, provide numerous insights into the mixture of guilt, pride, hesitation, pragmatism, determination, and resignation that led to the decision to grant Indian independence.

The next section, "New Nations and their Challenges," focuses on some of the political, religious, and economic problems that have confronted the new states of Africa and Asia after the demise of colonialism. The section begins with excerpts from the writings of C. Odumegwu Ojukwu, the leader of the Biafran movement for independence from Nigeria in the 1960s. He discusses one of the major impediments to political stability in Africa, and to a lesser degree in Asia, ethnic conflict. As this particular source reveals, such conflict was rooted in the colonial era, when peoples with different languages, religions, and tribal affiliations were lumped together into colonies with boundaries established by European officials with little knowledge of Africa. Such boundaries were maintained at the time of independence, with the result that Nigeria's population, for example, was divided among the Hausa-Fulani, the Yoruba, and the Igbo. Ojukwu's writings show how, despite delicate constitutional arrangements, the Igbos' grievances grew to the point that rebellion and the founding of an independent Biafra seemed to be their only option.

The section continues with excerpts from the writings of the Indian journalist Girilal Jain, who in the 1980s became a spokesman for the Bharatiya Janata (Indian Nationalist) Party and its Hindu fundamentalist principles. In its demand for the "Hinduization" of Indian society, the BJP challenged the Indian government's official secularism, and along with other Indian religious groups, has contributed to growing religious tension in India. Religious fundamentalism and religious conflict are by no means unique to newly independent states, but in states such as these, with a host of other problems, they can be especially disruptive.

Our next selection is made up of statistics on economic development based on information from the World Bank's *World Development Report* of 1978, 1987, and 1999–2000. It includes information on twenty-six nations, chosen to represent different regions and different levels of economic development. Topics include population, gross national product, education, agriculture, health, access to fresh water, infant mortality, life expectancy, and broad economic trends. Using the information, students should be able to evaluate what progress developing nations are making and whether the gap between poor and rich nations is widening or shrinking.

Our next section focuses on the experience of non-Western women in the late-twentieth century. Our three selections show that although industrialization, secularization, the end of colonialism, and momentous political changes transformed women's social, legal, and economic status, old customs and perceptions did not disappear. The ubiquity of change and the persistence of tradition created unique pressures and tensions for women in these societies.

The section begins with an editorial by an Iranian woman Zand Dokht, "The Revolution that Failed Women." It illustrates how fundamentalist religious movements, in this case the Islamic fundamentalism connected with Iran's revolution of 1979, have sought to keep women in their tradition-al roles. The next selection, a statement on genital mutilation by the Association of African Women for Research and Development, highlights a practice that has come to be seen as a major symbol of the abuse of women in Africa and other parts of the world. It also shows how well-meaning Western efforts to end the practice have sparked resentment among Africans, even among those who oppose the practice themselves. The final selection, a brief autobiography of a Chinese woman, Ming, illustrates the many ways Chinese women's lives have been affected by the political and economic upheavals in China during the late-twentieth century.

Our section on race focuses on the United States and South Africa. Although racial and ethnic tensions have contaminated human relationships in many parts of the world during the late-twentieth century, arguably they have been most disruptive and damaging in these two countries.

Including Nelson Mandela's Rivonia Trial Speech to illustrate South Africa's system of apartheid was an easy choice. Throughout his adult life he has been the political and spiritual leader to attain racial justice in South Africa. This speech, delivered in 1964, is a moving indictment of apartheid, but still did not prevent him from spending the next quarter of a century in government prisons. To illustrate the goals of the civil rights movement in the postwar United States, we have included excerpts from Martin Luther

King, Jr.'s "A Letter from a Birmingham Jail." No less than Mandela's Rivonia trial speech, it is a classic statement of a people's aspirations for justice.

The next section, "Another New Era: The Demise of Communism and the End of the Cold War," highlights the sweeping changes in international communism that took place in the late-1980s and early-1990s: the abandonment of Maoism in China; the reform and subsequent collapse of the Soviet Union; the collapse of communist regimes in eastern Europe; and the end of the cold war.

The section begins with excerpts from various writings and speeches by Deng Xiaoping, all from the mid-1980s. In them, China's most influential leader in the last two decades of the twentieth century explains China's need to abandon Mao's commitment to ideological purity and egalitarianism, and instead follow a new course designed to encourage technological develop-ment and economic growth. In the excerpts we have chosen, Deng reveals his hopes for China's economic future, his views of socialism and capitalism, and his reasons for opposing political liberalization and democracy.

Just as Deng Xiaoping and other moderates sought to set China on a new course by committing the country to economic development, Mikhail Gorbachev and his supporters in the mid-1980s attempted to rejuvenate communism in the Soviet Union by introducing *perestroika* (restructuring) and *glasnost* (openness) into Soviet society. The excerpts from Gorbachev's 1987 book, *Perestroika*, present his analysis of the problems facing the Soviet Union in the 1980s and his solutions. To say that Gorbachev's initiatives had unexpected results would be an extreme understatement. They set in motion a series of events that resulted not only in the end of the Soviet Union's control of Eastern Europe but the end of the Soviet Union itself.

Our two-volume collection of sources on global history fittingly ends with a section that deals with the earth itself. It presents excerpts from a debate that took place in 1992 between Juilan Simon, an America economist who believes that the "environmental crisis" has been overblown. Doomsayers are wrong, he says. The quality of human life has improved dramatically in the course of the twentieth century, and there is no reason why that improvement should not continue. Norman Myers, a British environmentalist, rejects Simon's optimism. In his view, resource depletion, species extinction, overpopulation, and pollution are all signs that the environmental crisis is no sham. Human beings can save the planet from devastation, but time is running out. These two selections will inspire critical thinking and spirited debate among our students.

Analyzing the Sources

George Kennan's Long Telegram paints a grim picture of the Soviet Union's intentions and strengths. Its leadership is committed to continual struggle with the capitalist powers, which they view as inherently and inevitably hostile to socialism. Kennan asserts at the very outset that the Soviets believe there can be no "permanent peaceful co-existence" with capitalism. As a result, Kennan expects the Soviet Union will concentrate all its efforts, both domestic and foreign, on this ongoing struggle against the capitalist states. In practice, this means the Soviet Union will continue to build its industrial economy, increase its armed forces, and single-mindedly pursue its interests in Europe, colonial Africa and Asia, the Middle East and South America. It also will mean clandestine efforts to destabilize and sew discord among the major Western powers. In all these endeavors, the Soviet leaders will be confident of victory. Their Marxist ideology teaches them that capitalism, with its internal flaws and contradictions, is doomed.

What historical forces have shaped the Soviet view of the world? According to Kennan, these forces are rooted in Russia's past and go much deeper than Marxism. The Kremlin's "neurotic" view of the world has resulted from long-held feelings of insecurity and inferiority. In the distant past its lack of natural barriers left its "peaceful agricultural people" vulnerable to outside attack from fierce nomads. More recently Russia has been threatened by the more advanced nations of Europe. The European "threat" was both external, in the sense of potential invasion, and internal, in the sense of revealing the weaknesses of the Russian government and economy.

Since the Russian Revolution of 1917, Marxism has simply reinforced traditional Russian feelings of paranoia and insecurity. With its view that conflict between the solitary socialist power, the USSR, and the capitalist world was inevitable, the Bolshevik leaders could justify their harsh dictatorship and large military expenditures. In a famous line, Kennan asserts that Marxism is "a fig leaf of their moral and intellectual respectability."

Kennan's message is not without hope. The Soviet system is as yet unproved, and in any case, the USSR is still far weaker than the West. But the Western powers must not become complacent or allow themselves to be weakened by internal conflict. Most importantly, the Western powers must be willing to use force to stop Soviet expansion. The Soviets, he claims, are "highly sensitive to [the] logic of force," and will back down in the face of effective resistance. This of course is the key component of Kennan's doctrine of "containment," which shaped the U.S. response to communism throughout the Cold War era.

If Kennan needed any proof of his claim that a sense of insecurity and paranoia characterized the post-World War II Soviet outlook, Novikov's letter of September 1946 certainly would have supplied it. The threat to the Soviet Union is no longer "fierce nomads" or western European powers, but the United States. Novikov believes that the United States, having defeated Germany and Japan, was, with probable help from England, preparing for another war, this time a war for nothing less than world domination. According to Novikov, the signs of American ambitions are clear: increases in military spending; congressional approval of a peacetime draft; the establishment of military bases in Europe and the Pacific region; co-ordinated military planning with England; and extension of U.S. military power in the oil-rich Near East.

All this is especially dangerous for the Soviet Union because U.S. leadership is convinced that its former ally will be its major adversary and stumbling block in its bid for world domination. Again Novikov can read the signs. U.S. policy in China, the Near East, and Europe is designed to surround and isolate the Soviet Union. Tactical training in the U.S. army is focused on preparing for a war against the Soviet Union. Anti-Soviet propaganda from government officials and the press is designed to encourage "war psychosis" among the masses and prepare them for a third world war against the Soviet Union.

Novikov's telegram differs from Kennan's in two important respects. First, it lacks any analysis of U.S. motives. Kennan devoted much of his telegram to discussing the historical reasons for Soviet policies. But Novikov provides no answers to the question of why the United States seeks world domination. Second, Novikov makes no recommendations about how the Soviet leaders should respond to the U.S. drive for world domination. But the implications of his analysis are fairly clear. There can be no co-operation or compromise between the Soviet Union and the United States. The people and leaders of the Soviet Union must prepare themselves for yet another struggle for its survival.

While the Cold War took leadership in international diplomacy out of the hands of the European powers, the demise of colonialism ended their control of Asia and Africa. Decolonization had two main causes: the growth of nationalism in the colonies themselves and the recognition on the part of European powers that they no longer had the will or mean to maintain their colonies. The growth of nationalism in Asia and Africa has been documented in previous chapters, so the selection we have included in this section illustrates what the Europeans were thinking.

The arguments presented in the 1947 Parliamentary debates in favor of granting Indian independence can be categorized as follows:

- *"We have done a fine job in India. The Indian people are ready for independence and we should grant it."* This is essentially the argument of the first speaker in our selection, Clement Davies. He asserts that during the colonial era the British had two goals in India: to improve living conditions and prepare the Indians for self-government (no mention of economic benefits for England, prestige, and missionary opportunities). Although he concedes that the British record in India has not been without blemishes, on the whole he considers it to have been honorable and beneficial to the Indians. Now the Britishers' work is done, and further control of India is unjustified and unnecessary.

- *"We have done the Indian people no favor by trying to run their affairs for close to two centuries. India is an ancient and highly cultured civilization, and the Indians themselves are best qualified to deal with their problems, many of which we have exacerbated."* This is one of several arguments set forth by Richard Sorensen.

- *"A commitment to self-government and freedom have characterized British politics for some time, and now that we have taught such concepts to the Indians we cannot very well deny the Indians independence."* Several speakers made this point.

- *"Holding on to India would mean a huge military undertaking, well beyond the capacity of postwar Great Britain."* This pragmatic argument was set forth by Richard Sorensen.

- *"Great Britain has more than its share of its own problems at home, so further embroilment in India would be folly."* This was one of several arguments made by Harold Davies, who in good socialist fashion described Britain as a "little old country...tottering and wounded as a result of the wars inherent in the capitalist system."

The opponents of Indian independence had their own arguments—India is not quite ready for self-rule; it won't do to divide the country into India and Pakistan; anarchy will reign after the British leave. They did not have the votes, however, and Great Britain's Labour government won the day.

* * *

C. Odumegwu Ojukwu's account of why the Biafrans seceded from Nigeria is a story filled with villains and martyrs. The first villains were the British. They were the ones who created the huge colony of Nigeria despite the fact that the Hausa-Fulani from the north had no interest in joining. In Ojukwu's view the British did this for economic reasons: they wanted to have a large unified market in the region. The British also prevented their colonial subjects from developing any sense of nationhood and common interests by maintaining separate educational systems and legal codes for the major ethnic groups.

But the list of villains does not end here. Also included were the statesmen (some British, some Nigerian), who created a constitution for independent Nigeria that divided the country into three provinces and guaranteed the northern province's dominance over the two southern provinces. This created an opportunity for northern politicians to oppress the southerners and enrich themselves along with their cronies and relatives. The list of villains concludes with those southern politicians who, in return for bribes and favors, went along with the system.

The people of eastern Nigeria are the martyrs in Ojukwu's story. Ojukwu claims, not inaccurately, that the easterners tended to be more highly educated, more successful in business, and more strongly represented in the professions than the northerners. They were, simply stated, more "progressive" and successful. As Ojukwu's tone clearly reveals, they also looked down on the northerners. Northerners were backward and needed the better-trained and more sophisticated easterners to bring them effective medical care, modern housing, and education.

The northerners' response was jealousy and hatred rather than gratitude. They used their political power to give every legal and economic advantage to themselves. According to Ojukwu, the situation had become so bad that some easterners had begun to dress and groom themselves like northerners to avoid oppression. But for most easterners the answer was not accommodation but secession.

What does Ojukwo hope for in terms of Biafra's future? Politically he wants democracy, a true sense of nationhood among the Biafrans, and a government free of corruption. Thus every effort must be made to wipe out the "twin evils" of tribalism and nepotism. He also dreams of a Biafran economy with industry, modern agriculture, and a viable infrastructure. In Ojukwu's view, only when an independent black nation has accomplished these things without outside help will Africans be able to claim respect from the rest of the world.

Just as Ojukwu's analysis of Nigerian politics in the 1960s had its share of villains, so too does Girilal Jain's appraisal of India during the 1980s. The two prime villains for Jain are India's political and intellectual elites and the West (especially Great Britain, but also the other Europe states, the United States, and even the Soviet Union). Both groups are more or less equally culpable for leading India astray. Jain has little regard for India's Muslims, but he considers them somewhat less blameworthy than the outside powers and India's intellectual and political elite. The Muslims simply have taken advantage of privileges and exemptions offered them first by the British colonialists and then by independent India's leaders.

Secularism, not Islam, is India's greatest curse in Jain's view. In his reading of Indian history, secularism was a bad solution to the problem of forging a sense of Indian nationalism in a society divided among Hindus, Muslims, Sikhs, and Christians. The secularists sought to forge loyalties between all these various groups and their government by making sure the government identified itself with the religious doctrines and practices of none of them. In doing so, Jain believes the government cut itself off from India's cultural roots. Strict secularism was favored, however, by the British and was eagerly embraced by India's intellectuals and politicians who, according to Jain, have always identified themselves with those in power. Nehru, who espoused the secularism of the British and the socialism of the Soviet Union, was according to Jain's view of things the archsymbol of India's betrayal by their leaders.

Jain is convinced that the supposedly neutral Indian government has been anything but even-handed in its religious policies. It has been overscrupulous in protecting the interests of the Muslims, especially those who live in the state of Jammu and Kashmir, where the Muslim population is relatively large. They have been allowed to live according to Islamic law and maintain their religious schools. But Hindus—the majority—have had their traditions and practices attacked.

Three things, according to Jain, have caused the Hindu majority finally to assert itself. They were the conversion of Harijans to Islam in southern India, the secessionist movements in Jammu and Kashmir, and the controversy over the destruction of the Ayodhya mosque that exists on the site of an ancient Hindu temple in honor of Ram. The result has been new vitality to Hindu nationalism and spectacular success at the polls.

Jain is not very specific about what he sees in a "Hinduized" India. Presumably, Muslims would lose all their special "privileges" and protection. The government would encourage the study of Hinduism in the schools and protect Hindu traditions. Efforts to blur caste distinctions and improve the lot of the untouchables would end. Most importantly, there would be a campaign to restrict the Indian people's accessibility to Western culture—music, cinema, literature, and fashion—and thereby halt the spread of secularism.

The statistics from the World Bank's *World Development Reports* are included in a section dealing with the economic problems of newly independent nations. But they also can be used to illuminate several other issues touched upon in this last chapter of *The Human Record*. For example, the statistics on literacy and life expectancy are broken down by gender and provide information about women's status in various societies. And the statistics on GNP per capita, tractors, energy consumption, life expectancy, and infant mortality can be used to evaluate the arguments of Julian Simon and Norman Myers (sources 123 and 124) over whether things are getting better or worse for humanity.

What can the statistics tell us about the economic achievements and prospects of the so-called developing nations? They show, first of all, that in some cases the recent economic record has been bleak, at least in terms of per capita GNP. In Sub-Saharan Africa, with the exception of Mali, increases have been modest, and in the case of Nigeria, GNP per capita has actually declined between 1976 and 1998. Asia, in contrast, has shown impressive gains, with Singapore, South Korea, and Thailand leading the way. The statistics on GNP per capita also show that the gap between the richest and poorest nations has increased over the past twenty years. This can be seen by comparing the average GNPs of the four richest and four poorest nations in 1976 and 1998.

How useful are the various types of data in terms of predicting economic development? There is a strong correlation between energy consumption and economic development. Nations showing the most dramatic increase in GNP per capita (South Korea, Singapore, and Thailand) also show the greatest gains in per capita energy usage. In contrast, the amount of energy consumed in the poorest nations remains extremely low. This is another area where the gap between rich and poor nations is large and getting larger.

The statistics on the relative weight of agriculture, manufacturing, and service of the various national economies highlight one of the most important areas of difference between industrial and developing nations— the percentage of the population involved in agriculture. The statistics also reveal the recent overall decline in the proportion of individuals directly involved in agriculture. This has resulted from several factors, including the mechanization of agriculture, the attraction of cities, and the growing gap between population levels and the amount of available arable land. These same figures also show a decline in developed nations, albeit a small one, in the percentage of GNP in manufacturing. This has resulted mainly in the shift of individuals to service-related occupations.

Another set of statistics deals with literacy and education. The figures show a dramatic rise in adult literacy since 1960 except in those developed societies that had already attained high levels of literacy in 1960. Similar, though somewhat less spectacular gains have been made in the percentage of populations attending secondary school. These same statistics also show how women continue to lag behind men in terms of literacy and educational opportunities. The gap was especially large in the poorest nations.

Just as the statistics on education provide possible reasons for optimism, so too do those on life expectancy and infant mortality. The people in developing societies are living longer, although on average they still die three decades sooner than people privileged to live in the world's wealthiest societies.

* * *

Nelson Mandela's self-defense at his Rivonia trial in 1964 is a classic description of the evils of apartheid and a description of how an essentially moderate and peaceful reform movement became violent. Mandela clearly and dispassionately explains how the African National Congress gradually abandoned Gandhi-inspired tactics of passive resistance for violence only after years of government intransigence convinced even the most optimistic blacks that peaceful change in South Africa was impossible. He freely admits his role in planning acts of sabotage but claims that previous state-sponsored violence against blacks justified his actions.

After explaining that the ANC welcomed support from Communist and Communist bloc nations but was not Communist itself, Mandela movingly concludes his speech. Here he goes beyond the numerous rules and regulations of the apartheid system and describes its human costs. Mandela deplores the political deprivation and economic inequities of apartheid. More than anything else, however, its most humiliating aspect was the racial assumption behind the political and economic realities—that white supremacy was justified by black inferiority.

A comparison of Martin Luther King, Jr.'s letter from a Birmingham Jail and Mandela's Rivonia trial speech shows a number of similarities and differences. Both men are attempting to justify their actions. Mandela is defending his advocacy of sabotage and his willingness to accept support from communists in a white courtroom. King is defending his campaign of "nonviolent direct action" against criticisms of black clergymen who believe he is going too far, too fast. Both men present moving descriptions of the emotional and psychological wounds caused by living in racially oppressive societies. Mandela describes the ways the apartheid system assaults human dignity, while King speaks of the psychological toll of "forever fighting a degenerating sense of 'nobodiness'."

The two men differ in their attitudes toward violence. Mandela describes how the African National Congress's views of violence evolved from its beginnings in the early part of the century. At first its members obeyed even unjust laws and sought change through strictly legal means, such as drawing up petitions and sending delegates to government conferences. After the implementation of the government's apartheid policy after 1949, the ANC adopted a Gandhian strategy of refusing to obey inequitable laws. Only after the Sharpeville massacre of 1960 and the repressive government measures that followed did the leaders of the now outlawed ANC turn to sabotage to further their cause.

King still hopes to avoid violence. Peaceful, passive resistance as preached by Gandhi and as taught in the Christian gospel of love offers the best hope of avoiding the racial violence preached by the black nationalists.

The two men also differ somewhat in the explanations they offer for their actions. Mandela justifies sabotage because peaceful strategies had failed and because the disenfranchised blacks had played no part in making the laws that governed them. King agrees that the laws he and his followers oppose are unjust because blacks had no role in making them. He writes, "An unjust law is a code inflicted on a minority which that minority had no part in enacting or creating...." In addition, King introduces the concept of natural law to justify resistance to inequitable laws. People are under no obligation to obey human laws that do not embody the higher principles of natural law (created by God and perceived by human reason) and morality. Segregation laws certainly fit into that category.

* * *

In their first reading of the three documents concerning late-twentieth-century women, students might conclude that the issues confronting women in Africa, Iran, and China were all quite different. Zand Dokht's 1981 editorial shows the potential for conflict between the goals of Western-inspired women's liberation movements and the values of fundamentalist religious groups. Specifically, she deplores the results of the 1979 Islamic revolution in Iran, which she and other women supported, but whose leaders promptly reimposed strict Islamic laws regulating women's dress, subservience to males, seclusion, divorce, marriage, and education. The statement by the Association of African Women for Research and Development deals with the issue of female circumcision, while the recollections of the Chinese woman, Ming, show how her life was affected not only by the patriarchical values of old China but also by the expectations and demands of the modern Chinese state.

Students should be able to see, however, that issues each document raises are similar in certain respects. All the sources, for example, describe problems that are deeply rooted in the past. Female circumcision in Africa, the wearing of the veil in Islamic countries, and the efforts of Chinese fathers to dominate and control their wives and daughters had existed for centuries.

Each source also shows just how difficult it has been to alter traditions regarding women, even in an age of momentous political and economic changes. Despite the efforts of the Pahlavi shahs to open up economic and educational opportunities for Iranian women, after 1979 the reinstatement of Islamic restrictions on women by the Khomeini regime had widespread support, even from many women. In China, as Ming's recollections make clear, despite forty years of communist rule, old practices and traditions remain. Parents still arrange marriages, female infanticide continues, fathers expect to control the lives of their daughters and wives, and abused wives, such as Ming's mother, have few options, other than continuing their unhappy marriage. Female circumcision in Africa continues despite opposition from Westerners and Africans alike.

All three sources also show how tensions between tradition and change have made women's lives more complex and, in a sense, more difficult in recent decades. An example of this is provided by the source concerning female circumcision in Africa. For centuries female circumcision had been practiced in Africa and other societies without protest or disapproval. Women performed the circumcision themselves and participated in the rites that accompanied it. In the twentieth century, Westerners and Western-educated Africans denounced the practice for medical and philosophical reasons and have pressured Africans to abandon it. This has raised the centuries-old issue that Spaniards had faced in the Americas, the British had faced in India, and European imperialists had faced throughout Africa— what right Westerners have, if any, to impose their values on others. It has also created problems for many young girls and women who face the decision whether to resist or give in to the pressure to go against their people's traditions.

The choices faced by Chinese women under communism have also become more complicated and difficult. Ming has the opportunity to attend school in her village, and because of her good record there, is admitted to a university. Such advanced studies would give her an opportunity to pursue a career in one of China's cities. But taking advantage of such opportunities necessitates breaking family ties and is a source of potential conflict with parents.

* * *

Our section on changes in the communist world in the late-twentieth century focuses on two key individuals: Deng Xiaoping, who assumed leadership in China after the death of Mao, and Mikhail Gorbachev, who in the mid-1980s plunged the Soviet Union into the uncharted waters of economic and political reform. Both men set their nations on new paths, but the changes Gorbachev engineered in the Soviet Union were more stunning to the outside world. This was in part due to the fact that the Soviet system that he began to dismantle had been in place since the late 1920s, whereas China's economic policies and priorities had already undergone several dramatic shifts under Communist rule. Furthermore, the transformation of the Soviet Union had broader international implications. It led not only to the collapse of communist regimes in eastern Europe, but also to the breakup of the Soviet Union and the end of the Cold War.

The selection by Deng Xiaoping is made up of excerpts from speeches he made between 1983 and 1987, that is, five to seven years after the Central Committee of the Chinese Communist Party in 1978 abandoned Maoism in favor of the "four modernizations" in agriculture, industry, science, and technology. Deng uses these speeches to defend his policies, review China's accomplishments, and chart a course for China's future.

Mao's priorities were achieving egalitarianism and maintaining revolutionary fervor. He favored China's economic development but not if it promoted inequality and encouraged bourgeois ways of thinking. Deng's priority was the elimination of poverty through what he calls the "development of productive forces." True communism, he claims, remains his ultimate goal but this will be achieved in China's distant future. In the meantime, social inequalities and uneven regional economic development will be unavoidable. In this respect his thinking is vaguely similar to Lenin's when in his New Economic Policy he took one step backward (in the direction of capitalism) to take two steps forward (in the direction of true socialism).

Deng is also superficially similar to Stalin in that both men put ideology aside to achieve rapid economic development in their respective countries. But the priorities and strategies of the two leaders were far different. For Stalin the focus of the Five-Year Plan was the development of heavy industry rather than the production of consumer goods and improvements in the people's standard of living. Agricultural production and pricing were regulated to serve the purposes of the industrial sector. And of course the Soviet economy was tightly controlled by the state and left no room for individual initiative or profit.

China's economic transformation under Deng began with agriculture, thus remaining true to the rural orientation of Chinese communism since the 1920s. China's post-1978 rural policy was a rejection of the principles of agricultural collectivization that China had adopted in part in imitation of the Soviet Union's rural collectives. According to Deng, the key to his agrarian policy was to "to bring the peasant's initiative into full play by introducing the responsibility system." In other words, peasants were to be given greater latitude in deciding what they could grow and how they could market their products. Similar rewards and incentives were introduced into industry and construction, where workers and managers would be rewarded on the basis of performance. Gone were the old days when "everyone ate out of the same pot." The new motto is "time is money, efficiency is life."

Deng's foreign policy differed from Stalin's and Mao's, and indeed was a conscious rejection of China's centuries-old tradition of economic self-sufficiency. Mao's China and Stalin's Soviet Union essentially had no economic dealings with capitalist nations; indeed one of their main goals was to prove the superiority of communism to capitalism by outproducing and outperforming the capitalists. Deng proclaims that China cannot achieve rapid economic development without the capital, technology, and business know-how the capitalists can offer. Not just China, but the whole world will benefit from increased trade, and the prospects for world peace will improve.

Where does socialism fit into Deng's market-oriented economic policies? As Deng points out, the state will continue to own and control a substantial part of the nation's economic assets. The state will also adopt tax policies to prevent people from becoming too prosperous; it will also "encourage" them to contribute money to worthwhile public works projects such as road and school building. Most important, says Deng, the Chinese must realize that the path to true socialism is a long one. A society must become wealthy before it can be truly communist, and this, says Deng with remarkable candor, will not be achieved until the middle of the twenty-first century.

Although Deng breaks with China's policy of isolation, he affirms its tradition of authoritarian politics. In the new China he envisions there will be no place for what he calls "bourgeois liberalization." By this he means there will be no free speech and no criticism of the regime. Democracy, he affirms, is China's long-term goal, but like true socialism, it is far in China's future. Meanwhile, one party rule and dictatorship democracy are necessary if China is to maintain political stability and respect in the international community.

In the excerpts from his 1987 book, *Perestroika*, Mikhail Gorbachev candidly admits that the Soviet system of socialism has failed. It stands in stark contrast to the pride and optimism of Joseph Stalin's speech of 1933 "The Results of the Five-Year Plan" (source 92) in which he boasts that the state economic planning implemented in the Five-Year Plans will enable the Soviet Union to outstrip the West. According to Gorbachev, the Soviet economy has stalled because too many Soviet workers lacked discipline and motivation; they knew that no matter how poorly they performed, they were guaranteed jobs, housing, health care, and education for their children. He also blames government and party officials for trying to ignore the problem or paper it over with empty pronouncements and slogans. Like Deng, he has concluded that a centralized economy with no room for individual initiative and profit is no long-term solution to economic development.

Gorbachev's proposals resemble Deng's to a degree. Like Deng, Gorbachev suggests that rewards should be determined by merit and performance, thus overcoming the "leveling tendency in pay and consumerism." He also calls for lightening the heavy hand of state economic planners and giving local officials and workers a greater voice in decision making.

In other respects, Gorbachev goes beyond the ideas of the Chinese reformers. His policy of *glasnost* advocates open debate of issues confronting Soviet society and even encourages criticism of party officials. Socialism is now to be tied with democracy, not dictatorship.

Gorbachev believed that communism could and should be saved. He saw perestroika and glasnost as ways to preserve the essentials of a socialist economy and party rule. Once adjustments were made, the people's commitment to their government would remain firm.

* * *

With its image of "spaceship earth" and its motto "Think globally, act locally," the modern environmental movement, more so than any other single development, has heightened global awareness and deepened a sense of human interrelatedness since the 1960s. Human beings now realize that destruction of the Amazon rain forest contributes to global warming; that global warming will cause melting of the polar icecaps; that the melting of the polar icecaps will raise the level of the oceans; and that raising the level of the oceans will lead to the flooding of coastal areas where people live, farm, and trade. They realize that the use of aerosol sprays depletes the ozone layer above the earth's poles and that this depletion will increase the worldwide incidence of skin cancer. They realize that political instability in the Middle East can drive up the price of oil; that the resulting inflation will cause interest rates to rise; that this will drive down stock prices; and that this will affect the wealth and income of millions of people throughout the world. The fortunes of human beings around the globe are inextricably linked.

It is only fitting that our two-volume survey of the human record ends with two sources that debate the earth's environmental future. Certainly it would be possible to approach these two sources in a more or less traditional way, posing to our students questions such: What is each debater's overall argument? What points does each make to buttress his point of view? What are the strengths and weaknesses of each man's argument? Who won the debate?

Such an approach, however, is probably not being the most effective way to use these sources. First of all, most of our students end up siding with Myers, whose "green" views are probably closer to their own. Second, without being able to review the various studies each debater cites, and without having an opportunity to verify their data, it is hard to evaluate the various points each man makes. The "debate" among students often ends up one-sided or else based more on emotion than analysis.

We tend to use the two sources as a jumping off point to have our students consider the broader issue of human progress since 1500 C.E. We sometimes have given our students the following exercise:

Check off the statement with which you agree, and then give five reasons why you chose it:

_____ 1. I believe that progress *has* characterized human history since 1500 for the following five reasons:

    a.

    b.

    c.

    d.

    e.

_____ 2. I believe that progress has *not* been a feature of human history since 1500 for the following five reasons:

    a.

    b.

    c.

    d.

    e.

In a somewhat different version, we use the two questions, "I am optimistic about humankind's future because…" and "I am pessimistic about humankind's future because…." Again, the students are required to offer five reasons for their choice.

We have found that students divide fairly evenly on these two questions, and that the ensuing discussion can serve as an opportunity to review some of the material we have covered during the semester and to prepare students for their final examination.

On the subject of progress, and whether the human condition is getting better or not, we should keep in mind that we have just finished another semester of world history. So things can't be all bad!

Other Ways to Use the Sources

1. The following four questions require students to stretch their minds beyond what is asked of them in the Questions for Analysis:

    a. Kennan and Novikov have an opportunity to comment on the way the Cold War turned out. How might they have attempted to relate their observations and predications with the actual events that unfolded?

b. What do you see as *Marxist* in Deng Xiaoping's writings and speeches and Gorbachev's *Perestroika*? What issues do they address that were *not* essential to Marx's philosophy?

c. What might Jules Ferry and Rudyard Kipling have said if they had been given an opportunity to participate in the 1947 British parliamentary debate on Indian independence?

d. Although the three selections on women's place in modern society seem to describe quite different issues, what underlying similarities do you see in the situations they describe?

2. The following two questions ask students to use the sources in Chapter 13 as basis for reviewing the material covered since the beginning of the semester. They could easily serve as the topics for a take-home final essay.

a. Do the various sources in this chapter seem to confirm or refute the theory that world history since 1500 has been marked by human progress?

b. It has been suggested by some historians that historical developments since the end of World War II mark a dramatic break in human affairs, introducing problems and challenges without precedent in the past. Based on your understanding of human history since 1500, do you agree or disagree with such an assertion?